THE KORAN

THE KORAN is a book apart, not only as Holy Scripture for Muslims throughout the world, but as the supreme classic of Arabic literature. In its 114 Suras, or chapters, it comprises the total of revelations believed to have been communicated to the prophet Muhammad as a final expression of God's will and purpose for man. The revelations were received over a number of years, the first dating from AD 610, the last shortly before Muhammad's death in AD 632, and the definitive canon was established some twenty years later.

ARTHUR J. ARBERRY (1905–69) was born at Buckland, Portsmouth, and educated at Pembroke College, Cambridge. In 1944 he was appointed to the chair of Persian at London University. In 1946 he became Professor of Arabic and Head of the Near and Middle East Department and in the following year he returned to Pembroke as Sir Thomas Adam's Professor of Arabic, a post which he held for the remainder of his life.

A profound and inspiring teacher, he was also an immensely prolific and versatile writer, publishing over sixty works on a wide range of topics in Arabic and Persian studies.

OXFORD WORLD'S CLASSICS

For over 100 years Oxford World's Classics have brought readers closer to the world's great literature. Now with over 700 titles—from the 4,000-year-old myths of Mesopotamia to the twentieth century's greatest novels—the series makes available lesser-known as well as celebrated writing.

The pocket-sized hardbacks of the early years contained introductions by Virginia Woolf, T. S. Eliot, Graham Greene, and other literary figures which enriched the experience of reading. Today the series is recognized for its fine scholarship and reliability in texts that span world literature, drama and poetry, religion, philosophy and politics. Each edition includes perceptive commentary and essential background information to meet the changing needs of readers.

OXFORD WORLD'S CLASSICS

The Koran
Interpreted

Translated with an Introduction by
ARTHUR J. ARBERRY

OXFORD
UNIVERSITY PRESS

OXFORD

UNIVERSITY PRESS

Great Clarendon Street, Oxford OX2 6DP

Oxford University Press is a department of the University of Oxford.
It furthers the University's objective of excellence in research, scholarship,
and education by publishing worldwide in

Oxford New York

Athens Auckland Bangkok Bogotá Buenos Aires Calcutta
Cape Town Chennai Dar es Salaam Delhi Florence Hong Kong Istanbul
Karachi Kuala Lumpur Madrid Melbourne Mexico City Mumbai
Nairobi Paris São Paulo Singapore Taipei Tokyo Toronto Warsaw

with associated companies in Berlin Ibadan

Oxford is a registered trade mark of Oxford University Press
in the UK and in certain other countries

Published in the United States
by Oxford University Press Inc., New York

First published 1955 by Allen & Unwin Ltd.
First published in the World's Classics by Oxford University Press 1964
First issued as a World's Classics paperback 1983
Reissued as an Oxford World's Classics paperback 1998
Reissued 2008

British Library Cataloguing in Publication Data

Data available

ISBN 978-0-19-953732-7

5

Printed in Great Britain by
Clays Ltd, St Ives plc

CONTENTS

CONTENTS

CONTENTS

CONTENTS

INTRODUCTION

THE Koran, the Sacred Book of Islam, comprises in its 114 Suras or chapters the total of revelations believed to have been communicated to the Prophet Muhammad, as a final expression of God's will and purpose for man. These revelations were supernaturally received, in circumstances of a trance-like nature, over a considerable number of years intermittently, the first (Sura XCVI) dating from about A.D. 610 and the last shortly before Muhammad's death in A.D. 632. It is uncertain whether the whole of the text was committed to writing during the Prophet's lifetime; he himself is said to have been illiterate, and merely to have 'recited' the words he heard out of heaven. Tradition relates that a few years after his death the scattered fragments were collected together from 'scraps of parchment and leather, tablets of stone, ribs of palm branches, camels' shoulder-blades and ribs, pieces of board, and the breasts of men'—this last phrase referring to the retentive memories of the Prophet's immediate followers. It was during the reign of the third caliph 'Uthmān (644–56) that the definitive canon was established by a panel of editors directed by the Prophet's amanuensis Zaid ibn Thābit. To these men belongs the responsibility for the accepted arrangement of the text, an arrangement which is very far from being chronological or rationally coherent; the principle followed seems to have been to place the Suras in diminishing order of their length with the solitary exception of the first Sura, called 'The Opening'. Apart from certain orthographical modifications of the originally somewhat primitive method of writing, intended to render unambiguous and easy the task of reading and recitation, the Koran as printed in the twentieth century is identical with the Koran as authorized by 'Uthmān more than 1,300 years ago.

Since the Koran is to the faithful Muslim the very Word of God, from earliest times orthodox opinion has rigidly maintained that it is untranslatable, a miracle of speech which it would be blasphemous to attempt to imitate. It is thus the duty of every believer to learn to understand its meaning in the original Arabic; to assist him in this not always easy labour he has at his disposal a great range of commentaries, some of immense length, compiled by learned exegetes in every century down to the present day. For all that, the Koran has been translated many times and into many languages, first into Latin *circa* 1143; the earliest English version appeared in 1657. The most esteemed English translations are those of Sale (1734), Rodwell (1861), Palmer (1880), and Pickthall (1930). In all these versions, with the exception of Rodwell's, the traditional order of the Suras has been followed; Rodwell attempted a chronological rearrangement, foreshadowing the far more radical recasting of Richard Bell (1937–9).

In making the present attempt to improve on the performance of my predecessors, and to produce something which might be accepted as echoing however faintly the sublime rhetoric of the Arabic Koran, I have been at pains to study the intricate and richly varied rhythms which—apart from the message itself—constitute the Koran's undeniable claim to rank amongst the greatest literary masterpieces of mankind. (The summary result of my investigation is printed in my *The Holy Koran*, published by Allen & Unwin in 1953.) This very characteristic feature —'that inimitable symphony', as the believing Pickthall described his Holy Book, 'the very sounds of which move men to tears and ecstasy'—has been almost totally ignored by previous translators; it is therefore not surprising that what they have wrought sounds dull and flat indeed in comparison with the splendidly decorated original. For the Koran is neither prose nor poetry, but a unique fusion of both. The verses into which it is divided—and the reckoning by fives and tens goes back to ancient times —are threaded together by loose rhymes into shorter or longer sequences within the Sura; the rhythms of those sequences vary sensibly according to the subject-matter, swinging from the steady march of straightforward narrative or enunciation (tales of the ancient prophets, formulations of ritual and law) to the impetuous haste of ecstatic ejaculation (the majesty of God, the imminence of the Last Day, the torments of Hell, and the delights of Paradise). I have striven to devise rhythmic patterns and sequence-groupings in correspondence with what the Arabic presents, paragraphing the grouped sequences as they seem to form original units of revelation.

The reader of the Koran, particularly if he has to depend upon a version, however accurate linguistically, is certain to be puzzled and dismayed by the apparently random nature of many of the Suras. This famous inconsequence has often been attributed to clumsy patchwork on the part of the first editors. I believe it to be rather of the very nature of the Book itself. In many passages it is stated that the Koran had been sent down 'confirming what was before it', by which was meant the Torah and the Gospel; the contents of the Jewish and Christian scriptures, excepting such falsifications as had been introduced into them, were therefore taken as true and known. All truth was thus present simultaneously within the Prophet's enraptured soul; all truth, however fragmented, revealed itself in his inspired utterance. The reader of the Muslim scriptures must strive to attain the same all-embracing apprehension. The sudden fluctuations of theme and mood will then no longer present such difficulties as have bewildered critics ambitious to measure the ocean of prophetic eloquence with the thimble of pedestrian analysis. Each Sura will now be seen to be a unity within itself, and the whole Koran will be recognized as a single revelation, self-consistent to the highest degree. Though half a mortal lifetime was needed for the message to be received and communicated, the message itself, being of the eternal, is one message in eternity, however heterogeneous its temporal expression may appear to be.

There is a repertory of familiar themes running through the whole Koran; each Sura elaborates or adumbrates one or more —often many—of these. To take a very straightforward instance: Sura XII consists almost entirely of a recital of the story of Joseph, with dramatic hiatuses emphasizing that the story is a familiar one, retold as a reminder of God's dealings with men and how He delivers out of evil and rewards His faithful messengers, a moral driven home in the epilogue. Sura XXVIII somewhat similarly relates incidents from the life of Moses, but the narrative is broken up to introduce a number of favourite *leitmotivs*: refutation of those who denied Muhammad's mission, the Last Day, and the Judgement, the Unity of God, woven backwards and forwards into the pattern of the composition. Sura XIX (and there are several others like it) follows a somewhat more complex scheme; episodes are sketched from the lives of a series of prophets in illustration of the Divine mercy, followed by a statement of the contrasting fates awaiting those who disbelieve and those who believe. The short Sura XCIII exhibits a simple but perfect rhetorical balance: an opening adjuration by contrasted light and darkness introduces three triplets matching exactly together. Sura LV, a triumphant hymn to the power and glory of God, the terrors of Hell, and the joys of Paradise, is knit together by a running refrain as the tension is built up from a quiet and meditative beginning to an unbearably tremendous close. So the pattern of each Sura can be methodically analysed into its component parts, seen as motives common to the whole Koran, treated in each context individually and with an astonishing wealth and variety of rhetoric and rhythm.

All previous versions of the Koran, like the original text itself, having been printed as continuous prose, the rhapsodic nature of its composition has been largely lost to ear and sight; by showing the text as here presented, some faint impression may be given of its dramatic impact and most moving beauty. I have called my version an interpretation, conceding the orthodox claim that the Koran (like all other literary masterpieces) is untranslatable; in making this interpretation I have considered the opinions of the learned commentators, and when (as not infrequently) they have differed, I have been eclectic in deciding between alternative explanations. I have tried to compose clear and unmannered English, avoiding the 'Biblical' style favoured by some of my predecessors. There is however one feature of antique usage which I have deliberately retained; it is absolutely necessary, if confusion is to be avoided, to mark the distinction between the second person singular and the second person plural. As footnotes and glosses do not interrupt the smooth flow of the Arabic Koran, so in this English interpretation footnotes and glosses have been deliberately avoided; readers anxious for further guidance should consult the earlier annotated versions.

This task was undertaken, not lightly, and carried to its conclusion at a time of great personal distress, through which it comforted and sustained the writer in a manner for which he will always be grateful. He therefore acknowledges his gratitude to whatever power or Power inspired the man and the Prophet who first recited these scriptures. I pray that this interpretation, poor echo though it is of the glorious original, may instruct, please, and in some degree inspire those who read it.

A. J. ARBERRY

I

THE OPENING

In the Name of God, the Merciful, the Compassionate

Praise belongs to God, the Lord of all Being,
the All-merciful, the All-compassionate,
    the Master of the Day of Doom.

5   Thee only we serve; to Thee alone we pray for succour.
    Guide us in the straight path,
the path of those whom Thou hast blessed,
not of those against whom Thou art wrathful,
    nor of those who are astray.

THE COW

In the Name of God, the Merciful, the Compassionate

Alif Lam Mim

That is the Book, wherein is no doubt,
    a guidance to the godfearing
who believe in the Unseen, and perform the prayer,
and expend of that We have provided them;
who believe in what has been sent down to thee
    and what has been sent down before thee,
        and have faith in the Hereafter;
    those are upon guidance from their Lord,
        those are the ones who prosper.

5 As for the unbelievers, alike it is to them
whether thou hast warned them or hast not warned them,
        they do not believe.
God has set a seal on their hearts and on their hearing,
        and on their eyes is a covering,
and there awaits them a mighty chastisement.

        And some men there are who say,
    'We believe in God and the Last Day';
        but they are not believers.
They would trick God and the believers,
    and only themselves they deceive,
        and they are not aware.
    In their hearts is a sickness,
        and God has increased their sickness,
and there awaits them a painful chastisement
    for that they have cried lies.
10 When it is said to them, 'Do not corruption in the land',
they say, 'We are only ones that put things right.'
    Truly, they are the workers of corruption

but they are not aware.
When it is said to them, 'Believe as the people believe',
they say, 'Shall we believe, as fools believe?'
　　Truly, they are the foolish ones,
　　　but they do not know.
When they meet those who believe, they say, 'We believe';
but when they go privily to their Satans, they say,
　　'We are with you; we were only mocking.'
　　God shall mock them, and shall lead them on
　　blindly wandering in their insolence.

15　　Those are they that have bought error
　　　at the price of guidance,
　　and their commerce has not profited them,
　　　and they are not right-guided.
The likeness of them is as the likeness of a man
who kindled a fire, and when it lit all about him
God took away their light, and left them in darkness
　　　　　unseeing,
　　　　deaf, dumb, blind—
　　　so they shall not return;
　　　or as a cloudburst out of heaven
in which is darkness, and thunder, and lightning—
　　they put their fingers in their ears
　　against the thunderclaps, fearful of death;
　　　and God encompasses the unbelievers;
the lightning wellnigh snatches away their sight;
whensoever it gives them light, they walk in it,
and when the darkness is over them, they halt;
　　had God willed, He would have taken away
　　　their hearing and their sight.
　　Truly, God is powerful over everything.

O you men, serve your Lord Who created you,
and those that were before you; haply so
　　you will be godfearing;
20　　who assigned to you the earth for a couch,
　　and heaven for an edifice, and sent down
　　out of heaven water, wherewith He brought forth
　　fruits for your provision; so set not up

compeers to God wittingly.
And if you are in doubt concerning that We have
sent down on Our servant, then bring a sura
like it, and call your witnesses, apart from
     God, if you are truthful.
And if you do not—and you will not—then
fear the Fire, whose fuel is men and stones,
     prepared for unbelievers.

Give thou good tidings to those who believe
and do deeds of righteousness, that for them
await gardens underneath which rivers flow;
whensoever they are provided with fruits therefrom
they shall say, 'This is that wherewithal
we were provided before'; that they shall be
given in perfect semblance; and there
for them shall be spouses purified; therein
     they shall dwell forever.

God is not ashamed to strike a similitude
even of a gnat, or aught above it.
As for the believers, they know it is the truth
from their Lord; but as for unbelievers,
they say, 'What did God desire by this
for a similitude?' Thereby He leads
many astray, and thereby He guides
many; and thereby He leads none astray
     save the ungodly
25   such as break the covenant of God
after its solemn binding, and such as cut
what God has commanded should be joined,
and such as do corruption in the land—
     they shall be the losers.

How do you disbelieve in God, seeing you were dead
and He gave you life, then He shall make you dead,
then He shall give you life, then unto Him
     you shall be returned?
It is He who created for you all that is

4

in the earth, then He lifted Himself to heaven
and levelled them seven heavens; and He has
knowledge of everything.

And when thy Lord said to the angels,
'I am setting in the earth a viceroy.'
They said, 'What, wilt Thou set therein one
who will do corruption there, and shed blood,
while We proclaim Thy praise and call Thee Holy?'
He said, 'Assuredly I know
that you know not.'
And He taught Adam the names, all of them;
then He presented them unto the angels
and said, 'Now tell Me the names of these,
if you speak truly.'
30   They said, 'Glory be to Thee! We know not
save what Thou hast taught us. Surely Thou art
the All-knowing, the All-wise.'
He said, 'Adam, tell them their names.'
And when he had told them their names
He said, 'Did I not tell you I know
the unseen things of the heavens and earth?
And I know what things you reveal, and
what you were hiding.'
And when We said to the angels, 'Bow
yourselves to Adam'; so they bowed
themselves, save Iblis; he refused,
and waxed proud, and so he became
one of the unbelievers.
And We said, 'Adam, dwell thou, and thy wife,
in the Garden, and eat thereof easefully
where you desire; but draw not nigh this tree,
lest you be evildoers.'
Then Satan caused them to slip therefrom
and brought them out of that they were in;
and We said, 'Get you all down, each
of you an enemy of each; and in
the earth a sojourn shall be yours, and
enjoyment for a time.'

35   Thereafter Adam received certain words
from his Lord, and He turned towards him;
truly He turns, and is All-compassionate.
We said, 'Get you down out of it, all together;
yet there shall come to you guidance from Me,
and whosoever follows My guidance,
no fear shall be on them, neither shall they sorrow.
As for the unbelievers who cry lies to Our signs,
those shall be the inhabitants of the Fire,
      therein dwelling forever.'

Children of Israel, remember My blessing
wherewith I blessed you, and fulfil My covenant
and I shall fulfil your covenant; and have awe of Me.
And believe in that I have sent down, confirming
that which is with you, and be not the first
to disbelieve in it. And sell not My signs
for a little price; and fear you Me.
And do not confound the truth with vanity,
and do not conceal the truth wittingly.

40   And perform the prayer, and pay the alms,
and bow with those that bow. Will you bid
others to piety, and forget yourselves
while you recite the Book? Do you not understand?
Seek you help in patience and prayer,
for grievous it is, save to the humble
who reckon that they shall meet their Lord
and that unto Him they are returning.

Children of Israel, remember My blessing
wherewith I blessed you, and that I
have preferred you above all beings;
and beware of a day when no soul for another

45   shall give satisfaction, and no intercession
shall be accepted from it, nor any counterpoise
be taken, neither shall they be helped.

And when We delivered you from the folk of Pharaoh
who were visiting you with evil chastisement,

slaughtering your sons, and sparing your women;
and in that was a grievous trial from your Lord.
And when We divided for you the sea
and delivered you, and drowned Pharaoh's folk
while you were beholding.
And when We appointed with Moses forty nights
then you took to yourselves the Calf after him
and you were evildoers;
then We pardoned you after that, that haply
you should be thankful.
50 And when We gave to Moses the Book
and the Salvation, that haply
you should be guided.
And when Moses said to his people,
'My people, you have done wrong against yourselves
by your taking the Calf; now turn to your Creator
and slay one another. That will be better for you
in your Creator's sight, and He will turn to you;
truly He turns, and is All-compassionate.'
And when you said, 'Moses, we will not believe thee
till we see God openly'; and the thunderbolt took you
while you were beholding.
Then We raised you up after you were dead, that haply
you should be thankful.
And We outspread the cloud to overshadow you,
and We sent down manna and quails upon you:
'Eat of the good things wherewith We have provided you.
And they worked no wrong upon Us, but
themselves they wronged.
55 And when We said, 'Enter this township,
and eat easefully of it wherever you will,
and enter in at the gate, prostrating,
and say, Unburdening; We will forgive you
your transgressions, and increase the good-doers.'
Then the evildoers substituted a saying
other than that which had been said to them;
so We sent down upon the evildoers
wrath out of heaven for their ungodliness.
And when Moses sought water for his people,

so We said, 'Strike with thy staff the rock';
and there gushed forth from it twelve fountains;
all the people knew now their drinking-place.
'Eat and drink of God's providing, and
mischief not in the earth, doing corruption.'
And when you said, 'Moses, we will not endure
one sort of food; pray to thy Lord for us, that He
may bring forth for us of that the earth produces—
green herbs, cucumbers, corn, lentils, onions.'
He said, 'Would you have in exchange what is meaner
for what is better? Get you down to Egypt;
you shall have there that you demanded.'
And abasement and poverty were pitched upon them,
and they were laden with the burden of God's anger;
that, because they had disbelieved the signs of God
and slain the Prophets unrightfully; that,
because they disobeyed, and were transgressors.
Surely they that believe, and those of Jewry,
and the Christians, and those Sabaeans,
whoso believes in God and the Last Day, and works
righteousness—their wage awaits them with their Lord,
and no fear shall be on them, neither shall they sorrow.

60   And when We took compact with you, and raised above you
the Mount: 'Take forcefully what We have given you, and
remember what is in it; haply you shall be godfearing.'
Then you turned away thereafter, and but for the bounty
and mercy of God towards you, you had been of the losers.
And well you know there were those among you
that transgressed the Sabbath, and We said to them,
'Be you apes, miserably slinking!'
And We made it a punishment exemplary
for all the former times and for the latter,
and an admonition to such as are godfearing.
And when Moses said to his people,
'God commands you to sacrifice a cow.' They said,
'Dost thou take us in mockery?' He said,
'I take refuge with God, lest I should be
one of the ignorant.' They said, 'Pray to thy Lord

8

for us, that He may make clear to us what she may be.'
He said, 'He says she is a cow neither old, nor virgin,
middling between the two; so do that you are bidden.'
65 They said, 'Pray to thy Lord for us, that He make clear
to us what her colour may be.' He said, 'He says
she shall be a golden cow, bright her colour,
gladdening the beholders.' They said, 'Pray
to thy Lord for us, that He make clear to us
what she may be; cows are much alike to us;
and, if God will, we shall then be guided.'
He said, 'He says she shall be a cow not broken
to plough the earth or to water the tillage,
one kept secure, with no blemish on her.' They said,
'Now thou hast brought the truth'; and therefore they
sacrificed her, a thing they had scarcely done.
And when you killed a living soul, and disputed
thereon—and God disclosed what you were hiding—
so We said, 'Smite him with part of it'; even so
God brings to life the dead, and He shows you
His signs, that haply you may have understanding.
Then your hearts became hardened thereafter
and are like stones, or even yet harder;
for there are stones from which rivers come gushing,
and others split, so that water issues from them,
and others crash down in the fear of God.
And God is not heedless of the things you do.

70 Are you then so eager that they should believe you,
seeing there is a party of them that heard
God's word, and then tampered with it, and that
after they had comprehended it, wittingly?
And when they meet those who believe, they say
'We believe'; and when they go privily
one to another, they say, 'Do you speak to them
of what God has revealed to you, that they may
thereby dispute with you before your Lord?
      Have you no understanding?'
Know they not that God knows what they keep secret
      and what they publish?

And some there are of them that are common folk
not knowing the Book, but only fancies
and mere conjectures. So woe to those
who write the Book with their hands, then say,
'This is from God,' that they may sell it
for a little price; so woe to them
for what their hands have written, and woe
  to them for their earnings.
And they say, 'The Fire shall not touch us
save a number of days.' Say: 'Have you taken
with God a covenant? God will not fail in His
covenant; or say you things against God
  of which you know nothing?

75   Not so; whoso earns evil, and is encompassed by
his transgression—those are the inhabitants of the Fire;
  there they shall dwell forever.
And those that believe, and do deeds of
righteousness—those are the inhabitants of Paradise;
  there they shall dwell forever.'

And when We took compact with the Children of Israel:
'You shall not serve any save God;
and to be good to parents, and the near kinsman,
and to orphans, and to the needy;
and speak good to men, and perform the prayer,
and pay the alms.' Then you turned away,
all but a few of you, swerving aside.
And when We took compact with you: 'You shall not
shed your own blood, neither expel your own
from your habitations'; then you confirmed it
and yourselves bore witness. Then there you are
killing one another, and expelling a party of you
from their habitations, conspiring against them
in sin and enmity; and if they come to you
as captives, you ransom them; yet their expulsion
was forbidden you. What, do you believe
in part of the Book, and disbelieve in part?
What shall be the recompense of those of you who
do that, but degradation in the present life,

and on the Day of Resurrection to be returned
unto the most terrible of chastisement?
And God is not heedless of the things you do.
80   Those who have purchased the present life at the price
of the world to come—for them the chastisement
shall not be lightened, neither shall they be helped.

And We gave to Moses the Book, and after him
sent succeeding Messengers; and We gave Jesus
son of Mary the clear signs, and confirmed him
with the Holy Spirit; and whensoever
there came to you a Messenger with that your souls
had not desire for, did you become arrogant,
and some cry lies to, and some slay?

And they say, 'Our hearts are uncircumcised.'
Nay, but God has cursed them for their unbelief;
little will they believe. When there came to them
a Book from God, confirming what was with them—
and they aforetimes prayed for victory
over the unbelievers—when there came to them
that they recognized, they disbelieved in it;
and the curse of God is on the unbelievers.
Evil is the thing they have sold themselves for,
disbelieving in that which God sent down,
grudging that God should send down of His bounty
on whomsoever He will of His servants,
and they were laden with anger upon anger;
and for unbelievers awaits a humbling chastisement.
85   And when they were told, 'Believe in that
God has sent down,' they said, 'We believe
in what was sent down on us'; and they disbelieve
in what is beyond that, yet it is the truth
confirming what is with them. Say: 'Why then
were you slaying the Prophets of God
in former time, if you were believers?'

And Moses came to you with the clear signs,
then you took to yourselves the Calf after him

and you were evildoers.
And when We took compact with you, and raised over you
the Mount: 'Take forcefully what We have given you
and give ear.' They said, 'We hear, and rebel';
and they were made to drink the Calf in their hearts
for their unbelief. Say: 'Evil is the thing
your faith bids you to, if you are believers.'
Say: 'If the Last Abode with God is yours
exclusively, and not for other people,
then long for death—if you speak truly.'
But they will never long for it, because of that
their hands have forwarded; God knows the evildoers;
90 and thou shalt find them the eagerest of men
for life. And of the idolaters; there is one of them
wishes if he might be spared a thousand years,
yet his being spared alive shall not remove him
from the chastisement. God sees the things they do.
Say: 'Whosoever is an enemy to Gabriel—
he it was that brought it down upon thy heart
by the leave of God, confirming what was before it,
and for a guidance and good tidings to the believers.
Whosoever is an enemy to God and His angels
and His Messengers, and Gabriel, and Michael—
surely God is an enemy to the unbelievers.'
And We have sent down unto thee signs, clear signs,
and none disbelieves in them except the ungodly.

Why, whensoever they have made a covenant,
does a party of them reject it?
Nay, but the most of them are unbelievers.
95 When there has come to them a Messenger from God
confirming what was with them, a party of them
that were given the Book reject the Book of God
behind their backs, as though they knew not,
and they follow what the Satans recited
over Solomon's kingdom. Solomon disbelieved not,
but the Satans disbelieved, teaching
the people sorcery, and that which was sent down
upon Babylon's two angels, Harut and Marut;

they taught not any man, without they said,
'We are but a temptation; do not disbelieve.'
From them they learned how they might divide
a man and his wife, yet they did not hurt
any man thereby, save by the leave of God,
and they learned what hurt them, and did not
profit them, knowing well that whoso buys it
shall have no share in the world to come;
evil then was that they sold themselves for,
    if they had but known.
Yet had they believed, and been godfearing,
a recompense from God had been better,
    if they had but known.

O believers', do not say, 'Observe us,'
but say, 'Regard us'; and give ear;
for unbelievers awaits a painful chastisement.

Those unbelievers of the People of the Book
and the idolaters wish not that any good
should be sent down upon you from your Lord;
but God singles out for His mercy whom He will;
    God is of bounty abounding.

100   And for whatever verse We abrogate
or cast into oblivion, We bring a better
or the like of it; knowest thou not that God
    is powerful over everything?
Knowest thou not that to God belongs
the kingdom of the heavens and the earth,
and that you have none, apart from God,
    neither protector nor helper?
Or do you desire to question your Messenger
as Moses was questioned in former time?
Whoso exchanges belief for unbelief has surely
    strayed from the right way.

Many of the People of the Book wish they might
restore you as unbelievers, after you have believed,

in the jealousy of their souls, after the truth
has become clear to them; yet do you pardon
and be forgiving, till God brings His command;
truly God is powerful over everything.
And perform the prayer, and pay the alms; whatever
good you shall forward to your souls' account,
you shall find it with God; assuredly God
     sees the things you do.

105   And they say, 'None shall enter Paradise
except that they be Jews or Christians.'
Such are their fancies. Say: 'Produce your proof,
     if you speak truly.'
Nay, but whosoever submits his will to God,
being a good-doer, his wage is with his Lord,
and no fear shall be on them, neither shall they sorrow.

The Jews say, 'The Christians stand not on anything';
the Christians say, 'The Jews stand not on anything';
yet they recite the Book. So too the ignorant
say the like of them. God shall decide between them
on the Day of Resurrection touching their differences.
And who does greater evil than he who bars
God's places of worship, so that His Name
be not rehearsed in them, and strives to destroy them?
Such men might never enter them, save in fear;
for them is degradation in the present world,
and in the world to come a mighty chastisement.

To God belong the East and the West;
whithersoever you turn, there is the Face of God;
     God is All-embracing, All-knowing.

110   And they say, 'God has taken to Him a son.'
Glory be to Him! Nay, to Him belongs
all that is in the heavens and the earth;
     all obey His will—
the Creator of the heavens and the earth;
and when He decrees a thing, He but says to it
     'Be,' and it is.

And they that know not say, 'Why does God not
speak to us? Why does a sign not come to us?'
So spoke those before them as these men say;
their hearts are much alike. Yet We have made
clear the signs unto a people who are sure.
We have sent thee with the truth, good tidings
to bear, and warning. Thou shalt not be questioned
     touching the inhabitants of Hell.
Never will the Jews be satisfied with thee,
neither the Christians, not till thou followest
their religion. Say: 'God's guidance
is the true guidance.' If thou followest
their caprices, after the knowledge that
has come to thee, thou shalt have against God
     neither protector nor helper.
115   Those to whom We have given the Book
and who recite it with true recitation,
they believe in it; and whoso disbelieves in it,
     they shall be the losers.

Children of Israel, remember My blessing
wherewith I blessed you, and that I
have preferred you above all beings;
and beware a day when no soul for another
shall give satisfaction, and no counterpoise
shall be accepted from it, nor any
intercession shall be profitable to it,
     neither shall they be helped.

And when his Lord tested Abraham
with certain words, and he fulfilled them.
He said, 'Behold, I make you a leader
for the people.' Said he, 'And of my seed?'
He said 'My covenant shall not reach
     the evildoers.'
And when We appointed the House to be
a place of visitation for the people,
     and a sanctuary,
and: 'Take to yourselves Abraham's station

for a place of prayer.' And We made covenant
with Abraham and Ishmael: 'Purify
My House for those that shall go about it
and those that cleave to it, to those who bow
    and prostrate themselves.'

120   And when Abraham said, 'My Lord, make this
a land secure, and provide its people
with fruits, such of them as believe in
    God and the Last Day.'
He said, 'And whoso disbelieves, to him
I shall give enjoyment a little, then I
shall compel him to the chastisement of the Fire—
    how evil a homecoming!'
And when Abraham, and Ishmael with him,
raised up the foundations of the House:
'Our Lord, receive this from us; Thou art
    the All-hearing, the All-knowing;
and, our Lord, make us submissive to Thee,
and of our seed a nation submissive
to Thee; and show us our holy rites, and
turn towards us; surely Thou turnest, and art
    All-compassionate;
and, our Lord, do Thou send among them
a Messenger, one of them, who shall recite
to them Thy signs, and teach them the Book
and the Wisdom, and purify them; Thou art
    the All-mighty, the All-wise.'
Who therefore shrinks from the religion
of Abraham, except he be foolish-minded?
Indeed, We chose him in the present world,
and in the world to come he shall be
    among the righteous.

125   When his Lord said to him, 'Surrender,'
he said, 'I have surrendered me to
    the Lord of all Being.'
And Abraham charged his sons with this
and Jacob likewise: 'My sons, God has chosen
for you the religion; see that you die not
    save in surrender.'

Why, were you witnesses, when death came
to Jacob? When he said to his sons,
'What will you serve after me?' They said,
'We will serve thy God and the God of thy fathers
Abraham, Ishmael and Isaac, One God;
    to Him we surrender.'
That is a nation that has passed away;
there awaits them that they have earned,
and there awaits you that you have earned;
you shall not be questioned concerning
    the things they did.

And they say, 'Be Jews or Christians and
you shall be guided.' Say thou: 'Nay, rather
the creed of Abraham, a man of pure faith;
    he was no idolater.'
130   Say you: 'We believe in God, and
in that which has been sent down on us
and sent down on Abraham, Ishmael,
Isaac and Jacob, and the Tribes,
and that which was given to Moses and Jesus
and the Prophets, of their Lord; we
make no division between any of them, and
    to Him we surrender.'
And if they believe in the like of that you
believe in, then they are truly guided; but if
they turn away, then they are clearly in schism;
God will suffice you for them; He is
    the All-hearing, the All-knowing;
the baptism of God; and who is there
that baptizes fairer than God?
    Him we are serving.
Say: 'Would you then dispute with us
concerning God, who is our Lord
and your Lord? Our deeds belong to us,
and to you belong your deeds; Him
    we serve sincerely.
Or do you say, "Abraham, Ishmael,
Isaac and Jacob, and the Tribes—

they were Jews, or they were Christians"?'
Say: 'Have you then greater knowledge,
or God? And who does greater evil than
he who conceals a testimony received
from God? And God is not heedless of
    the things you do.'

135   That is a nation that has passed away;
there awaits them that they have earned,
and there awaits you that you have earned;
you shall not be questioned concerning
    the things they did.

The fools among the people will say,
'What has turned them from the direction
they were facing in their prayers aforetime?'
        Say:
  'To God belong the East and the West;
He guides whomsoever He will
    to a straight path.'

Thus We appointed you a midmost nation
that you might be witnesses to the people,
and that the Messenger might be a witness
to you; and We did not appoint the direction
thou wast facing, except that We might know
who followed the Messenger from him who turned
on his heels—though it were a grave thing
save for those whom God has guided; but
God would never leave your faith to waste—
truly, God is All-gentle with the people,
    All-compassionate.
We have seen thee turning thy face about
in the heaven; now We will surely turn thee
to a direction that shall satisfy thee.
Turn thy face towards the Holy Mosque; and
wherever you are, turn your faces towards it.
Those who have been given the Book know it is
the truth from their Lord; God is not heedless of
    the things they do.

140   Yet if thou shouldst bring to those that have been
given the Book every sign, they will not follow
thy direction; thou art not a follower
of their direction, neither are they followers
of one another's direction. If thou followest
their caprices, after the knowledge
that has come to thee, then thou wilt surely be
      among the evildoers
whom We have given the Book, and they recognize it
as they recognize their sons, even though
there is a party of them conceal the truth
      and that wittingly.
The truth comes from thy Lord; then be not
      among the doubters.
Every man has his direction to which he turns;
so be you forward in good works. Wherever
you may be, God will bring you all together;
surely God is powerful over everything.
From whatsoever place thou issuest, turn
thy face towards the Holy Mosque; it is
the truth from thy Lord. God is not heedless of
      the things you do.

145   From whatsoever place thou issuest, turn
thy face towards the Holy Mosque; and
wherever you may be, turn your faces
towards it, that the people may not have
any argument against you, excepting
the evildoers of them; and fear you them not,
but fear you Me; and that I may perfect
My blessing upon you, and that haply so
      you may be guided;
as also We have sent among you, of yourselves,
a Messenger, to recite Our signs to you
and to purify you, and to teach you
the Book and the Wisdom, and to teach you
      that you knew not.
So remember Me, and I will remember
you; and be thankful to Me; and be you not
      ungrateful towards Me.

O all you who believe, seek you help
in patience and prayer; surely God is
    with the patient.
And say not of those slain in God's way,
'They are dead'; rather they are living,
    but you are not aware.

150   Surely We will try you with something of fear
and hunger, and diminution of goods
and lives and fruits; yet give thou good tidings
    unto the patient
who, when they are visited by an affliction,
say, 'Surely we belong to God, and
    to Him we return';
upon those rest blessings and mercy
from their Lord, and those—they are
    the truly guided.

Safa and Marwa are among the waymarks
of God; so whosoever makes the Pilgrimage
to the House, or the Visitation,
it is no fault in him to circumambulate
them; and whoso volunteers good, God is
    All-grateful, All-knowing

Those who conceal the clear signs and the guidance
that We have sent down, after We have shown them
clearly in the Book—they shall be cursed by
    God and the cursers,
155   save such as repent and make amends, and show
clearly—towards them I shall turn; I turn,
    All-compassionate.
But those who disbelieve, and die disbelieving—
upon them shall rest the curse of God
and the angels, and of men altogether,
therein dwelling forever; the chastisement
shall not be lightened for them; no respite
    shall be given them.

Your God is One God;

there is no god but He,
the All-merciful, the All-compassionate.

Surely in the creation of the heavens and the earth
and the alternation of night and day
and the ship that runs in the sea with profit
to men, and the water God sends down from heaven
therewith reviving the earth after it is dead
and His scattering abroad in it all manner of
crawling thing, and the turning about of the winds
and the clouds compelled between heaven and earth—
surely there are signs for a people having understanding.

160 Yet there be men who take to themselves compeers
apart from God, loving them as God is loved;
but those that believe love God more ardently.
O if the evildoers might see, when they see
the chastisement, that the power altogether
belongs to God, and that God is terrible
        in chastisement,
when those that were followed disown their followers,
and they see the chastisement, and their cords
        are cut asunder,
and those that followed say, 'O if only we might
return again and disown them, as they have disowned
us!' Even so God shall show them their works.
O bitter regrets for them! Never shall they
        issue from the Fire.

O men, eat of what is in the earth
lawful and good; and follow not the steps
of Satan; he is a manifest foe to you.
He only commands you to evil and indecency,
and that you should speak against God such things
        as you know not.

165 And when it is said to them, 'Follow what God
has sent down,' they say, 'No; but we will follow
such things as we found our fathers doing.'

What? And if their fathers had no understanding
of anything, and if they were not guided?
The likeness of those who disbelieve is as
the likeness of one who shouts to that
which hears nothing, save a call and a cry;
deaf, dumb, blind—they do not understand.

O believers, eat of the good things
wherewith We have provided you, and give thanks
to God, if it be Him that you serve.
These things only has He forbidden you:
carrion, blood, the flesh of swine,
what has been hallowed to other than God.
Yet whoso is constrained, not desiring
nor transgressing, no sin shall be on him;
God is All-forgiving, All-compassionate.

Those who conceal what of the Book God has sent down
on them, and sell it for a little price—they shall eat
naught but the Fire in their bellies; God shall not
speak to them on the Day of Resurrection
neither purify them; there awaits them
　　　a painful chastisement.
170　Those are they that have bought error at
the price of guidance, and chastisement at
the price of pardon; how patiently they
　　　shall endure the Fire!
That, because God has sent down the Book
with the truth; and those that are
at variance regarding the Book
　　　are in wide schism.

It is not piety, that you turn your faces
　　　to the East and to the West.
　　　True piety is this:
to believe in God, and the Last Day,
the angels, the Book, and the Prophets,
to give of one's substance, however cherished,
　　　to kinsmen, and orphans,

22

the needy, the traveller, beggars,
and to ransom the slave,
to perform the prayer, to pay the alms.
And they who fulfil their covenant
when they have engaged in a covenant,
and endure with fortitude
misfortune, hardship and peril,
these are they who are true in their faith,
these are the truly godfearing.

O believers, prescribed for you is
retaliation, touching the slain;
freeman for freeman, slave for slave,
female for female. But if aught is pardoned
a man by his brother, let the pursuing
be honourable, and let the payment be
with kindliness. That is a lightening
granted you by your Lord, and a mercy;
and for him who commits aggression
after that—for him there awaits
a painful chastisement.
175   In retaliation there is life for you,
men possessed of minds; haply you
will be godfearing.

Prescribed for you, when any of you
is visited by death, and he leaves behind
some goods, is to make testament
in favour of his parents and kinsmen
honourably—an obligation
on the godfearing.
Then if any man changes it after
hearing it, the sin shall rest upon
those who change it; surely God is
All-hearing, All-knowing.
But if any man fears injustice or
sin from one making testament, and so
makes things right between them, then
sin shall not rest upon him; surely God is

23

All-forgiving, All-compassionate.

O believers, prescribed for you is
the Fast, even as it was prescribed for
those that were before you—haply you
    will be godfearing—
180   for days numbered; and if any of you
be sick, or if he be on a journey,
then a number of other days; and for those
who are able to fast, a redemption
by feeding a poor man. Yet better
it is for him who volunteers good,
and that you should fast is better for you,
    if you but know;
the month of Ramadan, wherein the Koran
was sent down to be a guidance
to the people, and as clear signs
of the Guidance and the Salvation
So let those of you, who are present
at the month, fast it; and if any of you
be sick, or if he be on a journey,
then a number of other days; God desires
ease for you, and desires not hardship
for you; and that you fulfil the number, and
magnify God that He has guided you, and haply
    you will be thankful.

And when My servants question thee
concerning Me—I am near to answer
the call of the caller, when he calls
to Me; so let them respond to Me,
and let them believe in Me; haply so
    they will go aright.

Permitted to you, upon the night of
the Fast, is to go in to your wives;
they are a vestment for you, and you are
a vestment for them. God knows that you have been
betraying yourselves, and has turned to you

and pardoned you. So now lie with them,
and seek what God has prescribed for you.
And eat and drink, until the white thread
shows clearly to you from the black thread
at the dawn; then complete the Fast
unto the night, and do not lie with them
while you cleave to the mosques. Those are
God's bounds; keep well within them. So God
makes clear His signs to men; haply they
        will be godfearing.

Consume not your goods between you
in vanity; neither proffer it
to the judges, that you may sinfully
consume a portion of other men's goods,
        and that wittingly.

185   They will question thee concerning
the new moons. Say: 'They are appointed
times for the people, and the Pilgrimage.'

It is not piety to come to the houses
from the backs of them; but piety is
to be godfearing; so come to the houses
by their doors, and fear God; haply so
        you will prosper.

And fight in the way of God with those
who fight with you, but aggress not: God loves
        not the aggressors.
And slay them wherever you come upon them,
and expel them from where they expelled you;
persecution is more grievous than slaying.
But fight them not by the Holy Mosque
until they should fight you there;
then, if they fight you, slay them—
such is the recompense of unbelievers—
but if they give over, surely God is
All-forgiving, All-compassionate.

25

Fight them, till there is no persecution
and the religion is God's; then if they
give over, there shall be no enmity
    save for evildoers.
190   The holy month for the holy month;
holy things demand retaliation.
Whoso commits aggression against you,
do you commit aggression against him
like as he has committed against you;
and fear you God, and know that God is
    with the godfearing.

And expend in the way of God;
and cast not yourselves by your own hands
into destruction, but be good-doers; God
    loves the good-doers.

Fulfil the Pilgrimage and the Visitation
unto God; but if you are prevented,
then such offering as may be feasible.
And shave not your heads, till the offering
reaches its place of sacrifice. If any
of you is sick, or injured in his head,
then redemption by fast, or freewill offering,
or ritual sacrifice. When you are secure,
then whosoever enjoys the Visitation
until the Pilgrimage, let his offering
be such as may be feasible; or if he
finds none, then a fast of three days
in the Pilgrimage, and of seven when
you return, that is ten completely;
that is for him whose family are not
present at the Holy Mosque. And fear
God, and know that God is terrible
    in retribution.

The Pilgrimage is in months well-known;
whoso undertakes the duty of Pilgrimage
in them shall not go in to his womenfolk

nor indulge in ungodliness and disputing
in the Pilgrimage. Whatever good you do,
God knows it. And take provision;
but the best provision is godfearing,
so fear you Me, men possessed of minds!
It is no fault in you, that you should seek
bounty from your Lord; but when you press on
from Arafat, then remember God
at the Holy Waymark, and remember Him
as He has guided you, though formerly you
        were gone astray.

195   Then press on from where the people
press on, and pray for God's forgiveness;
God is All-forgiving, All-compassionate.
And when you have performed your holy rites
remember God, as you remember your fathers
or yet more devoutly. Now some men
there are who say, 'Our Lord, give to us
in this world'; such men shall have no part
        in the world to come.
And others there are who say, 'Our Lord,
give to us in this world good, and good
in the world to come, and guard us against the
        chastisement of the Fire';
those—they shall have a portion from
what they have earned; and God is swift
        at the reckoning.
And remember God during certain days
numbered. If any man hastens on
in two days, that is no sin in him;
and if any delays, it is not a sin
in him, if he be godfearing. And
fear you God, and know that unto Him
        you shall be mustered.

200   And some men there are whose saying
upon the present world pleases thee,
and such a one calls on God to witness
what is in his heart, yet he is most stubborn

        in altercation,
and when he turns his back, he hastens about
the earth, to do corruption there and to
destroy the tillage and the stock; and God
        loves not corruption;
and when it is said to him, 'Fear God',
vainglory seizes him in his sin.
So Gehenna shall be enough for him—how
        evil a cradling!
But other men there are that sell themselves
desiring God's good pleasure; and God is gentle
        with His servants.
O believers, enter the peace, all of you,
and follow not the steps of Satan;
205   he is a manifest foe to you. But
if you slip, after the clear signs
have come to you, know then that God is
        All-mighty, All-wise.

What do they look for, but that God
shall come to them in the cloud-shadows,
and the angels? The matter is determined,
and unto God all matters are returned.
Ask the Children of Israel how many a clear sign
We gave them. Whoso changes God's blessing
after it has come to him, God is terrible
        in retribution.
Decked out fair to the unbelievers
is the present life, and they deride
the believers; but those who were godfearing
shall be above them on the Resurrection Day;
and God provides whomsoever He will
        without reckoning.

The people were one nation; then God sent forth
the Prophets, good tidings to bear
and warning, and He sent down with them
the Book with the truth, that He might
decide between the people touching their differences;

 and only those who had been given it
were at variance upon it, after the
clear signs had come to them, being insolent
one to another; then God guided those
who believed to the truth, touching which
they were at variance, by His leave;
and God guides whomsoever He will
        to a straight path.

210 Or did you suppose you should enter Paradise
without there had come upon you the like
of those who passed away before you?
They were afflicted by misery and hardship
and were so convulsed, that the Messenger
and those who believed with him said,
'When comes God's help?' Ah, but surely
        God's help is nigh.

They will question thee concerning
what they should expend. Say: 'Whatsoever good
you expend is for parents and kinsmen,
orphans, the needy, and the traveller;
and whatever good you may do, God has
        knowledge of it.'

Prescribed for you is fighting, though it be
        hateful to you.
Yet it may happen that you will hate a thing
which is better for you; and it may happen that you
will love a thing which is worse for you; God knows,
        and you know not.

They will question thee concerning
the holy month, and fighting in it.
Say: 'Fighting in it is a heinous thing,
but to bar from God's way, and disbelief in Him,
and the Holy Mosque, and to expel its people
from it—that is more heinous in God's sight;
and persecution is more heinous than slaying.'
They will not cease to fight with you,

till they turn you from your religion,
if they are able; and whosoever of you
turns from his religion, and dies disbelieving—
their works have failed in this world and the next;
those are the inhabitants of the Fire; therein
    they shall dwell forever.

215   But the believers, and those who emigrate
and struggle in God's way—those have hope of
God's compassion; and God is All-forgiving,
    All-compassionate.

They will question thee concerning
wine, and arrow-shuffling. Say: 'In both
is heinous sin, and uses for men,
but the sin in them is more heinous
    than the usefulness.'

They will question thee concerning
what they should expend. Say: 'The abundance.'
So God makes clear His signs to you; haply
    you will reflect;
in this world, and the world to come.

They will question thee concerning
the orphans. Say: 'To set their affairs
    aright is good.
And if you intermix with them, they are
your brothers. God knows well
him who works corruption from him
who sets aright; and had He willed
He would have harassed you. Surely God is
    All-mighty, All-wise.'

220   Do not marry idolatresses, until
they believe; a believing slavegirl
is better than an idolatress, though
you may admire her. And do not marry
idolaters, until they believe. A believing
slave is better than an idolater, though

you may admire him.
Those call unto the Fire; and God calls unto
Paradise, and pardon, by His leave, and He
makes clear His signs to the people; haply
        they will remember.

They will question thee concerning
the monthly course. Say: 'It is hurt;
so go apart from women during
the monthly course, and do not approach them
till they are clean. When they have cleansed
themselves, then come unto them as God
has commanded you.' Truly, God loves
those who repent, and He loves those
        who cleanse themselves.
Your women are a tillage for you; so come
unto your tillage as you wish, and forward
for your souls; and fear God, and know that
you shall meet Him. Give thou good tidings
        to the believers.

Do not make God a hindrance, through your oaths,
to being pious and godfearing, and putting
things right between men. Surely God is
        All-hearing, All-knowing.
225 God will not take you to task for a slip
in your oaths; but He will take you to task
for what your hearts have earned; and God is
        All-forgiving, All-clement.

For those who forswear their women
a wait of four months; if they revert,
God is All-forgiving, All-compassionate;
but if they resolve on divorce, surely God is
        All-hearing, All-knowing.
Divorced women shall wait by themselves
for three periods; and it is not lawful
for them to hide what God has created
in their wombs; if they believe in God

and the Last Day. In such time their mates
have better right to restore them, if they
desire to set things right. Women have
such honourable rights as obligations, but
their men have a degree above them; God is
    All-mighty, All-wise.
Divorce is twice; then honourable retention
or setting free kindly. It is not lawful
for you to take of what you have given them
unless the couple fear they may not maintain
God's bounds; if you fear they may not maintain
God's bounds, it is no fault in them for her
to redeem herself. Those are God's bounds;
do not transgress them. Whosoever
transgresses the bounds of God—those
    are the evildoers.

230　　If he divorces her finally, she shall not
be lawful to him after that, until she
marries another husband. If he divorces her,
then it is no fault in them to return
to each other, if they suppose that they will
maintain God's bounds. Those are God's bounds;
He makes them clear unto a people
    that have knowledge.
When you divorce women, and they have reached
their term, then retain them honourably
or set them free honourably; do not retain them
by force, to transgress; whoever does that
has wronged himself. Take not God's signs
in mockery, and remember God's blessing
upon you, and the Book and the Wisdom He
has sent down on you, to admonish you.
And fear God, and know that God has knowledge
    of everything.
When you divorce women, and they have reached
their term, do not debar them from marrying
their husbands, when they have agreed together
honourably. That is an admonition for
whoso of you believes in God and the Last Day;

that is cleaner and purer for you; God knows,
  and you know not.

Mothers shall suckle their children two years
completely, for such as desire to fulfil
the suckling. It is for the father to provide them
and clothe them honourably. No soul is charged
save to its capacity; a mother shall not be pressed
for her child, neither a father for his child.
The heir has a like duty. But if the couple
desire by mutual consent and consultation
to wean, then it is no fault in them.
And if you desire to seek nursing
for your children, it is no fault in you
provide you hand over what you have given
honourably; and fear God, and know that God sees
  the things you do.

And those of you who die, leaving wives,
they shall wait by themselves for four months
and ten nights; when they have reached their term
then it is no fault in you what they may do
with themselves honourably. God is aware of
  the things you do.

235   There is no fault in you touching the proposal
to women you offer, or hide in your hearts;
God knows that you will be mindful of them;
but do not make troth with them secretly
without you speak honourable words.
And do not resolve on the knot of marriage
until the book has reached its term; and know
that God knows what is in your hearts,
so be fearful of Him; and know that God is
  All-forgiving, All-clement.

There is no fault in you, if you divorce
women while as yet you have not touched them
nor appointed any marriage-portion for them;

yet make provision for them, the affluent man
according to his means, and according to his means
the needy man, honourably—an obligation
     on the good-doers.
And if you divorce them before you have
touched them, and you have already appointed
for them a marriage-portion, then one-half
of what you have appointed, unless it be
they make remission, or he makes remission
in whose hand is the knot of marriage;
yet that you should remit is nearer
to godfearing. Forget not to be bountiful
one towards another. Surely God sees
     the things you do.

Be you watchful over the prayers,
and the middle prayer; and do you stand
     obedient to God.
240   And if you are in fear, then afoot
or mounted; but when you are secure, then
remember God, as He taught you the things
     that you knew not.

And those of you who die, leaving wives,
let them make testament for their wives,
provision for a year without expulsion; but if
they go forth, there is no fault in you what
they may do with themselves honourably; God is
     All-mighty, All-wise.
There shall be for divorced women
provision honourable—an obligation
     on the godfearing.

So God makes clear His signs for you; haply
     you will understand.

Hast thou not regarded those who went forth
from their habitations in their thousands
fearful of death? God said to them, 'Die!'

Then He gave them life. Truly God is bounteous
to the people, but most of the people
    are not thankful.

245   So fight in God's way, and know that God is
        All-hearing, All-knowing.
Who is he that will lend God a good loan,
and He will multiply it for him manifold?
God grasps, and outspreads; and unto Him
    you shall be returned.

Hast thou not regarded the Council
of the Children of Israel, after Moses,
when they said to a Prophet of theirs,
'Raise up for us a king, and we will fight
in God's way.' He said, 'Might it be
that, if fighting is prescribed for you,
you will not fight?' They said, 'Why should we
not fight in God's way, who have been
expelled from our habitations
and our children?' Yet when fighting was
prescribed for them, they turned their backs
except a few of them; and God has knowledge
    of the evildoers.
Then their Prophet said to them, 'Verily
God has raised up Saul for you as king.'
They said, 'How should he be king over us
who have better right than he to kingship,
seeing he has not been given amplitude
of wealth?' He said, 'God has chosen him
over you, and has increased him
broadly in knowledge and body. God gives
the kingship to whom He will; and God is
    All-embracing, All-knowing.'
And their Prophet said to them, 'The sign
of his kingship is that the Ark will come to you,
in it a Shechina from your Lord, and a remnant
of what the folk of Moses and Aaron's folk
left behind, the angels bearing it.
Surely in that shall be a sign for you, if

you are believers.'

250   And when Saul went forth with the hosts
he said, 'God will try you with a river;
whosoever drinks of it is not of me,
and whoso tastes it not, he is of me,
saving him who scoops up with his hand.'
But they drank of it, except a few
of them; and when he crossed it, and those
who believed with him, they said, 'We have no
power today against Goliath and his hosts.'
Said those who reckoned they should meet God,
'How often a little company has overcome
a numerous company, by God's leave! And God
    is with the patient.'
So, when they went forth against Goliath
and his hosts, they said, 'Our Lord, pour out
upon us patience, and make firm our feet,
and give us aid against the people of
    the unbelievers!'
And they routed them, by the leave of God,
and David slew Goliath; and God gave him
the kingship, and Wisdom, and He taught him
such as He willed. Had God not driven back
the people, some by the means of others,
the earth had surely corrupted; but God is bounteous
    unto all beings.

These are the signs of God We recite to thee
    in truth,
and assuredly thou art of the number
    of the Envoys.
And those Messengers, some We have preferred
    above others;
some there are to whom God spoke, and some He
    raised in rank.

And We gave Jesus son of Mary the clear signs,
and confirmed him with the Holy Spirit.
And had God willed, those who came after him

would not have fought one against the other
after the clear signs had come to them;
but they fell into variance, and some of them
believed, and some disbelieved; and had God willed
they would not have fought one against the other;
but God does whatsoever He desires.

255   O believers, expend of that wherewith
We have provided you, before there comes a day
wherein shall be neither traffick, nor friendship,
nor intercession; and the unbelievers—they
    are the evildoers.

    God
  there is no god but He, the
  Living, the Everlasting.
Slumber seizes Him not, neither sleep;
    to Him belongs
all that is in the heavens and the earth.
Who is there that shall intercede with Him
    save by His leave?
He knows what lies before them
  and what is after them,
and they comprehend not anything of His knowledge
  save such as He wills.
His Throne comprises the heavens and earth;
the preserving of them oppresses Him not;
He is the All-high, the All-glorious.

No compulsion is there in religion.
Rectitude has become clear from error.
So whosoever disbelieves in idols
and believes in God, has laid hold of
the most firm handle, unbreaking; God is
    All-hearing, All-knowing.

God is the Protector of the believers;
He brings them forth from the shadows
  into the light.

And the unbelievers—their protectors are
idols, that bring them forth from the light
    into the shadows;
those are the inhabitants of the Fire,
    therein dwelling forever.

260   Hast thou not regarded him who disputed
with Abraham, concerning his Lord,
that God had given him the kingship? When
Abraham said, 'My Lord is He who gives
life, and makes to die,' he said, 'I give
life, and make to die.' Said Abraham, 'God
brings the sun from the east; so bring thou
it from the west.' Then the unbeliever
was confounded. God guides not the people
    of the evildoers.
Or such as he who passed by a city
that was fallen down upon its turrets;
he said, 'How shall God give life to this
now it is dead?' So God made him die
a hundred years, then He raised him up,
saying, 'How long hast thou tarried?' He said,
'I have tarried a day, or part of a day.'
Said He, 'Nay; thou hast tarried a hundred years.
Look at thy food and drink—it has not spoiled;
and look at thy ass. So We would make thee
a sign for the people. And look at the bones,
how We shall set them up, and then clothe them
with flesh.' So, when it was made clear
to him, he said, 'I know that God is powerful
    over everything.'
And when Abraham said, 'My Lord, show me
how Thou wilt give life to the dead,' He said,
'Why, dost thou not believe?' 'Yes,' he said,
'but that my heart may be at rest.' Said He,
'Take four birds, and twist them to thee,
then set a part of them on every hill,
then summon them, and they will come to thee
running. And do thou know that God is

All-mighty, All-wise.'

The likeness of those who expend their wealth
in the way of God is as the likeness
of a grain of corn that sprouts seven ears,
in every ear a hundred grains. So God
multiplies unto whom He will; God is
      All-embracing, All-knowing.
Those who expend their wealth in the way of God
then follow not up what they have expended with
reproach and injury, their wage is with their Lord,
and no fear shall be on them, neither shall they sorrow.
Honourable words, and forgiveness, are better than
a freewill offering followed by injury; and God is
      All-sufficient, All-clement.
O believers, void not your freewill offerings
with reproach and injury, as one who expends
of his substance to show off to men
and believes not in God and the Last Day.
The likeness of him is as the likeness
of a smooth rock on which is soil,
and a torrent smites it, and leaves it barren.
They have no power over anything that they
have earned. God guides not the people
      of the unbelievers.
But the likeness of those who expend their
wealth, seeking God's good pleasure, and to
confirm themselves, is as the likeness
of a garden upon a hill; a torrent smites it
and it yields its produce twofold; if no
torrent smites it, yet dew; and God sees
      the things you do.
Would any of you wish to have a garden
of palms and vines, with rivers flowing
beneath it, and all manner of fruit there
for him, then old age smites him, and he has
seed, but weaklings, then a whirlwind with
fire smites it, and it is consumed?
So God makes clear the signs to you; haply

265

you will reflect.
O believers, expend of the good things
you have earned, and of that We
have produced for you from the earth,
and intend not the corrupt of it for
    your expending;
270   for you would never take it yourselves, except
you closed an eye on it; and know that God is
        All-sufficient, All-laudable.
Satan promises you poverty, and bids you
unto indecency; but God promises you
His pardon and His bounty; and God is
        All-embracing, All-knowing.
He gives the Wisdom to whomsoever He will,
and whoso is given the Wisdom, has been
given much good; yet none remembers but men
        possessed of minds.
And whatever expenditure you expend,
and whatever vow you vow, surely God
knows it. No helpers have the evildoers.
If you publish your freewill offerings, it is
excellent; but if you conceal them, and give them
to the poor, that is better for you, and will
acquit you of your evil deeds; God is aware of
        the things you do.

Thou art not responsible for guiding them;
but God guides whomsoever He will.

And whatever good you expend is for yourselves,
for then you are expending, being desirous
only of God's Face; and whatever good
you expend shall be repaid to you
in full, and you will not be wronged,
it being for the poor who are restrained
in the way of God, and are unable
to journey in the land; the ignorant man
supposes them rich because of their abstinence,
but thou shalt know them by their mark—

they do not beg of men importunately.
And whatever good you expend, surely God has
    knowledge of it.
275   Those who expend their wealth night and day, secretly
and in public, their wage awaits them with their Lord,
and no fear shall be on them, neither shall they sorrow.

Those who devour usury shall not rise again
except as he rises, whom Satan of the touch
prostrates; that is because they say,
'Trafficking is like usury.' God has
permitted trafficking, and forbidden usury.
Whosoever receives an admonition
from his Lord and gives over, he shall have
his past gains, and his affair is
committed to God; but whosoever reverts—
those are the inhabitants of the Fire,
    therein dwelling forever.
God blots out usury, but freewill offerings
He augments with interest. God loves not
    any guilty ingrate.

Those who believe and do deeds of righteousness,
and perform the prayer, and pay the alms—
their wage awaits them with their Lord,
and no fear shall be on them, neither shall they sorrow.

O believers, fear you God; and
give up the usury that is outstanding, if
    you are believers.
But if you do not, then take notice that
God shall war with you, and His Messenger; yet
if you repent, you shall have your principal,
    unwronging and unwronged.
280   And if any man should be in difficulties,
let him have respite till things are easier; but
that you should give freewill offerings is better for you,
    did you but know.

And fear a day wherein you shall be
returned to God, and every soul shall be
paid in full what it has earned; and they
  shall not be wronged.

O believers, when you contract a debt
one upon another for a stated term,
write it down, and let a writer
write it down between you justly,
and let not any writer refuse
to write it down, as God has taught him;
so let him write, and let the debtor
dictate, and let him fear God his Lord
and not diminish aught of it. And if
the debtor be a fool, or weak, or unable
to dictate himself, then let his guardian
dictate justly. And call in to witness
two witnesses, men; or if the two
be not men, then one man and two women,
such witnesses as you approve of,
that if one of the two women errs
the other will remind her; and let the witnesses
not refuse, whenever they are summoned.
And be not loth to write it down,
whether it be small or great, with its term;
that is more equitable in God's sight,
more upright for testimony, and likelier
that you will not be in doubt. Unless it be
merchandise present that you give and take
between you; then it shall be no fault in you
if you do not write it down. And take witnesses
when you are trafficking one with another.
And let not either writer or witness be
pressed; or if you do, that is ungodliness in you.
And fear God; God teaches you, and God has
  knowledge of everything.
And if you are upon a journey, and
you do not find a writer, then a pledge
in hand But if one of you trusts another,

let him who is trusted deliver his trust,
and let him fear God his Lord. And do not
conceal the testimony; whoso conceals it,
his heart is sinful; and God has knowledge of
    the things you do.
To God belongs all that is in the heavens and
earth. Whether you publish what is in your hearts
or hide it, God shall make reckoning with you
for it. He will forgive whom He will,
and chastise whom He will; God is powerful
    over everything.

285   The Messenger believes in what was sent down to
        him from his Lord,
and the believers; each one believes in God
    and His angels,
and in His Books and His Messengers; we
    make no division
between any one of His Messengers. They say,
    'We hear, and obey.
Our Lord, grant us Thy forgiveness; unto Thee
    is the homecoming.'

God charges no soul save to its capacity;
standing to its account is what it has earned,
and against its account what it has merited.

      Our Lord,
    take us not to task
if we forget, or make mistake.
      Our Lord,
    charge us not with a load such
as Thou didst lay upon those before us.
      Our Lord,
    do Thou not burden us
beyond what we have the strength to bear.
      And pardon us,
      and forgive us,

and have mercy on us;
Thou art our Protector.
And help us against the people
of the unbelievers.

III

THE HOUSE OF IMRAN

In the Name of God, the Merciful, the Compassionate

Alif Lam Mim

God
there is no god but He, the
Living, the Everlasting.

He has sent down upon thee the Book
with the truth, confirming what was before it,
and He sent down the Torah and the Gospel
aforetime, as guidance to the people,
    and He sent down the Salvation.

As for those who disbelieve in God's signs, for
them awaits a terrible chastisement; God is
    All-mighty, Vengeful.

From God nothing whatever is hidden
in heaven and earth. It is He who forms you
in the womb as He will. There is no god but He,
    the All-mighty, the All-wise.

5   It is He who sent down upon thee the Book,
wherein are verses clear that are the Essence
of the Book, and others ambiguous.
As for those in whose hearts is swerving,
they follow the ambiguous part, desiring
dissension, and desiring its interpretation;
and none knows its interpretation, save
only God. And those firmly rooted in
knowledge say, 'We believe in it; all
is from our Lord'; yet none remembers, but men
    possessed of minds.

Our Lord, make not our hearts to swerve
after that Thou hast guided us; and give us
     mercy from Thee;
     Thou art the Giver.
Our Lord, it is Thou that shall gather
mankind for a day whereon is no doubt;
     verily God will
     not fail the tryst.
As for the unbelievers, their riches
will not avail them, neither their children,
aught against God; those—they shall be
     fuel for the Fire
like Pharaoh's folk, and the people before them,
who cried lies to Our signs; God seized them
because of their sins; God is terrible
     in retribution.

10   Say to the unbelievers: 'You shall be
overthrown, and mustered into Gehenna—
     an evil cradling!'

There has already been a sign for you
in the two companies that encountered,
one company fighting in the way of God
and another unbelieving; they saw them
twice the like of them, as the eye sees,
but God confirms with His help whom He will.
Surely in that is a lesson for men
     possessed of eyes.

Decked out fair to men is the love of lusts—
women, children, heaped-up heaps of gold
and silver, horses of mark, cattle
and tillage. That is the enjoyment of
the present life; but God—with Him is
     the fairest resort.
Say: 'Shall I tell you of a better than that?'
For those that are godfearing, with their Lord
are gardens underneath which rivers flow,
therein dwelling forever, and spouses

purified, and God's good pleasure. And God
sees His servants
who say, 'Our Lord, we believe; forgive us
our sins, and guard us against the chastisement
of the Fire'—

15   men who are patient, truthful, obedient,
expenders in alms, imploring God's pardon
at the daybreak.

God bears witness that
there is no god but He—
and the angels, and men possessed of knowledge—
upholding justice;
there is no god but He,
the All-mighty, the All-wise.

The true religion with God is Islam.

Those who were given the Book were not at variance
except after the knowledge came to them,
being insolent one to another. And whoso
disbelieves in God's signs, God is swift
at the reckoning.
So if they dispute with thee, say: 'I have
surrendered my will to God, and whosoever
follows me.'
And say to those who have been given the Book
and to the common folk: 'Have you surrendered?'
If they have surrendered, they are right guided;
but if they turn their backs, thine it is only
to deliver the Message; and God
sees His servants.

20   Those who disbelieve in the signs of God
and slay the Prophets without right,
and slay such men as bid to justice—
do thou give them the good tidings of
a painful chastisement;
their works have failed in this world and the next;
they have no helpers.
Hast thou not regarded those who were given

a portion of the Book, being called to the Book
of God, that it might decide between them,
and then a party of them turned away,
    swerving aside?
That, because they said, 'The Fire shall not
touch us, except for a number of days';
and the lies they forged has deluded them
    in their religion.
But how will it be, when We gather them
for a day whereon is no doubt, and every soul
shall be paid in full what it has earned, and they
    shall not be wronged?

25 Say: 'O God, Master of the Kingdom,
Thou givest the Kingdom to whom Thou wilt,
and seizest the Kingdom from whom Thou wilt,
Thou exaltest whom Thou wilt, and Thou
abasest whom Thou wilt; in Thy hand
is the good; Thou art powerful
    over everything.
Thou makest the night to enter into the day
and Thou makest the day to enter into the night,
Thou bringest forth the living from the dead
and Thou bringest forth the dead from the living,
and Thou providest whomsoever Thou wilt
    without reckoning.'

Let not the believers take the unbelievers
for friends, rather than the believers—
for whoso does that belongs not to God in
anything—unless you have a fear of them.
God warns you that you beware of Him,
and unto God is the homecoming. Say:
'Whether you hide what is in your breasts
or publish it, God knows it. God knows
what is in the heavens and what is in
the earth; and God is powerful
    over everything.'

The day every soul shall find what it has done of good
brought forward, and what it has done of evil;
it will wish if there were only a far space
between it and that day. God warns you that you
beware of Him; and God is gentle with His servants.

Say: 'If you love God, follow me, and God
will love you, and forgive you your sins;
God is All-forgiving, All-compassionate.'
Say: 'Obey God, and the Messenger.' But
if they turn their backs, God loves not
  the unbelievers.

30   God chose Adam and Noah
   and the House of Abraham
   and the House of Imran
   above all beings, the
   seed of one another;
   God hears, and knows.

   When the wife of Imran
   said, 'Lord, I have vowed
   to Thee, in dedication,
   what is within my womb.
   Receive Thou this from me;
   Thou hearest, and knowest.'
   And when she gave birth to her
   she said, 'Lord, I have given
   birth to her, a female.'
   (And God knew very well
   what she had given birth to;
   the male is not as the female.)
   'And I have named her Mary,
   and commend her to Thee
   with her seed, to protect them
   from the accursed Satan.'
   Her Lord received the child
   with gracious favour,

and by His goodness
she grew up comely,
Zachariah taking
charge of her. Whenever
Zachariah went in to her
in the Sanctuary, he
found her provisioned.
'Mary,' he said,
'how comes this to thee?'
'From God,' she said.
Truly God provisions
whomsoever He will
without reckoning.
Then Zachariah
prayed to his Lord
saying, 'Lord, give me
of Thy goodness
a goodly offspring.
Yea, Thou hearest
prayer.' And the angels
called to him, standing
in the Sanctuary
at worship, 'Lo, God
gives thee good tidings
of John, who shall confirm
a Word of God,
a chief, and chaste,
a Prophet, righteous.'
35   'Lord,' said Zachariah,
'how shall I have a son,
seeing I am an old man
and my wife is barren?'
'Even so,' God said,
'God does what He will.'
'Lord,' said Zachariah,
'appoint to me a sign.'
'Thy sign,' God said,
'is that thou shalt not
speak, save by tokens,

to men for three days.
And mention thy Lord
oft, and give glory
at evening and dawn.'

And when the angels said,
'Mary, God has chosen
thee, and purified
thee; He has chosen
thee above all women.
Mary, be obedient to
thy Lord, prostrating
and bowing before Him.'
(That is of the tidings
of the Unseen, that We
reveal to thee; for thou
wast not with them, when
they were casting quills
which of them should have
charge of Mary; thou
wast not with them, when
they were disputing.)
40   When the angels said,
'Mary, God gives thee good
tidings of a Word from Him
whose name is Messiah,
Jesus, son of Mary;
high honoured shall he be
in this world and the next,
near stationed to God.
He shall speak to men
in the cradle, and of age,
and righteous he shall be.'
'Lord,' said Mary,
'how shall I have a son
seeing no mortal has
touched me?' 'Even so,'
God said, 'God
creates what He will.

When He decrees a thing
He does but say to it
"Be," and it is.
And He will teach him
the Book, the Wisdom,
the Torah, the Gospel,
to be a Messenger
to the Children of Israel
saying, "I have come to
you with a sign from
your Lord. I will create
for you out of clay as
the likeness of a bird;
then I will breathe into
it, and it will be a
bird, by the leave of God.
I will also heal
the blind and the leper,
and bring to life the
dead, by the leave of God.
I will inform you too
of what things you eat,
and what you treasure up
in your houses. Surely
in that is a sign for you,
if you are believers.
Likewise confirming the
truth of the Torah that
is before me, and to make
lawful to you certain
things that before were
forbidden unto you.
I have come to you with
a sign from your Lord;
so fear you God, and
obey you me. Surely
God is my Lord and
your Lord; so serve Him.
This is a straight path".'

45 And when Jesus perceived
their unbelief, he said,
'Who will be my helpers
unto God?' The Apostles
said, 'We will be helpers
of God; we believe in God;
witness thou our submission.
Lord, we believe in that
Thou hast sent down, and we
follow the Messenger.
Inscribe us therefore with
those who bear witness.'

And they devised, and God
devised, and God is
the best of devisers.

When God said, 'Jesus,
I will take thee to Me
and will raise thee to Me,
and I will purify thee
of those who believe not.
I will set thy followers
above the unbelievers
till the Resurrection Day.
Then unto Me shall you
return, and I will decide
between you, as to what
you were at variance on.
As for the unbelievers,
I will chastise them with
a terrible chastisement
in this world and the next;
they shall have no helpers.'

50 But as for the believers, who do
deeds of righteousness, He will pay them
in full their wages: and God loves not
the evildoers.

This We recite to thee
of signs and wise remembrance.
Truly, the likeness of
Jesus, in God's sight,
is as Adam's likeness;
He created him of dust,
then said He unto him,
'Be,' and he was.
The truth is of God;
be not of the doubters.
And whoso disputes with thee
concerning him, after the
knowledge that has come to thee,
say: 'Come now, let us call
our sons and your sons,
our wives and your wives,
our selves and your selves,
then let us humbly pray
and so lay God's curse
upon the ones who lie.'
55   This is the true story.
There is no god but God,
and assuredly God is
the All-mighty, the All-wise.
And if they turn their backs,
assuredly God knows
the workers of corruption.

Say: 'People of the Book! Come now to a word
common between us and you, that we serve
none but God, and that we associate not
aught with Him, and do not some of us take
others as Lords, apart from God.' And if
they turn their backs, say: 'Bear witness that
        we are Muslims.'

People of the Book! Why do you dispute
concerning Abraham? The Torah was not sent
down, neither the Gospel, but after him. What,

have you no reason?
Ha, you are the ones who dispute on what you
know; why then dispute you touching a matter
of which you know not anything? God knows,
 and you know not.
60 No; Abraham in truth was not a Jew,
neither a Christian; but he was a Muslim
and one pure of faith; certainly he was never
 of the idolaters.
Surely the people standing closest to Abraham
are those who followed him, and this Prophet,
and those who believe; and God is the Protector
 of the believers.

There is a party of the People of the Book
yearn to make you go astray; yet none
they make to stray, except themselves, but
 they are not aware.
People of the Book! Why do you disbelieve
in God's signs, which you yourselves witness?
People of the Book! Why do you confound
the truth with vanity, and conceal the truth
 and that wittingly?

65 There is a party of the People of the Book
say, 'Believe in what has been sent down upon
those who believe at the beginning of the
day, and disbelieve at the end of it; haply
 they will then return;
and believe not any but him who follows
your religion.' Say: 'The true guidance is
God's guidance—that anyone should be given
the like of what you have been given, or dispute
with you before your Lord.' Say: 'Surely bounty
is in the hand of God; He gives it unto
whomsoever He will; and God is
 All-embracing, All-knowing.
He singles out for His mercy whom He will;

God is of bounty abounding.'
And of the People of the Book is he who, if thou
trust him with a hundredweight, will restore it
thee; and of them is he who, if thou trust him with
one pound, will not restore it thee, unless ever thou
 standest over him.
That, because they say, 'There is no way over us as to
the common people.' They speak falsehood against God
 and that wittingly.

70 Nay, but whoso fulfils his covenant and fears God, God
 loves the godfearing.
Those that sell God's covenant, and their oaths,
for a little price, there shall be no share for them
in the world to come; God shall not speak to them
neither look on them on the Resurrection Day,
neither will He purify them; and for them awaits
 a painful chastisement.
And there is a sect of them twist their tongues
with the Book, that you may suppose it part of
the Book, yet it is not part of the Book; and they
say, 'It is from God,' yet it is not from God,
and they speak falsehood against God,
 and that wittingly.
It belongs not to any mortal that God should
give him the Book, the Judgment, the Prophethood,
then he should say to men, 'Be you servants to me
apart from God.' Rather, 'Be you masters in
that you know the Book, and in that you study.'
He would never order you to take the angels
and the Prophets as Lords; what, would He order
you to disbelieve, after you have surrendered?

75 And when God took compact with the Prophets:
 'That I have given you of Book and Wisdom;
then there shall come to you a Messenger confirming
what is with you—you shall believe in him
and you shall help him; do you agree?' He said.
'And do you take My load on you on that condition?'
They said, 'We do agree.' God said, 'Bear witness so,

and I shall be with you among the witnesses.'
Then whosoever turns his back after that—
    they are the ungodly.
What, do they desire another religion than God's,
and to Him has surrendered whoso is in the heavens
and the earth, willingly or unwillingly, and to Him
    they shall be returned?
Say: 'We believe in God, and that which has been sent
down on us, and sent down on Abraham and Ishmael,
Isaac and Jacob, and the Tribes, and in that which was
given to Moses and Jesus, and the Prophets, of their
Lord; we make no division between any of them, and
    to Him we surrender.'
Whoso desires another religion than Islam, it shall
not be accepted of him; in the next world he shall
    be among the losers.

80   How shall God guide a people who have disbelieved
after they believed, and bore witness that the
Messenger is true, and the clear signs came to them?
God guides not the people of the evildoers.
Those—their recompense is that there shall rest
on them the curse of God and of the angels
and of men, altogether, therein dwelling forever;
the chastisement shall not be lightened
for them; no respite shall be given them.
But those who repent thereafter, and make amends—
God is All-forgiving, All-compassionate.
Surely those who disbelieve after they have believed
and then increase in unbelief—their repentance
shall not be accepted; those are the ones who stray.

85   Surely those who disbelieve, and die disbelieving,
there shall not be accepted from any one of them
the whole earth full of gold, if he would ransom himself
thereby; for them awaits a painful chastisement, and
    they shall have no helpers.

You will not attain piety until you expend
of what you love; and whatever thing you expend,
    God knows of it.

All food was lawful to the Children of Israel
save what Israel forbade for himself
before the Torah was sent down. Say:
'Bring you the Torah now, and recite it,
if you are truthful.'
Whoso forges falsehood against God after that,
those are the evildoers.

Say: 'God has spoken the truth; therefore follow
the creed of Abraham, a man of pure faith
and no idolater.'
90 The first House established for the people
was that at Bekka, a place holy, and a guidance
to all beings.
Therein are clear signs—the station of Abraham,
and whosoever enters it is in security.
It is the duty of all men towards God to come
to the House a pilgrim, if he is able to
make his way there.
As for the unbeliever, God is All-sufficient
nor needs any being.

Say: 'People of the Book, why do you disbelieve
in the signs of God? Surely God is witness of
the things you do.'
Say: 'People of the Book, why do you bar from God's
way the believer, desiring to make it crooked,
yourselves being witnesses? God is not heedless of
the things you do.'

95 O believers, if you obey a sect of those
who have been given the Book, they will turn you,
after you have believed, into unbelievers.
How can you disbelieve, seeing you have God's signs
recited to you, and His Messenger among you?
Whosoever holds fast to God, he is guided
to a straight path.
O believers, fear God as He should be feared,
and see you do not die, save in surrender.

And hold you fast to God's bond, together,
and do not scatter; remember God's blessing
upon you when you were enemies, and He brought
your hearts together, so that by His blessing
    you became brothers.
You were upon the brink of a pit of Fire,
and He delivered you from it; even so God
makes clear to you His signs; so haply
    you will be guided.

100   Let there be one nation of you, calling to good,
and bidding to honour, and forbidding dishonour;
    those are the prosperers.
Be not as those who scattered and fell into variance
after the clear signs came to them; those there awaits
    a mighty chastisement,
the day when some faces are blackened, and some faces
                                      [whitened.
As for those whose faces are blackened—'Did you disbelieve
after you had believed? Then taste the chastisement for that
you disbelieved!' But as for those whose faces are whitened,
they shall be in God's mercy, therein dwelling forever.

These are the signs of God We recite to thee
        in truth,
and God desires not any injustice to
        living beings.

105   To God belongs all that is in the heavens
and in the earth, and unto Him all matters
        are returned.

You are the best nation ever brought forth
to men, bidding to honour, and forbidding
dishonour, and believing in God. Had the People
of the Book believed, it were better for them;
some of them are believers, but the most of
    them are ungodly.
They will not harm you, except a little hurt; and if
they fight with you, they will turn on you
their backs; then they will not be helped.

Abasement shall be pitched on them, wherever
they are come upon, except they be in a bond
of God, and a bond of the people; they will be laden
with the burden of God's anger, and poverty shall be
pitched on them; that, because they disbelieved in
God's signs, and slew the Prophets without right;
that, for that they acted rebelliously
    and were transgressors.
Yet they are not all alike; some of the People
of the Book are a nation upstanding, that
recite God's signs in the watches of the night,
    bowing themselves,

110 believing in God and in the Last Day,
bidding to honour and forbidding dishonour,
vying one with the other in good works; those
    are of the righteous.
And whatsoever good you do, you shall not
be denied the just reward of it; and God
    knows the godfearing.
As for the unbelievers, their riches shall not
avail them, neither their children, against God;
those are the inhabitants of the Fire,
    therein dwelling forever.
The likeness of that they expend in this present life
is as the likeness of a freezing blast that smites
the tillage of a people who wronged themselves,
and it destroyed that; God wronged them not, but
    themselves they wronged.

O believers, take not for your intimates
outside yourselves; such men spare nothing
to ruin you; they yearn for you to suffer.
Hatred has already shown itself of their mouths,
and what their breasts conceal is yet greater.
Now We have made clear to you the signs,
    if you understand.

115 Ha, there you are; you love them, and they
love you not; you believe in the Book, all of it,
and when they meet you they say, 'We believe,'

but when they go privily, they bite at you their
fingers, enraged. Say: 'Die in your rage; God knows
 the thoughts in the breasts.'
If you are visited by good fortune, it vexes them;
but if you are smitten by evil, they rejoice at it.
Yet if you are patient and godfearing, their
guile will hurt you nothing; God encompasses
 the things they do.

When thou wentest forth at dawn from thy people to lodge
the believers in their pitches for the battle—God is
 All-hearing, All-knowing—
when two parties of you were about to lose heart, though
God was their Protector—and in God let the believers
 put all their trust—
and God most surely helped you at Badr, when you
were utterly abject. So fear God, and haply
 you will be thankful.

120 When thou saidst to the believers, 'Is it not enough
for you that your Lord should reinforce you
with three thousand angels sent down upon you?
Yea; if you are patient and godfearing, and the foe
come against you instantly, your Lord will reinforce
you with five thousand swooping angels.' God wrought
this not, save as good tiding to you, and that your
hearts might be at rest; help comes only from God
 the All-mighty, the All-wise;
and that He might cut off a part of the unbelievers
or frustrate them, so that they turned in their
 tracks, disappointed.
No part of the matter is thine, whether He turns
towards them again, or chastises them; for
 they are evildoers.
To God belongs all that is in the heavens and earth;
He forgives whom He will, and chastises whom He will;
God is All-forgiving, All-compassionate.

125 O believers, devour not usury, doubled
and redoubled, and fear you God; haply so

you will prosper.
And fear the Fire prepared for the unbelievers,
and obey God and the Messenger; haply so
        you will find mercy.
And vie with one another, hastening to forgiveness
from your Lord, and to a garden whose breadth
is as the heavens and earth, prepared
        for the godfearing
who expend in prosperity and adversity in
almsgiving, and restrain their rage, and pardon
the offences of their fellowmen; and God
        loves the good-doers;
who, when they commit an indecency or wrong
themselves, remember God, and pray forgiveness for
their sins—and who shall forgive sins but God?—
and do not persevere in the things they did
        and that wittingly.
130   Those—their recompense is forgiveness from
their Lord, and gardens beneath which rivers flow,
        therein dwelling forever;
and how excellent is the wage of those who labour!

Divers institutions have passed away before you;
journey in the land, and behold how was the end of
        those that cried lies.

This is an exposition for mankind, and a guidance,
and an admonition for such as are godfearing.
Faint not, neither sorrow; you shall be the upper ones
        if you are believers.

If a wound touches you, a like wound already
has touched the heathen; such days We deal out
in turn among men, and that God may know
who are the believers, and that He may take
witnesses from among you; and God loves not
        the evildoers;
135   and that God may prove the believers, and blot out
        the unbelievers.

Or did you suppose you should enter Paradise
without God know who of you have struggled and
　　　who are patient?

You were longing for death before you met it;
now you have seen it, while you were beholding.

Muhammad is naught but a Messenger; Messengers
have passed away before him. Why, if he should die
or is slain, will you turn about on your heels?
If any man should turn about on his heels, he will
not harm God in any way; and God will recompense
　　　the thankful.
It is not given to any soul to die, save by the
leave of God, at an appointed time. Whoso desires
the reward of this world, We will give him of this;
and whoso desires the reward of the other world,
We will give him of that; and We will recompense
　　　the thankful.
140　Many a Prophet there has been, with whom thousands
manifold have fought, and they fainted not
for what smote them in God's way, neither
weakened, nor did they humble themselves; and God
　　　loves the patient.
Nothing else they said but, 'Lord, forgive us our
sins, and that we exceeded in our affair, and
　　　make firm our feet,
and help us against the people of the unbelievers.'
And God gave them the reward of this world and
the fairest reward of the world to come; and God
　　　loves the good-doers.

O believers, if you obey the unbelievers
they will turn you upon your heels, and you will
　　　turn about, losers.
No; but God is your Protector, and He is
　　　the best of helpers.
We will cast into the hearts of the unbelievers
terror, for that they have associated with God

that for which He sent down never authority;
their lodging shall be the Fire; evil is the lodging
    of the evildoers.

145   God has been true in His promise towards you
when you blasted them by His leave; until
you lost heart, and quarrelled about the matter,
and were rebellious, after He had shown you
    that you longed for.
Some of you there are that desire this world,
and some of you there are desire the next world.
Then He turned you from them, that He might try you;
and He has pardoned you; and God is bounteous
    to the believers.
When you were going up, not twisting about
for anyone, and the Messenger was calling you
in your rear; so He rewarded you with grief on grief
that you might not sorrow for what escaped you
neither for what smote you; and God is aware of
    the things you do.
Then He sent down upon you, after grief,
security—a slumber overcoming a party
of you; and a party themselves had grieved,
thinking of God thoughts that were not true
such as the pagans thought, saying, 'Have we
any part whatever in the affair?' Say:
'The affair belongs to God entirely.'
They were concealing in their hearts that
they show not to thee, saying, 'Ah, if we
had had a part in the affair, never
would we have been slain here.' Say: 'Even if
you had been in your houses, those for whom
slaying was appointed would have sallied forth
unto their last couches'; and that God might try
what was in your breasts, and that He might
prove what was in your hearts; and God knows
    the thoughts in the breasts.
Those of you who turned away the day the two hosts
encountered—Satan made them slip for somewhat

they had earned; but God has pardoned them; God is
All-forgiving, All-clement.

150 O believers, be not as the unbelievers
who say to their brothers, when they journey
in the land, or are upon expeditions, 'If
they had been with us, they would not have died
and not been slain'—that God may make that
an anguish in their hearts. For God gives
life, and He makes to die; and God sees
    the things you do.
If you are slain or die in God's way, forgiveness
and mercy from God are a better thing
    than that you amass;
surely if you die or are slain, it is unto God
    you shall be mustered.

It was by some mercy of God that thou wast
gentle to them; hadst thou been harsh
and hard of heart, they would have scattered
from about thee. So pardon them, and pray
forgiveness for them, and take counsel with them
in the affair; and when thou art resolved,
put thy trust in God; surely God loves those
    who put their trust.
If God helps you, none can overcome you;
but if He forsakes you, who then can help you
after Him? Therefore in God let the believers
    put all their trust.

155 It is not for a Prophet to be fraudulent;
whoso defrauds shall bring the fruits of his fraud
on the Day of Resurrection; then every soul
shall be paid in full what it has earned, and they
    shall not be wronged.
What, is he who follows God's good pleasure
like him who is laden with the burden
of God's anger, whose refuge is Gehenna?
    An evil homecoming!

They are in ranks with God; and God sees
    the things they do.
Truly God was gracious to the believers
when He raised up among them a Messenger
from themselves, to recite to them His signs
and to purify them, and to teach them
the Book and the Wisdom, though before they were
    in manifest error.

Why, when an affliction visited you, and you
had visited twice over the like of it,
did you say, 'How is this?' Say: 'This is
from your own selves; surely God is powerful
    over everything.'
160   And what visited you, the day the two hosts
encountered, was by God's leave, and that He might
    know the believers;
and that He might also know the hypocrites
when it was said of them, 'Come now, fight
in the way of God, or repel!' They said, 'If only
we knew how to fight, we would follow you.'
They that day were nearer to unbelief
    than to belief,
saying with their mouths that which never
was in their hearts; and God knows very well
    the things they hide;
who said of their brothers (and they themselves held
back), 'Had they obeyed us, they would not have been
slain.' Say: 'Then avert death from yourselves, if
    you speak truly.'
Count not those who were slain in God's way
as dead, but rather living with their Lord,
    by Him provided,
rejoicing in the bounty that God has given
them, and joyful in those who remain
behind and have not joined them, because
no fear shall be on them, neither shall they sorrow,
165   joyful in blessing and bounty from God,
and that God leaves not to waste the wage

of the believers.
And those who answered God and the Messenger
after the wound had smitten them—to all those
of them who did good and feared God, shall be
a mighty wage;
those to whom the people said, 'The people
have gathered against you, therefore fear them';
but it increased them in faith, and they said,
'God is sufficient for us; an excellent
Guardian is He.'
So they returned with blessing and bounty
from God, untouched by evil; they followed
the good pleasure of God; and God is
of bounty abounding.
That is Satan frightening his friends,
therefore do not fear them; but fear you Me,
if you are believers.

170   Let them not grieve thee that vie with one another
in unbelief; they will nothing hurt God;
God desires not to appoint for them a portion
in the world to come, and there awaits them
a mighty chastisement.
Those who buy unbelief at the price of faith,
they will nothing hurt God; and there awaits them
a painful chastisement.
And let not the unbelievers suppose that
the indulgence We grant them is better for them;
We grant them indulgence only that they may
increase in sin; and there awaits them
a humbling chastisement.

God will not leave the believers in the state
in which you are, till He shall distinguish the
corrupt from the good,
and God will not inform you of the Unseen;
but God chooses out of His Messengers
whom He will. Believe you then in God
and His Messengers; and if you believe

and are godfearing, there shall be for you
a mighty wage.

175 But as for those who are niggardly with
the bounty God has given them, let them not
suppose it is better for them; nay, it
is worse for them;
that they were niggardly with they shall have
hung about their necks on the Resurrection
Day; and to God belongs the inheritance
of the heavens and earth; and God is aware of
the things you do.

God has heard the saying of those who said,
'Surely God is poor, and we are rich.'
We shall write down what they have said,
and their slaying the Prophets without right,
and We shall say, 'Taste the chastisement
of the burning—
that, for what your hands have forwarded,
and for that God is never unjust
unto His servants.'
Those same men said, 'God has made covenant
with us, that we believe not any Messenger
until he brings to us a sacrifice
devoured by fire.'

180 Say: 'Messengers have come to you before me
bearing clear signs, and that you spoke of;
why therefore did you slay them, if
you speak truly?'
But if they cry lies to thee, lies were cried
to Messengers before thee, who came bearing
clear signs, and the Psalms, and the Book
Illuminating.

Every soul shall taste of death; you shall surely
be paid in full your wages on the Day
of Resurrection. Whosoever is removed
from the Fire and admitted to Paradise, shall
win the triumph. The present life is but the

joy of delusion.
You shall surely be tried in your possessions
and your selves, and you shall hear from those
who were given the Book before you, and from
those who are idolaters, much hurt; but if you
are patient and godfearing—surely that is
    true constancy.

And when God took compact with those who
had been given the Book: 'You shall make it
clear unto the people, and not conceal it.'
But they rejected it behind their backs
and sold it for a small price—how evil was
    that their selling!
185   Reckon not that those who rejoice in what
they have brought, and love to be praised
for what they have not done—do not reckon them
secure from chastisement; for them awaits
    a painful chastisement.

To God belongs the Kingdom of the heavens
and of the earth; and God is powerful
    over everything.
Surely in the creation of the heavens and earth
and in the alternation of night and day
there are signs for men possessed of minds
who remember God, standing and sitting
and on their sides, and reflect upon
the creation of the heavens and the earth:
'Our Lord, Thou hast not created this for
vanity. Glory be to Thee! Guard us against
    the chastisement
    of the Fire.
Our Lord, whomsoever Thou admittest
into the Fire, Thou wilt have abased;
    and the evildoers
    shall have no helpers.
190   Our Lord, we have heard a caller calling
us to belief, saying, "Believe you

in your Lord!"
And we believe.
Our Lord, forgive Thou us our sins
and acquit us of our evil deeds, and
    take us to Thee
    with the pious.
Our Lord, give us what Thou hast promised us
by Thy Messengers, and abase us not on the Day
    of Resurrection; Thou
    wilt not fail the tryst.'
And their Lord answers them: 'I waste not
the labour of any that labours among you,
be you male or female—the one of you
    is as the other.
And those who emigrated, and were expelled
from their habitations, those who suffered hurt
in My way, and fought, and were slain—
them I shall surely acquit of their evil deeds,
and I shall admit them to gardens underneath
    which rivers flow.'

195   A reward from God! And God—with Him is
    the fairest reward.

Let it not delude thee, that the unbelievers
go to and fro in the land; a little
enjoyment, then their refuge is Gehenna—
    an evil cradling!
But those who fear their Lord—for them shall be
gardens underneath which rivers flow, therein
dwelling forever—a hospitality God Himself
offers; and that which is with God is better
    for the pious.

And some there are of the People of the Book
who believe in God, and what has been sent down
unto you, and what has been sent down unto them,
men humble to God, not selling the signs of God
    for a small price;

those—their wage is with their Lord; God is swift
at the reckoning.

200   O believers, be patient, and vie you in
patience; be steadfast; fear God; haply
so you will prosper.

IV

WOMEN

In the Name of God, the Merciful, the Compassionate

Mankind, fear your Lord, who created you
of a single soul, and from it created
its mate, and from the pair of them scattered
abroad many men and women; and fear God
by whom you demand one of another,
and the wombs; surely God ever
   watches over you.

Give the orphans their property, and do not
exchange the corrupt for the good; and devour
not their property with your property; surely
   that is a great crime.
If you fear that you will not act justly
towards the orphans, marry such women
as seem good to you, two, three, four;
but if you fear you will not be equitable,
then only one, or what your right hands own;
so it is likelier you will not be partial.
And give the women their dowries as a gift
spontaneous; but if they are pleased
to offer you any of it, consume it
   with wholesome appetite.
But do not give to fools their property
that God has assigned to you to manage;
provide for them and clothe them out of it,
and speak to them honourable words.
5 Test well the orphans, until they reach
the age of marrying; then, if you perceive
in them right judgment, deliver to them
their property; consume it not wastefully
   and hastily
ere they are grown. If any man is rich,

let him be abstinent; if poor, let him
    consume in reason.
And when you deliver to them their property,
take witnesses over them; God suffices
    for a reckoner.

To the men a share of what parents and kinsmen
leave, and to the women a share of what
parents and kinsmen leave, whether it be
little or much, a share apportioned;
and when the division is attended by
kinsmen and orphans and the poor,
make provision for them out of it,
and speak to them honourable words.
10   And let those fear who, if they left
behind them weak seed, would be afraid
on their account, and let them fear
God, and speak words hitting the mark.
Those who devour the property of orphans
unjustly, devour Fire in their bellies,
and shall assuredly roast in a Blaze.

God charges you, concerning your children:
to the male the like of the portion
of two females, and if they be women
above two, then for them two-thirds
of what he leaves, but if she be one
then to her a half; and to his parents
to each one of the two the sixth
of what he leaves, if he has children;
but if he has no children, and his
heirs are his parents, a third to his
mother, or, if he has brothers, to his
mother a sixth, after any bequest
he may bequeath, or any debt.
Your fathers and your sons—you know not
which out of them is nearer in profit
to you. So God apportions; surely God is
    All-knowing, All-wise.

And for you a half of what your wives
leave, if they have no children; but
if they have children, then for you of what
they leave a fourth, after any bequest
they may bequeath, or any debt.
And for them a fourth of what you leave,
if you have no children; but if you
have children, then for them of what
you leave an eighth, after any bequest
you may bequeath, or any debt.

15   If a man or a woman have no heir
direct, but have a brother or a sister,
to each of the two a sixth; but if they
are more numerous than that, they share
equally a third, after any bequest
he may bequeath, or any debt not
prejudicial; a charge from God. God is
        All-knowing, All-clement.

Those are God's bounds. Whoso obeys God
and His Messenger, He will admit him
to gardens underneath which rivers flow,
therein dwelling forever; that is
        the mighty triumph.
But whoso disobeys God, and His Messenger,
and transgresses His bounds, him He will
admit to a Fire, therein dwelling
forever, and for him there awaits
        a humbling chastisement.

Such of your women as commit indecency,
call four of you to witness against them;
and if they witness, then detain them
in their houses until death takes them
or God appoints for them a way.

20   And when two of you commit indecency,
punish them both; but if they repent
and make amends, then suffer them to be;
God turns, and is All-compassionate.

74

God shall turn only towards those who do
evil in ignorance, then shortly repent;
God will return towards those; God is
        All-knowing, All-wise.
But God shall not turn towards those
who do evil deeds until, when one of them
is visited by death, he says, 'Indeed
now I repent,' neither to those who die
disbelieving; for them We have prepared
        a painful chastisement.

O believers, it is not lawful for you
to inherit women against their will;
neither debar them, that you may go off
with part of what you have given them,
except when they commit a flagrant indecency.
Consort with them honourably; or if
you are averse to them, it is possible
you may be averse to a thing, and God set
        in it much good.
And if you desire to exchange a wife
in place of another, and you have given
to one a hundredweight, take of it nothing.
What, will you take it by way of calumny
        and manifest sin?

25   How shall you take it, when each of you has been
privily with the other, and they have taken from you
        a solemn compact?
And do not marry women that your fathers
married, unless it be a thing of the past;
surely that is indecent and hateful,
        an evil way.

Forbidden to you are your mothers and daughters,
your sisters, your aunts paternal and maternal,
your brother's daughters, your sister's daughters,
your mothers who have given suck to you,
your suckling sisters, your wives' mothers,
your stepdaughters who are in your care

being born of your wives you have been in to—
but if you have not yet been in to them
it is no fault in you—and the spouses
of your sons who are of your loins,
and that you should take to you two sisters
together, unless it be a thing of the past;
God is All-forgiving, All-compassionate;
and wedded women, save what your right hands own.
So God prescribes for you. Lawful for you,
beyond all that, is that you may seek,
using your wealth, in wedlock and not
in licence. Such wives as you enjoy thereby,
give them their wages apportionate; it is no
fault in you in your agreeing together,
after the due apportionate. God is
     All-knowing, All-wise.

Any one of you who has not the affluence
to be able to marry believing freewomen
in wedlock, let him take believing handmaids
that your right hands own; God knows very well
your faith; the one of you is as the other.
So marry them, with their people's leave,
and give them their wages honourably
as women in wedlock, not as in licence
     or taking lovers.
30   But when they are in wedlock, if they
commit indecency, they shall be liable
to half the chastisement of freewomen.
That provision is for those of you who fear
fornication; yet it is better for you
to be patient. God is All-forgiving
     All-compassionate.
God desires to make clear to you, and to
guide you in the institutions of those
before you, and to turn towards you; God is
     All-knowing, All-wise;
and God desires to turn towards you, but
those who follow their lusts desire you

to swerve away mightily. God desires
to lighten things for you, for man was
    created a weakling.

O believers, consume not your goods
between you in vanity, except there be
trading, by your agreeing together.
And kill not one another. Surely God is
    compassionate to you.
But whosoever does that in transgression
and wrongfully, him We shall certainly
roast at a Fire; and that for God is
    an easy matter.

35 If you avoid the heinous sins that
are forbidden you, We will acquit you
of your evil deeds, and admit you by
    the gate of honour.

Do not covet that whereby God in bounty
has preferred one of you above another.
To the men a share from what they have earned,
and to the women a share from what they
have earned. And ask God of His bounty;
    God knows everything.

To everyone We have appointed heirs
of that which parents and kinsmen leave,
and those with whom you have sworn compact.
So give to them their share; God is witness
    over everything.

Men are the managers of the affairs of women
for that God has preferred in bounty
one of them over another, and for that
they have expended of their property.
Righteous women are therefore obedient,
guarding the secret for God's guarding.
And those you fear may be rebellious
admonish; banish them to their couches,

and beat them. If they then obey you,
look not for any way against them; God is
    All-high, All-great.
And if you fear a breach between the two,
bring forth an arbiter from his people
and from her people an arbiter, if they
desire to set things right; God will
compose their differences; surely God is
    All-knowing, All-aware.

40   Serve God,
    and associate naught with Him.

Be kind to parents, and the near kinsman,
and to orphans, and to the needy,
and to the neighbour who is of kin,
and to the neighbour who is a stranger,
and to the companion at your side,
and to the traveller, and to that your
right hands own. Surely God loves not
    the proud and boastful
such as are niggardly, and bid other men
to be niggardly, and themselves conceal
the bounty that God has given them.
We have prepared for the unbelievers
    a humbling chastisement,
and such as expend of their substance
to show off to men, and believe not
in God and the Last Day. Whosoever
has Satan for a comrade, an evil
    comrade is he.
Why, what would it harm them, if they
believed in God and the Last Day, and
expended of that God has provided them?
    God knows them.
Surely God shall not wrong so much as the
weight of an ant; and if it be a good deed
He will double it, and give from Himself
    a mighty wage.

45 How then shall it be, when We bring forward from every
    nation a witness, and bring thee to witness against those?
    Upon that day the unbelievers, those who have disobeyed
    the Messenger, will wish that the earth might be levelled
    with them; and they will not conceal from God one tiding.

> O believers, draw not near to prayer
> when you are drunken until you know
> what you are saying, or defiled—unless
> you are traversing a way—until you
> have washed yourselves; but if you are
> sick, or on a journey, or if any of you
> comes from the privy, or you have touched
> women, and you can find no water,
> then have recourse to wholesome dust
> and wipe your faces and your hands; God is
>   All-pardoning, All-forgiving.

> Hast thou not regarded those who were given
> a share of the Book purchasing error,
> and desiring that you should also err
> from the way? God knows well your enemies;
> God suffices as a protector, God suffices
>   as a helper.
> Some of the Jews pervert words from their meanings
> saying, 'We have heard and we disobey'
> and 'Hear, and be thou not given to hear'
> and 'Observe us,' twisting with their tongues and
>   traducing religion.
> If they had said, 'We have heard and obey'
> and 'Hear' and 'Regard us,' it would have been
> better for them, and more upright; but God has
> cursed them for their unbelief, so they believe not
>   except a few.

50 You who have been given the Book, believe
    in what We have sent down, confirming
    what is with you, before We obliterate
    faces, and turn them upon their backs, or
    curse them as We cursed the Sabbath-men, and

79

God's command is done.
God forgives not that aught should be with Him
associated; less than that He forgives
to whomsoever He will. Whoso associates
with God anything, has indeed forged
a mighty sin.

Hast thou not regarded those who purify
themselves? Nay; only God purifies
whom He will; and they shall not be wronged
a single date-thread.
Consider how they forge falsehood
against God; and that suffices for
a manifest sin.

Hast thou not regarded those who were given
a share of the Book believing in demons
and idols, and saying to the unbelievers,
'These are more rightly guided on the way
than the believers'?

55   Those are they whom God has cursed; he whom God
has cursed, thou wilt not find for him
any helper.
Or have they a share in the Kingdom?
If that is so, they do not give the people
a single date-spot.
Or are they jealous of the people
for the bounty that God has given them?
Yet We gave the people of Abraham
the Book and the Wisdom, and We gave them
a mighty kingdom.
And some of them there are that believe, and
some of them that bar from it; Gehenna suffices
for a Blaze!
Surely those who disbelieve in Our signs—We
shall certainly roast them at a Fire; as often
as their skins are wholly burned, We shall
give them in exchange other skins, that they
may taste the chastisement. Surely God is

All-mighty, All-wise.

60   And those that believe, and do deeds of righteousness,
them We shall admit to gardens underneath
which rivers flow, therein dwelling forever and ever;
therein for them shall be spouses purified,
and We shall admit them to a shelter
      of plenteous shade.

God commands you to deliver trusts
back to their owners; and when you judge
between the people, that you judge with justice.
Good is the admonition God gives you; God is
      All-hearing, All-seeing.

O believers, obey God, and obey the Messenger
and those in authority among you. If you
should quarrel on anything, refer it to God
and the Messenger, if you believe in God
and the Last Day; that is better, and fairer
      in the issue.
Hast thou not regarded those who assert
that they believe in what has been sent down
to thee, and what was sent down before thee,
desiring to take their disputes to idols,
yet they have been commanded to disbelieve
in them? But Satan desires to lead them astray
      into far error.
And when it is said to them, 'Come now to
what God has sent down, and the Messenger,'
then thou seest the hypocrites barring
      the way to thee.

65   How shall it be, when they are visited
by an affliction for what their own hands
have forwarded, then they come to thee
swearing by God, We sought only kindness and
      conciliation'?
Those—God knows what is in their hearts;
so turn away from them, and admonish them,

and say to them penetrating words
 about themselves.
We sent not ever any Messenger, but
that he should be obeyed, by the leave of God.
If, when they wronged themselves, they had
come to thee, and prayed forgiveness of God,
and the Messenger had prayed forgiveness
for them, they would have found God turns,
 All-compassionate.
But no, by thy Lord! they will not believe
till they make thee the judge regarding
the disagreement between them, then they
shall find in themselves no impediment
touching thy verdict, but shall surrender
 in full submission.
But had We prescribed for them, saying,
'Slay yourselves' or 'Leave your habitations,'
they would not have done it, save a few of them;
yet if they had done as they were admonished
it would have been better for them, and stronger
 confirming them,
70 and then We surely would have given them
from Us a mighty wage, and guided them
 on a straight path.
Whosoever obeys God, and the Messenger—
they are with those whom God has blessed,
Prophets, just men, martyrs, the righteous;
 good companions they!
That is the bounty from God; God suffices
 as One who knows.

O believers, take your precautions; then
move forward in companies, or move forward
 all together.
Some of you there are that are dilatory;
then, if an affliction visits you, he says,
'God has blessed me, in that I was not
 a martyr with them.'
75 But if a bounty from God visits you, he

will surely say, as if there had never been
any affection between you and him,
'Would that I had been with them, to attain
 a mighty triumph!'
So let them fight in the way of God who
sell the present life for the world to come;
and whosoever fights in the way of God
and is slain, or conquers, We shall bring him
 a mighty wage.
How is it with you, that you do not fight
in the way of God, and for the men,
women, and children who, being abased,
say, 'Our Lord, bring us forth from this city
whose people are evildoers, and appoint to us
a protector from Thee, and appoint to us
 from Thee a helper'?
The believers fight in the way of God,
and the unbelievers fight in the idols' way.
Fight you therefore against the friends
of Satan; surely the guile of Satan
 is ever feeble.
Hast thou not regarded those to whom it was said,
'Restrain your hands, and perform the prayer,
and pay the alms'? Then, as soon as fighting
is prescribed for them, there is a party
of them fearing the people as they would
fear God, or with a greater fear, and they say,
'Our Lord, why hast thou prescribed fighting for us?
Why not defer us to a near term?'
Say: 'The enjoyment of this world is little;
the world to come is better for him
who fears God; you shall not be wronged
 a single date-thread.'
80 Wherever you may be, death will overtake you,
though you should be in raised-up towers.
And if a good thing visits them, they say,
'This is from God'; but if an evil thing
visits them, they say, 'This is from thee.'
Say: 'Everything is from God.' How is it

with this people? They scarcely understand
    any tiding.
Whatever good visits thee, it is of God;
whatever evil visits thee is of thyself.
And We have sent thee to men a Messenger; God
    suffices for a witness.

Whosoever obeys the Messenger, thereby
obeys God; and whosoever turns his
back—We have not sent thee to be a
    watcher over them.
They say, 'Obedience'; but when they sally
forth from thee, a party of them meditate
all night on other than what thou sayest. God
writes down their meditations; so turn away from
them, and put thy trust in God; God suffices
    for a guardian.
What, do they not ponder the Koran?
If it had been from other than God
surely they would have found in it much
    inconsistency.
85   When there comes to them a matter, be it
of security or fear, they broadcast it;
if they had referred it to the Messenger
and to those in authority among them, those
of them whose task it is to investigate
would have known the matter. And but for
the bounty of God to you, and His mercy,
you would surely have followed Satan,
    except a few.

So do thou fight in the way of God;
thou art charged only with thyself.
And urge on the believers; haply God
will restrain the unbelievers' might;
God is stronger in might, more terrible
    in punishing.

Whoso intercedes with a good intercession

shall receive a share of it; whosoever
intercedes with a bad intercession, he
shall receive the like of it; God has power
    over everything.

And when you are greeted with a greeting
greet with a fairer than it, or return it;
surely God keeps a watchful count
    over everything.

    God—
there is no god but He.
He will surely gather you
to the Resurrection Day,
    no doubt of it.
And who is truer in tidings than God?

90   How is it with you, that you are two parties
touching the hypocrites, and God has overthrown
them for what they earned? What, do you desire
to guide him whom God has led astray?
Whom God leads astray, thou wilt not find
    for him a way.
They wish that you should disbelieve as
they disbelieve, and then you would be
equal; therefore take not to yourselves
friends of them, until they emigrate in
the way of God; then, if they turn their backs,
take them, and slay them wherever you find them;
take not to yourselves any one of them
    as friend or helper
except those that betake themselves to a people
who are joined with you by a compact,
or come to you with breasts constricted
from fighting with you or fighting their people.
Had God willed, He would have given them
authority over you, and then certainly
they would have fought you. If they withdraw
from you, and do not fight you, and offer you

peace, then God assigns not any way
　　to you against them.
You will find others desiring to be secure
from you, and secure from their people, yet
whenever they are returned to temptation, they
are overthrown in it. If they withdraw not
from you, and offer you peace, and restrain
their hands, take them, and slay them wherever
you come on them; against them We have given you
　　a clear authority.

It belongs not to a believer to slay
a believer, except it be by error.
If any slays a believer by error, then
let him set free a believing slave,
and bloodwit is to be paid to his family
unless they forgo it as a freewill offering.
If he belong to a people at enmity
with you and is a believer, let the slayer
set free a believing slave. If he belong
to a people joined with you by a compact,
then bloodwit is to be paid to his family
and the slayer shall set free a believing slave.
But if he finds not the means, let him fast
two successive months—God's turning; God is
　　All-knowing, All-wise.
95　And whoso slays a believer wilfully,
his recompense is Gehenna, therein
dwelling forever, and God will be wroth with him
and will curse him, and prepare for him
　　a mighty chastisement.

O believers, when you are journeying
in the path of God, be discriminating,
and do not say to him who offers you
a greeting, 'Thou art not a believer,'
seeking the chance goods of the present life.
With God are spoils abundant. So you were
aforetime; but God has been gracious to you.

So be discriminating; surely God is aware of
    the things you do.

Such believers as sit at home—unless
they have an injury—are not the equals
of those who struggle in the path of God
with their possessions and their selves.
God has preferred in rank those who struggle
with their possessions and their selves
over the ones who sit at home; yet to each
God has promised the reward most fair;
and God has preferred those who struggle
over the ones who sit at home for the bounty
    of a mighty wage,
in ranks standing before Him, forgiveness
and mercy; surely God is All-forgiving,
    All-compassionate.

And those the angels take, while still they
are wronging themselves—the angels will say,
'In what circumstances were you?' They will say,
'We were abased in the earth.' The angels
will say, 'But was not God's earth wide,
so that you might have emigrated in it?'
Such men, their refuge shall be Gehenna—
    an evil homecoming!—

100   except the men, women, and children
who, being abased, can devise nothing
and are not guided to a way; haply
them God will yet pardon, for God is
    All-pardoning, All-forgiving.
Whoso emigrates in the way of God
will find in the earth many refuges
and plenty; whoso goes forth from his house
an emigrant to God and His Messenger,
and then death overtakes him, his wage
shall have fallen on God; surely
God is All-forgiving, All-compassionate.

And when you are journeying in the land
there is no fault in you that you shorten
the prayer, if you fear the unbelievers
may afflict you; the unbelievers are for you
    a manifest foe.
When thou art amongst them, and performest
for them the prayer, let a party of them
stand with thee, and let them take their weapons.
When they bow themselves, let them be behind you;
and let another party who have not prayed
come and pray with thee, taking their precautions
and their weapons. The unbelievers wish
that you should be heedless of your weapons
and your baggage, then they would wheel on you
all at once. There is no fault in you,
if rain molests you, or you are sick, to
lay aside your weapons; but take your precautions.
God has prepared for the unbelievers
    a humbling chastisement.
When you have performed the prayer, remember
God, standing and sitting and on your sides.
Then, when you are secure, perform the prayer;
surely the prayer is a timed prescription
    for the believers.

105   Faint not in seeking the heathen; if you
are suffering, they are also suffering as
you are suffering, and you are hoping from God
for that for which they cannot hope; God is
    All-knowing, All-wise.

Surely We have sent down to thee the Book
with the truth, so that thou mayest judge
between the people by that God has shown thee.
So be not an advocate for the traitors;
and pray forgiveness of God; surely
God is All-forgiving, All-compassionate.
And do not dispute on behalf of those

who betray themselves; surely God loves not
     the guilty traitor.
They hide themselves from men, but hide not
themselves from God; for He is with them
while they meditate at night discourse
unpleasing to Him; God encompasses
     the things they do.
Ha, there you are; you have disputed
on their behalf in the present life; but
who will dispute with God on their behalf
on the Resurrection Day, or who will be
     a guardian for them?

110   Whosoever does evil, or wrongs himself,
and then prays God's forgiveness, he shall find
God is All-forgiving, All-compassionate.
And whosoever earns a sin, earns it
against himself only; and God is ever
     All-knowing, All-wise.
And whosoever earns a fault or a sin
and then casts it upon the innocent,
thereby has laid upon himself calumny
     and manifest sin.

But for God's bounty to thee and His mercy
a party of them purposed to lead thee
astray; but they lead only themselves astray;
they do not hurt thee in anything.
God has sent down on thee the Book and
the Wisdom, and He has taught thee that
thou knewest not; God's bounty to thee
     is ever great.
No good is there in much of their conspiring,
except for him who bids to freewill
offering, or honour, or setting things right
between the people. Whoso does that, seeking
God's good pleasure, We shall surely give him
     a mighty wage.
115   But whoso makes a breach with the Messenger

after the guidance has become clear to him,
and follows a way other than the believers',
him We shall turn over to what he has turned to
and We shall roast him in Gehenna—
 an evil homecoming!

God forgives not that aught should be with Him
associated; less than that He forgives
to whomsoever He will. Whoso associates
with God anything, has gone astray
 into far error.
In stead of Him, they pray not except to
female beings; they pray not except to
 a rebel Satan
accursed by God. He said, 'Assuredly
I will take unto myself a portion
appointed of Thy servants, and I will
lead them astray, and fill them with fancies,
and I will command them and they will cut off
the cattle's ears; I will command them
and they will alter God's creation.'
Whoso takes Satan to him for a friend,
instead of God, has surely suffered
 a manifest loss.
He promises them and fills them with fancies,
but there is nothing Satan promises them
 except delusion.
120 Such men—their refuge shall be Gehenna,
and they shall find no asylum from it.
But those that believe, and do deeds of righteousness,
them We shall admit to gardens underneath
which rivers flow, therein dwelling for ever and ever;
God's promise in truth; and who is truer
 in speech than God?
It is not your fancies, nor the fancies
of the People of the Book. Whosoever
does evil shall be recompensed for it,
and will not find for him, apart from God,
 a friend or helper.

And whosoever does deeds of righteousness,
be it male or female, believing—
they shall enter Paradise, and not be wronged
    a single date-spot.
And who is there that has a fairer religion
than he who submits his will to God
being a good-doer, and who follows
the creed of Abraham, a man of pure faith?
And God took Abraham for a friend.

125   To God belongs all that is in the heavens
and in the earth, and God encompasses
    everything.

They will ask thee for a pronouncement
concerning women. Say: 'God pronounces
to you concerning them, and what is recited
to you in the Book concerning the orphan
women to whom you give not what is prescribed
for them, and yet desire to marry them,
and the oppressed children, and that you secure
justice for orphans. Whatever good you do,
    God knows of it.'

If a woman fear rebelliousness or aversion
in her husband, there is no fault in them
if the couple set things right between them;
right settlement is better; and souls are very
prone to avarice. If you do good
and are godfearing, surely God is aware of
    the things you do.
You will not be able to be equitable
between your wives, be you ever so eager;
yet do not be altogether partial
so that you leave her as it were suspended.
If you set things right, and are godfearing,
God is All-forgiving, All-compassionate.
But if they separate, God will enrich
each of them of His plenty; God is

All-embracing, All-wise.

130   To God belongs all that is in the heavens
and in the earth. We have charged those
who were given the Book before you,
and you, 'Fear God.' If you disbelieve,
to God belongs all that is in the heavens
and in the earth; God is All-sufficient,
      All-laudable.
To God belongs all that is in the heavens
and in the earth; God suffices
      for a guardian.
If He will, He can put you away, O men,
and bring others; surely God is powerful
      over that.
Whoso desires the reward of this world,
with God is the reward of this world
and of the world to come; God is
      All-hearing, All-seeing.

O believers, be you securers of
justice, witnesses for God, even though
it be against yourselves, or your parents
and kinsmen, whether the man be rich
or poor; God stands closest to either.
Then follow not caprice, so as to swerve;
for if you twist or turn, God is aware of
      the things you do.

135   O believers, believe in God and His Messenger
and the Book He has sent down on His Messenger
and the Book which He sent down before.
Whoso disbelieves in God and His angels
and His Books, and His Messengers,
and the Last Day, has surely gone astray
      into far error.
Those who believe, and then disbelieve,
and then believe, and then disbelieve,
and then increase in unbelief—God is not

likely to forgive them, neither to guide them
on any way.

Give thou good tidings to the hypocrites that
for them awaits a painful chastisement.
Those who take unbelievers for their friends
instead of believers—do they seek glory
in them? But glory altogether
belongs to God.
He has sent down upon you in the Book:
'When you hear God's signs being disbelieved
and made mock of, do not sit with them
until they plunge into some other talk, or
else you will surely be like to them.' God
will gather the hypocrites and the unbelievers
all in Gehenna.

140　　Those who wait upon you and, if a victory comes
to you from God, say, 'Were we not with you?'
but if the unbelievers get a share, they say,
'Did we not gain the mastery over you, and
did we not defend you from the believers?' God
will judge between you on the Resurrection Day,
and God will not grant the unbelievers any way
over the believers.
The hypocrites seek to trick God, but God
is tricking them. When they stand up to pray
they stand up lazily, showing off to the people
and not remembering God save a little; wavering
all the time—not to these, not to those;
and whom God leads astray, thou wilt not find
for him a way.
O believers, take not the unbelievers
as friends instead of the believers; or
do you desire to give God over you
a clear authority?
Surely the hypocrites will be in the lowest
reach of the Fire; thou wilt not find for them
any helper;

145　　save such as repent, and make amends, and

hold fast to God, and make their religion
sincerely God's; those are with the believers,
and God will certainly give the believers
    a mighty wage.
What would God do with chastising you
if you are thankful, and believe? God is
    All-thankful, All-knowing.

God likes not the shouting of evil words
unless a man has been wronged; God is
    All-hearing, All-knowing.

If you do good openly or.in secret
or pardon an evil, surely God is
    All-pardoning, All-powerful.

Those who disbelieve in God and His Messengers
and desire to make division between God
and His Messengers, and say, 'We believe
in part, and disbelieve in part,' desiring
to take between this and that a way—
150   those in truth are the unbelievers;
and We have prepared for the unbelievers
    a humbling chastisement.
And those who believe in God and His Messengers
and make no division between any of them,
those—We shall surely give them their wages;
God is All-forgiving, All-compassionate.

The People of the Book will ask thee to bring down
upon them a Book from heaven; and they asked
Moses for greater than that, for they said,
'Show us God openly.' And the thunderbolt
took them for their evildoing. Then they took
to themselves the Calf, after the clear signs
had come to them; yet We pardoned them
that, and We bestowed upon Moses
    a clear authority.
And We raised above them the Mount, taking

compact with them; and We said to them, 'Enter in
at the gate, prostrating'; and We said to them,
'Transgress not the Sabbath'; and We took from them
  a solemn compact.
So, for their breaking the compact, and disbelieving
in the signs of God, and slaying the Prophets
without right, and for their saying, 'Our hearts
are uncircumcised'—nay, but God sealed them
for their unbelief, so they believe not,
  except a few—
155 and for their unbelief, and their uttering
against Mary a mighty calumny,
and for their saying, 'We slew the Messiah,
Jesus son of Mary, the Messenger of God'—
yet they did not slay him, neither crucified him,
only a likeness of that was shown to them.
Those who are at variance concerning him surely
are in doubt regarding him; they have no knowledge
of him, except the following of surmise;
and they slew him not of a certainty—
no indeed; God raised him up to Him; God is
  All-mighty, All-wise.
There is not one of the People of the Book
but will assuredly believe in him before his
death, and on the Resurrection Day he will be
  a witness against them.
And for the evildoing of those of Jewry, We
have forbidden them certain good things that
were permitted to them, and for their barring
  from God's way many,
and for their taking usury, that they were
prohibited, and consuming the wealth
of the people in vanity; and We have
prepared for the unbelievers among them
  a painful chastisement.
160 But those of them that are firmly rooted in
knowledge, and the believers believing in
what has been sent down to thee, and what was
sent down before thee, that perform the prayer

and pay the alms, and those who believe in God
and the Last Day—them We shall surely give
    a mighty wage.

We have revealed to thee as We revealed
to Noah, and the Prophets after him,
and We revealed to Abraham, Ishmael,
Isaac, Jacob, and the Tribes,
Jesus and Job, Jonah and Aaron
and Solomon, and We gave to David
    Psalms,
and Messengers We have already told thee of
before, and Messengers We have not told thee of;
and unto Moses God spoke directly—
Messengers bearing good tidings, and warning,
so that mankind might have no argument
against God, after the Messengers; God is
    All-mighty, All-wise.
But God bears witness to that He has sent down
to thee; He has sent it down with His knowledge;
and the angels also bear witness; and God suffices
    for a witness.

165   Surely those who disbelieve, and bar
from the way of God, have gone astray
    into far error.
Surely the unbelievers, who have done evil,
God would not forgive them, neither guide them
    on any road
but the road to Gehenna, therein dwelling
forever and ever; and that for God is
    an easy matter.

O men, the Messenger has now come to you
with the truth from your Lord; so believe;
better is it for you. And if you disbelieve,
to God belongs all that is in the heavens
and in the earth; and God is
    All-knowing, All-wise.

People of the Book, go not beyond the bounds
in your religion, and say not as to God
but the truth. The Messiah, Jesus son of Mary,
was only the Messenger of God, and His Word
that He committed to Mary, and a Spirit from
Him. So believe in God and His Messengers,
and say not, 'Three.' Refrain; better is it
for you. God is only One God. Glory be
to Him—that He should have a son!
To Him belongs all that is in the heavens
and in the earth; God suffices
        for a guardian.

170   The Messiah will not disdain to be a servant
of God, neither the angels who are near
        stationed to Him.
Whosoever disdains to serve Him, and waxes
proud, He will assuredly muster them to
        Him, all of them.
As for the believers, who do deeds of righteousness,
He will pay them in full their wages,
and He will give them more, of His bounty;
and as for them who disdain, and wax proud,
them He will chastise with a painful chastisement,
and they shall not find for them, apart from God,
        a friend or helper.

O men, a proof has now come to you from your Lord;
We have sent down to you a manifest light.
As for those who believe in God, and hold fast
to Him, He will surely admit them to mercy
from Him, and bounty, and will guide them to Him
        on a straight path.

175   They will ask thee for a pronouncement.
Say: 'God pronounces to you concerning
the indirect heirs. If a man perishes
having no children, but he has a sister,
she shall receive a half of what he leaves,
and he is her heir if she has no children.

If there be two sisters, they shall receive
two-thirds of what he leaves; if there be
brothers and sisters, the male shall receive
the portion of two females. God makes clear
to you, lest you go astray; God has knowledge
of everything.

V

THE TABLE

In the Name of God, the Merciful, the Compassionate

O believers, fulfil your bonds.

Permitted to you is the beast of the flocks,
except that which is now recited to you,
so that you deem not game permitted to be
hunted when you are in pilgrim sanctity.
God decrees whatsoever He desires.
O believers, profane not God's waymarks
nor the holy month, neither the offering,
nor the necklaces, nor those repairing to
the Holy House seeking from their Lord bounty
    and good pleasure.
But when you have quit your pilgrim sanctity,
    then hunt for game.

Let not detestation for a people who
barred you from the Holy Mosque move you
to commit aggression. Help one another to
piety and godfearing; do not help each other
to sin and enmity. And fear God; surely God is
    terrible in retribution.

    Forbidden to you are
carrion, blood, the flesh of swine,
what has been hallowed to other than God,
the beast strangled, the beast beaten down,
the beast fallen to death, the beast gored,
and that devoured by beasts of prey—
excepting that you have sacrificed duly—
as also things sacrificed to idols,
and partition by the divining arrows;
    that is ungodliness.

Today the unbelievers have despaired of
your religion; therefore fear them not,
    but fear you Me.
5   Today I have perfected your religion
for you, and I have completed My blessing
upon you, and I have approved Islam for
    your religion.

But whosoever is constrained in emptiness
and not inclining purposely to sin—
God is All-forgiving, All-compassionate.

They will question thee what is permitted them.
Say: 'The good things are permitted you; and
such hunting creatures as you teach, training
them as hounds, and teaching them as God has
taught you—eat what they seize for you, and
mention God's Name over it. Fear God; God is
    swift at the reckoning.'
Today the good things are permitted you,
and the food of those who were given the Book
is permitted to you, and permitted to them
is your food. Likewise believing women
in wedlock, and in wedlock women of
them who were given the Book before you
if you give them their wages, in wedlock
and not in licence, or as taking lovers.
Whoso disbelieves in the faith, his work has
failed, and in the world to come he shall
    be among the losers.

O believers, when you stand up to pray
wash your faces, and your hands up to the
elbows, and wipe your heads, and your feet
up to the ankles. If you are defiled,
purify yourselves; but if you are sick
or on a journey, or if any of you
comes from the privy, or you have touched
women, and you can find no water,

then have recourse to wholesome dust
and wipe your faces and your hands with it.
God does not desire to make any impediment
for you; but He desires to purify you, and
that He may complete His blessing upon you;
 haply you will be thankful.

10 And remember God's blessing upon you,
and His compact which He made with you
when you said, 'We have heard and we obey.'
And fear you God; surely God knows
 the thoughts in the breasts.

O believers, be you securers of
justice, witnesses for God. Let not
detestation for a people move you
not to be equitable; be equitable—
that is nearer to godfearing.
And fear God; surely God is aware of
 the things you do.
God has promised those that believe, and do
deeds of righteousness; they shall have forgiveness
 and a mighty wage.
And the unbelievers, who cried lies to Our
signs—they shall be the inhabitants of
 Hell.
O believers, remember God's blessing
upon you, when a certain people purposed
to stretch against you their hands, and He
restrained their hands from you; and fear
God; and in God let the believers
 put all their trust.

15 God took compact with the Children of Israel;
and We raised up from among them twelve
chieftains. And God said, 'I am with you.
Surely, if you perform the prayer, and pay
the alms, and believe in My Messengers
and succour them, and lend to God
a good.loan, I will acquit you of

your evil deeds, and I will admit you
to gardens underneath which rivers flow.
So whosoever of you thereafter
disbelieves, surely he has gone astray
  from the right way.'
So for their breaking their compact We cursed them
and made their hearts hard, they perverting
words from their meanings; and they have forgotten
a portion of that they were reminded of;
and thou wilt never cease to light upon
some act of treachery on their part, except
  a few of them.
Yet pardon them, and forgive; surely God
  loves the good-doers.
And with those who say 'We are Christians'
We took compact; and they have forgotten
a portion of that they were reminded of.
So We have stirred up among them enmity
and hatred, till the Day of Resurrection;
and God will assuredly tell them of
  the things they wrought.

People of the Book, now there has come to you
Our Messenger, making clear to you many things
you have been concealing of the Book,
and effacing many things. There has come
to you from God a light, and a Book Manifest
whereby God guides whosoever follows
His good pleasure in the ways of peace,
and brings them forth from the shadows into
the light by His leave; and He guides them
  to a straight path.
  They are unbelievers
who say, 'God is the Messiah, Mary's son.'
Say: 'Who then shall overrule God in any way
if He desires to destroy the Messiah,
Mary's son, and his mother, and all those
  who are on earth?'
20 For to God belongs the kingdom of the heavens

and of the earth, and all that is between them,
creating what He will. God is powerful
    over everything.

    Say the Jews and Christians,
'We are the sons of God, and His beloved ones.'
Say: 'Why then does He chastise you for your sins?
No; you are mortals, of His creating;
He forgives whom He will, and He chastises
    whom He will.'
For to God belongs the kingdom of the heavens
and of the earth, and all that is between them;
    to Him is the homecoming.

People of the Book, now there has come to you
Our Messenger, making things clear to you,
upon an interval between the Messengers
lest you should say, 'There has not come to us
any bearer of good tidings, neither any warner.'
Indeed, there has come to you a bearer of
good tidings and a warner; God is powerful
    over everything.

And when Moses said to his people,
'O my people, remember God's blessing
upon you, when He appointed among you
Prophets, and appointed you kings, and gave you
such as He had not given to any being.
O my people, enter the Holy Land
which God has prescribed for you, and turn not
back in your traces, to turn about losers.'
25   They said, 'Moses, there are people in it
very arrogant; we will not enter it
until they depart from it; if they depart from it
    then we will enter.'
Said two men of those that feared God
whom God had blessed, 'Enter against them
the gate! When you enter it, you will be

victors. Put you all your trust in God,
    if you are believers.'
They said, 'Moses, we will never enter it
so long as they are in it. Go forth, thou
and thy Lord, and do battle; we will
    be sitting here.'
He said, 'O my Lord, I rule no one
except myself and my brother. So do Thou
divide between us and the people
    of the ungodly.'
Said He, 'Then it shall be forbidden them
for forty years, while they are wandering
in the earth; so grieve not for the people
    of the ungodly.'

30   And recite thou to them the story
of the two sons of Adam truthfully,
when they offered a sacrifice, and it was
accepted of one of them, and not accepted
of the other. 'I will surely slay thee,'
said one. 'God accepts only of the godfearing,'
    said the other.
'Yet if thou stretchest out thy hand against
me, to slay me, I will not stretch out my hand
against thee, to slay thee; I fear God,
    the Lord of all Being.
I desire that thou shouldest be laden
with my sin and thy sin, and so become
an inhabitant of the Fire; that is the recompense
    of the evildoers.'
Then his soul prompted him to slay
his brother, and he slew him, and became
    one of the losers.
Then God sent forth a raven, scratching
into the earth, to show him how he might
conceal the vile body of his brother.
He said, 'Woe is me! Am I unable
to be as this raven, and so conceal
my brother's vile body?' And he became

one of the remorseful.

35   Therefore We prescribed for the Children of Israel
that whoso slays a soul not to retaliate
for a soul slain, nor for corruption
done in the land, shall be as if he had
slain mankind altogether; and whoso
gives life to a soul, shall be as if he had
given life to mankind altogether.
Our Messengers have already come to them
with the clear signs; then many of them
thereafter commit excesses in the earth.

This is the recompense of those who fight
against God and His Messenger, and hasten
about the earth, to do corruption there:
they shall be slaughtered, or crucified,
or their hands and feet shall alternately
be struck off, or they shall be banished
from the land. That is a degradation for them
in this world; and in the world to come awaits them
        a mighty chastisement,
except for such as repent, before you
have power over them. So know you that
God is All-forgiving, All-compassionate.

O believers, fear God, and seek the means
to come to Him, and struggle in His way;
        haply you will prosper.

40   The unbelievers, though they possessed all
that is in the earth, and the like of it with it,
to ransom themselves from the chastisement
of the Day of Resurrection thereby, it would
not be accepted of them; for them awaits
        a painful chastisement.
They will desire to come forth from the Fire, but
they will not come forth from it; for them awaits
        a lasting chastisement.

And the thief, male and female: cut off the hands
of both, as a recompense for what they have earned,
and a punishment exemplary from God; God is
     All-mighty, All-wise.
But whoso repents, after his evildoing,
and makes amends, God will turn towards him;
God is All-forgiving, All-compassionate.
Knowest thou not that to God belongs
the kingdom of the heavens and the earth?
He chastises whom He will, and forgives
whom He will; and God is powerful
     over everything.

45   O Messenger, let them not grieve thee
that vie with one another in unbelief,
such men as say with their mouths 'We believe'
but their hearts believe not; and the Jews
who listen to falsehood, listen to other folk,
who have not come to thee, perverting words
from their meanings, saying, 'If you are given
this, then take it; if you are not given it,
beware!' Whomsoever God desires to try,
thou canst not avail him anything with God.
Those are they whose hearts God desired not
to purify; for them is degradation
in this world; and in the world to come awaits them
     a mighty chastisement;
who listen to falsehood, and consume the unlawful.
If they come to thee, judge thou between them,
or turn away from them; if thou turnest
away from them, they will hurt thee nothing;
and if thou judgest, judge justly between them;
     God loves the just.
Yet how will they make thee their judge
seeing they have the Torah, wherein is God's
judgment, then thereafter turn their backs?
     They are not believers.
Surely We sent down the Torah, wherein is
guidance and light; thereby the Prophets

who had surrendered themselves gave judgment
for those of Jewry, as did the masters
and the rabbis, following such portion
of God's Book as they were given to keep
and were witnesses to. So fear not men,
but fear you Me; and sell not My signs
for a little price. Whoso judges not
according to what God has sent down—
      they are the unbelievers.
And therein We prescribed for them:
'A life for a life, an eye for an eye,
a nose for a nose, an ear for an ear,
a tooth for a tooth, and for wounds
retaliation'; but whosoever forgoes it
as a freewill offering, that shall be for him
an expiation. Whoso judges not
according to what God has sent down—
      they are the evildoers.

50   And We sent, following
      in their footsteps, Jesus
      son of Mary, confirming
      the Torah before him;
      and We gave to him
      the Gospel, wherein
      is guidance and light,
      and confirming the Torah
      before it, as a guidance
      and an admonition
      unto the godfearing.
So let the People of the Gospel judge
according to what God has sent down
therein. Whosoever judges not
according to what God has sent down—
      they are the ungodly.

And We have sent down to thee the Book
with the truth, confirming the Book
that was before it, and assuring it.

So judge between them according to what
God has sent down, and do not follow
their caprices, to forsake the truth
that has come to thee. To every one
of you We have appointed a right way
     and an open road.
If God had willed, He would have made you
one nation; but that He may try you
in what has come to you. So be you forward
in good works; unto God shall you
return, all together; and He will tell you
of that whereon you were at variance.
And judge between them according to what
God has sent down, and do not follow
their caprices, and beware of them
lest they tempt thee away from any
of what God has sent down to thee.
But if they turn their backs, know that God
desires only to smite them for some sin
they have committed; surely, many men
     are ungodly.

55   Is it the judgment of pagandom then
that they are seeking? Yet who is fairer
in judgment than God, for a people
     having sure faith?

O believers, take not Jews and Christians
as friends; they are friends of each other.
Whoso of you makes them his friends
is one of them. God guides not the people
     of the evildoers.
Yet thou seest those in whose hearts is sickness
vying with one another to come to them,
saying, 'We fear lest a turn of fortune
should smite us.' But it may be that God
will bring the victory, or some commandment
from Him, and then they will find themselves,
for that they kept secret within them,
     remorseful,

and the believers will say, 'What, are these
the ones who swore by God most earnest oaths
that they were with you? Their works have failed;
    now they are losers.'

O believers, whosoever of you turns
from his religion, God will assuredly
bring a people He loves, and who love Him,
humble towards the believers, disdainful
towards the unbelievers, men who struggle
in the path of God, not fearing the reproach
of any reproacher. That is God's bounty;
He gives it unto whom He will; and God is
    All-embracing, All-knowing.

60   Your friend is only God, and His Messenger,
and the believers who perform the prayer
and pay the alms, and bow them down.
Whoso makes God his friend, and His Messenger,
and the believers—the party of God,
    they are the victors.
O believers, take not as your friends those
of them, who were given the Book before you,
and the unbelievers, who take your religion
in mockery and as a sport—and fear God,
    if you are believers—
and when you call to prayer, take it
in mockery and as a sport; that is
because they are a people who have
    no understanding.

Say: 'People of the Book, do you blame us
for any other cause than that we believe
in God, and what has been sent down to us,
and what was sent down before, and that most of
    you are ungodly?'
65   Say: 'Shall I tell you of a recompense
with God, worse than that? Whomsoever
God has cursed, and with whom He is wroth,
and made some of them apes and swine,

and worshippers of idols—they are worse
situated, and have gone further astray
      from the right way.'

When they come to you, they say, 'We believe';
but they have entered in unbelief, and so
they have departed in it; God knows very well
      what they were hiding.
Thou seest many of them vying in sin
and enmity, and how they consume
the unlawful; evil is the thing
      they have been doing.
Why do the masters and the rabbis
not forbid them to utter sin, and consume
the unlawful? Evil is the thing
      they have been working.

The Jews have said, 'God's hand is fettered.'
Fettered are their hands, and they are cursed
for what they have said. Nay, but His hands
are outspread; He expends how He will.
And what has been sent down to thee from
thy Lord will surely increase many of them
in insolence and unbelief; and We have cast
between them enmity and hatred, till the Day
of Resurrection. As often as they light
a fire for war, God will extinguish it.
They hasten about the earth, to do
corruption there; and God loves not the
      workers of corruption.
70   But had the People of the Book believed
and been godfearing, We would have acquitted
them of their evil deeds, and admitted them
to Gardens of Bliss. Had they performed
the Torah and the Gospel, and what was
sent down to them from their Lord, they would
have eaten both what was above them, and
what was beneath their feet. Some of them are

a just nation; but many of them—evil are
    the things they do.

O Messenger, deliver that which has
been sent down to thee from thy Lord;
for if thou dost not, thou wilt not have
delivered His Message. God will protect thee
from men. God guides not the people
    of the unbelievers.
Say: 'People of the Book, you do not stand
on anything, until you perform
the Torah and the Gospel, and what was sent
down to you from your Lord.' And what has been
sent down to thee from thy Lord will surely
increase many of them in insolence
and unbelief; so grieve not for the people
    of the unbelievers.
Surely they that believe, and those of Jewry,
and the Sabaeans, and those Christians,
whosoever believes in God and
the Last Day, and works righteousness—
no fear shall be on them, neither shall they sorrow.

And We took compact with the Children of Israel,
and We sent Messengers to them. Whensoever there
came to them a Messenger with that their souls
had not desire for, some they cried lies to,
    and some they slew.
75   And they supposed there should be no trial;
but blind they were, and deaf. Then God turned
towards them; then again blind they were,
many of them, and deaf; and God sees
    the things they do.

    They are unbelievers
who say, 'God is the Messiah, Mary's son.'
    For the Messiah said,
    'Children of Israel,
    serve God, my Lord and

your Lord. Verily
whoso associates
with God anything,
God shall prohibit him
entrance to Paradise,
and his refuge shall be
the Fire; and wrongdoers
shall have no helpers.'

They are unbelievers
who say, 'God is the Third of Three.'
No god is there but
One God.
If they refrain not from what they say, there
shall afflict those of them that disbelieve
a painful chastisement.
Will they not turn to God and pray His forgiveness?
God is All-forgiving, All-compassionate.

The Messiah, son of Mary, was only
a Messenger; Messengers before him
passed away; his mother was a just woman;
they both ate food. Behold, how We make clear
the signs to them; then behold, how they
perverted are!

80   Say: 'Do you serve, apart from God,
that which cannot hurt or profit you? God is
the All-hearing, the All-knowing.'
Say: 'People of the Book, go not beyond the
bounds in your religion, other than the truth,
and follow not the caprices of a people
who went astray before, and led astray
many, and now again have gone astray
from the right way.'
Cursed were the unbelievers of the Children
of Israel by the tongue of David, and
Jesus, Mary's son; that, for their rebelling
and their transgression.

They forbade not one another any dishonour
that they committed; surely evil were
    the things they did.
Thou seest many of them making unbelievers
their friends. Evil is that they have forwarded
to their account, that God is angered
against them, and in the chastisement they
    shall dwell forever.
Yet had they believed in God and the Prophet
and what has been sent down to him, they would
not have taken them as friends; but many of them
    are ungodly.

85   Thou wilt surely find the most hostile
of men to the believers are the Jews
and the idolaters; and thou wilt surely find
the nearest of them in love to the believers
are those who say 'We are Christians'; that,
because some of them are priests and monks, and
    they wax not proud,
and when they hear what has been sent down
to the Messenger, thou seest their eyes
overflow with tears because of the truth
they recognize. They say, 'Our Lord,
we believe; so do Thou write us down
    among the witnesses.
Why should we not believe in God and the
truth that has come to us, and be eager
that our Lord should admit us with
    the righteous people?'
And God rewards them for what they say
with gardens underneath which rivers flow,
    therein dwelling forever;
that is the recompense of the good-doers.
But those who disbelieve, and cry lies
to Our signs—they are the inhabitants of
    Hell.

O believers, forbid not such good things as God
has permitted you; and transgress not; God

113

loves not transgressors.
90   Eat of what God has provided you
lawful and good; and fear God, in whom
        you are believers.

God will not take you to task for a slip
in your oaths; but He will take you to task
for such bonds as you have made by oaths,
whereof the expiation is to feed ten
poor persons with the average of the food
you serve to your families, or to clothe them,
or to set free a slave; or if any finds not
the means, let him fast for three days.
That is the expiation of your oaths
when you have sworn; but keep your oaths.
So God makes clear to you His signs; haply
        you will be thankful.

O believers, wine and arrow-shuffling,
idols and divining-arrows are an abomination,
some of Satan's work; so avoid it; haply
        so you will prosper.
Satan only desires to precipitate enmity
and hatred between you in regard to wine
and arrow-shuffling, and to bar you from
the remembrance of God, and from prayer.
Will you then desist? And obey God
and obey the Messenger, and beware;
but if you turn your backs, then know that
it is only for Our Messenger to deliver
        the Message Manifest.

There is no fault in those who believe and
do deeds of righteousness what they may eat, if
they are godfearing, and believe, and do deeds of
righteousness, and then are godfearing and believe,
and then are godfearing and do good; God
        loves the good-doers.

114

95   O believers, God will surely try you
with something of the game that your hands and
lances attain, that God may know who
fears Him in the Unseen. Whoso thereafter
commits transgression, there awaits him
       a painful chastisement.
O believers, slay not the game while you
are in pilgrim sanctity; whosoever of you
slays it wilfully, there shall be recompense—
the like of what he has slain, in flocks
as shall be judged by two men of equity
among you, an offering to reach the Kaaba;
or expiation—food for poor persons
or the equivalent of that in fasting, so that
·he may taste the mischief of his action.
God has pardoned what is past; but whoever offends
again, God will take vengeance on him; God is
       All-mighty, Vengeful.
Permitted to you is the game of the sea
and the food of it, as a provision for you
and for the journeyers; but forbidden to you
is the game of the land, so long as you remain
in pilgrim sanctity; and fear God, unto whom
       you shall be mustered.
God has appointed the Kaaba, the Holy House,
as an establishment for men, and the holy month,
the offering, and the necklaces—that, that you
may know that God knows all that is in the heavens
and in the earth, and that God has knowledge
       of everything.
Know God is terrible in retribution, and
God is All-forgiving, All-compassionate.

It is only for the Messenger to deliver
the Message; and God knows what you reveal
       and what you hide.
100   Say: 'The corrupt and the good are not equal,
though the abundance of the corrupt please thee.'
So fear God, O men possessed of minds; haply

so you will prosper.

O believers, question not concerning things
which, if they were revealed to you, would vex you;
yet if you question concerning them when the Koran
is being sent down, they will be revealed to you.
God has effaced those things; for God is
     All-forgiving, All-clement.
A people before you questioned concerning them,
     then disbelieved in them.
God has not appointed cattle dedicated
to idols, such as Bahira, Sa'iba,
Wasila, Hami; but the unbelievers
forge against God falsehood, and most of them
     have no understanding.
And when it is said to them, 'Come now to
what God has sent down, and the Messenger,
they say, 'Enough for us is what we found
     our fathers doing.'
What, even if their fathers had knowledge of naught
     and were not guided?
O believers, look after your own souls.
He who is astray cannot hurt you, if you
are rightly guided. Unto God shall you
return, all together, and He will tell you
     what you were doing.

105   O believers, the testimony between you
when any of you is visited by death,
at the bequeathing, shall be two men
of equity among you; or two others from
another folk, if you are journeying in the land
and the affliction of death befalls you.
Them you shall detain after the prayer, and
they shall swear by God, if you are doubtful,
'We will not sell it for a price, even though
it were a near kinsman, nor will we hide the
testimony of God, for then we would surely be
     among the sinful.'

But if it be discovered that both of them
have merited the accusation of any sin,
then two others shall stand in their place,
these being the nearest of those most concerned,
and they shall swear by God, 'Our testimony
is truer than their testimony, and we have not
transgressed, for then we would assuredly be
    among the evildoers.'
So it is likelier that they will bear testimony
in proper form, or else they will be afraid
that after their oaths oaths may be rebutted.
Fear God, and hearken; God guides not the people
    of the ungodly.

The day when God shall gather the Messengers, and say,
'What answer were you given?' They shall say, 'We have
no knowledge; Thou art the Knower of the things unseen.'

    When God said, 'Jesus
    Son of Mary, remember
    My blessing upon thee
    and upon thy mother,
    when I confirmed thee
    with the Holy Spirit,
    to speak to men in
    the cradle, and of age;
110   and when I taught thee
    the Book, the Wisdom,
    the Torah, the Gospel;
    and when thou createst
    out of clay, by My
    leave, as the likeness
    of a bird, and thou
    breathest into it,
    and it is a bird, by My
    leave; and thou healest
    the blind and the leper
    by My leave, and thou
    bringest the dead forth

by My leave; and when I
restrained from thee
the Children of Israel
when thou camest unto
them with the clear
signs, and the unbelievers
among them said, "This is
nothing but sorcery,
manifest." And when I
inspired the Apostles:
"Believe in Me and My
Messenger"; they said,
"We believe; witness
Thou our submission." '
And when the Apostles
said, 'O Jesus son of
Mary, is thy Lord able
to send down on us a
Table out of heaven?'
He said, 'Fear you God,
if you are believers.'
They said, 'We desire
that we should eat of it
and our hearts be at rest;
and that we may know that
thou hast spoken true to
us, and that we may be
among its witnesses.'
Said Jesus son of Mary,
'O God, our Lord, send
down upon us a Table
out of heaven, that shall
be for us a festival, the
first and last of us,
and a sign from Thee.
And provide for us; Thou
art the best of providers.'
115 God said, 'Verily I
do send it down on you;

whoso of you hereafter
disbelieves, verily I
shall chastise him with a
chastisement wherewith I
chastise no other being.'
And when God said, 'O
Jesus son of Mary,
didst thou say unto men,
"Take me and my mother
as gods, apart from God"?'
He said, 'To Thee be
glory! It is not mine to
say what I have no right
to. If I indeed said it,
Thou knowest it, knowing
what is within my soul,
and I know not what is
within Thy soul; Thou
knowest the things unseen
I only said to them what
Thou didst command me:
"Serve God, my Lord and
your Lord." And I was a
witness over them, while
I remained among them;
but when Thou didst take
me to Thyself, Thou wast
Thyself the watcher over
them; Thou Thyself art
witness of everything.
If Thou chastisest them,
they are Thy servants; if
Thou forgivest them, Thou
art the All-mighty, the
All-wise.' God said,
'This is the day the
truthful shall be profited
by their truthfulness.
For them await gardens

underneath which rivers
flow, therein dwelling
forever and ever, God being
well-pleased with them and
they well-pleased with Him;
that is the mighty triumph.'

To God belongs the kingdom of the heavens
and of the earth, and all that is in them,
and He is powerful over everything.

VI

CATTLE

In the Name of God, the Merciful, the Compassionate

   Praise belongs to God
  who created the heavens and the earth
  and appointed the shadows and light;
then the unbelievers ascribe equals to their Lord.
   It is He who created you of
  clay, then determined a term
  and a term is stated with Him; yet
    thereafter you doubt.
  He is God in the heavens and the earth;
He knows your secrets, and what you publish,
  and He knows what you are earning.

Not a sign of their Lord comes to them, but
   they turn away from it.
They cried lies to the truth when it came to
them, but there shall come to them news of
   that they were mocking.
Have they not regarded how We destroyed before
them many a generation We established in the
earth, as We never established you, and how We
loosed heaven upon them in torrents, and made
the rivers to flow beneath them? Then We destroyed
them because of their sins, and raised up after them
   another generation.
Had We sent down on thee a Book on parchment
and so they touched it with their hands, yet
the unbelievers would have said, 'This is naught
   but manifest sorcery.'
'Why has an angel not been sent down on him?'
they say; yet had We sent down an angel, the matter
would have been determined, and then no respite
   would be given them.

121

And had We made him an angel, yet assuredly
We would have made him a man, and confused
for them the thing which they themselves
   are confusing.

10   Messengers indeed were mocked at before thee;
but those that scoffed at them were encompassed by
   that they mocked at.
Say: 'Journey in the land, then behold
how was the end of them that cried lies.'
Say: 'To whom belongs what is in the heavens
and in the earth?' Say: 'It is God's.
He has prescribed for Himself mercy. He will
surely gather you to the Resurrection Day, of
which is no doubt. Those who have lost their souls,
   they do not believe.
And to Him belongs whatsoever inhabits
the night and the day; and He is
   the All-hearing, the All-knowing.'
Say: 'Shall I take to myself as protector
other than God, the Originator of the heavens
and of the earth, He who feeds and is not fed?'
Say: 'I have been commanded to be the first
of them that surrender: "Be not thou
   of the idolaters." '
15   Say: 'Indeed I fear, if I should rebel
against my Lord, the chastisement
   of a dreadful day.'
From whomsoever it is averted on that day,
He will have mercy on him; that is
   the manifest triumph.

And if God visits thee with affliction
none can remove it but He; and if He
visits thee with good, He is powerful
   over everything.
He is Omnipotent over His servants, and He is
   the All-wise, the All-aware.
Say: 'What thing is greatest in testimony?'

Say: 'God is witness between me and you,
and this Koran has been revealed to me
that I may warn you thereby, and whomsoever
it may reach. Do you indeed testify
that there are other gods with God?'
Say: 'I do not testify.' Say: 'He is only
One God, and I am quit of that
    you associate.'

20   Those to whom We have given the Book
recognize it as they recognize their sons.
Those who have lost their own souls,
    they do not believe.
And who does greater evil than he who
forges against God a lie, or cries lies
to His signs? They shall not prosper,
    the evildoers.
And on the day when We shall muster them all together,
then We shall say unto those who associated other gods
with God, 'Where are your associates whom you were
                          [asserting?'
Then they shall have no proving, but to say, 'By God our
Lord, we never associated other gods with Thee.'
Behold how they lie against themselves, and how that
which they were forging has gone astray from them!

25   And some of them there are that listen to
thee, and We lay veils upon their hearts
lest they understand it, and in their ears
heaviness; and if they see any sign
whatever, they do not believe in it, so that
when they come to thee they dispute with thee,
the unbelievers saying, 'This is naught
but the fairy-tales of the ancient ones.'
And they forbid it, and keep afar from it,
and it is only themselves they destroy, but
    they are not aware.
If thou couldst see when they are stationed
before the Fire, and they say, 'Would that we
might be returned, and then not cry lies to

the signs of our Lord, but that we might be
    among the believers!'
No; that which they were concealing before
has now appeared to them; and even if
they were returned, they would again commit
the very thing they were prohibited;
    they are truly liars.
And they say, 'There is only our present life;
    we shall not be raised.'

30   If thou couldst see when they are stationed
before their Lord! He will say, 'Is not this
the truth?' They will say, 'Yes indeed, by our
Lord!' He will say, 'Then taste the chastisement
    for your unbelief.'
Lost indeed are they that cried lies to the
encounter with God, so that when the Hour comes
to them suddenly they shall say, 'Alas for us,
that we neglected it!' On their backs
they shall be bearing their loads; O how evil
    the loads they bear!
The present life is naught but a sport
and a diversion; surely the Last Abode is
better for those that are godfearing. What,
    do you not understand?

We know indeed that it grieves thee
the things they say; yet it is not thee
they cry lies to, but the evildoers—
it is the signs of God that they deny.
Messengers indeed were cried lies to
before thee, yet they endured patiently
that they were cried lies to, and were hurt,
until Our help came unto them.
No man can change the words of God; and
there has already come to thee some tiding
    of the Envoys.

35   And if their turning away is distressful
for thee, why, if thou canst seek out
a hole in the earth, or a ladder

in heaven, to bring them some sign—
but had God willed, He would have gathered
them to the guidance; so be not thou
    one of the ignorant.
Answer only will those who hear; as for the dead,
God will raise them up, then unto Him
    they will be returned.

They also say, 'Why has no sign been sent
down upon him from his Lord?' Say: 'Surely
God is able to send down a sign, but
    most of them know not.'

No creature is there crawling on the earth,
   no bird flying with its wings,
but they are nations like unto yourselves.
We have neglected nothing in the Book;
then to their Lord they shall be mustered.

And those who cry lies to Our signs
are deaf and dumb, dwelling in the shadows.
Whomsoever God will, He leads astray,
and whomsoever He will, He sets him
    on a straight path.

40   Say: 'What think you? If God's chastisement
comes upon you, or the Hour comes upon you,
will you call upon any other than God
    if you speak truly?'
No; upon Him you will call, and He will
remove that for which you call upon Him
if He will, and you will forget that you
    associate with Him.

Indeed We sent to nations before thee,
and We seized them with misery and hardship
   that haply they might be humble;
if only, when Our might came upon them, they
had been humble! But their hearts were
hard, and Satan decked out fair to them

what they were doing.
So, when they forgot what they were reminded of,
We opened unto them the gates of everything
until, when they rejoiced in what they were
given, We seized them suddenly, and behold, they
     were sore confounded.
45   So the last remnant of the people who did
evil was cut off. Praise belongs to God
     the Lord of all Being.
Say: 'What think you? If God seizes
your hearing and sight, and sets a seal upon
your hearts, who is a god other than God
to give it back to you?' Behold how We
turn about the signs! Yet thereafter they
     are turning away.
Say: 'What think you? If God's chastisement
comes upon you, suddenly or openly,
shall any be destroyed, except the people
     of the evildoers?'

We do not send the Envoys, except good
tidings to bear, and warning; whoever believes
     and makes amends—
no fear shall be on them, neither shall they sorrow.
But those who cry lies to Our signs, them
the chastisement shall visit, for that
     they were ungodly.
50   Say: 'I do not say to you, "I possess
the treasuries of God"; I know not the Unseen.
And I say not to you, "I am an angel";
I only follow what is revealed to me.'
Say: 'Are the blind and the seeing man equal?
     Will you not reflect?'

And warn therewith those who fear they shall be
mustered to their Lord; they have, apart from
God, no protector and no intercessor; haply
     they will be godfearing.
And do not drive away those who call

upon their Lord at morning and evening
desiring His countenance; nothing of their
account falls upon thee, and nothing of
thy account falls upon them, that thou
shouldst drive them away, and so become
     one of the evildoers.
Even so We have tried some of them by others
that they may say, 'Are these the ones God
has been gracious to among us?' Knows not God
     very well the thankful?
And when those who believe in Our signs come
to thee, say, 'Peace be upon you. Your Lord has
prescribed for Himself mercy. Whosoever of you
does evil in ignorance, and thereafter repents
and makes amends, He is All-forgiving,
     All-compassionate.'
55   Thus We distinguish Our signs, that the sinners'
     way may be manifest.

Say: 'I am forbidden to serve those you call on
     apart from God.'
Say: 'I do not follow your caprices, or
else I had gone astray, and would not be
     of the right-guided.'
Say: 'I stand upon a clear sign from my Lord,
and you have cried lies to it. Not with me
is that you seek to hasten; the judgment is
God's alone. He relates the truth, and He is
     the Best of deciders.'
Say: 'If what you seek to hasten were
with me, the matter between you and me
would be decided; and God knows very well
     the evildoers.'

With Him are the keys of the Unseen;
     none knows them but He.
He knows what is in land and sea;
not a leaf falls, but He knows it.

Not a grain in the earth's shadows,
not a thing, fresh or withered,
but it is in a Book Manifest.
60   It is He who recalls you by night,
and He knows what you work by day;
then He raises you up therein, that
a stated term may be determined;
then unto Him shall you return,
then He will tell you of what
    you have been doing.
He is the Omnipotent over His servants.
    He sends recorders over you till,
when any one of you is visited
by death, Our messengers take him
    and they neglect not.
Then they are restored to God
their Protector, the True. Surely
His is the judgment; He is the swiftest
    of reckoners.

Say: 'Who delivers you from the shadows
of land and sea? You call upon Him
humbly and secretly, "Truly, if Thou
deliverest from these, we shall be
    among the thankful." '
Say: 'God delivers you from them and
from every distress; then you assign
    Him associates.'
65   Say: 'He is able to send forth upon you
chastisement, from above you or from under
your feet, or to confuse you in sects
and to make you taste the violence
    of one another.'
Behold how We turn about the signs; haply
    they will understand.
Thy people have cried it lies; yet it is
the truth. Say: 'I am not a guardian over
you. Every tiding has its time appointed;
    you will surely know.'

When thou seest those who plunge into Our
signs, turn away from them until they plunge
into some other talk; or if Satan
should make thee forget, do not sit,
after the reminding, with the people
    of the evildoers.
Nothing of their account falls upon those
that are godfearing; but a reminding; haply
    they will be godfearing.
Leave alone those who take their religion
for a sport and a diversion, and whom
the present life has deluded. Remind
hereby, lest a soul should be given up
to destruction for what it has earned;
apart from God, it has no protector
and no intercessor; though it offer
any equivalent, it shall not be taken
from it. Those are they who are given up
to destruction for what they have earned;
for them awaits a draught of boiling water
and a painful chastisement, for that
    they were unbelievers.

70   Say: 'Shall we call, apart from God,
on that which neither profits nor hurts us,
and shall we be turned back on our heels
after that God has guided us?—Like one
lured to bewilderment in the earth
by Satans, though he has friends who
call him to guidance, "Come to us!" '
Say: 'God's guidance is the true guidance,
and we are commanded to surrender to
    the Lord of all Being,
and: "Perform the prayer, and fear Him;
it is unto Him you shall be mustered." '

It is He who created the heavens and the earth
in truth; and the day He says 'Be', and it is;
His saying is true, and His is the Kingdom

the day the Trumpet is blown; He is Knower
of the Unseen and the visible; He is
      the All-wise, the All-aware.

And when Abraham said to his father Azar,
'Takest thou idols for gods? I see thee,
and thy people, in manifest error.'
75   So We were showing Abraham the kingdom
of the heavens and earth, that he might be
      of those having sure faith.
When night outspread over him he saw a star
      and said, 'This is my Lord.'
But when it set he said, 'I love not the setters.'
When he saw the moon rising, he said,
      'This is my Lord.' But when
it set he said, 'If my Lord does not guide me
I shall surely be of the people gone astray.'
When he saw the sun rising, he said,
      'This is my Lord; this is greater!'
But when it set he said, 'O my people,
surely I am quit of that you associate.
I have turned my face to Him who originated
the heavens and the earth, a man of pure faith;
      I am not of the idolaters.'
80   His people disputed with him. He said, 'Do you
dispute with me concerning God, and He has
guided me? I fear not what you associate
with Him, except my Lord will aught.
My Lord embraces all things in His knowledge;
      will you not remember?
How should I fear what you have associated,
seeing you fear not that you have associated
with God that whereon He has not sent down on
      you any authority?'

Which of the two parties has better title
to security, if you have any knowledge?
Those who believe, and have not confounded
their belief with evildoing—to them belongs

the true security; they are rightly guided.
That is Our argument, which We bestowed
upon Abraham as against his people.
We raise up in degrees whom We will;
surely thy Lord is All-wise, All-knowing.
And We gave to him Isaac and Jacob—
  each one We guided,
And Noah We guided before; and of his seed
David and Solomon, Job and Joseph,
  Moses and Aaron—
even so We recompense the good-doers—
85 Zachariah and John, Jesus and Elias; each
  was of the righteous;
Ishmael and Elisha, Jonah and Lot—
each one We preferred above all beings;
and of their fathers, and of their seed,
  and of their brethren;
and We elected them, and We guided them
  to a straight path.

That is God's guidance; He guides by it
whom He will of His servants; had they been
idolaters, it would have failed them,
  the things they did.
Those are they to whom We gave the Book,
the Judgment, the Prophethood; so if these
disbelieve in it, We have already
entrusted it to a people who do not
  disbelieve in it.
90 Those are they whom God has guided; so
follow their guidance. Say: 'I ask of you
no wage for it; it is but a reminder
  unto all beings.'
They measured not God with His true measure
when they said, 'God has not sent down aught
on any mortal.' Say: 'Who sent down the Book
that Moses brought as a light and a guidance
to men? You put it into parchments, revealing
them, and hiding much; and you were taught

that you knew not, you and your fathers.'
Say: 'God.' Then leave them alone, playing
 their game of plunging.

This is a Book We have sent down, blessed
and confirming that which was before it,
and for thee to warn the Mother of Cities
and those about her; and those who believe
in the world to come believe in it, and
 watch over their prayers.
And who does greater evil than he who forges
against God a lie, or says, 'To me it has been
revealed', when naught has been revealed to him,
or he who says, 'I will send down the like of
what God has sent down'? If thou couldst only
see when the evildoers are in the agonies of
death, and the angels are stretching out their
hands: 'Give up your souls! Today you shall be
recompensed with the chastisement of humiliation
for what you said untruly about God, waxing
 proud against His signs.'
'Now you have come to Us one by one, as We created you
upon the first time, and you have left what We conferred
on you behind your backs. We do not see with you your
intercessors, those you asserted to be associates
in you; the bond between you is now broken; that
which you ever asserted has now gone astray from you.'

95 It is God who splits the grain and the date-stone,
   brings forth the living from the dead; He
   brings forth the dead too from the living.
  So that then is God; then how are you perverted?
   He splits the sky into dawn,
   and has made the night for a repose,
   and the sun and moon for a reckoning.
That is the ordaining of the All-mighty, the All-knowing.
  It is He who has appointed for you the stars, that
   by them you might be guided in
   the shadows of land and sea.

We have distinguished the signs for a people who know.
> It is He who produced you from one living soul,
>> and then a lodging-place,
>> and then a repository.

We have distinguished the signs for a people who understand.
> It is He who sent down out of heaven water, and
>> thereby We have brought forth
>> the shoot of every plant,

and then We have brought forth the green leaf of it,
> bringing forth from it
> close-compounded grain,

and out of the palm-tree, from the spathe of it,
> dates thick-clustered,
> ready to the hand, and
>> gardens of vines,
> olives, pomegranates,
> like each to each, and
>> each unlike to each.

Look upon their fruits when they fructify and ripen!
Surely, in all this are signs for a people who do believe.

100 Yet they ascribe to God, as associates, the
jinn, though He created them; and they impute
to Him sons and daughters without any knowledge.
> Glory be to Him!

High be He exalted above what they describe!
The Creator of the heavens and the earth—
> how should He have a son,

seeing that He has no consort, and He created
all things, and He has knowledge of everything?

> That then is God your Lord;
> there is no god but He,
> the Creator of everything.
>> So serve Him,
> for He is Guardian over everything.

The eyes attain Him not, but He attains the eyes;
> He is the All-subtle, the All-aware.

Clear proofs have come to you from your Lord.
Whoso sees clearly, it is to his own gain,
and whoso is blind, it is to his own loss;
    I am not a watcher over you.

105   So We turn about the signs, that they may say,
'Thou hast studied'; and that We may make it clear
        to a people having knowledge.
Follow thou what has been revealed to thee
from thy Lord; there is no god but He;
and turn thou away from the idolaters.
Had God willed, they were not idolaters;
and We have not appointed thee a watcher over them,
        neither art thou their guardian.

Abuse not those to whom they pray, apart from God,
or they will abuse God in revenge without knowledge.
So We have decked out fair to every nation
their deeds; then to their Lord they shall return,
and He will tell them what they have been doing.
They have sworn by God the most earnest oaths
if a sign comes to them they will believe in it.
Say: 'Signs are only with God.' What will make you
realize that, when it comes, they will not believe?
110   We shall turn about their hearts and their eyes,
even as they believed not in it the first time;
and We shall leave them in their insolence
        wandering blindly.
Though We had sent down the angels to them,
and the dead had spoken with them, had We mustered
against them every thing, face to face, yet
they would not have been the ones to believe,
unless God willed; but most of them are ignorant.
So We have appointed to every Prophet an enemy—
Satans of men and jinn, revealing tawdry
speech to each other, all as a delusion;
yet, had thy Lord willed, they would never
have done it. So leave them to their forging,
and that the hearts of those who believe not

in the world to come may incline to it,
and that they may be well-pleased with it,
and that they may gain what they are gaining.
What, shall I seek after any judge but God?
For it is He who sent down to you the Book
well-distinguished; and those whom We have given
the Book know it is sent down from thy Lord
with the truth; so be not thou of the doubters.

115   Perfect are the words of thy Lord in truthfulness
and justice; no man can change His words; He is
     the All-hearing, the All-knowing.
If thou obeyest the most part of those on earth
they will lead thee astray from the path of God;
they follow only surmise, merely conjecturing.
Thy Lord knows very well who goes astray from
His path; He knows very well the right-guided.

Eat of that over which God's Name has been
mentioned, if you believe in His signs.
How is it with you, that you do not eat of
that over which God's Name has been mentioned,
seeing that He has distinguished for you that
He has forbidden you, unless you are constrained
to it? But surely, many lead astray
by their caprices, without any knowledge;
thy Lord knows very well the transgressors.

120   Forsake the outward sin, and the inward;
surely the earners of sin shall be recompensed
     for what they have earned.
And eat not of that over which God's Name
has not been mentioned; it is ungodliness.
The Satans inspire their friends to dispute
with you; if you obey them, you are idolaters.

Why, is he who was dead, and We gave him life,
and appointed for him a light to walk by
among the people as one whose likeness is in
the shadows, and comes not forth from them?

So it is decked out fair to the unbelievers
    the things they have done.

And even so We appointed in every city
great ones among its sinners, to devise there;
but they devised only against themselves,
    and they were not aware.
And when a sign came to them, they said,
'We will not believe until we are given the
like of what God's Messengers were given.'
God knows very well where to place His Message;
and humiliation in God's sight shall befall
the sinners, and a terrible chastisement,
    for what they devised.

125   Whomsoever God desires to guide,
    He expands his breast to Islam;
    whomsoever He desires to lead astray,
    He makes his breast narrow, tight,
    as if he were climbing to heaven.
    So God lays abomination
    upon those who believe not.
This is the path of thy Lord; straight; We have
distinguished the signs to a people who remember.
Theirs is the abode of peace with their Lord,
    and He is their Protector for
        that they were doing.

On the day when He shall muster them all together:
'Company of jinn, you have made much of mankind.'
Then their friends among mankind will say, 'Our Lord,
we have profited each of the other, and we
have reached the term determined by Thee for us.'
He will say: 'The Fire is your lodging, therein to dwell
forever'—except as God will; surely thy Lord is
    All-wise, All-knowing.
So We make the evildoers friends of each other
    for what they have earned.

130 'Company of jinn and mankind, did not Messengers

come to you from among you, relating to you My signs
and warning you of the encounter of this your day?'
They shall say, 'We bear witness against ourselves.'
They were deluded by the present life, and they
bear witness against themselves that they were unbelievers.

That is because thy Lord would never destroy
the cities unjustly, while their inhabitants
were heedless. All have degrees according to
what they have done; thy Lord is not heedless of
    the things they do.
Thy Lord is All-sufficient, Merciful. If He will,
He can put you away, and leave after you, to
succeed you, what He will, as He produced you
from the seed of another people. The thing
you are promised, that will surely come;
    you cannot frustrate it.

135   Say: 'O my people, act according to your station;
I am acting. And assuredly you will know
who shall possess the Abode Ultimate.
Surely the evildoers will not prosper.'
They appoint to God, of the tillage and cattle
that He multiplied, a portion, saying,
'This is for God'—so they assert—'and
this is for our associates.' So what is
for their associates reaches not God; and
what is for God reaches their associates.
    Evil is their judgment!
Thus those associates of theirs have decked out
fair to many idolaters to slay their children,
to destroy them, and to confuse their religion
for them. Had God willed, they would not have
done so; so leave them to their forging.
They say, 'These are cattle and tillage
sacrosanct; none shall eat them, but whom
we will'—so they assert—'and cattle
whose backs have been forbidden, and cattle
over which they mention not the Name of God.'

All that they say, forging against God;
He will assuredly recompense them for
    what they were forging.
140   And they say, 'What is within the bellies
of these cattle is reserved for our males
and forbidden to our spouses; but if it be
dead, then they all shall be partners in it.'
He will assuredly recompense them for
their describing; surely He is
      All-wise, All-knowing.
Losers are they who slay their children in
folly, without knowledge, and have forbidden
what God has provided them, forging against God;
they have gone astray, and are not right-guided.

It is He who produces gardens
    trellised, and untrellised,
palm-trees, and crops diverse
      in produce,
    olives, pomegranates,
    like each to each, and
      each unlike to each.
Eat of their fruits when they fructify, and
pay the due thereof on the day of its harvest;
and be not prodigal; God loves not the prodigal.
And of the cattle, for burthen and for
slaughter, eat of what God has provided you;
and follow not the steps of Satan;
    he is a manifest foe to you.

Eight couples: two of sheep, of goats two.
Say: 'Is it the two males He has forbidden
    or the two females?
Or what the wombs of the two females contain?
Tell me with knowledge, if you speak truly.'
145   Of camels two, of oxen two.
Say: 'Is it the two males He has forbidden
    or the two females?
Or what the wombs of the two females contain?

Or were you witnesses when God charged you
with this? Then who does greater evil than he
who forges against God a lie, in order that he
may lead mankind astray without any knowledge?
Surely God guides not the people of the evildoers.'
Say: 'I do not find, in what is revealed to me,
aught forbidden to him who eats thereof
except it be carrion, or blood outpoured,
    or the flesh of swine—
that is an abomination—or an ungodly thing
that has been hallowed to other than God;
yet whoso is constrained, not desiring nor
transgressing, surely thy Lord is All-forgiving,
    All-compassionate.'
And to those of Jewry We have forbidden
every beast with claws; and of oxen and sheep
We have forbidden them the fat of them, save
what their backs carry, or their entrails,
or what is mingled with bone; that We
recompensed them for their insolence; surely
    We speak truly.
So, if they cry thee lies, say: 'Your Lord is
of mercy all-embracing, and His might
will never be turned back from the people
    of the sinners.'

The idolaters will say, 'Had God willed,
we would not have been idolaters, neither our
fathers, nor would we have forbidden aught.'
Even so the people before them cried lies
until they tasted Our might. Say: 'Have you
any knowledge, for you to bring forth for us?
You follow only surmise, merely conjecturing.'
150   Say: 'To God belongs the argument conclusive;
for had He willed, He would have guided you all.'
Say: 'Produce your witnesses, those who testify
God has forbidden this.' Then if they testify,
bear not witness with them; and do not thou
follow the caprices of those who cried lies

to Our signs, and who believe not in
the world to come, and ascribe equals
    to their Lord.
Say: 'Come, I will recite what your Lord has
forbidden you: that you associate not
anything with Him, and to be good to your
parents, and not to slay your children
because of poverty; We will provide you and them;
and that you approach not any indecency
outward or inward, and that you slay not
the soul God has forbidden, except by right.
That then He has charged you with; haply you
    will understand.
And that you approach not the property of
the orphan, save in the fairer manner, until
he is of age. And fill up the measure and
the balance with justice. We charge not any soul
save to its capacity. And when you speak,
be just, even if it should be to a
near kinsman. And fulfil God's covenant.
That then He has charged you with; haply you
    will remember.
And that this is My path, straight; so do you
follow it, and follow not divers paths
lest they scatter you from His path.
That then He has charged you with; haply you
    will be godfearing.'

155   Then We gave Moses the Book, complete
for him who does good, and distinguishing
every thing, and as a guidance and a mercy;
haply they would believe in the encounter
    with their Lord.

This is a Book We have sent down, blessed;
so follow it, and be godfearing; haply so
    you will find mercy;
lest you should say, 'The Book was sent down
only upon two parties before us, and we

have indeed been heedless of their study';
or lest you say, 'If the Book had been sent
down upon us, we had surely been more rightly
guided than they.' Yet indeed a clear sign
has come to you from your Lord, and a guidance
and a mercy; and who does greater evil than
he who cries lies to God's signs, and turns
away from them? We shall surely recompense
those who turn away from Our signs with an evil
chastisement for their turning away. What,
do they look for the angels to come to them,
nothing less, or that thy Lord should come,
or that one of thy Lord's signs should come?
On the day that one of thy Lord's signs comes
it shall not profit a soul to believe that
never believed before, or earned some good
    in his belief.
Say: 'Watch and wait; We too are waiting.'

160   Those who have made divisions in their religion
and become sects, thou art not of them in
anything; their affair is unto God, then
He will tell them what they have been doing.
Whoso brings a good deed shall have ten the like
of it; and whoso brings an evil deed shall
only be recompensed the like of it; they
    shall not be wronged.

Say: 'As for me, my Lord has guided me
to a straight path, a right religion,
the creed of Abraham, a man of pure faith;
    he was no idolater.'
Say: 'My prayer, my ritual sacrifice,
my living, my dying—all belongs to God,
    the Lord of all Being.
No associate has He. Even so I have been
commanded, and I am the first of those
    that surrender.'

Say: 'Shall I seek after a Lord other
than God, who is the Lord of all things?'

Every soul earns only to its own account;
no soul laden bears the load of another.
Then to your Lord shall you return, and
He will tell you of that whereon you
       were at variance.

165   It is He who has appointed you viceroys
in the earth, and has raised some of you
in rank above others, that He may try you
in what He has given you. Surely thy Lord
is swift in retribution; and surely
He is All-forgiving, All-compassionate.

VII

THE BATTLEMENTS

In the Name of God, the Merciful, the Compassionate

Alif Lam Mim Sad

A Book sent down to thee—
so let there be no impediment in thy breast
because of it—
to warn thereby, and as a reminder to believers:
Follow what has been sent down to you from your
Lord, and follow no friends other than He; little
do you remember.
How many a city We have destroyed! Our might came
upon it at night, or while they took their ease
in the noontide,
and they but cried, when Our might came upon them,
'We were evildoers.'
5 So We shall question those unto whom a Message was sent,
and We shall question the Envoys,
and We shall relate to them with knowledge; assuredly
We were not absent.
The weighing that day is true; he whose scales are heavy—
they are the prosperers,
and he whose scales are light—they have lost their souls
for wronging Our signs.

We have established you in the earth
and there appointed for you livelihood;
little thanks you show.
10 We created you, then We shaped you,
then We said to the angels: 'Bow yourselves
to Adam'; so they bowed themselves,
save Iblis—he was not of those
that bowed themselves.
Said He, 'What prevented thee to

143

bow thyself, when I commanded thee?'
Said he, 'I am better than he; Thou
createdst me of fire, and him Thou
     createdst of clay.'
Said He, 'Get thee down out of it;
it is not for thee to wax proud here,
so go thou forth; surely thou art
     among the humbled.'
Said he, 'Respite me till the day
     they shall be raised.'
Said He, 'Thou art among the ones
     that are respited.'

15   Said he, 'Now, for Thy perverting me,
I shall surely sit in ambush for them
     on Thy straight path;
then I shall come on them from before them
and from behind them, from their right hands
and their left hands; Thou wilt not find
     most of them thankful.'
Said He, 'Go thou forth from it, despised
and banished. Those of them that follow
thee—I shall assuredly fill Gehenna
     with all of you.'

'O Adam, inherit, thou and thy wife,
the Garden, and eat of where you will,
but come not nigh this tree, lest you be
     of the evildoers.'
Then Satan whispered to them, to reveal
to them that which was hidden from them
of their shameful parts. He said, 'Your Lord
has only prohibited you from this tree
lest you become angels, or lest you
     become immortals.'

20   And he swore to them, 'Truly, I am for you
     a sincere adviser.'
So he led them on by delusion; and when
they tasted the tree, their shameful parts
revealed to them, so they took to stitching

upon themselves leaves of the Garden.
And their Lord called to them, 'Did not I
prohibit you from this tree, and say
to you, "Verily Satan is for you
     a manifest foe"?'
They said, 'Lord, we have wronged ourselves,
and if Thou dost not forgive us, and
have mercy upon us, we shall surely be
     among the lost.'
Said He, 'Get you down, each of you
an enemy to each. In the earth a sojourn
shall be yours, and enjoyment
     for a time.'
Said He, 'Therein you shall live, and
therein you shall die, and from there you
     shall be brought forth.'

25   Children of Adam! We have sent down on you
a garment to cover your shameful parts,
and feathers; and the garment of godfearing—
that is better; that is one of God's signs;
     haply they will remember.
Children of Adam! Let not Satan tempt you
as he brought your parents out of the Garden,
stripping them of their garments to show them
their shameful parts. Surely he sees you,
he and his tribe, from where you see them not.
We have made the Satans the friends of those
     who do not believe.
And whenever they commit an indecency
they say, 'We found our fathers practising it,
and God has commanded us to do it.'
Say: 'God does not command indecency;
what, do you say concerning God such things
     as you know not?'
Say: 'My Lord has commanded justice.
Set your faces in every place of worship
and call on Him, making your religion
sincerely His. As He originated you

so you will return; a part He guided,
and a part justly disposed to error—they
have taken Satans for friends instead of God,
    and think them guided.'
Children of Adam! Take your adornment
at every place of worship; and eat
and drink, but be you not prodigal; He
    loves not the prodigal.

30   Say: 'Who has forbidden the ornament of God
which He brought forth for His servants, and
the good things of His providing?' Say:
'These, on the Day of Resurrection, shall be
exclusively for those who believed in this
present life. So We distinguish the signs for
    a people who know.'
Say: 'My Lord has only forbidden indecencies,
the inward and the outward, and sin,
and unjust insolence, and that you associate
with God that for which He sent down never
authority, and that you say concerning God
    such as you know not.'
To every nation a term; when their term comes
they shall not put it back by a single hour
    nor put it forward.
Children of Adam! If there should come to you
Messengers from among you, relating to you
My signs, then whosoever is godfearing
    and makes amends—
no fear shall be on them, neither shall they sorrow.
And those that cry lies to Our signs, and
    wax proud against them—
those shall be the inhabitants of the Fire,
    therein dwelling forever.

35   And who does greater evil than he who forges
against God a lie, or cries lies to His
signs? Those—their portion of the Book
shall reach them; till, when Our messengers
come to them, to take them away, they say,
'Where is that you were calling on, beside God?'

They will say, 'They have gone astray from us,'
and they will bear witness against themselves
   that they were unbelievers.

He will say, 'Enter among nations that
passed away before you, jinn and mankind,
   into the Fire.'
Whenever any nation enters, it curses
   its sister-nation;
till, when they have all successively
come there, the last of them shall say
   to the first of them,
'O our Lord, these led us astray;
so give them a double chastisement
   of the Fire.'
He will say, 'Unto each a double,
   but you know not.'
The first of them shall say to the last
   of them, 'You have
no superiority over us, then;
so taste the chastisement for what you
   have been earning.'
Those that cry lies to Our signs and wax
   proud against them—
the gates of heaven shall not be opened
to them, nor shall they enter Paradise
until the camel passes through the eye
of the needle. Even so We recompense
   the sinners;
Gehenna shall be their cradle, above them
coverings. Even so We recompense
   the evildoers.
40   And those who believe, and do deeds
of righteousness—We charge not any
soul, save according to its capacity;
those are the inhabitants of Paradise,
   therein dwelling forever;
We shall strip away all rancour that is
   in their breasts;

and underneath them rivers flowing;
    and they will say,
'Praise belongs to God, who guided
us unto this; had God not guided
us, we had surely never been guided.
Indeed, our Lord's Messengers came
    with the truth.'
And it will be proclaimed: 'This
is your Paradise; you have been
given it as your inheritance
    for what you did.'
The inhabitants of Paradise will call
to the inhabitants of the Fire:
'We have found that which our Lord
promised us true; have you found
what your Lord promised you true?'
    'Yes,' they will say.
And then a herald shall proclaim
between them: 'God's curse is on
    the evildoers
who bar from God's way, desiring
to make it crooked, disbelieving in
    the world to come.'
And between them is a veil, and
on the Ramparts are men knowing
    each by their mark,
who shall call to the inhabitants
of Paradise: 'Peace be upon you!
They have not entered it, for all
    their eagerness.'
45   And when their eyes are turned
towards the inhabitants of the Fire
they shall say, 'Our Lord, do not
Thou assign us with the people
    of the evildoers.'
And the dwellers on the Battlements
shall call to certain men they know
by their sign: 'Your amassing
has not availed you, neither your

waxing proud.
Are these the ones that you swore
God would never reach with mercy?'
'Enter Paradise; no fear upon you,
    nor shall you sorrow.'
The inhabitants of the Fire shall
call to the inhabitants of Paradise:
'Pour on us water, or of that God
    has provided you!'
They will say: 'God has forbidden them
    to the unbelievers
who have taken their religion as
a diversion and a sport, and whom
the present life has deluded.'—
Therefore today We forget them
as they forgot the encounter
of this their day, and that they
    denied Our signs.

50   And We have brought to them a Book
that We have well distinguished,
resting on knowledge, a guidance
and a mercy unto a people
    that believe.
Do they look for aught else but its
    interpretation?
The day its interpretation comes,
those who before forgot it shall say,
'Indeed, our Lord's Messengers came
    with the truth.
Have we then any intercessors to
intercede for us, or shall we be
returned, to do other than that
    we have done?'
They have indeed lost their souls, and
that which they were forging has gone
    astray from them.

Surely your Lord is God, who created the heavens
    and the earth in six days—

then sat Himself upon the Throne,
covering the day with the night
   it pursues urgently—
and the sun, and the moon, and the stars
subservient, by His command.
Verily, His are the creation and the command.
     Blessed be God,
   the Lord of all Being.
Call on your Lord, humbly and secretly; He
   loves not transgressors.
Do not corruption in the land, after
   it has been set right;
and call on Him fearfully, eagerly—
   surely the mercy of God is nigh
   to the good-doers.

55   It is He who looses the winds, bearing good tidings
   before His mercy,
till, when they are charged with heavy clouds, We drive it
   to a dead land
and therewith send down water, and bring forth therewith
   all the fruits.
Even so We shall bring forth the dead; haply
   you will remember.
And the good land—its vegetation comes forth by the
   leave of its Lord,
and the corrupt—it comes forth but scantily.
Even so We turn about the signs for a people
   that are thankful.

And We sent Noah to his people;
and he said, 'O my people, serve God!
You have no god other than He;
truly, I fear for you the chastisement
   of a dreadful day.'
Said the Council of his people, 'We see thee
   in manifest error.'
Said he, 'My people, there is no error

in me; but I am a Messenger from
　　the Lord of all Being.

60　　I deliver to you the Messages
of my Lord, and I advise you
sincerely; for I know from God
　　that you know not.
What, do you wonder that a reminder
from your Lord should come to you
by the lips of a man from among you?
That he may warn you, and you be godfearing,
　　haply to find mercy.'
But they cried him lies; so We delivered him,
and those with him, in the Ark,
and We drowned those who cried lies
to Our signs; assuredly they were
　　a blind people.

And to Ad their brother Hood;
he said, 'O my people, serve God!
You have no god other than He;
　　will you not be godfearing?'
Said the Council of the unbelievers
of his people, 'We see thee
in folly, and we think that thou art
　　one of the liars.'
65　　Said he, 'My people, there is no folly
in me; but I am a Messenger from
　　the Lord of all Being.
I deliver to you the Messages
of my Lord; I am your adviser
　　sincere, faithful.
What, do you wonder that a reminder
from your Lord should come to you
by the lips of a man from among you?
That he may warn you; and remember
when He appointed you as successors
after the people of Noah, and increased you
in stature broadly; remember God's bounties;
　　haply you will prosper.'

They said, 'Why, hast thou come to us
that we may serve God alone,
and forsake that our fathers served?
Then bring us that thou promisest us, if
    thou speakest truly.'
Said he, 'Anger and wrath from your Lord
have fallen upon you. What, do you dispute
with me regarding names you have named,
you and your fathers, touching which God
has sent down never authority?
Then watch and wait; I shall be with you
    watching and waiting.'
70   So We delivered him, and those with him,
    by a mercy from Us;
and We cut off the last remnant of
those who cried lies to Our signs and
    were not believers.

And to Thamood their brother Salih;
he said, 'O my people, serve God!
You have no god other than He;
there has now come to you a clear sign
from your Lord—this is the She-camel
of God, to be a sign for you. Leave her
that she may eat in God's earth, and do not
touch her with evil, lest you be seized by
    a painful chastisement.
And remember when He appointed you
successors after Ad, and lodged you
in the land, taking to yourselves castles
of its plains, and hewing its mountains
into houses. Remember God's bounties,
and do not mischief in the earth,
    working corruption.'
Said the Council of those of his people
who waxed proud to those that were abased,
to those of them who believed, 'Do you know
that Salih is an Envoy from his Lord?'
They said, 'In the Message he has been sent with

we are believers.'
Said the ones who waxed proud, 'As for
us, we are unbelievers in the thing in
   which you believe.'
75 So they hamstrung the She-camel
and turned in disdain from the commandment
of their Lord, saying, 'O Salih,
bring us that thou promisest us, if
   thou art an Envoy.'
So the earthquake seized them, and
morning found them in their habitation
   fallen prostrate.
So he turned his back on them, and said,
'O my people, I have delivered to you
the Message of my Lord, and advised you
sincerely; but you do not love
   sincere advisers.'

And Lot, when he said to his people,
'What, do you commit such indecency
as never any being in all the world
   committed before you?
See, you approach men lustfully
instead of women; no, you are a people
   that do exceed.'
80 And the only answer of his people
was that they said, 'Expel them
from your city; surely they are folk that
   keep themselves clean!'
So We delivered him and his family,
except his wife; she was one of
   those that tarried.
And We rained down upon them a rain;
so behold thou, how was the end
   of the sinners!

And to Midian their brother Shuaib;
he said, 'O my people, serve God!
You have no god other than He;

there has now come to you a clear sign
from your Lord. So fill up the measure
and the balance, and diminish not
the goods of the people; and do not
corruption in the land, after it
has been set right; that is better for you,
    if you are believers.
And do not sit in every path, threatening
and barring from God's way those who believe
in Him, desiring to make it crooked.
And remember when you were few, and He
multiplied you; and behold, how was the end of
    the workers of corruption.

85   And if there is a party of you who believe
in the Message I have been sent with,
and a party who believe not, be patient
till God shall judge between us; He is
    the best of judges.'
Said the Council of those of his people
who waxed proud, 'We will surely expel thee,
O Shuaib, and those who believe with thee,
from our city, unless you return
into our creed.' He said, 'What, even
    though we detest it?
We should have forged against God a lie
if we returned into your creed, after
God delivered us from it. It is not for us
to return into it, unless God our Lord
so will. Our Lord embraces all things
in His knowledge. In God we have put
our trust. Our Lord, give true deliverance
between us and our people; Thou art
    the best of deliverers.'
Said the Council of those of his people
who disbelieved, 'Now, if you follow
Shuaib, assuredly in that case
    you will be losers.'
So the earthquake seized them, and
morning found them in their habitation

fallen prostrate,
those who cried lies to Shuaib, as if never
they dwelt there; those who cried lies to Shuaib,
        they were the losers.
So he turned his back on them, and said,
'O my people, I have delivered to you
the Messages of my Lord, and advised you
sincerely; how should I grieve for a people
        of unbelievers?'

We have sent no Prophet to any city
but that We seized its people with misery
and hardship, that haply they might be humble;
then We gave them in the place of evil
good, till they multiplied, and said, 'Hardship
and happiness visited our fathers.'
So We seized them suddenly, unawares.
Yet had the peoples of the cities believed
and been godfearing, We would have opened
upon them blessings from heaven and earth;
but they cried lies, and so We seized them
        for what they earned.
Do the people of the cities feel secure
Our might shall not come upon them at night
        while they are sleeping?
Do the people of the cities feel secure
Our might shall not come upon them in daylight
        while they are playing?
Do they feel secure against God's devising?
None feels secure against God's devising but
        the people of the lost.
Is it not a guidance to those who inherit
the earth after those who inhabited it
that, did We will, We would smite them
because of their sins, sealing their hearts
        so they do not hear?
Those cities We relate to thee tidings of;
their Messengers came to them with the clear signs,
but they were not the ones to believe in that

they had cried lies before; so God seals the hearts
of the unbelievers.

100 We found no covenant in the most part
of them; indeed, We found the most part
of them ungodly.

Then We sent, after them, Moses
with Our signs to Pharaoh and his Council,
but they did them wrong;
so behold thou, how was the end of
the workers of corruption!

Moses said, 'Pharaoh, I am a Messenger from
the Lord of all Being,
worthy to say nothing regarding God
except the truth. I have brought a clear sign
to you from your Lord; so send forth with me
the Children of Israel.'

Said he, 'If thou hast brought a sign, produce it,
if thou speakest truly.'

So he cast his staff; and behold, it was
a serpent manifest.

105 And he drew forth his hand, and lo, it was white
to the beholders.

Said the Council of the people of Pharaoh,
'Surely this man is a cunning sorcerer
who desires to expel you from your land;
what do you command?'

They said, 'Put him and his brother off a while,
and send among the cities musterers,
to bring thee every cunning sorcerer.'

110 And the sorcerers came to Pharaoh, saying,
'We shall surely have a wage, if we
should be the victors?'

He said, 'Yes, indeed; and you shall be among
the near-stationed.'

They said, 'Moses, wilt thou cast, or shall
we be the casters?'

He said, 'You cast.' And when they cast
they put a spell upon the people's eyes,
and called forth fear of them, and produced

a mighty sorcery.
And We revealed to Moses: 'Cast thy staff.'
And lo, it forthwith swallowed up their
    lying invention.
115 So the truth came to pass, and false was proved
    what they were doing.
So they were vanquished there, and they
    turned about, humbled.
And the sorcerers were cast down,
    bowing themselves.
They said, 'We believe in
    the Lord of all Being,
the Lord of Moses and Aaron.'
120 Said Pharaoh, 'You have believed in Him
before I gave you leave. Surely this is
a device you have devised in the city
that you may expel its people from it.
        Now you shall know!
I shall assuredly cut off alternately
your hands and feet, then I shall crucify
    you all together.'
They said, 'Surely unto our Lord
    we are turning.
Thou takest vengeance upon us only
because we have believed in the signs
of our Lord when they came to us.
Our Lord, pour out upon us
patience, and gather us unto Thee
    surrendering.'
Then said the Council of the people of Pharaoh,
'Wilt thou leave Moses and his people
to work corruption in the land, and leave
    thee and thy gods?'
Said he, 'We shall slaughter their sons
and spare their women; surely we are
    triumphant over them!'
125 Said Moses to his people, 'Pray for succour
to God, and be patient; surely the earth
is God's and He bequeaths it to whom He will

157

among His servants. The issue ultimate
    is to the godfearing.'
They said, 'We have been hurt before thou
camest to us, and after thou camest to us.'
He said, 'Perchance your Lord will destroy
your enemy, and will make you successors
in the land, so that He may behold
    how you shall do.'
Then seized We Pharaoh's people with years
of dearth, and scarcity of fruits, that haply
    they might remember.
So, when good came to them, they said,
    'This belongs to us';
but if any evil smote them, they would augur
ill by Moses and those with him. Why, surely
their ill augury was with God; but the most
    of them knew not.
And they said, 'Whatsoever sign thou
bringest to us, to cast a spell upon us,
    we will not believe thee.'
130   So We let loose upon them the flood
and the locusts, the lice and the frogs,
the blood, distinct signs; but they waxed proud
    and were a sinful people.
And when the wrath fell upon them, they said,
'Moses, pray to thy Lord for us
by the covenant He has made with thee.
If thou removest from us the wrath, surely
we will believe thee, and send forth with thee
    the Children of Israel.'
But when We removed from them the wrath
unto a term that they should come to, lo,
    they broke their troth.
So We took vengeance on them, and drowned them
in the sea, for that they cried lies to Our signs
    and heeded them not.
And We bequeathed upon the people
that were abased all the east and the west
of the land We had blessed; and perfectly

was fulfilled the most fair word of thy Lord
upon the Children of Israel, for that they
endured patiently; and We destroyed utterly
the works of Pharaoh and his people, and what
    they had been building.
And We brought the Children of Israel
over the sea, and they came upon a people
cleaving to idols they had. They said,
'Moses, make for us a god, as they have gods.'
Said he, 'You are surely a people
    who are ignorant.

135   Surely this they are engaged upon
shall be shattered, and void is what
    they have been doing.'
He said, 'What, shall I seek a god for you
other than God, who has preferred you
    above all beings?'
And when We delivered you from the folk of Pharaoh
who were visiting you with evil chastisement,
slaying your sons, and sparing your women—
and in that was a grievous trial
    from your Lord.
And We appointed with Moses thirty nights
and We completed them with ten, so the
appointed time of his Lord was forty nights;
and Moses said to his brother Aaron,
'Be my successor among my people, and put things
right, and do not follow the way of
    the workers of corruption.'
And when Moses came to Our appointed time
and his Lord spoke with him, he said,
'Oh my Lord, show me, that I may behold Thee!'
Said He, 'Thou shalt not see Me; but behold
the mountain—if it stays fast in its place,
    then thou shalt see Me.'
And when his Lord revealed Him to the mountain
He made it crumble to dust; and Moses
    fell down swooning.

140   So when he awoke, he said, 'Glory be

to Thee! I repent to Thee; I am the first
    of the believers.'
Said He, 'Moses, I have chosen thee
above all men for My Messages and
My Utterance; take what I have given thee,
    and be of the thankful.'
And We wrote for him on the Tablets of everything
an admonition, and a distinguishing
of everything: 'So take it forcefully,
and command thy people to take the fairest
of it. I shall show you the habitation
    of the ungodly.

I shall turn from My signs those who
wax proud in the earth unjustly; though they
see every sign, they will not believe in it,
and though they see the way of rectitude
they will not take it for a way, and though
they see the way of error, they will take
    it for a way.
That, because they have cried lies to Our signs
    and heeded them not.'

145   Those who cry lies to Our signs, and the encounter
in the world to come—their works have failed;
shall they be recompensed, except according to
    the things they have done?
And the people of Moses took to them, after him,
of their ornaments a Calf—a mere body
that lowed. Did they not see it spoke not
to them, neither guided them upon any way?
Yet they took it to them, and were evildoers.
And when they smote their hands, and saw that
they had gone astray, they said, 'If our Lord
has not mercy on us, and forgives us not, surely
    we shall be of the lost.'
And when Moses returned to his people, angry
and sorrowful, he said, 'Evilly have you done
in my place, after me; what, have you outstripped
your Lord's commandment?' And he cast down
the Tablets, and laid hold of his brother's head,

dragging him to him. He said, 'Son of my mother,
surely the people have abased me, and wellnigh
slain me. Make not my enemies to gloat
over me, and put me not among the people
     of the evildoers.'

150   He said, 'O my Lord, forgive me and my brother
and enter us into Thy mercy; Thou art the most merciful
     of the merciful.'
'Surely those who took to themselves the Calf—
anger shall overtake them from their Lord, and
abasement in this present life; so We recompense
     those who are forgers.
And those who do evil deeds, then repent
thereafter and believe, surely thereafter
thy Lord is All-forgiving, All-compassionate.'
And when Moses' anger abated in him, he took
the Tablets; and in the inscription of them
was guidance, and mercy unto all those who
     hold their Lord in awe.
And Moses chose of his people seventy men
for Our appointed time; and when the earthquake
seized them, he said, 'My Lord, hadst Thou willed
Thou wouldst have destroyed them before, and me.
Wilt Thou destroy us for what the foolish ones
of us have done? It is only Thy trial, whereby
Thou leadest astray whom Thou wilt, and guidest
whom Thou wilt. Thou art our Protector; so
forgive us, and have mercy on us, for Thou art
     the best of forgivers.

155   And prescribe for us in this world good, and in
the world to come; we have repented unto Thee.'
Said He, 'My chastisement—I smite with it
whom I will; and My mercy embraces all things, and
I shall prescribe it for those who are godfearing
and pay the alms, and those who indeed believe
in Our signs, those who follow the Messenger,
the Prophet of the common folk, whom they find
written down with them in the Torah and the Gospel,
bidding them to honour, and forbidding them

dishonour, making lawful for them the good things
and making unlawful for them the corrupt things,
and relieving them of their loads, and the fetters
that were upon them. Those who believe in him
and succour him and help him, and follow
the light that has been sent down with him—
     they are the prosperers.'

Say: 'O mankind, I am the Messenger of God
     to you all,
of Him to whom belongs the kingdom of the heavens
     and of the earth.
     There is no god but He.
     He gives life, and makes to die.
Believe then in God, and in His Messenger,
the Prophet of the common folk, who believes
in God and His words, and follow him; haply
     so you will be guided.'

Of the people of Moses there is a nation who
guide by the truth, and by it act with justice.

160   And We cut them up into twelve tribes, nations.
And We revealed to Moses, when his people asked him
for water: 'Strike with thy staff the rock';
and there gushed forth from it twelve fountains;
all the people knew now their drinking-place.
And We outspread the cloud to overshadow them,
and We sent down manna and quails upon them:
'Eat of the good things wherewith We have supplied you.'
And they worked no wrong upon Us, but
     themselves they wronged.
And when it was said to them, 'Dwell in this township
and eat of it wherever you will; and say,
Unburdening; and enter in at the gate, prostrating;
We will forgive you your transgressions, and
     increase the good-doers.'
Then the evildoers of them substituted a saying
other than that which had been said to them;

so We sent down upon them wrath out of heaven
for their evildoing.
And question them concerning the township which
was bordering the sea, when they transgressed
the Sabbath, when their fish came to them
on the day of their Sabbath, swimming shorewards,
but on the day they kept not Sabbath, they came not
unto them. Even so We were trying them
for their ungodliness.
And when a certain nation of them said, 'Why
do you admonish a people God is about to destroy
or to chastise with a terrible chastisement?'
They said, 'As an excuse to your Lord; and haply
they will be godfearing.'

165 So, when they forgot that they were reminded of,
We delivered those who were forbidding wickedness,
and We seized the evildoers with evil chastisement
for their ungodliness.
And when they turned in disdain from that forbidding
We said to them, 'Be you apes, miserably slinking!'
And when thy Lord proclaimed He would send forth
against them, unto the Day of Resurrection,
those who should visit them with evil chastisement.
Surely thy Lord is swift in retribution; surely
He is All-forgiving, All-compassionate.
And We cut them up into nations in the earth,
some of them righteous, and some of them otherwise;
and We tried them with good things and evil, that
haply they should return.
And there succeeded after them a succession
who inherited the Book, taking the chance goods
of this lower world, and saying, 'It will be
forgiven us'; and if chance goods the like of them
come to them, they will take them. Has not the compact
of the Book been taken touching them, that they
should say concerning God nothing but the truth?
And they have studied what is in it; and the Last
Abode is better for those who are godfearing.
Do you not understand?

And those who hold fast to the Book, and perform
the prayer—surely We leave not to waste the wage
    of those who set aright.
170   And when We shook the mountain above them
as if it were a canopy, and they supposed
it was about to fall on them: 'Take forcefully
what We have given you, and remember what is in it;
    haply you will be godfearing.'

And when thy Lord took from the Children of Adam,
from their loins, their seed, and made them testify
touching themselves, 'Am·I not your Lord?'
They said, 'Yes, we testify'—lest you should say
on the Day of Resurrection, 'As for us, we
    were heedless of this,'
or lest you say, 'Our fathers were idolaters
aforetime, and we were seed after them.
What, wilt Thou then destroy us for the deeds
    of the vain-doers?'

So We distinguish the signs; and haply
    they will return.

And recite to them the tiding of him to whom
We gave Our signs, but he cast them off,
and Satan followed after him, and he became
    one of the perverts.
175   And had We willed, We would have raised him up
thereby; but he inclined towards the earth
and followed his lust. So the likeness of him
is as the likeness of a dog; if thou attackest it
it lolls its tongue out, or if thou leavest it
it lolls its tongue out. That is that people's likeness
who cried lies to Our signs. So relate the story;
    haply they will reflect.
An evil likeness is the likeness of
the people who cried lies to Our signs, and
    themselves were wronging.

Whomsoever God guides,
   he is rightly guided;
and whom He leads astray—
   they are the losers.
We have created for Gehenna
   many jinn and men;
they have hearts, but understand
   not with them;
they have eyes, but perceive
   not with them;
they have ears, but they hear
   not with them.
They are like cattle; nay, rather
   they are further astray.
Those—they are the heedless.

To God belong the Names Most Beautiful;
   so call Him by them,
and leave those who blaspheme His Names—
they shall assuredly be recompensed
   for the things they did.

180   Of those We created are a nation
who guide by the truth, and by it
   act with justice.
And those who cry lies to Our signs
We will draw them on little by little
   whence they know not;
and I respite them—assuredly
   My guile is sure.
Have they not reflected? No madness
   is in their comrade;
he is naught but a plain warner.
Or have they not considered
the dominion of the heaven and
of the earth, and what things
God has created, and that it may be
their term is already nigh?

In what manner of discourse then
will they after this believe?

185   Whomsoever God leads astray,
           no guide he has;
        He leaves them in their insolence
           blindly wándering.

They will question thee concerning
the Hour, when it shall berth.
Say: 'The knowledge of it is only
with my Lord; none shall reveal it
at its proper time, but He.
Heavy is it in the heavens and the earth;
it will not come on you but—suddenly!'
They will question thee, as though
thou art well-informed of it.
Say: 'The knowledge of it is only
with God, but most men know not.'
Say: 'I have no power to profit
for myself, or hurt, but as God will.
Had I knowledge of the Unseen
I would have acquired much good,
and evil would not have touched me.
I am only a warner, and a bearer of
good tidings, to a people believing.'

It is He who created you out of one living soul,
        and made of him his spouse
        that he might rest in her.
Then, when he covered her, she bore a light burden
        and passed by with it;
        but when it became heavy
they cried to God their Lord, 'If Thou givest us
        a righteous son, we indeed
        shall be of the thankful.'
190   Thereafter, when He gave them a righteous son, they
        assigned Him associates
        in that He had given them;

but God is high exalted above that they associate.
What, do they associate
that which creates nothing
and themselves are created, and that have no power
to help them, neither
they help themselves?
If you call them to guidance they will not follow you;
equal it is to you
whether you call them,
or whether you are silent. Those on whom you call
apart from God, are
servants the likes of you;
call them and let them answer you, if you speak truly.
What, have they feet
wherewith they walk,
or have they hands wherewith they lay hold,
or have they eyes
wherewith they see,
or have they ears wherewith they give ear?
Say: 'Call you then
to your associates;
then try your guile on me, and give me no respite.
195   My Protector is God
who sent down the Book,
and He takes into His protection the righteous.
And those on whom you
call, apart from God,
have no power to help you, neither they help themselves.'

If you call them to the guidance
they do not hear;
and thou seest them looking at
thee, unperceiving.
Take the abundance, and bid to
what is honourable,
and turn away from the ignorant.
If a provocation
from Satan should provoke thee,
seek refuge in God;

He is All-hearing, All-seeing.

200   The godfearing,
when a visitation of Satan
    troubles them,
remember, and then see clearly;
    and their brothers
they lead on into error, then
    they stop not short.
And when thou bringest them not
    a sign, they say,
'Why hast thou not chosen one?'
    Say: 'I follow
only what is revealed to me
    from my Lord; this
is clear testimony from your Lord,
    guidance, and mercy
for a people of believers.'
    And when the Koran
is recited, give you ear to it
    and be silent;
haply so you will find mercy.

Remember thy Lord
in thy soul, humbly and fearfully,
    not loud of voice,
at morn and eventide. Be not thou
    among the heedless.
205   Surely those who are with thy Lord
    wax not too proud
to serve Him; they chant His praise,
    and to Him they bow.

VIII

THE SPOILS

In the Name of God, the Merciful, the Compassionate

They will question thee concerning
the spoils. Say: 'The spoils belong to
God and' the Messenger; so fear you God,
and set things right between you, and
obey you God and His Messenger,
    if you are believers.'
Those only are believers who, when God
is mentioned, their hearts quake, and
when His signs are recited to them, it
increases them in faith, and in their Lord
    they put their trust,
those who perform the prayer, and expend of
    what We have provided them,
those in truth are the believers; they have
degrees with their Lord, and forgiveness,
    and generous provision.

5   As thy Lord brought, thee forth from thy house
with the truth, and a part of the believers
    were averse to it,
disputing with thee concerning the truth
after it had become clear, as though
they were being driven into death with
    their eyes wide open.
And when God promised you one of the two
parties should be yours, and you were wishing
that the one not accoutred should be yours;
but God was desiring to verify the truth
by His words, and 'to cut off the unbelievers
    to the last remnant,
and that He might verify the truth and
prove untrue the untrue, though the sinners

were averse to it.
When you were calling upon your Lord for
succour, and He answered you, 'I shall
reinforce you with a thousand angels
  riding behind you.'

10 God wrought this not, save as good tidings
and that your hearts thereby might be at rest;
help comes only from God; surely God is
  All-mighty, All-wise.
When He was causing slumber to overcome you
as a security from Him, and sending
down on you water from heaven, to purify
you thereby, and to put away
from you the defilement of Satan,
and to strengthen your hearts, and to
  confirm your feet.
When thy Lord was revealing to the angels,
'I am with you; so confirm the believers.
I shall cast into the unbelievers' hearts
terror; so smite above the necks, and smite
  every finger of them!'
That, because they had made a breach
with God and with His Messenger; and
whosoever makes a breach with God and with
His Messenger, surely God is terrible
  in retribution.
That for you; therefore taste it; and
that the chastisement of the Fire is
  for the unbelievers.

15 O believers, when you encounter
the unbelievers marching to battle, turn
  not your backs to them.
Whoso turns his back that day to them,
unless withdrawing to fight again
or removing to join another host,
he is laden with the burden of God's

anger, and his refuge is Gehenna—
an evil homecoming!

You did not slay them, but God slew them;
and when thou threwest, it was not
thyself that threw, but God threw, and
that He might confer on the believers
a fair benefit; surely God is
All-hearing, All-knowing.
That for you; and that God weakens the
unbelievers' guile.

If victory you are seeking, victory
has already come upon you; and if
you give over, it is better for you.
But if you return, We shall return,
and your host will avail you nothing
though it be numerous; and that God is
with the believers

20 O believers, obey God and His Messenger,
and do not turn away from Him, even
as you are listening;
and be not as those who say, 'We hear,'
and they hear not.
Surely the worst of beasts in God's sight
are those that are deaf and dumb and
do not understand.
If God had known of any good in them
He would have made them hear; and if
He had made them hear, they would have turned
away, swerving aside.
O believers, respond to God and the Messenger
when He calls you unto that which will
give you life; and know that God stands
between a man and his heart, and that to Him
you shall be mustered.
25 And fear a trial which shall surely not
smite in particular the evildoers

among you; and know that God is terrible
in retribution.
And remember when you were few and
abased in the land, and were fearful
that the people would snatch you away;
but He gave you refuge, and confirmed you
with His help, and provided you
with the good things, that haply
     you might be thankful.
O believers, betray not God and the
Messenger, and betray not your trusts
     and that wittingly;
and know that your wealth and your children
are a trial, and that with God is
     a mighty wage.
O believers, if you fear God, He will assign
you a salvation, and acquit you of your
evil deeds, and forgive you; and God is
     of bounty abounding.

30   And when the unbelievers were devising
against thee, to confine thee, or slay thee,
or to expel thee, and were devising,
and God was devising; and God is
     the best of devisers.
And when Our signs were being recited to
them, they said, 'We have already heard;
if we wished, we could say the like of
this; this is naught but the fairy-tales
     of the ancients.'
And when they said, 'O God, if this be
indeed the truth from Thee, then rain down
upon us stones out of heaven, or bring us
     a painful chastisement.'
But God would never chastise them, with thee
among them; God would never chastise them as
     they begged forgiveness.
But what have they now, that God should
not chastise them, when they are barring from

the Holy Mosque, not being its protectors?
Its only protectors are the godfearing; but
    most of them know not.
And their prayer at the House is nothing
but a whistling and a clapping of hands—
therefore taste you now the chastisement
    for your unbelief!

35   The unbelievers expend their wealth
to bar from God's way, and still they will
expend it, till it is an anguish for them,
    then be overthrown,
and the unbelievers will be mustered
    into Gehenna,
that God may distinguish the corrupt
from the good, and place the corrupt
one upon another, and so heap them up
all together, and put them in Gehenna;
    those are the losers.

Say to the unbelievers, if they give over
He will forgive them what is past; but
if they return, the wont of the ancients
    is already gone!

40   Fight them, till there is no persecution
and the religion is God's entirely;
then if they give over, surely God sees
    the things they do;
but if they turn away, know that God is
your Protector—an excellent Protector,
    an excellent Helper!

Know that, whatever booty you take, the
fifth of it is God's, and the Messenger's,
and the near kinsman's, and the orphans',
and for the needy, and the traveller,
if you believe in God and that We
sent down upon Our servant on the day
of salvation, the day the two hosts
encountered; and God is powerful

over everything;
when you were on the nearer bank, and they
were on the farther bank, and the cavalcade
was below you; and had you made tryst
together, you would have surely failed
the tryst; but that God might determine a
    matter that was done,
that whosoever perished might perish
by a clear sign, and by a clear sign
he might live who lived; and surely God is
    All-hearing, All-knowing.

45   When God showed thee them in thy dream
as few; and had He shown them as many
you would have lost heart, and quarrelled
about the matter; but God saved; He knows
    the thoughts in the breasts.
When God showed you them in your eyes as
few, when you encountered, and made you
few in their eyes, that God might determine
a matter that was done; and unto God all
    matters are returned.

O believers, whensoever you
encounter a host, then stand firm, and
remember God frequently; haply
    so you will prosper.
And obey God, and His Messenger,
and do not quarrel together, and
so lose heart, and your power depart;
and be patient; surely God is
    with the patient.
Be not as those who went forth from
their habitations swaggering boastfully
to show off to men, and barring
from God's way; and God encompasses
    the things they do.

50   And when Satan decked out their deeds
fair to them, and said, 'Today no man
shall overcome you, for I shall be

your neighbour.' But when the two hosts
sighted each other, he withdrew upon
his heels, saying, 'I am quit of you;
for I see what you do not see.
I fear God; and God is terrible
    in retribution.'

When the hypocrites, and those in whose
hearts was sickness, said, 'Their religion
has deluded them'; but whosoever
puts his trust in God, surely God is
    All-mighty, All-wise.
If thou couldst only see when the angels
take the unbelievers, beating their faces
and their backs: 'Taste the chastisement
    of the burning—
that, for what your hands have forwarded,
and for that God is never unjust
    unto His servants.'
Like Pharaoh's folk, and the people before him,
who disbelieved in God's signs; God seized them
because of their sins; God is strong, terrible
    in retribution.
55   That is because God would never change His favour
that He conferred on a people until they changed
what was within themselves; and that God is
    All-hearing, All-knowing.
Like Pharaoh's folk, and the people before him,
who cried lies to the signs of their Lord,
so We destroyed them because of their sins,
and We drowned the folk of Pharaoh; and
    all were evildoers.

Surely the worst of beasts in God's sight
are the unbelievers, who will not believe,
those of them with whom thou hast made compact
then they break their compact every time,
    not being godfearing.
So, if thou comest upon them anywhere

in the war, deal with them in such wise
as to scatter the ones behind them; haply
    they will remember.

60   And if thou fearest treachery any way
at the hands of a people, dissolve it
with them equally; surely God loves
    not the treacherous.

And thou art not to suppose that they who
disbelieve have outstripped Me; they cannot
    frustrate My will.

Make ready for them whatever force and
strings of horses you can, to terrify thereby
the enemy of God and your enemy, and others
besides them that you know not; God knows them.
And whatsoever you expend in the way
of God shall be repaid you in full;
    you will not be wronged.

And if they incline to peace, do thou incline
to it; and put thy trust in God; He is
    the All-hearing, the All-knowing.

And if they desire to trick thee, God is
sufficient for thee; He has confirmed thee
with His help, and with the believers, and
brought their hearts together. Hadst thou
expended all that is in the earth, thou couldst
not have brought their hearts together; but
God brought their hearts together; surely He is
    All-mighty, All-wise.

65   O Prophet, God suffices thee, and the believers
    who follow thee.

O Prophet, urge on the believers to fight.
If there be twenty of you, patient men,
they will overcome two hundred; if there be
a hundred of you, they will overcome
a thousand unbelievers, for they are a people
    who understand not.

Now God has lightened it for you, knowing
that there is weakness in you. If there be
a hundred of you, patient men, they will

overcome two hundred; if there be of you
a thousand, they will overcome two thousand
by the leave of God; God is with the patient.

It is not for any Prophet to have prisoners
until he make wide slaughter in the land.
You desire the chance goods of the present world,
and God desires the world to come; and God is
     All-mighty, All-wise.
Had it not been for a prior prescription from
God, there had afflicted you, for what you took,
     a mighty chastisement.
70   Eat of what you have taken as booty, such as
is lawful and good; and fear you God; surely
God is All-forgiving, All-compassionate.

O Prophet, say to the prisoners in your hands:
'If God knows of any good in your hearts
He will give you better than what has been taken
from you, and He will forgive you; surely
God is All-forgiving, All-compassionate.'

And if they desire treachery against thee,
they have tricked God before; but He has
given thee power over them; and God is
     All-knowing, All-wise.

Those who believe, and have emigrated
and struggled with their possessions
and their selves in the way of God,
and those who have given refuge and help—
those are friends one of another.
And those who believe, but have not
emigrated—you have no duty of friendship
towards them till they emigrate; yet if
they ask you for help, for religion's sake,
it is your duty to help them, except
against a people between whom and you
there is a compact; and God sees

the things you do.
As for the unbelievers, they are friends
one of another. Unless you do this,
there will be persecution in the land
and great corruption.

75 And those who believe, and have emigrated
and struggled in the way of God.
those who have given refuge and help—
those in truth are the believers,
and theirs shall be forgiveness
and generous provision.
And those who have believed afterwards
and emigrated, and struggled with you—
they belong to you; but those related
by blood are nearer to one another
in the Book of God; surely God has knowledge
of everything.

IX

REPENTANCE

An acquittal, from God and His Messenger,
unto the idolaters with whom you made covenant:
'Journey freely in the land for four months;
and know that you cannot frustrate the will
of God, and that God degrades the unbelievers.'

A proclamation, from God and His Messenger,
unto mankind on the day of the Greater Pilgrimage:
'God is quit, and His Messenger, of the idolaters.
So if you repent, that will be better for you; but
if you turn your backs, know that you cannot frustrate
        the will of God.

And give thou good tidings to the unbelievers of
        a painful chastisement;
excepting those of the idolaters with whom
you made covenant, then they failed you naught
neither lent support to any man against you.
With them fulfil your covenant till their term; surely
        God loves the godfearing.
5 Then, when the sacred months are drawn away,
slay the idolaters wherever you find them,
and take them, and confine them, and lie in wait
for them at every place of ambush. But if they
repent, and perform the prayer, and pay the alms, then
        let them go their way;
God is All-forgiving, All-compassionate.
And if any of the idolaters seeks of thee
protection, grant him protection till he hears
the words of God; then do thou convey him to his
place of security—that, because they are a people
        who do not know.
How should the idolaters have a covenant with God
        and His Messenger?—

excepting those with whom you made covenant
at the Holy Mosque; so long as they go straight
with you, do you go straight with them; surely
      God loves the godfearing.
How? If they get the better of you, they will not
observe towards you any bond or treaty,
giving you satisfaction with their mouths
but in their hearts refusing; and the most
      of them are ungodly.
They have sold the signs of God for a small price,
and have barred from His way; truly evil is that
      they have been doing,

10   observing neither bond nor treaty towards a believer;
      they are the transgressors.
Yet if they repent, and perform the prayer,
and pay the alms, then they are your brothers
in religion; and We distinguish the signs for
      a people who know.
But if they break their oaths after their covenant
and thrust at your religion, then fight the leaders
of unbelief; they have no sacred oaths; haply
      they will give over.
Will you not fight a people who broke their oaths
and purposed to expel the Messenger, beginning
the first time against you? Are you afraid of them?
You would do better to be afraid of God,
      if you are believers.
Fight them, and God will chastise them at your hands
and degrade them, and He will help you
against them, and bring healing to the breasts of
      a people who believe,

15   and He will remove the rage within their hearts;
and God turns towards whomsoever He will; God is
      All-knowing, All-wise
Or did you suppose you would be left in peace,
and God knows not as yet those of you who have
struggled, and taken not—apart from God and His
Messenger and the believers—any intimate? God is
      aware of what you do.

It is not for the idolaters to inhabit God's places of
worship, witnessing against themselves unbelief;
those—their works have failed them, and in the Fire
        they shall dwell forever.
Only he shall inhabit God's places of worship
who believes in God and the Last Day, and
performs the prayer, and pays the alms, and fears
none but God alone; it may be that those will
        be among the guided.
Do you reckon the giving of water to pilgrims
and the inhabiting of the Holy Mosque as the same
as one who believes in God and the Last Day
and struggles in the way of God? Not equal are they
in God's sight; and God guides not the people
        of the evildoers.
20   Those who believe, and have emigrated, and have struggled
in the way of God with their possessions and their selves
are mightier in rank with God; and those—
        they are the triumphant;
their Lord gives them good tidings of mercy from Him
and good pleasure; for them await gardens wherein
        is lasting bliss,
therein to dwell forever and ever; surely with God
        is a mighty wage.

O believers, take not your fathers and brothers
to be your friends, if they prefer unbelief to belief;
whosoever of you takes them for friends, those—
        they are the evildoers.
Say: 'If your fathers, your sons, your brothers, your wives,
your clan, your possessions that you have gained,
commerce you fear may slacken, dwellings you love—
if these are dearer to you than God and His Messenger,
and to struggle in His way, then wait till God
brings His command; God guides not the people
        of the ungodly.'

25   God has already helped you on many fields, and on
the day of Hunain, when your multitude was pleasing

to you, but it availed you naught, and the land
for all its breadth was strait for you, and you
     turned about, retreating.
Then God sent down upon His Messenger His Shechina,
and upon the believers, and He sent down
legions you did not see, and He chastised
the unbelievers; and that is the recompense
     of the unbelievers;
then God thereafter turns towards whom He will;
God is All-forgiving, All-compassionate.
O believers, the idolaters are indeed unclean; so
let them not come near the Holy Mosque after this
year of theirs. If you fear poverty, God shall surely
enrich you of His bounty, if He will; God is
     All-knowing, All-wise.
Fight those who believe not in God and the Last Day
and do not forbid what God and His Messenger
have forbidden—such men as practise not the
religion of truth, being of those who have been given
the Book—until they pay the tribute out of hand
     and have been humbled.

30   The Jews say, 'Ezra is the Son of God';
the Christians say, 'The Messiah is the Son of God.'
That is the utterance of their mouths, conforming
with the unbelievers before them. God assail them!
     How they are perverted!
They have taken their rabbis and their monks as lords
apart from God, and the Messiah, Mary's son—
and they were commanded to serve but One God;
there is no god but He; glory be to Him, above
     that they associate—
desiring to extinguish with their mouths God's light;
and God refuses but to perfect His light, though
     the unbelievers be averse.
It is He who has sent His Messenger with
the guidance and the religion of truth, that
He may uplift it above every religion, though
     the unbelievers be averse.

O believers, many of the rabbis and monks indeed
consume the goods of the people in vanity
and bar from God's way. Those who treasure up
gold and silver, and do not expend them in
the way of God—give them the good tidings of
      a painful chastisement,
35 the day they shall be heated in the fire of Gehenna
and therewith their foreheads and their sides and their
backs shall be branded: 'This is the thing you have
treasured up for yourselves; therefore taste you now
      what you were treasuring!'

The number of the months, with God, is twelve
in the Book of God, the day that He created
the heavens and the earth; four of them are sacred.
That is the right religion. So wrong not each other
during them. And fight the unbelievers totally
even as they fight you totally; and know that God
      is with the godfearing.
The month postponed is an increase of unbelief
whereby the unbelievers go astray; one year they make it
profane, and hallow it another, to agree with
the number that God has hallowed, and so profane
what God has hallowed. Decked out fair to them
are their evil deeds; and God guides not the people
      of the unbelievers.

O believers, what is amiss with you, that when
it is said to you, 'Go forth in the way of God,'
you sink down heavily to the ground? Are you
so content with this present life, rather than
the world to come? Yet the enjoyment of this
present life, compared with the world to come,
      is a little thing.
If you go not forth, He will chastise you
with a painful chastisement, and instead of you
He will substitute another people; and you
will not hurt Him anything, for God is powerful
      over everything.

40 If you do not help him, yet God has helped him
already, when the unbelievers drove him forth
the second of two, when the two were in the Cave,
when he said to his companion, 'Sorrow not; surely
God is with us.' Then God sent down on him His Shechina,
and confirmed him with legions you did not see;
and He made the word of the unbelievers the lowest;
and God's word is the uppermost; God is
            All-mighty, All-wise.
Go forth, light and heavy! Struggle in God's way
with your possessions and your selves; that is better
        for you, did you know.

Were it a gain near at hand, and an easy journey,
they would have followed thee; but the distance
was too far for them. Still they will swear by God,
'Had we been able, we would have gone out with you,'
so destroying their souls; and God knows that
        they are truly liars.
God pardon thee! Why gavest thou them leave, till it
was clear to thee which of them spoke the truth, and
        thou knewest the liars?
Those who believe in God and the Last Day
ask not leave of thee, that they may struggle
with their possessions and their selves; and God
        knows the godfearing.
45 They only ask leave of thee who believe not in
God and the Last Day, those whose hearts are filled
with doubt, so that in their doubt they go
        this way and that.
If they had desired to go forth, they would have
made some preparation for it; but God was
averse that they should be aroused, so He made them
pause, and it was said to them, 'Tarry you
        with the tarriers.'
Had they gone forth among you, they would only have
increased you in trouble, and run to and fro in your
midst, seeking to stir up sedition between you;
and some of you would listen to them; and God

knows the evildoers.
They sought to stir up sedition already
before, and turned things upside down for thee,
until the truth came, and God's command appeared,
though they were averse.

Some of them there are that say, 'Give me leave
and do not tempt me.' Have not such men fallen
into temptation? And surely Gehenna encompasses
the unbelievers.

50 If good fortune befalls thee, it vexes them;
but if thou art visited by an affliction,
they say, 'We took our dispositions before,' and
turn away, rejoicing.
Say: 'Naught shall visit us but what God has prescribed
for us; He is our Protector; in God let the believers
put all their trust.'
Say: 'Are you awaiting for aught to come to us but
one of the two rewards most fair? We are awaiting
in your case too, for God to visit you with chastisement
from Him, or at our hands; so await; we are
awaiting with you.'
Say: 'Expend willingly, or unwillingly, it shall
not be accepted from you; you are surely
a people ungodly.'
And naught prevents that their expendings should
be accepted from them, but that they believe not
in God and His Messenger, and perform not the prayer
save lazily, and that they expend not without
they are averse.

55 So let not their possessions or their children
please thee; God only desires thereby to chastise them
in this present life, and that their souls should depart
while they are unbelievers.
They swear by God that they belong with you,
but they are not of you; they are a people
that are afraid.
If they could find a shelter, or some caverns, or
any place to creep into, they would turn about and

bolt away to it.

Some of them find fault with thee touching the
freewill offerings; if they are given a share of them
they are well-pleased, but if they are given none
    then they are angry.
O were they well-pleased with what God and His Messenger
have brought them, saying, 'Enough for us is God; God
will bring us of His bounty, and His Messenger; to
    God we humbly turn.'
60 The freewill offerings are for the poor and needy,
those who work to collect them, those whose hearts are
brought together, the ransoming of slaves, debtors, in
God's way, and the traveller; so God ordains; God is
    All-knowing, All-wise.

And some of them hurt the Prophet, saying,
'He is an ear!' Say: 'An ear of good for you;
he believes in God, and believes the believers,
and he is a mercy to the believers among you.
Those who hurt God's Messenger—for them awaits
    a painful chastisement.'

They swear to you by God, to please you; but God and His
Messenger—more right is it they should please Him,
    if they are believers.
Do they not know that whosoever opposes God
and His Messenger—for him awaits the fire
of Gehenna, therein to dwell forever? That is
    the mighty degradation.
65 The hypocrites are afraid, lest a sura should be
sent down against them, telling thee what is in
their hearts. Say: 'Mock on; God will bring forth
    what you fear.'
And if thou questionest them, then assuredly
they will say, 'We were only plunging and playing.'
Say: 'What, then were you mocking God, and His signs,
    and His Messenger?
Make no excuses. You have disbelieved

after your believing. If We forgive one party
of you, We will chastise another party for that
      they were sinners.'
The hypocrites, the men and the women, are as
one another; they bid to dishonour, and forbid
honour; they keep their hands shut; they have forgotten
God, and He has forgotten them. The hypocrites—
      they are the ungodly.
God has promised the hypocrites, men and women,
and the unbelievers, the fire of Gehenna,
therein to dwell forever. That is enough for them;
God has cursed them; and there awaits them
      a lasting chastisement.

70   Like those before you, who were stronger than you
in might, and more abundant in wealth and children;
they took enjoyment in their share; so do you
take enjoyment in your share, as those before you
took enjoyment in their share. You have plunged
as they plunged. Those—their works have failed
in this world and in the world to come; those—
      they are the losers.
Has there not come to you the tidings of those
who were before you—the people of Noah, Ad,
Thamood, the people of Abraham, the men of Midian
and the subverted cities? Their Messengers came to
them with the clear signs; God would not wrong them, but
      themselves they wronged.

And the believers, the men and the women, are friends
one of the other; they bid to honour, and forbid
dishonour; they perform the prayer, and pay the alms,
and they obey God and His Messenger.
Those—upon them God will have mercy; God is
      All-mighty, All-wise.
God has promised the believers, men and women,
gardens underneath which rivers flow, forever
therein to dwell, and goodly dwelling-places in the
Gardens of Eden; and greater, God's good pleasure;
      that is the mighty triumph.

O Prophet, struggle with the unbelievers and hypocrites,
and be thou harsh with them; their refuge is Gehenna—
  an evil homecoming!

75 They swear by God that they said nothing,
but they indeed said the word of unbelief
and disbelieved, after they had surrendered.
They purposed what they never attained to, and
they took revenge only that God enriched them,
and His Messenger, of His bounty. So if they
repent it will be better for them; if they turn away
God will chastise them with a painful chastisement
in this world and the next; on the earth they have
  no protector or helper.
And some of them have made covenant with God: 'If
He gives us of His bounty, we will make offerings
  and be of the righteous.'
Nevertheless, when He gave them of His bounty
they were niggardly of it, and turned away,
  swerving aside.
So as a consequence He put hypocrisy
into their hearts, until the day they meet Him,
for that they failed God in that they promised Him
  and they were liars.
Did they not know that God knows their secret and
what they conspire together, and that God knows
  the things unseen?

80 Those who find fault with the believers
who volunteer their freewill offerings, and
those who find nothing but their endeavour they
deride—God derides them; for them awaits
  a painful chastisement.
Ask pardon for them, or ask not pardon for them;
if thou askest pardon for them seventy times, God
will not pardon them; that, because they disbelieved
in God and His Messenger; God guides not the people
  of the ungodly.

Those who were left behind rejoiced in tarrying

behind the Messenger of God, and were averse
to struggle with their possessions and their selves
in the way of God. They said, 'Go not forth in
the heat.' Say: 'Gehenna's fire is hotter, did
      they but understand.'
Therefore let them laugh little, and weep much,
in recompense for what they have been earning.
So, if God returns thee to a party of them
and they ask leave of thee to go forth, say:
'You shall not go forth with me ever, and
you shall not fight with me any enemy. You were
well-pleased to tarry the first time, so now
      tarry with those behind.'
85   And pray thou never over any one of them
when he is dead, nor stand over his grave; they
disbelieved in God and His Messenger, and died
      while they were ungodly.
And let not their possessions and their children
please thee; God only desires thereby to chastise them
in this present world, and that their souls should depart
      while they are unbelievers.
And when a sura is sent down, saying, 'Believe in God,
and struggle with His Messenger,' the affluent
among them ask leave of thee, saying, 'Let us be
      with the tarriers.'
They are well-pleased to be with those behind,
and a seal has been set upon their hearts, so
      they understand not.
But the Messenger, and the believers with him,
have struggled with their possessions and their selves,
and those—for them await the good things; those—
      they are the prosperers.
90   God has prepared for them gardens underneath
which rivers flow, therein to dwell forever;
      that is the mighty triumph.

And the Bedouins came with their excuses, asking
for leave; those who lied to God and His Messenger
tarried; there shall befall the unbelievers of them

a painful chastisement.

There is no fault in the weak and the sick
and those who find nothing to expend, if they
are true to God and to His Messenger.
There is no way against the good-doers—
God is All-forgiving, All-compassionate—
neither against those who, when they came to thee, for
thee to mount them, thou saidst to them, 'I find not
whereon to mount you'; they turned away, their eyes
overflowing with tears of sorrow, because they found
        nothing to expend.
The way is open only against those who ask leave of
thee, being rich; they are well-pleased to be with
those behind; God has set a seal on their hearts,
        so they know not.

95   They will excuse themselves to you, when you return
to them. Say: 'Do not excuse yourselves; we will not
believe you. God has already told us tidings of you.
God will surely see your work, and His Messenger,
then you will be returned to Him who knows.
the unseen and the visible, and He will tell you
        what you were doing.'
They will swear to you by God, when you turn back to
them, that you may turn aside from them. So turn
aside from them, for they are an abomination, and
their refuge is Gehenna—a recompense for what
        they have been earning.
They will swear to you, that you may be well-pleased
with them; but if you are well-pleased with them,
God will surely not be well-pleased with the people
        of the ungodly.

The Bedouins are more stubborn in unbelief
and hypocrisy, and apter not to know the bounds of
what God has sent down on His Messenger; and God is
        All-knowing, All-wise.
Some of the Bedouins take what they expend for a
fine, and await the turns of fortune to go against

you. Theirs shall be the evil turn; God is
    All-hearing, All-knowing.

100   And some of the Bedouins believe in God and the
Last Day, and take what they expend for offerings
bringing them near to God, and the prayers of the
Messenger. Surely they are an offering for them,
and God will admit them into His mercy;
God is All-forgiving, All-compassionate.
And the Outstrippers, the first of the Emigrants
and the Helpers, and those who followed them
in good-doing—God will be well-pleased with them
and they are well-pleased with Him; and He has
prepared for them gardens underneath which
rivers flow, therein to dwell forever and ever;
    that is the mighty triumph.
And some of the Bedouins who dwell around you
are hypocrites; and some of the people
of the City are grown bold in hypocrisy. Thou
knowest them not; but We know them, and We shall
chastise them twice, then they will be returned to
    a mighty chastisement.
And other have confessed their sins; they have
mixed a righteous deed with another evil.
It may be that God will turn towards them;
God is All-forgiving, All-compassionate.
Take of their wealth a freewill offering, to purify
them and to cleanse them thereby, and pray for them;
thy prayers are a comfort for them; God is
    All-hearing, All-knowing.

105   Do they not know that God is He who accepts
repentance from His servants, and takes the freewill
offerings, and that God—He turns, and is
    All-compassionate?
Say: 'Work; and God will surely see your work,
and His Messenger, and the believers,
and you will be returned to Him who knows
the unseen and the visible, and He will tell you
    what you were doing.'
And others are deferred to God's commandment, whether

He chastises them, or turns towards them; God is
       All-knowing, All-wise.

And those who have taken a mosque in opposition
and unbelief, and to divide the believers,
and as a place of ambush for those who fought
God and His Messenger aforetime—they will swear
'We desired nothing but good'; and God testifies
       they are truly liars.
Stand there never. A mosque that was founded
upon godfearing from the first day is worthier
for thee to stand in; therein are men who love
to cleanse themselves; and God loves those
       who cleanse themselves.
110 Why, is he better who founded his building upon
the fear of God and His good pleasure, or he
who founded his building upon the brink of a
crumbling bank that has tumbled with him into the
fire of Gehenna? And God guides not the people
       of the evildoers.
The buildings they have built will not cease to be
a point of doubt within their hearts, unless it
be that their hearts are cut into pieces; God is
       All-knowing, All-wise.

God has bought from the believers their selves
and their possessions against the gift of Paradise;
they fight in the way of God; they kill, and are
killed; that is a promise binding upon God
in the Torah, and the Gospel, and the Koran;
and who fulfils his covenant truer than God?
So rejoice in the bargain you have made with Him;
       that is the mighty triumph.
Those who repent, those who serve, those who pray, those
who journey, those who bow, those who prostrate themselves,
those who bid to honour and forbid dishonour, those
who keep God's bounds—and give thou good tidings
       to the believers.

It is not for the Prophet and the believers
to ask pardon for the idolaters, even
though they be near kinsmen, after that it
has become clear to them that they will be the
   inhabitants of Hell.

115 Abraham asked not pardon for his father except
because of a promise he had made to him; and when
it became clear to him that he was an enemy of God,
he declared himself quit of him; Abraham was
   compassionate, clement.
God would never lead a people astray after that
He has guided them, until He makes clear to them
as to what they should be godfearing; surely God
   knows everything.
Surely to God belongs the kingdom of the heavens
and of the earth; He gives life, and makes to die;
and you have not, apart from God, either
   protector or helper.

God has turned towards the Prophet and the Emigrants
and the Helpers who followed him in the hour of
difficulty, after the hearts of a part of them
wellnigh swerved aside; then He turned towards them;
surely He is Gentle to them, and All-compassionate.
And to the three who were left behind, until,
when the earth became strait for them, for all its
breadth, and their souls became strait for them, and
they thought that there was no shelter from God
except in Him, then He turned towards them, that
they might also turn; surely God turns, and is
   All-compassionate.

120 O believers, fear God, and be with the truthful ones.

It is not for the people of the City
and for the Bedouins who dwell around them
to stay behind God's Messenger, and to prefer
their lives to his; that is because they are smitten

neither by thirst, nor fatigue, nor emptiness
in the way of God, neither tread they any tread
enraging the unbelievers, nor gain any gain from any
enemy, but a righteous deed is thereby written
to their account; God leaves not to waste the wage
       of the good-doers.
Nor do they expend any sum, small or great, nor do they
traverse any valley, but it is written to their
account, that God may recompense them the best of
       what they were doing.

It is not for the believers to go forth totally;
but why should not a party of every section of them
go forth, to become learned in religion, and to
warn their people when they return to them, that
       haply they may beware?

125   O believers, fight the unbelievers who are near to you,
and let them find in you a harshness; and know that God
       is with the godfearing.
Whenever a sura is sent down to thee, some of them
say, 'Which of you has this increased in belief?'
As for the believers, them it has increased in belief,
       and they are joyful.
But as for those in whose heart is sickness,
them it has increased in abomination added
to their abomination, and they have died
       while they were unbelievers.
Do they not see that they are tried every year
once or twice? Yet still they do not repent,
       nor do they remember.
And whenever a sura is sent down, they look
one at another: 'Does anyone see you?'
Then they turn away. God has turned away
their hearts, for that they are a people who
       do not understand.

Now there has come to you a Messenger from among
yourselves; grievous to him is your suffering;

anxious is he over you, gentle to the believers,
    compassionate.

130   So if they turn their backs, say: 'God is enough for me.
There is no god but He. In Him I have put my trust.
    He is the Lord of the Mighty Throne.'

X

JONAH

In the Name of God, the Merciful, the Compassionate

Alif Lam Ra
Those are the signs of the Wise Book.

Was it a wonder to the people
that We revealed to a man from among them:
'Warn the people, and give thou good tidings
to the believers that they have a sure footing
with their Lord'? The unbelievers say,
      'This is a manifest sorcerer.'

Surely your Lord is God, who created
the heavens and the earth in six days,
then sat Himself upon the Throne,
directing the affair. Intercessor
there is none, save after His leave.
that then is God, your Lord; so serve Him.
     Will you not remember?
To Him shall you return, all together—
God's promise, in truth. He originates
creation, then He brings it back again
that He may recompense those who believe
and do deeds of righteousness, justly. And
those who disbelieve—for them awaits a draught
of boiling water, and a painful chastisement,
     for their disbelieving.

5   It is He who made the sun a radiance,
         and the moon a light,
and determined it by stations, that you
might know the number of the years
         and the reckoning.
God created that not save with the truth,

distinguishing the signs
to a people who know.
In the alternation of night and day, and
what God has created in the heavens and
the earth—surely there are signs for
a godfearing people.

Surely those who look not to encounter Us
and are well-pleased with the present life
and are at rest in it, and those who are
heedless of Our signs,
those—their refuge is the Fire, for that
they have been earning.
Surely those who believe, and do deeds
of righteousness, their Lord will guide them
for their belief; beneath them rivers flowing
in gardens of bliss;
10   their cry therein, 'Glory to Thee, O God,'
their greeting, 'Peace,'
and their cry ends, 'Praise belongs to God,
the Lord of all Being.'

If God should hasten unto men evil
as they would hasten good, their term
would be already decided for them.
But We leave those, who look not
to encounter Us, in their insolence
wandering blindly.
When affliction visits a man, he calls Us
on his side, or sitting, or standing;
but when We have removed his affliction
from him, he passes on, as if he never
called Us to an affliction that visited him.
So decked out fair to the prodigal is that
they have been doing.

We destroyed the generations before you
when they did evil, and their Messengers
came to them with the clear signs, but they

would not believe; so We recompense the people
of the sinners.

15   Then We appointed you viceroys in the earth
after them, that We might behold
      how you would do.

And when Our signs are recited to them,
clear signs, those who look not to encounter
Us say, 'Bring a Koran other than this,
or alter it.' Say: 'It is not for me
to alter it of my own accord. I follow
nothing, except what is revealed to me.
Truly I fear, if I should rebel
against my Lord, the chastisement
      of a dreadful day.'
Say: 'Had God willed I would not have recited it
to you, neither would He have taught you it;
I abode among you a lifetime before it—
      will you not understand?'
And who does greater evil than he who
forges against God a lie, or cries lies
to His signs? Surely the sinners
      do not prosper.
They serve, apart from God, what hurts them not
neither profits them, and they say,
'These are our intercessors with God.'
Say: 'Will you tell God what He knows not
either in the heavens or in the earth?'
Glory be to Him! High be He exalted above
      that they associate!

20   Mankind were only one nation, then
they fell into variance. But for a word
that preceded from thy Lord, it had been
decided between them already touching
      their differences.

They say, 'Why has a sign not been
sent down upon him from his Lord?' Say:

'The Unseen belongs only to God.
Then watch and wait; I shall be with you
    watching and waiting.'
When We let the people taste mercy
after hardship has visited them, lo,
they have a device concerning Our signs.
Say: 'God is swifter at devising;
surely Our messengers are writing down
    what you are devising.'

It is He who conveys you
    on the land and the sea;
and when you are in the ship—
and the ships run with them
    with a fair breeze,
    and they rejoice in it,
there comes upon them a strong wind,
and waves come on them from every side,
and they think they are encompassed;
    they call upon God,
making their religion His sincerely:
'If Thou deliverest us from these, surely
    we shall be among the thankful.'
Nevertheless when He has delivered them
    behold, they are insolent
    in the earth, wrongfully.
    O men, your insolence is
    only against yourselves;
the enjoyment of this present life,
then unto Us you shall return,
    then We shall tell you
    what you were doing.

25 The likeness of this present life is as water that
            We send down out of heaven,
    and the plants of the earth mingle with it
            whereof men and cattle eat,
    till, when the earth has taken on its glitter
            and has decked itself fair,

and its inhabitants think they have power over it,
    Our command comes upon it
by night or day, and We make it stubble, as though
    yesterday it flourished not.
Even so We distinguish the signs for a people
    who reflect.

And God summons to the Abode of Peace,
and He guides whomsoever He will
    to a straight path;
to the good-doers the reward most fair
and a surplus; neither dust nor abasement
    shall overspread their faces.
Those are the inhabitants of Paradise,
    therein dwelling forever.
And for those who have earned evil deeds
    the recompense of an evil deed
    shall be the like of it;
    abasement shall overspread them,
neither have they any defender from God,
    as if their faces were covered
    with strips of night shadowy.
Those are the inhabitants of the Fire,
    therein dwelling forever.

And the day We shall muster them all, then We shall say
to those who associate other gods with God:
'Get you to your place, you and your associates!'
Then We shall set a space between them, and their associates
will say, 'Not us you were serving. God is a sufficient witness
between us and you; assuredly we were heedless of your
                                         ⌈service.'
There every soul shall prove its past deeds; and they
shall be restored to God, their Protector, the True,
and there shall go astray from them that they were forging.

Say: 'Who provides you out of heaven and earth,
or who possesses hearing and sight, and
who brings forth the living from the dead

and brings forth the dead from the living,
and who directs the affair?'
They will surely say, 'God.' Then say:
'Will you not be godfearing?'
That then is God, your Lord, the True;
what is there, after truth, but error? Then
how are you turned about?
Thus the word of thy Lord is realized
against the ungodly
that they believe not.

35   Say: 'Is there any of your associates
who originates creation,
then brings it back again?'
Say: 'God—He originates creation,
then brings it back again;
so how are you perverted?'
Say: 'Is there any of your associates
who guides to the truth?'
Say: 'God—He guides to the truth;
and which is worthier to be followed—
He who guides to the truth, or he who
guides not unless he is guided? What then
ails you, how you judge?'
And the most of them follow only surmise,
and surmise avails naught against truth.
Surely God knows
the things they do.

This Koran could not have been forged
apart from God; but it is a confirmation
of what is before it, and a distinguishing
of the Book, wherein is no doubt, from
the Lord of all Being.
Or do they say, 'Why, he has forged it'?
Say: 'Then produce a sura like it, and
call on whom you can, apart from God,
if you speak truly.'

40   No; but they have cried lies to that whereof
they comprehended not the knowledge, and whose

interpretation has not yet come to them.
Even so those that were before them
cried lies; then behold how was the end
 of the evildoers!
And some of them believe in it, and some
believe not in it. Thy Lord knows very well
 those who do corruption.
If they cry lies to thee, then do thou say:
'I have my work, and you have your work;
you are quit of what I do, and I am quit
 of what you do.'
And some of them give ear to thee;
what, wilt thou make the deaf to hear, though
 they understand not?
And some of them look unto thee;
what, wilt thou then guide the blind, though
 they do not see?

45 Surely God wrongs not men anything, but
   themselves men wrong.

And the day He shall muster them, as if they had not tarried
but an hour of the day, mutually recognizing one another;
lost will be those who cried lies to the encounter with God,
   and were not guided.

Whether We show thee a part of that We
promise them, or We call thee unto Us, to
Us they shall return; then God is witness of
  the things they do.

Every nation has its Messenger; then,
when their Messenger comes, justly
the issue is decided between them, and
  they are not wronged.

They say 'When will this promise be,
 if you speak truly?'
50 Say: 'I have no power to profit

for myself, or hurt, but as God will.
To every nation a term; when their term comes
they shall not put it back by a single hour
        nor put it forward.'
Say: 'Have you considered? If His
chastisement comes upon you by night or
day, what part of it will the sinners
        seek to hasten?
What, when it has come to pass, will you then
believe in it? Now, when already you seek
        to hasten it!'
Then it will be said to the evildoers:
'Taste the chastisement of eternity! Are
you recompensed for aught but that you
        have been earning?'
They ask thee to tell them, 'Is it true?'
Say: 'Yes, by my Lord! It is true; you
        cannot frustrate Him.'

55   If every soul that has done evil
        possessed all that is in the earth,
        he would offer it for his ransom;
        and they will be secretly remorseful
        when they see the chastisement, and justly
        the issue is decided between them, and
                they are not wronged.
        Why, surely to God belongs everything
        that is in the heavens and earth. Why, surely
        God's promise is true; but the most of them
                have no knowledge.
        He gives life, and makes to die, and to Him
                you shall be returned.

        O men, now there has come to you
        an admonition from your Lord, and
        a healing for what is in the breasts,
        and a guidance, and a mercy
                to the believers.
        Say: 'In the bounty of God, and His mercy—

in that let them rejoice; it is better than
    that they amass.'
60   Say: 'Have you considered the provision
God has sent down for you, and you have made
some of it unlawful, and some lawful?'
Say: 'Has God given you leave, or do you
    forge against God?'
What will they think, who forge falsehood
against God, on the Day of Resurrection?
God is bountiful to men; but most of them
    are not thankful.

Thou art not upon any occupation,
neither recitest thou any Koran of it,
nor do you any work, without that We are
witnesses over you when you press on it;
and not so much as the weight of an ant in
earth or heaven escapes from thy Lord, neither
is aught smaller than that, or greater, but
    in a Manifest Book.

Surely God's friends—no fear shall be on them,
    neither shall they sorrow.
Those who believe, and are godfearing—
65   for them is good tidings in the present life
    and in the world to come.
There is no changing the words of God;
    that is the mighty triumph.

And do not let their saying grieve thee;
the glory belongs altogether to God; He is
    the All-hearing, the All-knowing.
Why, surely to God belongs everyone that is
in the heavens and in the earth; they follow,
who call upon associates, apart from God—
they follow nothing but surmise, merely
    conjecturing.

It is He who made for you the night

to repose in it,
and the day, to see;
surely in that are signs for a people
who have ears.

They say, 'God has taken to Him a son.'
Glory be to Him! He is All-sufficient;
to Him belongs all that is in the heavens
and in the earth; you have no authority
for this. What, do you say concerning God
that you know not?

70   Say: 'Those who forge against God falsehood
shall not prosper.'
Some enjoyment in this world; then unto Us
they shall return; then We shall let them
taste the terrible chastisement, for that they
were unbelievers.

And recite to them the story of Noah
when he said to his people, 'My people,
if my standing here is grievous to you
and my reminding you of the signs of God,
in God have I put my trust; so resolve
on your affair, with your associates,
then let not your affair be a worry
to you, but make decision unto me, and
respite me not.
Then if you turn your backs, I have not asked
you for any wage; my wage falls only on God,
and I have been commanded to be of
those that surrender.'
But they cried him lies; so We delivered him,
and those with him, in the Ark, and We
appointed them as viceroys, and We
drowned those who cried lies to Our signs;
then behold how was the end of them
that were warned!

75   Then We sent forth, after him, Messengers

to their people, and they brought them
the clear signs; but they were not
men to believe in that they had cried
lies to before. So We seal the hearts
     of the transgressors.
Then We sent forth, after them, Moses
and Aaron to Pharaoh and his Council with
Our signs, but they waxed proud, and were
     a sinful people.
So, when the truth came to them
from Us, they said, 'Surely this is
     a manifest sorcery.'
Moses said, 'What, do you say this
to the truth, when it has come to you?
Is this a sorcery? But sorcerers
     do not prosper.'
They said, 'Art thou come to us to
turn us from that we found our fathers
practising, and that the domination in
the land might belong to you two? We
     do not believe you.'
80   Pharaoh said, 'Bring me every cunning
sorcerer.' Then, when the sorcerers came,
Moses said to them, 'Cast you down
     what you will cast.'
Then, when they had cast, Moses said,
'What you have brought is sorcery; God
will assuredly bring it to naught.
God sets not right the work of those
     who do corruption.
God verifies the truth by His words, though
     sinners be averse.'
So none believed in Moses, save a seed
of his people, for fear of Pharaoh and
their Council, that they would persecute them;
and Pharaoh was high in the land, and he was
     one of the prodigals.
Moses said, 'O my people, if you believe
in God, in Him put your trust, if

you have surrendered.'

85 They said, 'In God we have put our trust. Our
Lord, make us not a temptation to the people
   of the evildoers,
and deliver us by Thy mercy from the people
   of the unbelievers.'
And We revealed to Moses and his brother,
'Take you, for your people, in Egypt
certain houses; and make your houses
a direction for men to pray to; and perform
the prayer; and do thou give good tidings
   to the believers.'
Moses said, 'Our Lord, Thou hast given
to Pharaoh and his Council adornment
and possessions in this present life.
Our Lord, let them go astray
from Thy way; Our Lord, obliterate
their possessions, and harden their hearts
so that they do not believe, till they see
   the painful chastisement.'
He said, 'Your prayer is answered; so
go you straight, and follow not the way of
   those that know not.'
90 And We brought the Children of Israel
over the sea; and Pharaoh and his hosts
followed them insolently and impetuously
till, when the drowning overtook him, he said,
'I believe that there is no god but He in whom
the Children of Israel believe; I am of
   those that surrender.'
'Now? And before thou didst rebel, being of those
   that did corruption.
So today We shall deliver thee with thy
body, that thou mayest be a sign to those
after thee. Surely many men are heedless
   of Our signs.'
And We settled the Children of Israel
in a sure settlement, and We provided them
with good things; so they differed not

until the knowledge came to them. Surely
thy Lord will decide between them
on the Day of Resurrection touching
    their differences.

So, if thou art in doubt regarding
what We have sent down to thee, ask
those who recite the Book before thee.
The truth has come to thee from thy Lord;
    so be not of the doubters,
nor be of those who cry lies to God's signs
    so as to be of the losers.

95 Those against whom thy Lord's word is realized
        will not believe,
though every sign come to them, till they see
        the painful chastisement.

Why was there never a city that believed,
and its belief profited it?—Except
the people of Jonah; when they believed,
We removed from them the chastisement
of degradation in this present life,
and We gave unto them enjoyment
    for a time.

And if thy Lord had willed, whoever
is in the earth would have believed,
all of them, all together. Wouldst thou
then constrain the people, until
    they are believers?

100 It is not for any soul to believe
save by the leave of God; and He lays
abomination upon those who have
    no understanding.
Say: 'Behold what is in the heavens
and in the earth!' But neither signs
nor warnings avail a people who
    do not believe.
So do they watch and wait for aught

but the like of the days of those
who passed away before them? Say:
'Then watch and wait; I shall be with you
  watching and waiting.'
Then We shall deliver Our Messengers
and the believers. Even so, as is
Our bounden duty, We shall deliver
  the believers.

Say: 'O men, if you are in doubt
regarding my religion, I serve
not those you serve apart from God,
but I serve God, who will gather you
to Him, and I am commanded to be
  of the believers,
105 and: "Set thy face to the religion,
a man of pure faith, and be thou not
  of the idolaters;
and do not call, apart from God, on
that which neither profits nor hurts thee,
for if thou dost, then thou wilt surely be
  of the evildoers.
And if God visits thee with affliction,
 none can remove it but He;
and if He desires any good for thee,
 none can repel His bounty;
He causes it to fall upon whomsoever
  He will of His servants."
He is the All-forgiving, the All-compassionate.'

Say: 'O men, the truth has come to you
from your Lord. Whosoever is guided
is guided only to his own gain,
and whosoever goes astray, it is only
to his own loss. I am not a guardian
  over you.'

And follow thou what is revealed to thee;

and be thou patient
until God shall judge; and He is
the best of judges.

XI

HOOD

In the Name of God, the Merciful, the Compassionate

Alif Lam Ra

A Book whose verses are set clear,
  and then distinguished,
from One All-wise, All-aware:
  'Serve you none but God'
(I am to you a warner from Him
and a bearer of good tidings)
and: 'Ask forgiveness of your Lord,
  then repent to Him,
and He will give you fair enjoyment
  unto a term stated,
and He will give of His bounty
  to every man of grace.
But if you should turn your backs
I fear for you the chastisement
  of a mighty day; to
God shall you return; He is powerful
  over everything.'

5   Behold, they fold their breasts, to
          hide them from Him;
        behold, when they wrap themselves in
        their garments He knows what they secrete
          and what they publish;
        surely He knows all the thoughts
          within the breasts.
        No creature is there crawling on the
        earth, but its provision rests on God;
          He knows its lodging-place
          and its repository. All
          is in a Manifest Book.

And it is He who created
the heavens and the earth in six days,
and His Throne was upon the waters—
that He might try you, which one of
you is fairer in works.

10   And if thou sayest, 'You shall surely be
raised up after death,' the unbelievers will say,
'This is naught but a manifest sorcery.'
And if We postpone the chastisement from them
till a reckoned moment they will say 'What is
detaining it?' Surely, the day it shall come
to them, it shall not be turned aside from
them, and they shall be encompassed by
         that they mocked at.
And if We let a man taste mercy from Us,
and then We wrest it from him, he is
         desperate, ungrateful.
But if We let him taste prosperity after
hardship that has visited him, he will say,
'The evils have gone from me'; behold, he is
         joyous, boastful—
save such as are patient, and do deeds of
righteousness; for them awaits forgiveness
         and a mighty wage.

15   Perchance thou art leaving part of what is revealed
to thee, and thy breast is straitened by it,
because they say, 'Why has a treasure not been sent
down upon him, or an angel not come with him?'
Thou art only a warner; and God is a Guardian
         over everything.
Or do they say, 'He has forged it'? Say:
'Then bring you ten suras the like of it, forged;
and call upon whom you are able, apart from God,
         if you speak truly.'
Then, if they do not answer you, know that it has been
sent down with God's knowledge, and that there is

no god but He. So
have you surrendered?

Whoso desires the present life and its adornment, We
will pay them in full for their works therein, and
    they shall not be defrauded there;
those are they for whom in the world to come there is
only the Fire; their deeds there will have failed,
    and void will be their works.

20   And what of him who stands upon a clear sign
from his Lord, and a witness from Him recites it,
and before him is the Book of Moses for an ensample
and a mercy? Those believe in it; but whosoever
disbelieves in it, being one of the partisans,
his promised land is the Fire. So be thou not
in doubt of it; it is the truth from thy Lord,
    but most men do not believe.

And who does greater evil than he who forges
against God a lie? Those shall be presented
before their Lord, and the witnesses will say,
'Those are they who lied against their Lord.'
Surely the curse of God shall rest upon
    the evildoers
who bar from God's way, desiring to make it
crooked; they disbelieve in the world to come;
they are unable to frustrate Him on earth
and they have no protectors, apart from God.
For them the chastisement shall be doubled;
they could not hear, neither did they see.
Those are they that have lost their souls, and
that they forged has gone astray from them;
they without doubt will be the greatest losers
    in the world to come.

25   But those who believe, and do righteous deeds,
and have humbled themselves unto their Lord—
they shall be the inhabitants of Paradise,
    therein dwelling forever.
    The likeness of the two parties

is as the man blind and deaf, and the man who
sees and hears; are they equal in likeness?
Will you not remember?

And We sent Noah to his people:
'I am for you a warner, and a bearer
    of good tidings:
Serve you none but God. I fear
for you the chastisement of
    a painful day.'
Said the Council of the unbelievers
of his people, 'We see thee not
other than a mortal like ourselves,
and we see not any following thee
but the vilest of us, inconsiderately.
We do not see you have over us
any superiority; no, rather we
        think you are liars.'

30   He said, 'O my people, what think you?
If I stand upon a clear sign
from my Lord, and He has given me
mercy from Him, and it has been obscured
for you, shall we compel you to it while
        you are averse to it?
O my people, I do not ask of you
wealth for this; my wage falls only
upon God. I will not drive away
those who believe; they shall surely
meet their Lord. But I see you are
        an ignorant people.
O my people, who would help me
against God, if I drive you away?
        Will you not remember?
I do not say to you, "I possess the
treasuries of God"; I know not the Unseen;
and I do not say, "I am an angel."
Nor do I say to those your eyes despise,
"God will not give them any good";
God knows best what is in their hearts.

Surely in that case I should be
      among the evildoers.'
They said, 'Noah, thou hast disputed with
us and make much disputation with us.
Then bring us that thou promisest us, if
      thou speakest truly.'
35   He said, 'God will bring you it if He will;
      you cannot frustrate Him.
And my sincere counsel will not profit
you, if I desire to counsel you
sincerely, if God desires to pervert
you; He is your Lord, and unto Him
      you shall be returned.'
(Or do they say, 'He has forged it'?
Say: 'If I have forged it, upon me
falls my sin; and I am quit of
      the sins you do.')
And it was revealed to Noah, saying,
'None of thy people shall believe
but he who has already believed;
so be thou not distressed by that
      they may be doing.
Make thou the Ark under Our eyes,
and as We reveal; and address Me not
concerning those who have done evil;
      they shall be drowned.'
40   So he was making the Ark; and whenever
a council of his people passed by him
they scoffed at him. He said, 'If you
scoff at us, we shall surely scoff at
      you, as you scoff,
and you shall know to whom will come
a chastisement degrading him,
and upon whom there shall alight a
      lasting chastisement.'
Until, when Our command came, and
the Oven boiled, We said, 'Embark
in it two of every kind, and thy
family—except for him against

whom the word has already been
spoken—and whosoever believes.'
And there believed not with him
 except a few.
He said, 'Embark in it! In God's Name
shall be its course and its berthing.
Surely my Lord is All-forgiving,
 All-compassionate.'
So it ran with them amid waves like
mountains; and Noah called to his son,
who was standing apart, 'Embark with
us, my son, and be thou not with
 the unbelievers!'

45   He said, 'I will take refuge in
a mountain, that shall defend me
from the water.' Said he, 'Today
there is no defender from God's command
but for him on whom He has mercy.' And
the waves came between them, and he was
 among the drowned.
And it was said, 'Earth, swallow thy
waters; and, heaven, abate!' And the
waters subsided, the affair was
accomplished, and the Ark settled on El-Judi,
and it was said: 'Away with the people
 of the evildoers!'
And Noah called unto his Lord, and
said, 'O my Lord, my son is of my
family, and Thy promise is surely
the truth. Thou art the justest of
 those that judge.'
Said He, 'Noah, he is not of
thy family; it is a deed not
righteous. Do not ask of Me that
whereof thou hast no knowledge.
I admonish thee, lest thou shouldst be
 among the ignorant.'
He said, 'My Lord, I take refuge
with Thee, lest I should ask of Thee

that whereof I have no knowledge;
for if Thou forgivest me not, and
hast not mercy on me, I shall be
    among the losers.'

50 It was said, 'Noah, get thee down in
peace from Us, and blessings upon thee
and on the nations of those with thee; and
nations—We shall give them enjoyment,
then there shall visit them from Us a
    painful chastisement.'
(That is of the tidings of the Unseen,
that We reveal to thee; thou didst not
know it, neither thy people, before this.
So be patient; the issue ultimate is
    to the godfearing.)

And to Ad their brother Hood;
he said, 'O my people, serve God!
You have no god other than He;
    you are but forgers.
O my people, I do not ask of you
a wage for this; my wage falls only
upon Him who did originate me;
    will you not understand?
And, O my people, ask forgiveness
of your Lord, then repent to Him,
and He will loose heaven in
    torrents upon you,
55 and He will increase you in strength
unto your strength; and turn not your
    backs as sinners.'
They said, 'Hood, thou hast not brought
us a clear sign, and we will not leave
our gods for what thou sayest; we do
    not believe thee.
We say nothing, but that one of our
gods has smitten thee with some evil.'
He said, 'I call God to witness;
and witness you, that I am quit of

that you associate
apart from Him; so try your guile on
me, all together, then you shall
          give me no respite.
Truly, I have put my trust in God,
my Lord and your Lord; there is no
creature that crawls, but He takes it
by the forelock. Surely my Lord is
          on a straight path.
60   But if you turn your backs, I have
delivered to you that I was sent with
unto you, and my Lord will make a people
other than you successors; you will not
hurt Him anything. My Lord is Guardian
          over everything.'
And when Our command came, We delivered
Hood and those who believed with him by a
mercy from Us, and delivered them from a
          harsh chastisement.
That was Ad; they denied the signs of
their Lord, and rebelled against His Messengers,
and followed the command of every
          froward tyrant.
And there was sent following after them
in this world a curse, and upon the Day
of Resurrection: 'Surely Ad disbelieved
in their Lord: so away with Ad, the
          people of Hood!'

And to Thamood their brother Salih;
he said, 'O my people, serve God!
You have no god other than He.
It is He who produced you from the earth
and has given you to live therein;
so ask forgiveness of Him, then repent
to Him; surely my Lord is nigh, and
          answers prayer.'
65   They said, 'Salih, thou hast hitherto
been a source of hope among us. What,

dost thou forbid us to serve that
our fathers served? Truly we are in
doubt, concerning what thou callest us
    to, disquieting.'
He said, 'O my people, what think you?
If I stand upon a clear sign
from my Lord, and He has given me
mercy from Him, who shall help me.
against God if I rebel against Him?
You would do nothing for me, except
    increase my loss.
O my people, this is the She-camel of
God, to be a sign for you. Leave her that
she may eat in God's earth, and touch her
not with evil, lest you be seized by a
    nigh chastisement.'
But they hamstrung her; and he said,
'Take your joy in your habitation
three days—that is a promise not
    to be belied.'
And when Our command came, We delivered
Salih and those who believed with him by a
mercy from Us, and from the degradation
of that day; thy Lord is the All-strong,
    the All-mighty.
70   And the evildoers were seized by the Cry,
and morning found them in their habitations
    fallen prostrate
as if they never dwelt there: 'Surely
Thamood disbelieved in their Lord, so
    away with Thamood!'

Our messengers came to Abraham
with the good tidings; they said, 'Peace!'
'Peace,' he said; and presently he brought
    a roasted calf.
And when he saw their hands not reaching
towards it, he was suspicious of them and
conceived a fear of them. They said,

'Fear not; we have been sent to the
    people of Lot.'
And his wife was standing by; she
laughed, therefore We gave her the
glad tidings of Isaac, and, after
    Isaac, of Jacob.

75   She said, 'Woe is me! Shall I bear,
being an old woman, and this my husband
is an old man? This assuredly is
    a strange thing.'
They said, 'What, dost thou marvel at
God's command? The mercy of God
and His blessings be upon you, O
people of the House! Surely He is
    All-laudable, All-glorious.'
So, when the awe departed from Abraham
and the good tidings came to him,
he was disputing with Us concerning
the people of Lot; Abraham was clement,
    compassionate, penitent.
'O Abraham, turn away from this; thy
Lord's command has surely come, and
there is coming upon them a chastisement
    not to be turned back.'
And when Our messengers came to Lot,
he was troubled on their account and
distressed for them, and he said,
    'This is a fierce day.'

80   And his people came to him, running
towards him; and erstwhile they
had been doing evil deeds. He said,
'O my people, these are my daughters;
they are cleaner for you. So fear God,
and do not degrade me in my guests.
What, is there not one man among you
    of a right mind?'
They said, 'Thou knowest we have no right
to thy daughters, and thou well knowest
    what we desire.'

He said, 'O would that I had power
against you, or might take refuge
 in a strong pillar!'
They said, 'Lot, we are messengers
of thy Lord. They shall not reach thee;
so set forth, thou with thy family,
in a watch of the night, and let not
any one of you turn round, excepting
thy wife; surely she shall be smitten
by that which smites them. Their
promised time is the morning; is the
 morning not nigh?'
So when Our command came, We turned it
uppermost nethermost, and rained on it
stones of baked clay, one on another,
marked with thy Lord, and never far
 from the evildoers.

85 And to Midian their brother Shuaib;
he said, 'O my people, serve God!
You have no god other than He.
And diminish not the measure and the
balance. I see you are prospering; and
I fear for you the chastisement of an
 encompassing day.
O my people, fill up the measure
and the balance justly, and do not
diminish the goods of the people,
and do not mischief in the land,
 working corruption.
God's remainder is better for you, if
 you are believers.
And I am not a guardian over you.'
They said, 'Shuaib, does thy prayer
command thee that we should leave that
our fathers served, or to do as we will
with our goods? Thou art the clement one,
 the right-minded.'
90 He said, 'O my people, what think you?

If I stand upon a clear sign
from my Lord, and He has provided me
with fair provision from Him—and I
desire not to come behind you, betaking
me to that I forbid you; I desire only
to set things right, so far as I am able.
My succour is only with God; in Him
I have put my trust, and to Him I
      turn, penitent.
O my people, let not the breach with me
move you, so that there smite you the like
of what smote the people of Noah, or
the people of Hood, or the people of
Salih; and the people of Lot are not
      far away from you.
And ask forgiveness of your Lord, then
repent to Him; surely my Lord is
All-compassionate, All-loving.'
They said, 'Shuaib, we do not understand
much of what thou sayest. Truly we see
thee weak among us; but for thy tribe
we would have stoned thee; for thou art not
      strong against us.'
He said, 'O my people, is my tribe
stronger against you than God? And Him—
have you taken Him as something to be
thrust behind you? My Lord encompasses
      the things you do.
O my people, act according to your
station; I am acting; and certainly
      you will know
to whom will come the chastisement
degrading him, and who is a liar.
And be upon the watch; I shall be
      with you, watching.'
And when Our command came, We delivered
Shuaib and those who believed with him by a
      mercy from Us,
and the evildoers were seized by the Cry,

95

and morning found them in their habitations
    fallen prostrate
as if they had never dwelt there:
'So away with Midian, even as Thamood
    was done away!'

And We sent Moses with Our signs,
and a manifest authority, to Pharaoh
and his Council; but they followed Pharaoh's
command, and Pharaoh's command was
    not right-minded.

100   He shall go before his people on the Day
of Resurrection, and will have led them down
to the Fire—evil the watering-place to
    be led down to!
And there was sent following after them
in this world a curse, and upon the Day
of Resurrection—evil the offering
    to be offered!

That is of the tidings of the cities
We relate to thee; some of them are standing
    and some stubble.
And We wronged them not, but they wronged
themselves; their gods availed them not
that they called upon, apart from God,
anything, when the command of thy Lord
came; and they increased them not, save
    in destruction.
Such is the seizing of thy Lord, when He
seizes the cities that are evildoing;
surely His seizing is painful, terrible.

105   Surely in that is a sign for him who fears
the chastisement in the world to come;
that is a day mankind are to be gathered to,
    a day to witness,
and We shall not postpone it, save to
    a term reckoned;
the day it comes, no soul shall speak save

by His leave; some of them shall be wretched
and some happy.
As for the wretched, they shall be in the
Fire, wherein there shall be for them
moaning and sighing,
therein dwelling forever, so long as
the heavens and earth abide, save as thy
Lord will; surely thy Lord accomplishes
what He desires.

110   And as for the happy, they shall be in
Paradise, therein dwelling forever,
so long as the heavens and earth abide,
save as thy Lord will—for a
gift unbroken.
So be thou not in doubt concerning
what these men serve; they serve only
as their fathers served before; and We
shall surely pay them in full their
portion undiminished.

And We gave Moses the Book; and there was
difference regarding it, and but for a word
that preceded from thy Lord, it had been
decided between them; and they are in doubt
of it disquieting.
Surely each one of them—thy Lord will pay
them in full for their works; He is aware of
the things they do.
So go thou straight, as thou hast been
commanded, and whoso repents with thee;
and be you not insolent; surely He sees
the things you do.

115   And lean not on the evildoers, so
that the Fire touches you—you have no
protectors apart from God—and then you
will not be helped.

And perform the prayer at the two ends of the day
and nigh of the night; surely the good deeds will

drive away the evil deeds. That is a remembrance
    unto the mindful.
And be thou patient; God will not leave to waste the
    wage of the good-doers.
Or if there had been, of the generations before
you, men of a remainder forbidding corruption
in the earth—except a few of those whom We
delivered of them; but the evildoers
followed the ease they were given to exult in
    and became sinners.
Yet thy Lord would never destroy the cities
unjustly, while as yet their people were
    putting things right.
120 Had thy Lord willed, He would have made mankind
one nation; but they continue in their differences
excepting those on whom thy Lord has mercy.
To that end He created them, and perfectly
is fulfilled the word of thy Lord: 'I shall
assuredly fill Gehenna with jinn and men
    all together.'

And all that We relate to thee of
the tidings of the Messengers is that
whereby We strengthen thy heart; in
these there has come to thee the truth
and an admonition, and a reminder
    to the believers.
And say to the unbelievers: 'Act you
according to your station; we are acting.
And watch and wait; we are also
    watching and waiting.'

To God belongs the Unseen in the heavens and the earth.
To Him the whole matter shall be returned; so serve Him,
and put thy trust in Him. Thy Lord is not heedless of
    the things you do.

XII

JOSEPH

In the Name of God, the Merciful, the Compassionate

Alif Lam Ra

Those are the signs of the Manifest Book.
We have sent it down as an Arabic Koran;
      haply you will understand.

We will relate to thee the fairest of stories
in that We have revealed to thee this Koran,
though before it thou wast one of the heedless.

When Joseph said to his father, 'Father, I saw
eleven stars, and the sun and the moon; I saw them
      bowing down before me.'
5 He said, 'O my son, relate not thy vision
to thy brothers, lest they devise against thee
some guile. Surely Satan is to man
      a manifest enemy.
So will thy Lord choose thee, and teach thee
the interpretation of tales, and perfect His
blessing upon thee and upon the House of Jacob,
as He perfected it formerly on thy fathers
Abraham and Isaac; surely thy Lord is
      All-knowing, All-wise.'
(In Joseph and his brethren were signs for those
      who ask questions.)
When they said, 'Surely Joseph and his brother
are dearer to our father than we, though
we are a band. Surely our father is
      in manifest error.
Kill you Joseph, or cast him forth into
some land, that your father's face may be
free for you, and thereafter you may be

a righteous people.'

10　One of them said, 'No, kill not Joseph,
but cast him into the bottom of the pit
and some traveller will pick him out,
　　　if you do aught.'
They said, 'Father, what ails thee, that thou
trustest us not with Joseph? Surely we are his
　　　sincere well-wishers.
Send him forth with us tomorrow, to
frolic and play; surely we shall be
　　　watching over him.'
He said, 'It grieves me that you should go with him,
and I fear the wolf may eat him, while you
　　　are heedless of him.'
They said, 'If the wolf eats him, and we a band,
　　　then are we losers!'
15　So when they went with him, and agreed to put him
in the bottom of the well, and We revealed to him,
'Thou shalt tell them of this their doing
　　　when they are unaware.'
And they came to their father in the evening,
　· and they were weeping.
They said, 'Father, we went running races, and
left Joseph behind with our things; so the wolf
ate him. But thou wouldst never believe us,
　　　though we spoke truly.'
And they brought his shirt with false blood on it.
He said, 'No; but your spirits tempted you
to do somewhat. But come, sweet patience!
And God's succour is ever there to seek against
　　　that you describe.'
Then came travellers, and they sent one of them,
a water-drawer, who let down his bucket.
'Good news!' he said. 'Here is a young man.'
So they hid him as merchandise; but God knew
　　　what they were doing.
20　Then they sold him for a paltry price, a
handful of counted dirhams; for they set
　　　small store by him.

He that bought him, being of Egypt,
said to his wife, 'Give him goodly lodging,
and it may be that he will profit us,
or we may take him for our own son.'
So We established Joseph in the land, and
that We might teach him the interpretation
of tales. God prevails in His purpose, but
most men know not.
And when he was fully grown, We gave him
judgment and knowledge. Even so We recompense
the good-doers.

Now the woman in whose house he was
solicited him, and closed the doors on them.
'Come,' she said, 'take me!' 'God be my refuge,'
he said. 'Surely my lord has given me
a goodly lodging. Surely the evildoers
do not prosper.'
For she desired him; and he would have taken her,
but that he saw the proof of his Lord.
So was it, that We might turn away from him
evil and abomination; he was one of
Our devoted servants.

25   They raced to the door; and she tore his shirt
from behind. They encountered her master
by the door. She said, 'What is the recompense
of him who purposes evil against thy folk,
but that he should be imprisoned, or
a painful chastisement?'
Said he, 'It was she that solicited me';
and a witness of her folk bore witness,
'If his shirt has been torn from before
then she has spoken truly, and he is
one of the liars;
but if it be that his shirt has been torn
from behind, then she has lied, and he is
one of the truthful.'
When he saw his shirt was torn from behind
he said, 'This is of your women's guile; surely

your guile is great.
Joseph, turn away from this; and thou, woman,
ask forgiveness of thy crime; surely thou art
    one of the sinners.'
30 Certain women that were in the city said,
'The Governor's wife has been soliciting her
page; he smote her heart with love; we see her
    in manifest error.'
When she heard their sly whispers, she sent
to them, and made ready for them a repast,
then she gave to each one of them a knife.
'Come forth, attend to them,' she said.
And when they saw him, they so admired him
that they cut their hands, saying, 'God save us!
This is no mortal; he is no other
    but a noble angel.'
'So now you see,' she said. 'This is he you
blamed me for. Yes, I solicited him, but
he abstained. Yet if he will not do what I
command him, he shall be imprisoned, and be
    one of the humbled.'
He said, 'My Lord, prison is dearer to me
than that they call me to; yet if Thou
turnest not from me their guile, then I
shall yearn towards them, and so become
    one of the ignorant.'
So his Lord answered him, and He turned
away from him their guile; surely He is
    the All-hearing, the All-knowing.
35 Then it seemed good to them, after they had
seen the signs, that they should imprison
    him for a while.
And there entered the prison with him
two youths. Said one of them, 'I dreamed
that I was pressing grapes.' Said the other,
'I dreamed that I was carrying on my head
bread, that birds were eating of. Tell us
its interpretation; we see that thou art
    of the good-doers.'

He said, 'No food shall come to you
for your sustenance, but ere it comes to you
I shall tell you its interpretation.
That I shall tell you is of what God
has taught me. I have forsaken the creed
of a people who believe not in God
and who moreover are unbelievers in
   the world to come.
And I have followed the creed of my fathers,
Abraham, Isaac and Jacob. Not ours is it
to associate aught with God. That is of God's
bounty to us, and to men; but most men
   are not thankful.
Say, which is better, my fellow-prisoners—
many gods at variance, or God the One,
   the Omnipotent?
40 That which you serve, apart from Him, is
nothing but names yourselves have named,
you and your fathers; God has sent down
no authority touching them. Judgment
belongs only to God; He has commanded
that you shall not serve any but Him.
That is the right religion; but
   most men know not.
Fellow-prisoners, as for one of you, he shall
pour wine for his lord; as for the other,
he shall be crucified, and birds will eat
of his head. The matter is decided
   whereon you enquire.'
Then he said to the one he deemed
should be saved of the two, 'Mention me
in thy lord's presence.' But Satan caused him
to forget to mention him to his master,
so that he continued in the prison
   for certain years.

And the king said, 'I saw in a dream
seven fat kine, and seven lean ones
devouring them; likewise seven green ears

of corn, and seven withered. My counsellors,
pronounce to me upon my dream, if you are
  expounders of dreams.'
'A hotchpotch of nightmares!' they said.
'We know nothing of the interpretation
  of nightmares.'

45 Then said the one who had been delivered,
remembering after a time, 'I will
myself tell you its interpretation;
  so send me forth.'

'Joseph, thou true man, pronounce to us
regarding seven fat kine, that seven lean ones
were devouring, seven green ears of corn, and
seven withered; haply I shall return to the men,
  haply they will know.'
He said, 'You shall sow seven years
after your wont; what you have harvested
leave in the ear, excepting a little
  whereof you eat.
Then thereafter there shall come upon you
seven hard years, that shall devour what
you have laid up for them, all but a little
  you keep in store.
Then thereafter there shall come a year
wherein the people will be succoured
  and press in season.'

50 The king said, 'Bring him to me!' And
when the messenger came to him, he
said, 'Return unto thy lord, and ask
of him, "What of the women who cut
their hands?" Surely my Lord has knowledge
  of their guile.'
'What was your business, women,' he said,
'when you solicited Joseph?' 'God save us!'
they said. 'We know no evil against him.'
The Governor's wife said, 'Now the truth

is at last discovered; I solicited him; he
is a truthful man.'
'That, so that he may know I betrayed him not
secretly, and that God guides not the guile
of the treacherous.
Yet I claim not that my soul was innocent—
surely the soul of man incites to evil—
except inasmuch as my Lord had mercy;
truly my Lord is All-forgiving,
All-compassionate.'
The king said, 'Bring him to me! I would
attach him to my person.' Then, when he
had spoken with him, he said, 'Today
thou art established firmly in our favour
and in our trust.'

55   He said, 'Set me over the land's storehouses; I
am a knowing guardian.'
So We established Joseph in the land, to
make his dwelling there wherever he would.
We visit with Our mercy whomsoever We
will, and We leave not to waste the wage
of the good-doers.
Yet is the wage of the world to come better
for those who believe, and are godfearing.

And the brethren of Joseph came, and
entered unto him, and he knew them, but
they knew him not.
When he had equipped them with their equipment
he said, 'Bring me a certain brother of yours
from your father. Do you not see
that I fill up the measure, and am
the best of hosts?

60   But if you bring him not to me, there shall
be no measure for you with me, neither shall
you come nigh me.'
They said, 'We will solicit him of our father;
that we will do.'
He said to his pages, 'Put their merchandise

in their saddlebags; haply they will recognize it
when they have turned to their people; haply
     they will return.'
So, when they had returned to their father,
they said, 'Father, the measure was denied
to us; so send with us our brother, that we
may obtain the measure; surely we shall be
     watching over him.'
He said, 'And shall I entrust him to you
otherwise than as I entrusted before
his brother to you? Why, God is the best
guardian, and He is the most merciful
     of the merciful.'
65   And when they opened their things, they found
their merchandise, restored to them. 'Father,'
they said, 'what more should we desire?
See, our merchandise here is restored to us.
We shall get provision for our family,
and we shall be watching over our brother;
we shall obtain an extra camel's load—that
     is an easy measure.'
He said, 'Never will I send him with you
until you bring me a solemn pledge by God
that you will surely bring him back to me
unless it be that you are encompassed.'
When they had brought him their solemn pledge
he said, 'God shall be Guardian
     over what we say.'
He also said, 'O my sons, enter not
by one door; enter by separate doors.
Yet I cannot avail you anything
against God; judgment belongs not to any
but God. In Him I have put my trust;
and in Him let all put their trust
     who put their trust.'

And when they entered after the manner
their father commanded them, it availed them
nothing against God; but it was a need

in Jacob's soul that he so satisfied.
Verily he was possessed of a knowledge
for that We had taught him; but
        most men know not.
And when they entered unto Joseph, he said,
taking his brother into his arms,
'I am thy brother; so do not despair of
        that they have done.'

70   Then, when he had equipped them with
their equipment, he put his drinking-cup
into the saddlebag of his brother.
Then a herald proclaimed, 'Ho, cameleers,
        you are robbers!'
They said, turning to them, 'What is it that
        you are missing?'
They said, 'We are missing the king's goblet.
Whoever brings it shall receive a camel's load;
        that I guarantee.'
'By God,' they said, 'you know well that we
came not to work corruption in the land.
        We are not robbers.'
They said, 'And what shall be its recompense
        if you are liars?'

75   They said, 'This shall be its recompense—
in whoever's saddlebag the goblet is found,
he shall be its recompense. So we recompense
        the evildoers.'
So he made beginning with their sacks, before
his brother's sack, then he pulled it out
of his brother's sack. So We contrived
for Joseph's sake; he could not have taken his
brother, according to the king's doom, except
that God willed. Whomsoever We will, We
raise in rank; over every man of knowledge
        is One who knows.
They said, 'If he is a thief, a brother of his
was a thief before.' But Joseph secreted it
in his soul and disclosed it not to them, saying,
'You are in a worse case; God knows very well

what you are describing.'
They said, 'Mighty prince, he has a father,
aged and great with years; so take one of us
in his place; we see that thou art one
    of the good-doers.'
He said, 'God forbid that we should take
any other but him in whose possession
we found the goods; for if we did so, we
    would be evildoers.'

80   When they despaired of moving him, they
conferred privily apart. Said the eldest of
them, 'Do you not know how your father has taken
a solemn pledge from you by God, and aforetime
you failed regarding Joseph? Never will I
quit this land, until my father gives me
leave, or God judges in my favour; He is
    the best of judges.
Return you all to your father, and say,
"Father, thy son stole; we do not testify
except that we know; we were no guardians
    of the Unseen.
Enquire of the city wherein we were, and the
caravan in which we approached; surely
    we are truthful men".'

'No!' he said. 'But your spirits tempted you
to do somewhat. But come, sweet patience!
Haply God will bring them all to me; He is
    the All-knowing, the All-wise.'
And he turned away from them, and said,
'Ah, woe is me for Joseph!' And his eyes
turned white because of the sorrow that
    he choked within him.

85   'By God,' they said, 'thou wilt never cease
mentioning Joseph till thou art consumed, or
    among the perishing.'
He said, 'I make complaint of my anguish
and my sorrow unto God; I know from God
    that you know not.

Depart, my sons, and search out tidings
of Joseph and his brother. Do not despair
of God's comfort; of God's comfort
no man despairs, excepting the people
      of the unbelievers.'

So, when they entered unto him, they said,
'O mighty prince, affliction has visited us
and our people. We come with merchandise
of scant worth. Fill up to us the measure,
and be charitable to us; surely God recompenses
      the charitable.'
He said, 'Are you aware of what you did
with Joseph and his brother, when you
      were ignorant?'

90   They said, 'Why, art thou indeed Joseph?'
'I am Joseph,' he said. 'This is my brother.
God has indeed been gracious unto us.
Whosoever fears God, and is patient—
surely God leaves not to waste the wage
      of the good-doers.'
'By God,' they said, 'God has indeed
preferred thee above us, and certainly
      we have been sinful.'
He said, 'No reproach this day shall be on you;
God will forgive you; He is the most merciful
      of the merciful.
Go, take this shirt, and do you cast it
on my father's face, and he shall recover
his sight; then bring me your family
      all together.'

So, when the caravan set forth, their father
said, 'Surely I perceive Joseph's scent, unless
      you think me doting.'

95   They said, 'By God, thou art certainly in
      thy ancient error.'
But when the bearer of good tidings came

to him, and laid it on his face, forthwith
    he saw once again.
He said, 'Did I not tell you I know from God
   . that you know not?'
They said, 'Our father, ask forgiveness
of our crimes for us; for certainly
    we have been sinful.'
He said, 'Assuredly I will ask my Lord
to forgive you; He is the All-forgiving,
    the All-compassionate.'

100   So, when they entered unto Joseph,
he took his father and mother into his arms
saying, 'Enter you into Egypt, if God will,
    in security.'
And he lifted his father and mother
upon the throne; and the others fell down
prostrate before him. 'See, father,' he said,
'this is the interpretation of my vision
of long ago; my Lord has made it true.
He was good to me when He brought me forth
from the prison, and again when He
brought you out of the desert, after that
Satan set at variance me and my brethren.
My Lord is gentle to what He will; He is
    the All-knowing, the All-wise.
O my Lord, Thou hast given me to rule,
and Thou hast taught me the interpretation
of tales. O Thou, the Originator of the
heavens and earth, Thou art my Protector
in this world and the next. O receive me
to Thee in true submission, and join me
    with the righteous.'

That is of the tidings of the Unseen that
We reveal to thee; thou wast not with them
when they agreed upon their plan, devising.
Yet, be thou ever so eager, the most part of
    men believe not.

Thou askest of· them no wage for it;
it is nothing but a reminder
    unto all beings.

105   How many a ·sign there is in the heavens
and in the earth that they pass by, turning
    away from it!
And the most part of them believe not in God,
    but they associate
other gods with Him. Do they feel secure
that there shall come upon them no enveloping
of the chastisement of God, or that the
Hour shall not come upon them suddenly
    when they are unaware?

    Say: 'This is my way.
I call to God with sure knowledge,
I and whoever follows after me.
To God be glory! And I am not
    among the idolaters.'

We sent not forth any before thee, but
men We revealed to of the people living
in the cities. Have they not journeyed
in the land? Have they not beheld
how was the end of those before them? Surely
the abode of the world to come is better
for those that are godfearing. What,
    do you not understand?

110   Till, when the Messengers despaired, deeming
they were counted liars, Our help came to them
and whosoever We willed was delivered. Our
might will never be turned back from the people
    of the sinners.
In their stories is surely a lesson to
men possessed of minds; it is not a tale
forged, but a confirmation of what is before
it, and a distinguishing of every thing,
and a guidance, and a mercy to a people
    who believe.

XIII

THUNDER

In the Name of God, the Merciful, the Compassionate

Alif Lam Mim Ra

Those are the signs of the Book;
and that which has been sent down to thee
from thy Lord is the truth, but most men
do not believe.

God is He who raised up the heavens
without pillars you can see,
then He sat Himself upon the Throne.
He subjected the sun and the moon,
each one running to a term stated.
He directs the affair; He
distinguishes the signs;
haply you will have faith in the encounter
with your Lord.

It is He who stretched out the earth
and set therein
firm mountains and rivers,
and of every fruit He placed there two kinds,
covering the day with the night.
Surely in that are signs for a people who reflect.
And on the earth are tracts neighbouring
each to each,
and gardens of vines,
and fields sown,
and palms in pairs, and palms single,
watered with one water;
and some of them We prefer in produce
above others.
Surely in that are signs for a people who understand.

5   If thou wouldst wonder, surely wonderful
    is their saying, 'What, when we are dust
    shall we indeed then be raised up again
        in new creation?'
Those are they that disbelieve in their
    Lord; those—on their necks are fetters;
    those shall be the inhabitants of the Fire,
        therein dwelling forever.
They would have thee hasten the evil ere the good;
yet there have passed away before them examples.
Thy Lord is forgiving to men, for all their evil-doing,
    and thy Lord is terrible in retribution.

The unbelievers say, 'Why has a sign not been
sent down upon him from his Lord?' Thou art only
    a warner, and a guide to every people.

    God knows what every female bears,
    and the wombs' shrinking and swelling;
    everything with Him has its measure—
10   the Knower of the unseen and the visible,
        the All-great, the All-exalted.
Alike of you is he who conceals his
    saying, and he who proclaims it, he
    who hides himself in the night, and
        he who sallies by day;
he has attendant angels, before him and behind him,
    watching over him by God's command.
God changes not what is in a people, until they
    change what is in themselves.
Whensover God desires evil for a people, there is
        no turning it back;
apart from Him, they have no protector.

It is He who shows you the lightning, for fear and hope,
    and produces the heavy clouds;
the thunder proclaims His praise, and the angels,
        in awe of Him.

He looses the thunderbolts, and smites with them
    whomsoever He will; yet they
dispute about God, who is mighty in power.
    To Him is the call of truth;
and those upon whom they call, apart from Him,
    answer them nothing,
but it is as a man who stretches out his hands to water
    that it may reach his mouth,
and it reaches it not. The prayer of the unbelievers
    goes only astray.
15 To God bow all who are in the heavens and the earth,
    willingly or unwillingly,
as do their shadows also in the mornings and the evenings.

Say: 'Who is the Lord of the heavens and of the earth?'
    Say: 'God.'
Say: 'Then have you taken unto you others beside Him
    to be your protectors, even
such as have no power to profit or hurt themselves?'
    Say: 'Are the blind and the seeing man
equal, or are the shadows and the light equal?
    Or have they ascribed to God
associates who created as He created, so that creation
    is all alike to them?'
Say: 'God is the Creator of everything, and He is
    the One, the Omnipotent.'

He sends down out of heaven water,
and the wadis flow each in its measure,
and the torrent carries a swelling scum;
and out of that over which they kindle
fire, being desirous of ornament or ware,
out of that rises a scum the like of it.
So God strikes both the true and the false.
As for the scum, it vanishes as jetsam,
and what profits men abides in the earth.
Even so God strikes His similitudes.
For those who answer their Lord, the reward
most fair; and those who answer Him not—

if they possessed all that is in the earth,
and the like of it with it, they would
offer it for their ransom. Those—
theirs shall be the evil reckoning,
and their refuge shall be Gehenna—
    an evil cradling!

What, is he who knows what is sent down to thee
from thy Lord is the truth, like him who is blind?
    Only men possessed of minds remember;
20   who fulfil God's covenant, and break not the compact,
who join what God has commanded shall be joined,
and fear their Lord, and dread the evil reckoning,
patient men, desirous of the Face of their Lord,
who perform the prayer, and expend of that
We have provided them, secretly and in public,
and who avert evil with good—theirs shall be
        the Ultimate Abode,
Gardens of Eden which they shall enter;
and those who were righteous of their fathers,
and their wives, and their seed, shall enter them,
    and the angels shall enter unto them
        from every gate:
'Peace be upon you, for that you were patient.'
    Fair is the Ultimate Abode.
25   And those who break the covenant of God
after His compact, and who snap what God
has commanded to be joined, and who work
corruption in the earth—theirs shall be the curse,
        and theirs the Evil Abode.
God outspreads and straitens His provision
unto whomsoever He will. They rejoice in
this present life; and this present life,
beside the world to come, is naught but
        passing enjoyment.

The unbelievers say, 'Why has a sign not
been sent down upon him from his Lord?'
Say: 'God leads astray whomsoever He will,

and He guides to Him all who are penitent.'
Those who believe, their hearts being at rest
in God's remembrance—in God's remembrance
are at rest the hearts of those who believe
and do righteous deeds; theirs is blessedness
and a fair resort.

Thus We have sent thee among a nation before
which other nations have passed away, to
recite to them that We have revealed to thee;
and yet they disbelieve in the All-merciful.
Say:
'He is my Lord—
there is no god but He. In
Him I have put my trust,
and to Him I turn.'

30   If only a Koran whereby the mountains were
set in motion, or the earth were cleft, or
the dead were spoken to—nay, but God's
is the affair altogether. Did not the
believers know that, if God had willed, He
would have guided men all together? And
still the unbelievers are smitten by a
shattering for what they wrought, or it
alights nigh their habitation, until God's
promise comes; and God will not fail the tryst.
Messengers indeed were scoffed at before thee,
and I respited the unbelievers; then I seized
them—and how was my retribution?

What, He who stands over every soul for what
it has earned?—And yet they ascribe
to God associates. Say: 'Name them! Or
will you tell Him what He knows not in the
earth? Or in apparent words?' Nay; but
decked out fair to the unbelievers is
their devising, and they are barred from
the way; and whomsoever God leads astray,
no guide has he.

For them is chastisement in the present life;
and the chastisement of the world to come is
yet more grievous; they have none to defend
     them from God.

35   The likeness of Paradise, that is promised
to the godfearing: beneath it rivers flow,
its produce is eternal, and its shade.
That is the requital of the godfearing;
and the requital of the unbelievers is—
     the Fire!

And those to whom We have given the Book
rejoice in what is sent down unto thee;
and of the parties some reject some of it.
    Say: 'I have only been commanded
    to serve God, and not to associate
    aught with Him. To Him I call, and
      to Him I turn.'
    Even so We have sent it down as an
    Arabic judgment. And if thou dost
    follow their caprices, after the
    knowledge that has come to thee,
    thou shalt have no protector against
      God, and no defender.
And We sent Messengers before thee, and We
assigned to them wives, and seed; and it was
not for any Messengers to bring a sign, but
by God's leave. Every term has a Book.
    God blots out, and He establishes
whatsoever He will; and with Him is the
     Essence of the Book.

40   Whether We show thee a part of that We
promise them, or We call thee to Us, it is
thine only to deliver the Message, and
     Ours the reckoning.
Have they not seen how We come to the land
diminishing it in its extremities? God
judges; none repels His judgment; He is swift
    at the reckoning.

Those that were before them devised; but God's
is the devising altogether. He knows what
every soul earns. The unbelievers shall
assuredly know whose will be the Ultimate
Abode.

The unbelievers say, 'Thou art not an Envoy.'
Say: 'God suffices as a witness between me and
you, and whosoever possesses knowledge of
the Book.'

XIV

ABRAHAM

In the Name of God, the Merciful, the Compassionate

Alif Lam Ra

A Book We have sent down to thee
that thou mayest bring forth mankind
from the shadows to the light
by the leave of their Lord,
to the path of the All-mighty, the All-laudable,
God, to whom belongs
all that is in the heavens and all that is in the earth.
And woe to the unbelievers
for a terrible chastisement,
such as prefer the present life over the world to come,
and bar from God's way, desiring to make it crooked—
they are in far error. And
We have sent no Messenger
save with the tongue of his people,
that he might make all clear to them;
then God leads astray whomsoever He will, and
He guides whomsoever He will; and He is
the All-mighty, the All-wise.

5   And We sent Moses with Our signs—
'Bring forth thy people
from the shadows to the light
and remind thou them of the Days of God.'.
Surely in that are signs for every man
enduring, thankful!

And when Moses said to his people,
'Remember God's blessing upon you
when He delivered you from the folk
of Pharaoh, who were visiting you with

evil chastisement, slaughtering your
sons, and sparing your women—and in
that was a grievous trial from your
Lord. And when your Lord proclaimed,
"If you are thankful, surely I will
increase you, but if you are thankless
My chastisement is surely terrible." '
And Moses said, 'If you are thankless,
you and whoso is on earth, all together,
yet assuredly God is All-sufficient,
        All-laudable.'

Has there not come to you the tidings of those
who were before you—the people of Noah,
Ad, Thamood, and of those after them whom
none knows but God? Their Messengers
came to them with the clear signs; but they
thrust their hands into their mouths, saying,
'We certainly disbelieve in the Message
you have been sent with, and we are in
doubt, concerning that you call us unto,
        disquieting.'
Their Messengers said, 'Is there any doubt
regarding God, the Originator of the
heavens and the earth, who calls you so
that He may forgive you your sins, and
defer you to a term stated?' They said,
'You are nothing but mortals, like us;
you desire to bar us from that our fathers
served; then bring us a manifest authority.'
Their Messengers said to them, 'We are nothing
but mortals, like you; but God is gracious
unto whomsoever He will of His servants.
It is not for us to bring you an authority
save by the leave of God; and in God
let the believers put all their trust.
And why should we not put our trust
in God, seeing that He has guided us
in our ways? We will surely endure

10

15

patiently, whatever you hurt us; and in God
let all put their trust who put their trust.'
The unbelievers said to their Messengers,
'We will assuredly expel you from our land,
or you will surely return into our creed.'
Then did their Lord reveal unto them:
'We will surely destroy the evildoers,
and We will surely make you to dwell
in the land after them—that, for him
who fears My station and fears My threat.'
They sought a judgment; then was disappointed
every froward tyrant—beyond him Gehenna,
and he is given to drink of oozing pus,

20   the which he gulps, and can scarce swallow,
and death comes upon him from every side,
yet he cannot die; and still beyond him is
        a harsh chastisement.

The likeness of those who disbelieve in their Lord:
     their works are as ashes,
   whereon the wind blows strong
   upon a tempestuous day;
they have no power over that they have earned—
     that is the far error!
   Hast thou not seen that God created
   the heavens and the earth in truth?
   If He will, He can put you away
   and bring a new creation; that
   is surely no great matter for God.

   They sally forth unto God, all together;
   then say the weak to those who waxed proud,
   'We were your followers; will you avail us
   against the chastisement of God anything?'

25   They say, 'If God had guided us, we
   would have guided you. Alike it is for us
   whether we cannot endure, or whether
   we are patient; we have no asylum.'
   And Satan says, when the issue is decided,

'God surely promised you a true promise;
and I promised you, then I failed you,
for I had no authority over you, but
that I called you, and you answered me.
So do not blame me, but blame yourselves;
I cannot aid you, neither can you aid me.
I disbelieved in your associating me with
    God aforetime.'
As for the evildoers, for them awaits a
    painful chastisement;
but as for those who believe, and do deeds
of righteousness, they shall be admitted
to gardens underneath which rivers flow,
   therein dwelling forever,
by the leave of their Lord, their greeting
   therein: 'Peace!'

Hast thou not seen how God has struck
a similitude? A good word
  is as a good tree—
  its roots are firm,
and its branches are in heaven;
30 it gives its produce every season
  by the leave of its Lord.
So God strikes similitudes for men;
  haply they will remember.
And the likeness of a corrupt word
  is as a corrupt tree—
  uprooted from the earth,
  having no stablishment.
God confirms those who believe with
the firm word, in the present life
  and in the world to come;
and God leads astray the evildoers;
  and God does what He will.
Hast thou not seen those who exchanged
the bounty of God with unthankfulness,
and caused their people to dwell in
  the abode of ruin?—

Gehenna, wherein they are roasted;
    an evil stablishment!
35   And they set up compeers to God, that
they might lead astray from His way.
Say: 'Take your joy! Your homecoming
    shall be—the Fire!'
Say to My servants who believe, that
they perform the prayer, and expend of
that We have provided them, secretly
and in public, before a day comes
wherein shall be neither bargaining
    nor befriending.

It is God who created the heavens and the earth,
   · and sent down out of heaven water
wherewith He brought forth fruits to be your sustenance.
    And He subjected to you the ships
    to run upon the sea at His commandment;
    and He subjected to you the rivers
and He subjected to you the sun and moon
    constant upon their courses,
and He subjected to you the night and day,
    and gave you of all you asked Him.
If you count God's blessing, you will never number it;
    surely man is sinful, unthankful!

And when Abraham said, 'My Lord,
make this land secure, and turn me
and my sons away from serving idols;
my Lord, they have led astray many men.
Then whoso follows me belongs to me;
and whoso rebels against me, surely Thou
art All-forgiving, All-compassionate.
40   Our Lord, I have made some of my seed to
dwell in a valley where is no sown land
by Thy Holy House; Our Lord, let them
perform the prayer, and make hearts of
men yearn towards them, and provide them

with fruits; haply they will be thankful.
Our Lord, Thou knowest what we keep secret
and what we publish; from God nothing
whatever is hidden in earth and heaven.
Praise be to God, who has given me,
though I am old, Ishmael and Isaac;
surely my Lord hears the petition.
My Lord, make me a performer of the
prayer, and of my seed. Our Lord,
and receive my petition. Our Lord,
forgive Thou me and my parents, and
the believers, upon the day when
the reckoning shall come to pass.'

Deem not that God is heedless of what the evildoers work;
He is only deferring them to a day when eyes shall stare,
when they shall run with necks outstretched and heads erect,
their glances never returned on themselves, their hearts void.
And warn mankind of the day when the chastisement comes
⌈on them,

45　And those who did evil shall say, 'Our Lord, defer us
to a near term, and we will answer Thy call, and follow
the Messengers.' 'Ah, but did you not swear aforetime
there should be no removing for you? And you dwelt
in the dwelling-places of those who wronged themselves,
and it became clear to you how We did with them, and
how We struck similitudes for you. They devised
their devising, and their devising is known to God,
though their devising were such as to remove mountains.'
So do not deem that God will fail in His promise to
His Messengers; surely God is All-mighty, Vengeful.
Upon the day the earth shall be changed to other than the
⌈earth,
and the heavens and they sally forth unto God,
　　the One, the Omnipotent.
50　And thou shalt see the sinners that day coupled in fetters,
of pitch their shirts, their faces enveloped by the Fire,
that God may recompense every soul for its earnings; surely
　　God is swift at the reckoning.

This is a Message to be delivered to mankind
    that they may be warned by it,
    and that they may know that He
      is One God,
and that all possessed of minds may remember.

XV

EL-HIJR

In the Name of God, the Merciful, the Compassionate

Alif Lam Ra

Those are the signs of the Book
and of a manifest Koran.

Perchance the unbelievers will wish that
they had surrendered:
leave them to eat, and to take their joy,
and to be bemused by hope; certainly
they will soon know!
Never a city have We destroyed, but it
had a known decree,
5   and no nation outstrips its term, nor
do they put it back.

They say:
'Thou, upon whom the Remembrance is sent down,
thou art assuredly possessed!
Why dost thou not bring the angels unto us, if
thou speakest truly?'
We send not down the angels, save with truth;
then they would not be respited.
It is We who have sent down the Remembrance,
and We watch over it.
10   Indeed, We sent Messengers before thee, among
the factions of the ancients,
and not a single Messenger came to them, but
they mocked at him;
even so We cause it to enter into the hearts
of the sinners—
they believe not in it, though the wont of the
ancients is already gone.

Though We opened to them a gate in heaven, and
    still they mounted through it,
15   yet would they say, 'Our eyes have been dazzled;
    nay, we are a people bewitched!'

We have set in heaven constellations
and decked them out fair to the beholders,
and guarded them from every accursed Satan
excepting such as listens by stealth—
and he is pursued by a manifest flame.
And the earth—We stretched it forth, and cast
    on it firm mountains,
and We caused to grow therein of every thing
    justly weighed, and
20   there appointed for you livelihood, and for those
    you provide not for.
Naught is there, but its treasuries are with Us,
    and We send it not down
    but in a known measure.
And We loose the winds fertilising,
and We send down out of heaven water,
then We give it to you to drink, and
you are not its treasurers. It is
We who give life, and make to die,
and it is We who are the inheritors.
We know the ones of you who press forward, and
    We know the laggards;
25   and it is thy Lord shall muster them, and He is
    All-wise, All-knowing.

Surely We created man of a clay
    of mud moulded,
and the jinn created We before
    of fire flaming.
And when thy Lord said to the angels,
'See, I am creating a mortal of a clay
    of mud moulded.
When I have shaped him, and breathed My spirit in
him, fall you down, bowing before him!'

30   Then the angels bowed themselves
              all together,
     save Iblis; he refused to be among
              those bowing.
     Said He, 'What ails thee, Iblis, that
     thou art not among those bowing?'
     Said he, 'I would never bow myself
              before a mortal
     whom Thou hast created of a clay
              of mud moulded.'
     Said He, 'Then go thou forth hence;
              thou art accursed.
35   Upon thee shall rest the curse, till
              the Day of Doom.'
     Said he, 'My Lord, respite me till the day
              they shall be raised.'
     Said He, 'Thou art among the ones
     that are respited unto the day
              of a known time.'
     Said he, 'My Lord, for Thy perverting me
              I shall deck all fair
              to them in the earth,
     and I shall pervert them, all together,
40   excepting those Thy servants among them
              that are devoted.'
     Said He, 'This is for Me a straight path:
              over My servants
     thou shalt have no authority, except those
              that follow thee,
              being perverse;
     Gehenna shall be their promised land
              all together.
     Seven gates it has, and unto each gate
              a set portion
              of them belongs.'
45   But the godfearing shall be amidst gardens
              and fountains:
     'Enter you them, in peace and security!'
     We shall strip away all rancour that is

in their breasts;
as brothers they shall be upon couches
        set face to face;
no fatigue there shall smite them, neither
shall they ever be driven forth from there.
        Tell My servants
I am the All-forgiving, the All-compassionate,
50   and that My chastisement
        is the painful chastisement.

And tell them of the guests of Abraham,
when they entered unto him, saying,
'Peace!' He said, 'Behold, we are
afraid of you.' They said, 'Be not
afraid; behold, we give thee good tidings
of a cunning boy.' He said, 'What,
do you give me good tidings, though
old age has smitten me? Of what do you
55   give me good tidings?' They said, 'We
give thee good tidings of truth. Be not
of those that despair.' He said, 'And who
despairs of the mercy of his Lord,
excepting those that are astray?'
He said, 'And what is your business,
envoys?' They said, 'We have been sent
unto a people of sinners, excepting
the folk of Lot; them we shall deliver
60   all together, excepting his wife—
we have decreed, she shall surely be
of those that tarry.' So, when the envoys
came to the folk of Lot, he said,
'Surely you are a people unknown to me!'
They said, 'Nay, but we have brought thee
that concerning which they were doubting.
We have come to thee with the truth,
and assuredly we speak truly.
65   So set forth, thou with thy family,
in a watch of the night, and follow
after the backs of them, and let not

any one of you turn round; and depart
unto the place you are commanded.'
And We decreed for him that commandment,
that the last remnant of those should be
cut off in the morning. And the people
of the city came rejoicing. He said,
'These are my guests; put me not to shame,
and fear God, and do not degrade me.'
70 They said, 'Have we not forbidden thee all
beings?' He said, 'These are my daughters,
if you would be doing.' By thy life,
they wandered blindly in their dazzlement,
and the Cry seized them at the sunrise,
and We turned it uppermost nethermost
and rained on it stones of baked clay.
75 Surely in that are signs for such as mark;
surely it is on a way yet remaining;
surely in that is a sign for believers.

Certainly the dwellers in the Thicket were evildoers,
and We took vengeance on them. The two of them were
upon a roadway manifest.

80 The dwellers in El-Hijr cried lies
to the Envoys. We brought them Our
signs, and they turned away from them.
They were hewing the mountains into
houses, therein dwelling securely;
and the Cry seized them in the morning;
that they earned did not avail them.

85 We created not the heavens and the earth, and all
that is between them, save in truth. Surely the Hour
is coming; so pardon thou, with a gracious pardoning.
Surely thy Lord, He is the All-creator, the All-knowing.

We have given thee seven of the oft-repeated,
and the mighty Koran.

Stretch not thine eyes to that We have given
    pairs of them to enjoy;
and do not sorrow for them, and lower thy wing
    unto the believers,
and say, 'Surely, I am the manifest warner.'
90   So We sent it down
to the partitioners, who have broken the Koran
    into fragments.
Now by thy Lord, We shall surely question them
    all together
concerning that they were doing. So shout that
    thou art commanded
and turn thou away from the idolaters.
95   We suffice thee
against the mockers, even against those who
    set up with God
another god. Certainly they will soon know!
    We know indeed
thy breast is straitened by the things they say.

Proclaim thy Lord's praise,
and be of those that bow,
and serve thy Lord, until
the Certain comes to thee.

XVI

THE BEE

In the Name of God, the Merciful, the Compassionate

> God's command comes;
> so seek not to hasten it.
> Glory be to Him!

High be He exalted above that they associate with Him!
He sends down the angels with the Spirit of His command
upon whomsoever He will among His servants, saying:

> Give you warning
> that there is no God but I;
> so fear you Me!

He created the heavens and the earth in truth;
high be He exalted above that they associate with Him!
He created man of a sperm-drop; and, behold,
he is a manifest adversary. And the cattle—
5   He created them for you; in them is warmth, and uses
various, and of them you eat, and there is beauty
in them for you, when you bring them home to rest
and when you drive them forth abroad to pasture;
and they bear your loads unto a land that you
never would reach, excepting with great distress.
Surely your Lord is All-clement, All-compassionate.
And horses, and mules, and asses, for you to ride,
and as an adornment; and He creates what you know not.

> God's it is to show the way;
> and some do swerve from it.
> If He willed, He would have
> guided you all together.

10   It is He who sends down to you out of heaven water
      of which you have to drink,

and of which trees, for you to pasture your herds,
      and thereby He brings forth
for you crops, and olives, and palms, and vines,
      and all manner of fruit.
Surely in that is a sign for a people who reflect.
And He subjected to you the night and day, and
the sun and moon; and the stars are subjected
      by His command.
Surely in that are signs for a people who understand.
And that which He has multiplied for you in the earth
      of diverse hues.
Surely in that is a sign for a people who remember.
It is He who subjected to you the sea, that you
      may eat of it
fresh flesh, and bring forth out of it ornaments
      for you to wear;
and thou mayest see the ships cleaving through it;
      and that you may seek
of His bounty, and so haply you will be thankful.
15   And He cast on the earth firm mountains, lest it
      shake with you,
and rivers and ways; so haply you will be guided;
and waymarks; and by the stars they are guided.
      Is He who creates as
he who does not create? Will you not remember?
If you count God's blessing, you will never number it;
surely God is All-forgiving, All-compassionate.

    And God knows what you keep secret
      and what you publish.
20   And those they call upon, apart from God,
created nothing, and themselves are created,
dead, not alive, and are not aware when
      they shall be raised.

    Your God is One God.
And they who believe not in the world to come,
their hearts deny, and they have waxed proud.
    Without a doubt God

knows what they keep secret
and what they publish;
He loves not those that wax proud.
And when it is said to them, 'What has your
Lord sent down?' they say, 'Fairy-tales
of the ancients.'
That they may bear their loads complete
on the Day of Resurrection, and some of
the loads of those that they lead astray
without any knowledge. O evil the
load they bear!

Those that were before them contrived; then God
came upon their building from the foundations,
and the roof fell down on them from over them,
and the chastisement came upon them from whence
they were not aware.

Then on the Day of Resurrection He will degrade them,
saying, 'Where are My associates concerning which you
made a breach together?' Those that were given the
knowledge will say, 'Degradation today and evil
are on the unbelievers, whom the angels take while
still they are wronging themselves.' Then they will offer
surrender: 'We were doing nothing evil.' 'Nay;
but surely God has knowledge of the things you did.
So enter the gates of Gehenna, there to dwell forever.'
Evil is the lodging of those that wax proud. And
it shall be said to the godfearing, 'What has your
Lord sent down?' They will say, 'Good! For those
who do good in this world good; and surely the abode
of the world to come is better; excellent is the abode
of the godfearing—Gardens of Eden they shall enter,
underneath which rivers flow, wherein they shall have
all they will. So God recompenses the godfearing, whom
the angels take while they are goodly, saying, 'Peace
be on you! Enter Paradise for that you were doing.'

Do they look for aught but that the angels

shall come to them, or thy Lord's command
shall come? So did those before them, and God
wronged them not, but themselves they wronged.
So the evil things that they wrought
smote them, and they were encompassed by
      that they mocked at.

The idolators say, 'If God had willed
we would not have served, apart from Him,
anything, neither we nor our fathers,
nor would we have forbidden, apart from Him,
anything.' So did those before them; yet
is aught for the Messengers, but to deliver
      the manifest Message?
Indeed, We sent forth among every nation
a Messenger, saying: 'Serve you God,
and eschew idols.' Then some of them
God guided, and some were justly disposed
to error. So journey in the land,
and behold how was the end of them
      that cried lies.
Though thou art ever so eager to guide them,
God guides not those whom He leads astray;
      they have no helpers.

40   They have sworn by God the most earnest oaths
God will never raise up him who dies; nay,
it is a promise binding upon Him, but
      most men know not,
so that He may make clear to them that
whereon they were at variance, 'and that
the unbelievers may know that they
      were truly liars.
The only words We say to a thing, when We
desire it, is that We say to it 'Be,'
      and it is.
And those that emigrated in God's cause
after they were wronged—We shall surely
lodge them in this world in a goodly lodging,
and the wage of the world to come is greater,

did they but know;
even such men as are patient, and put their
    trust in their Lord.

45   We sent not any before thee, except men
to whom We revealed: 'Question the people
of the Remembrance, if it should be that
    you do not know'—
with the clear signs, and the Psalms; and
We have sent down to thee the Remembrance
that thou mayest make clear to mankind
what was sent down to them; and so haply
    they will reflect.

Do they feel secure, those who devise
evil things, that God will not cause the earth
to swallow them, or that the chastisement
will not come upon them, from whence
    they are not aware?
Or that He will not seize them in their
going to and fro, and they will not be able
    to frustrate Him?
Or that He will not seize them, little by little
destroying them? Surely thy Lord is All-clement,
    All-compassionate.

50   Have they not regarded all things that God has created
casting their shadows to the right and to the left,
bowing themselves before God in all lowliness?
To God bows everything in the heavens, and every
creature crawling on the earth, and the angels.
They have not waxed proud; they fear their Lord
above them, and they do what they are commanded.

    God says:
    'Take not to you two gods.
    He is only One God;
    so have awe of Me.'

To Him belongs all that is in the heavens and earth;
His is the religion for ever. Then
will you fear other than God?
55   Whatsoever blessing you have, it comes from God;
then when affliction visits you
it is unto Him that you groan.
Then, when He removes the affliction from you,
lo, a party of you assign
associates to their Lord,
that they may show unthankfulness for that We have
given them. So take your joy;
certainly you will soon know!
And they appoint a share of that We have provided
them to what they know not.
By God, you shall be questioned
as to that you forged. And they assign to God
daughters; glory be to Him!—
and they have their desire;
60   and when any of them is given the good tidings of
a girl, his face is darkened
and he chokes inwardly, as
he hides him from the people because of the evil
of the good tidings that
have been given unto him,
whether he shall preserve it in humiliation, or
trample it into the dust.
Ah, evil is that they judge!

Those who believe not in the world to come, theirs
is the evil likeness; God's is the loftiest likeness;
He is the All-mighty, the All-wise.
If God should take men to task for their evildoing, He
would not leave on the earth one creature that crawls;
but He is deferring
them to a term stated; and when their term is come
they shall not put it back by a single hour
nor put it forward.

They assign to God that they themselves dislike;

and their tongues describe
falsehood, that the reward
most fair shall be theirs. Without any doubt
theirs shall be the Fire,
and they are hastened in.
65 By God, assuredly We sent Messengers to nations
before thee, but Satan
decked out fair to them
their deeds; he is their protector today, and
there yet awaits them
a painful chastisement.
And We have not sent down upon thee the Book
except that thou mayest
make clear to them that
whereon they were at variance, and as a guidance
and as a mercy to
a people who believe.

And it is God who sends down out of heaven water,
and therewith revives the
earth after it is dead.
Surely in that is a sign for a people who have ears.
And surely in the cattle there is a lesson for you;
We give you to drink of
what is in their bellies,
between filth and blood, pure milk, sweet to drinkers.
And of the fruits of the palms and the vines, you take
therefrom an intoxicant
and a provision fair.
Surely in that is a sign for a people who understand.
70 And thy Lord revealed unto the bees, saying:
'Take unto yourselves,
of the mountains, houses,
and of the trees, and of what they are building.
Then eat of all manner of fruit, and follow
the ways of your Lord
easy to go upon.'
Then comes there forth out of their bellies a drink
of diverse hues wherein

is healing for men.
Surely in that is a sign for a people who reflect.

God created you; then He will gather you
to Him; and some of you will be kept back
unto the vilest state of life, that after
knowing somewhat, they may know nothing;
    God is All-knowing, All-powerful.
And God has preferred some of you over others
in provision; but those that were preferred
shall not give over their provision
to that their right hands possess, so that
they may be equal therein. What, and do they
        deny God's blessing?
God has appointed for you of yourselves wives,
and He has appointed for you of your wives
sons and grandsons, and He has provided you
of the good things. What, do they believe
in vanity, and do they disbelieve
        in God's blessing?
75   And do they serve, apart from God,
that which has no power to provide them
anything from the heavens and the earth
        and can do nothing?
So strike not any similitudes for God;
        surely God knows,
        and you know not.

God has struck a similitude: a servant
possessed by his master, having no power
        over anything,
and one whom We have provided of Ourselves
with a provision fair, and he expends of it
        secretly and openly.
Are they equal? Praise belongs to God! Nay,
        most of them know not.
God has struck a similitude: two men,
one of them dumb, having no power over
anything, and he is a burden upon his

master—wherever he despatches him,
    he brings no good.
Is he equal to him who bids to justice, and is
    on a straight path?

To God belongs the Unseen in the heavens
    and in the earth.
And the matter of the Hour is as a twinkling of
    the eye, or nearer.
Surely God is powerful over everything.

80   And it is God who brought you forth,
       knowing nothing, from your mothers' wombs,
    and He appointed for you hearing,
       and sight, and hearts,
    that haply so you will be thankful.

Have they not regarded the birds, that are subjected
    in the air of heaven?
    Naught holds them but God;
surely in that are signs for a people who believe.

And it is God who has appointed
    a place of rest
for you of your houses, and He has
    appointed for you
of the skins of the cattle houses
    you find light
on the day that you journey, and on
    the day you abide,
and of their wool, and of their fur,
    and of their hair
furnishing and an enjoyment for a while.
And it is God who has appointed
    for you coverings
of the things He created, and He has
    appointed for you
of the mountains refuges, and He has
    appointed for you

shirts to protect you from the heat, and
    shirts to protect
you from your own violence. Even so He
    perfects His blessing
upon you, that haply you will surrender.
    So, if they turn
their backs, thine it is only to deliver
    the manifest Message.

85   They recognize the blessing of God,
    then they deny it,
and the most of them are the unthankful.

And the day We shall raise up from every nation a witness,
then to the unbelievers no leave shall be given, nor shall they
be suffered to make amends. And when the evildoers behold
the chastisement, it shall not be lightened for them, and no
respite shall be given them. And when the idolaters behold
their associates, they shall say, 'Our Lord, these are our
associates on whom we called apart from Thee.' They will fling
back at them the saying, 'Surely, you are truly liars."
And they will offer God surrender that day, and there shall go
90 astray from them that they were forging. Those that disbelieve
and bar from the way of God—them We shall give increase of
chastisement upon chastisement, for that they were doing
corruption. And the day We shall raise up from every nation
a witness against them from amongst them, and We shall bring
    thee as a witness against those.

And We have sent down on thee the Book
making clear everything, and as a guidance
and a mercy, and as good tidings to
    those who surrender.
Surely God bids to justice and good-doing
and giving to kinsmen; and He forbids
indecency, dishonour, and insolence,
admonishing you, so that haply
    you will remember.
Fulfil God's covenant, when you make

covenant, and break not the oaths
after they have been confirmed, and you
have made God your surety; surely God knows
    the things you do.
And be not as a woman who breaks
her thread, after it is firmly spun,
into fibres, by taking your oaths
as mere mutual deceit, one nation being
more numerous than another nation. God
only tries you thereby; and certainly
He will make clear to you upon the
Day of Resurrection that whereon you
    were at variance.

95   If God had willed, He would have made you
one nation; but He leads astray
whom He will, and guides whom He will;
and you will surely be questioned about
    the things you wrought.
Take not your oaths as mere mutual
deceit, lest any foot should slip after
it has stood firm, and you should taste
evil, for that you barred from the way
of God, and lest there should await you
    a mighty chastisement.
And do not sell the covenant of God
for a small price; surely what is
with God—that is better for you,
    did you but know.
What is with you comes to an end, but
what is with God abides; and surely
We shall recompense those who were patient
their wage, according to the best
    of what they did.
And whosoever does a righteous deed,
be it male or female, believing, We
shall assuredly give him to live a
goodly life; and We shall recompense them
their wage, according to the best
    of what they did.

100 When thou recitest the Koran, seek refuge in God
   from the accursed Satan; he has
no authority over those who believe and trust
   in their Lord; his authority
is over those who take him for their friend
   and ascribe associates to God.

And when We exchange a verse
in the place of another verse—
and God knows very well
what He is sending down—
they say, 'Thou art a mere
forger!' Nay, but the most
of them have no knowledge.
Say: 'The Holy Spirit
sent it down from thy Lord
in truth, and to confirm
those who believe, and to be
a guidance and good tidings
to those who surrender.'

105 And We know very well that
they say, 'Only a mortal
is teaching him.' The speech
of him at whom they hint
is barbarous; and this is
speech Arabic, manifest.

Those that believe not in the signs of God
God will not guide; there awaits them
   a painful chastisement.
They only forge falsehood, who believe
not in the signs of God, and those—
   they are the liars.
Whoso disbelieves in God, after
he has believed—excepting him
who has been compelled, and his heart
is still at rest in his belief—
but whosoever's breast is expanded
in unbelief, upon them shall rest

anger from God, and there awaits them
 a mighty chastisement;
that, because they have preferred
the present life over the world to come,
and that God guides not the people
 of the unbelievers.
110 Those—God has set a seal on their
hearts, and their hearing, and their eyes,
and those—they are the heedless ones;
without a doubt, in the world to come they
 will be the losers.
Then, surely thy Lord—unto those
who have emigrated after persecution,
then struggled and were patient—surely
thy Lord thereafter is All-forgiving,
 All-compassionate.

The day that every soul shall come disputing in its
own behalf; and every soul shall be paid in full
for what it wrought, and they shall not be wronged.

God has struck a similitude: a city
that was secure, at rest, its provision
coming to it easefully from every place,
then it was unthankful for the blessings
of God; so God let it taste the garment
of hunger and of fear, for the things
 that they were working.
There came indeed to them a Messenger from
amongst them, but they cried him lies; so
they were seized by the chastisement while
 they were evildoers.

115 So eat of what God has provided you
lawful and good; and be you thankful
for the blessing of God, if it be
 Him that you serve.
These things only He has forbidden you:
carrion, blood, the flesh of swine,

what has been hallowed to other than God.
Yet whoso is constrained, not desiring
nor transgressing, God is All-forgiving,
    All-compassionate.
And do not say, as to what your tongues
falsely describe, 'This is lawful, and
this is forbidden,' so that you may
forge against God falsehood; surely
those who forge against God falsehood
    shall not prosper.
A little enjoyment, then for them awaits
    a painful chastiṣement.
And those of Jewry—We have forbidden
them what We related to thee before,
and We wronged them not, but they
    wronged themselves.

120 Then, surely thy Lord—unto those who
did evil in igrɔrance, then repented
after that and put things right—surely
thy Lord thereafter is All-forgiving,
    All-compassionate.

Surely, Abraham was a nation
obedient unto God, a man of pure faith
    and no idolater,
showing thankfulness for His blessings;
He chose him, and He guided him
    to a straight path.
And We gave him in this world good,
and in the world to come he shall be
    among the righteous.
Then We revealed to thee: 'Follow thou
the creed of Abraham, a man of pure faith
    and no idolater.'

125 The Sabbath was only appointed for those
who were at variance thereon; surely
thy Lord will decide between them
on the Day of Resurrection, touching
    their differences.

Call thou to the way of thy Lord
with wisdom and good admonition,
   and dispute with them
   in the better way.
Surely thy Lord knows very well
those who have gone astray from
His way, and He knows very well
   those who are guided.
And if you chastise, chastise
even as you have been chastised;
   and yet assuredly
   if you are patient,
better it is for those patient.
   And be patient;
yet is thy patience only with
   the help of God.
   And do not sorrow
for them, nor be thou straitened
for what they devise. Surely
   God is with those
who are godfearing, and those
   who are good-doers.

XVII

THE NIGHT JOURNEY

In the Name of God, the Merciful, the Compassionate

Glory be to Him, who carried His servant by night
from the Holy Mosque to the Further Mosque
the precincts of which We have blessed,
that We might show him some of Our signs.
He is the All-hearing, the All-seeing.

And We gave Moses the Book, and made it
a guidance to the Children of Israel:
'Take not unto yourselves any guardian
      apart from Me.'
The seed of those We bore with Noah; he was
      a thankful servant.
And We decreed for the Children of Israel
in the Book: 'You shall do corruption
in the earth twice, and you shall ascend
      exceeding high.'
So, when the promise of the first of these
came to pass, We sent against you servants
of Ours, men of great might, and they went
through the habitations, and it was a
      promise performed.
Then We gave back to you the turn to
prevail over them, and We succoured you
with wealth and children, and We made you
      a greater host.
'If you do good, it is your own souls
you do good to, and if you do evil
it is to them likewise.' Then, when
the promise of the second came to pass,
We sent against you Our servants
to discountenance you, and to enter the
Temple, as they entered it the first time,

5

and to destroy utterly that which they
    ascended to.
Perchance your Lord will have mercy upon
you; but if you return, We shall return;
and We have made Gehenna a prison for
    the unbelievers.

Surely this Koran guides to the way that is straightest
    and gives good tidings to the believers
10   who do deeds of righteousness, that theirs
        shall be a great wage,
and that those who do not believe in the
world to come—we have prepared for them
    a painful chastisement.

Man prays for evil, as he prays for good;
    man is ever hasty.
We have appointed the night and the day
as two signs; then We have blotted out
the sign of the night, and made the sign
of the day to see, and that you may seek
bounty from your Lord, and that you may know
the number of the years, and the reckoning;
and everything We have distinguished
    very distinctly.
And every man—We have fastened to him
his bird of omen upon his neck; and We
shall bring forth for him, on the Day
of Resurrection, a book he shall find
    spread wide open.
15   'Read thy book! Thy soul suffices thee
this day as a reckoner against thee.'
Whosoever is guided, is only guided
to his own gain, and whosoever goes
astray, it is only to his own loss;
no soul laden bears the load of another.
We never chastise, until We send forth
    a Messenger.

And when We desire to destroy a city, We
command its men who live at ease, and they
commit ungodliness therein, then the Word
is realized against it, and We destroy
     it utterly.
How many generations We have destroyed
after Noah! Thy Lord suffices as one
who is aware of and sees the sins of
     His servants.
Whosoever desires this hasty world,
We hasten for him therein what We will
unto whomsoever We desire; then
We appoint for him Gehenna
wherein he shall roast, condemned
     and rejected.
And whosoever desires the world to come
and strives after it as he should,
being a believer—those, their striving
     shall be thanked.
Each We succour, these and those, from
thy Lord's gift; and thy Lord's gift
     is not confined.
Behold, how We prefer some of them
over others! And surely the world
to come is greater in ranks, greater
     in preferment.

20

     Set not up with God
     another god, or thou
     wilt sit condemned
     and forsaken.
     Thy Lord has decreed
     you shall not serve
     any but Him,
and to be good to parents,
whether one or both of them
attains old age with thee;
     say not to them 'Fie'
     neither chide them, but

speak unto them words
respectful,
25   and lower to them the
wing of humbleness
out of mercy and say,
  'My Lord,
have mercy upon them,
as they raised me up
when I was little.'
Your Lord knows very well what is in your hearts
if you are righteous,
for He is All-forgiving to those who are penitent.
And give the kinsman his right,
and the needy, and the traveller;
and never squander;
the squanderers are brothers of
Satan, and Satan is unthankful
to his Lord.
30   But if thou turnest from them,
seeking mercy from thy Lord that
thou hopest for, then speak unto
them gentle words.
And keep not thy hand chained
to thy neck, nor outspread it
widespread altogether, or thou
wilt sit reproached
and denuded.
Surely thy Lord outspreads and straitens His provision
unto whom He will;
surely He is aware of and sees His servants.

And slay not your children for fear of poverty;
We will provide for you and them;
surely the slaying of them is a grievous sin.
And approach not fornication;
surely it is an indecency, and evil as a way.
35   And slay not the soul God has
forbidden, except by right. Whosoever is slain
unjustly, We have appointed to

his next-of-kin authority; but let him not exceed
in slaying; he shall be helped.

And do not approach the property of the orphan
save in the fairest manner, until he is of age.
And fulfil the covenant; surely the covenant
    shall be questioned of.
And fill up the measure when you measure, and
weigh with the straight balance; that is better
    and fairer in the issue.
And pursue not that thou hast no knowledge of;
the hearing, the sight, the heart—all of those
    shall be questioned of.
And walk not in the earth exultantly; certainly
thou wilt never tear the earth open, nor attain
    the mountains in height.
40   All of that—the wickedness of it is hateful
    in the sight of thy Lord.

That is of the wisdom thy Lord has revealed to thee:
        set not up with God
        another god, or thou
        wilt be cast into
        Gehenna, reproached
            and rejected.

What, has your Lord favoured you with sons
and taken to Himself from the angels
females? Surely it is a monstrous thing
        you are saying!
We have turned about in this Koran, that
they may remember; and it increases them
        only in aversion.
Say: 'If there had been other gods with Him,
as they say, in that case assuredly
they would have sought a way unto the
        Lord of the Throne.'
        Glory be to Him!

45   High indeed be He exalted above that they say!
The seven heavens and the earth, and whosoever
in them is, extol Him; nothing is, that does not
proclaim His praise, but you do not understand their
extolling. Surely He is All-clement, All-forgiving.

When thou recitest the Koran, We place
between thee, and those who do not
believe in the world to come, a curtain
        obstructing,
and We lay veils upon their hearts
lest they understand it, and in their ears
        heaviness.
And when thou mentionest thy Lord only
in the Koran, they turn in their traces
        in aversion.

50   We know very well how they listen
when they listen to thee, and when
they conspire, when the evildoers
say, 'You are only following a man
        bewitched!'
Behold, how they strike similitudes
for thee, and go astray, and cannot
        find a way!
They say, 'What, when we are bones
and broken bits, shall we really
be raised up again in a new
        creation?'
Say: 'Let you be stones, or iron,
or some creation yet more monstrous
in your minds!' Then they will say,
'Who will bring us back?' Say: 'He
who originated you the first time.'
Then they will shake their heads at thee,
and they will say, 'When will it be?'
Say: 'It is possible that it may
        be nigh,
on the day when He will call you, and
you will answer praising Him, and

you will think you have but tarried
    a little.'

55   And say to My servants, that they say
words that are kindlier. For surely
Satan provokes strife between them,
and Satan is ever a manifest
       foe to man.
Your Lord knows you very well;
if He will, He will have mercy on you,
or, if He will, He will chastise you.
We sent thee not to be a guardian
       over them.
And thy Lord knows very well all
who are in the heavens and the earth;
and We have preferred some Prophets
over others; and We gave to David
       Psalms.

Say: 'Call on those you asserted
apart from Him; they have no power
to remove affliction from you, or to
       transfer it.'
Those they call upon are themselves
seeking the means to come to their Lord,
which of them shall be nearer; they hope
for His mercy, and fear His chastisement.
Surely thy Lord's chastisement is a thing
       to beware of.

60   No city is there, but We shall destroy it
before the Day of Resurrection, or
We shall chastise it with a terrible
chastisement; that is in the Book
       inscribed.

Naught prevented Us from sending the signs
but that the ancients cried lies to them;
and We brought Thamood the She-camel
visible, but they did her wrong.

And We do not send the signs, except
to frighten.
And when We said to thee, 'Surely
thy Lord encompasses men,' and We made
the vision that We showed thee and the
tree cursed in the Koran to be only
a trial for men; and We frighten them,
but it only increases them in great
insolence.
And when We said to the angels, 'Bow
yourselves to Adam'; so they bowed
themselves, save Iblis; he said, 'Shall I
bow myself unto one Thou hast created
of clay?'
He said, 'What thinkest Thou? This whom
Thou hast honoured above me—if Thou
deferrest me to the Day of Resurrection
I shall assuredly master his seed,
save a few.'

65　　　Said He, 'Depart! Those of them
that follow thee—surely Gehenna
shall be your recompense, an ample
recompense!
And startle whomsoever of them thou
canst with thy voice; and rally
against them thy horsemen and thy foot,
and share with them in their wealth
and their children, and promise them!'
But Satan promises them naught, except
delusion.
'Surely over My servants thou shalt have
no authority.' Thy Lord suffices as
a guardian.

Your Lord it is who drives for you the ships on the sea
that you may seek His bounty; surely
He is All-compassionate towards you.
And when affliction visits you upon the sea, then
there go astray those on whom you call

except Him; and when He delivers you
to land, you turn away; man is ever unthankful.
70   Do you feel secure that He will not
cause the shore to swallow you up,
or loose against you a squall of pebbles, then
you will find no guardian for you?
Or do you feel secure that He will
not send you back into it a second time, and loose
against you a hurricane of wind and
drown you for your thanklessness,
then you will find no prosecutor for you against Us?

We have honoured the Children of Adam
and carried them on land and sea,
and provided them with good things,
and preferred them greatly over many of
those We created.
On the day when We shall call all men
with their record, and whoso is given his
book in his right hand—those shall read
their book, and they shall not be wronged
a single date-thread.
And whosoever is blind in this world
shall be blind in the world to come,
and he shall be even further astray
from the way.
75   Indeed they were near to seducing thee
from that We revealed to thee, that thou
mightest forge against Us another, and
then they would surely have taken thee
as a friend;
and had We not confirmed thee, surely
thou wert near to inclining unto them
a very little;
then would We have let thee taste the double
of life and the double of death; and then
thou wouldst have found none to help thee
against Us.
Indeed they were near to startling thee

from the land, to expel thee from it,
and then they would have tarried after thee
    only a little—
the wont of those We sent before thee of
Our Messengers; thou wilt find no change
    to Our wont.

80   Perform the prayer
at the sinking of the sun to the darkening of the night
    and the recital of dawn;
    surely the recital of dawn is witnessed.
        And as for the night,
keep vigil a part of it, as a work of supererogation for thee;
    it may be that thy Lord will
    raise thee up to a laudable station.
        And say: 'My Lord,
lead me in with a just ingoing, and lead me out with a
    just outgoing; grant me
    authority from Thee, to help me.'
        And say:
'The truth has come, and falsehood has vanished away;
    surely falsehood
    is ever certain to vanish.'

    And We send down, of the Koran,
    that which is a healing and a mercy
    to the believers; and the unbelievers
    it increases not, except in loss.
85   And when We bless man, he turns
    away, and withdraws aside; but when
    evil visits him, he is in despair.
    Say: 'Every man works according to
    his own manner; but your Lord knows
    very well what man is best guided
        as to the way.'

    They will question thee concerning
    the Spirit. Say: 'The Spirit is of
    the bidding of my Lord. You have

been given of knowledge nothing
except a little.'

If We willed, We could take away that
We have revealed to thee, then thou
wouldst find none thereover to guard
      thee against Us,
excepting by some mercy of thy Lord;
surely His favour to thee is great.
90   Say: 'If men and jinn banded together
to produce the like of this Koran,
they would never produce its like,
not though they backed one another.'
We have indeed turned about for men
in this Koran every manner of
similitude; yet most men refuse all
      but unbelief.
They say, 'We will not believe thee till
thou makest a spring to gush forth from
      the earth for us,
or till thou possessest a garden
of palms and vines, and thou makest
rivers to gush forth abundantly
      all amongst it,
or till thou makest heaven to fall,
as thou assertest, on us in fragments,
or thou bringest God and the angels
      as a surety,
95   or till thou possessest a house of gold
ornament, or till thou goest up into
heaven; and we will not believe thy
going up till thou bringest down on us
a book that we may read. Say: 'Glory be
to my Lord! Am I aught but a mortal,
      a Messenger?'
And naught prevented men from believing
when the guidance came to them, but that
they said, 'Has God sent forth a mortal
      as Messenger?'

Say: 'Had there been in the earth angels
walking at peace, We would have sent down
upon them out of heaven an angel
     as Messenger.'
Say: 'God suffices as a witness between me
and you; surely He is aware of and sees
     His servants.'

Whomsoever God guides,
    he is rightly guided;
and whom He leads astray—
    thou wilt not find for them
    protectors, apart from Him.
And We shall muster them
on the Resurrection Day
    upon their faces,
    blind, dumb, deaf;
their refuge shall be Gehenna,
and whensoever it abates
We shall increase for them
    the Blaze.
100   That is their recompense
because they disbelieved in
    Our signs
and said, 'What, when we are bones
and broken bits, shall we really
be raised up again in a new
    creation?'
Have they not seen that God,
who created the heavens
and earth, is powerful to
create the like of them?
He has appointed for them
a term, no doubt of it;
yet the unbelievers refuse
    all but unbelief.
Say: 'If you possessed the
treasuries of my Lord's
mercy, yet would you

hold back for fear of
expending; and man is
ever niggardly.'

And We gave Moses nine signs,
clear signs. Ask the Children of Israel
when he came to them, and Pharaoh
said to him, 'Moses, I think thou art
bewitched.'
He said, 'Indeed thou knowest that none
sent these down, except the Lord
of the heavens and earth, as clear
proofs; and, Pharaoh, I think thou art
accursed.'
105 . He desired to startle them from the land;
and We drowned him and those with him, all
together.
And We said to the Children of Israel
after him, 'Dwell in the land; and
when the promise of the world to come
comes to pass, We shall bring you
a rabble.'

With the truth We have sent it down,
and with the truth it has come down;
and We have sent thee not, except
good tidings to bear, and warning;
and a Koran We have divided,
for thee to recite it to mankind
at intervals, and We have sent it down
successively.
Say: 'Believe in it, or believe not;
those who were given the knowledge before it
when it is recited to them, fall down
upon their faces prostrating, and say,
"Glory be to our Lord! Our Lord's promise is
performed."
And they fall down upon their faces

weeping; and it increases them in
    humility.'
110   Say: 'Call upon God, or call upon
the Merciful; whichsoever you call
upon, to Him belong the Names Most
    Beautiful.'

And be thou not loud in thy prayer,
    nor hushed therein,
but seek thou for a way between that.
    And say:
'Praise belongs to God, who has not
    taken to Him a son,
and who has not any associate in the
    Kingdom,
nor any protector out of humbleness.'
    And magnify Him
      with repeated magnificats.

XVIII

THE CAVE

In the Name of God, the Merciful, the Compassionate

Praise belongs to God
who has sent down upon His servant the Book
and has not assigned unto it any
crookedness;
right, to warn of great violence
from Him, and to give good tidings
unto the believers, who do righteous deeds,
that theirs shall be a goodly wage
therein to abide for
ever,
and to warn those who say, 'God has taken to Himself
a son';
they have no knowledge of it, they
nor their fathers; a monstrous word
it is, issuing out of their mouths;
they say nothing but a lie.

5   Yet perchance, if they believe not
in this tiding, thou wilt consume
thyself, following after them, of
grief.
We have appointed all that is on the earth
for an adornment for it, and that We may
try which of them is fairest in
works;
and We shall surely make all that is on it
barren dust.

Or dost thou think the Men of the Cave
and Er-Rakeem were among Our signs a
wonder?
When the youths took refuge in the Cave
saying, 'Our Lord, give us mercy from Thee,

and furnish us with rectitude in our
    affair.'

10   Then We smote their ears many years in
    the Cave.

Afterwards We raised them up again, that
We might know which of the two parties
would better calculate the while they had
    tarried.

We will relate to thee their tidings
truly. They were youths who believed
in their Lord, and We increased them in
    guidance.

And We strengthened their hearts, when
they stood up and said, 'Our Lord is
the Lord of the heavens and earth;
we will not call upon any god, apart
from Him, or then we had spoken
    outrage.

These our people have taken to them
other gods, apart from Him. Ah, if only
they would bring some clear authority
regarding them! But who does greater
evil than he who forges against God
    a lie?

15   So, when you have gone apart from them
and that they serve, excepting God,
take refuge in the Cave, and your Lord
will unfold to you of His mercy, and will
furnish you with a gentle issue of your
    affair.'

And thou mightest have seen the sun,
when it rose, inclining from their Cave
towards the right, and, when it set,
passing them by on the left, while they
were in a broad fissure of the Cave.
That was one of God's signs; whomsoever
God guides, he is rightly guided,
and whomsoever He leads astray, thou
wilt not find for him a protector to

direct.
Thou wouldst have thought them awake,
as they lay sleeping, while We turned them
now to the right, now to the left,
and their dog stretching its paws on
the threshold. Hadst thou observed them
surely thou wouldst have turned thy back on
them in flight, and been filled with terror
    of them.
And even so We raised them up again
that they might question one another.
One of them said, 'How long have you
tarried?' They said, 'We have tarried
a day, or part of a day.' They said,
'Your Lord knows very well how long
you have tarried. Now send one of you
forth with this silver to the city,
and let him look for which of them has
purest food, and bring you provision thereof;
let him be courteous, and apprise no man
    of you.
If they should get knowledge of you
they will stone you, or restore you to
their creed, then you will not prosper
    ever.'
20 And even so We made them stumble upon
them, that they might know that God's
promise is true, and that the Hour—
there is no doubt of it. When they were
contending among themselves of their affair
then they said, 'Build over them a
building; their Lord knows of them very well.'
Said those who prevailed over their affair,
'We will raise over them a place of
    worship.'
(They will say, 'Three; and their dog
was the fourth of them.' They will say,
'Five; and their dog was the sixth of them.'
guessing at the Unseen. They will say,

'Seven; and their dog was the eighth of them.'
Say: 'My Lord knows very well their
number, and none knows them, except
       a few.'
So do not dispute with them, except
in outward disputation, and ask not
any of them for a pronouncement
       on them.
And do not say, regarding anything,
'I am going to do that tomorrow,'
but only, 'If God will'; and mention
thy Lord, when thou forgettest, and say,
'It may be that my Lord will guide me
unto something nearer to rectitude
       than this.')
And they tarried in the Cave three
hundred years, and to that they added
       nine more.
25   Say: 'God knows very well how long
they tarried. To Him belongs the Unseen
in the heavens and in the earth.
How well He sees! How well He hears!
They have no protector, apart from Him,
and He associates in His government
       no one.'

Recite what has been revealed to thee of the Book of thy Lord;
no man can change His words. Apart from Him, thou wilt find
       no refuge.
And restrain thyself with those who call upon their Lord
at morning and evening, desiring His countenance,
and let not thine eyes turn away from them, desiring
the adornment of the present life; and obey not him
whose heart We have made neglectful of Our remembrance
so that he follows his own lust, and his affair has become
       all excess.
Say: 'The truth is from your Lord; so let whosoever will
believe, and let whosoever will disbelieve.' Surely We
have prepared for the evildoers a fire, whose pavilion

encompasses them; if they call for succour, they will be
succoured with water like molten copper, that shall
scald their faces—how evil a potion, and how evil a
resting-place!
Surely those who believe, and do deeds of righteousness—
surely We leave not to waste the wage of him who does
good works;

30 those—theirs shall be Gardens of Eden, underneath which
rivers flow; therein they shall be adorned with bracelets
of gold, and they shall be robed in green garments
of silk and brocade, therein reclining upon couches—
O, how excellent a reward! And O, how fair a
resting-place!

And strike for them a similitude:
two men.
To one of them We assigned two gardens of
vines, and surrounded them with palm-trees,
and between them We set a sown field;
each of the two gardens yielded its produce
and failed naught in any wise; and We
caused to gush amidst them a river.
So he
had fruit; and he said to his fellow,
as he was conversing with him, 'I have
more abundance of wealth than thou
and am mightier in respect of men.'
And he entered his garden, wronging
himself; he said, 'I do not think that
this will ever perish; I do not think
that the Hour is coming; and if I
am indeed returned to my Lord, I shall
surely find a better resort than this.'

35 Said his fellow,
as he was conversing with him, 'What,
disbelievest thou in Him who created
thee of dust, then of a sperm-drop,
then shaped thee as a man? But lo,
He is God, my Lord,

292

and I will not associate with my Lord
        any one.
Why, when thou wentest into thy garden,
didst thou not say, "As God will;
there is no power except in God"?
If thou seest me, that I am less
than thou in wealth and children, yet
it may be that my Lord will give me
better than thy garden, and loose on it
a thunderbolt out of heaven, so that
in the morning it will be a slope
        of dust,
or in the morning the water of it will
be sunk into the earth, so that thou
wilt not be able to seek it out.'
And his fruit was all encompassed,
and in the morning he was wringing
his hands for that he had expended
upon it, and it was fallen down upon
its trellises, and he was saying,
'Would I had not associated with my Lord
        any one!'
But there was no host to help him,
apart from God, and he was helpless.
Thereover protection belongs only to God
the True; He is best rewarding, best in
        the issue.

And strike for them the similitude of
        the present life:
it is as water that We send down
out of heaven, and the plants of
the earth mingle with it; and in
the morning it is straw the winds
scatter; and God is omnipotent over
        everything.

Wealth and sons are the adornment of the present world;
but the abiding things, the deeds of righteousness,

are better with God in reward, and better in hope.

45 And on the day We shall set the mountains in motion,
and thou seest the earth coming forth, and We muster them
so that We leave not so much as one of them behind;
and they shall be presented before their Lord in ranks—
'You have come to Us, as We created you upon the first time;
nay, you asserted We should not appoint for you a tryst.'
And the Book shall be set in place; and thou wilt see
the sinners fearful at what is in it, and saying,
'Alas for us! How is it with this Book, that it leaves
nothing behind, small or great, but it has numbered it?'
And they shall find all they wrought present, and thy Lord
       shall not wrong anyone.

      And when We said to the angels, 'Bow
      yourselves to Adam'; so they bowed
      themselves, save Iblis; he was one of
      the jinn, and committed ungodliness
      against his Lord's command. What,
      and do you take him and his seed
      to be your friends, apart from Me,
      and they an enemy to you? How evil
      is that exchange for the evildoers!
      I made them not witnesses of the
      creation of the heavens and earth,
      neither of the creation of themselves;
      I would not ever take those who lead
      others astray to be My supporters.

50 And on the day He shall say, 'Call on My associates whom
you asserted'; and then they shall call on them, but they
will not answer them, and We shall set a gulf between them.
Then the evildoers will see the Fire, and think that they
are about to fall into it, and will find no escape from it.

      We have indeed turned about for men
      in this Koran every manner of
      similitude; man is the most disputatious
        of things.

And naught prevented men from believing
when the guidance came unto them,
and seeking their Lord's forgiveness,
but that the wont of the ancients
should come upon them, or that the
chastisement should come upon them
   face to face.
And We send not the Envoys, but
good tidings to bear, and warning.
Yet do the unbelievers dispute
with falsehood, that they may rebut
thereby the truth. They have taken
My signs, and what they are warned of,
   in mockery.

55 And who does greater evil than he
who, being reminded of the signs
of his Lord, turns away from them and
forgets what his hands have forwarded?
Surely We have laid veils on their hearts
lest they understand it, and in their ears
   heaviness;
and though thou callest them to the
guidance, yet they will not be guided
   ever.
But thy Lord is the All-forgiving,
full of mercy. If He should take them
to task for that they have earned, He would
hasten for them the chastisement; but they
have a tryst, from which they will find no
   escape.
And those cities, We destroyed them when they
did evil, and appointed for their destruction
   a tryst.

And when Moses said to his page,
'I will not give up until I reach
the meeting of the two seas,
though I go on for many years.'
60 Then, when they reached their meeting,

they forgot their fish, and it took
its way into the sea, burrowing.
When they had passed over, he said
to his page, 'Bring us our breakfast;
indeed, we have encountered
weariness from this our journey.'
He said, 'What thinkest thou? When we
took refuge in the rock, then I
forgot the fish—and it was Satan
himself that made me forget it
so that I should not remember it—
and so it took its way into
the sea in a manner marvellous.'
Said he, 'This is what we were
seeking!' And so they returned
upon their tracks, retracing them.
Then they found one of Our servants
unto whom We had given mercy
from Us, and We had taught him
knowledge proceeding from Us.
65   Moses said to him, 'Shall I follow thee
so that thou teachest me, of what
thou hast been taught, right judgment?'
Said he, 'Assuredly thou wilt not
be able to bear with me patiently.
And how shouldst thou bear patiently
that thou hast never encompassed
in thy knowledge?' He said,
'Yet thou shalt find me, if God
will, patient; and I shall not
rebel against thee in anything.'
Said he, 'Then if thou followest
me, question me not on anything
until I myself introduce
the mention of it to thee.'
70   So they departed; until, when
they embarked upon the ship,
he made a hole in it. He said,
'What, hast thou made a hole in it

so as to drown its passengers? Thou
hast indeed done a grievous thing.'
Said he, 'Did I not say that thou
couldst never bear with me patiently?'
He said, 'Do not take me to task
that I forgot, neither constrain me
to do a thing too difficult.'
So they departed; until, when
they met a lad, he slew him.
He said, 'What, hast thou slain
a soul innocent, and that not to
retaliate for a soul slain? Thou
hast indeed done a horrible thing.'
Said he, 'Did I not say that thou
couldst never bear with me patiently?'
75 He said, 'If I question thee
on anything after this,
then keep me company no more;
thou hast already experienced
excuse sufficient on my part.'
So they departed; until, when
they reached the people of a city,
they asked the people for food,
but they refused to receive them
hospitably. There they found
a wall about to tumble down,
and so he set it up. He said,
'If thou hadst wished, thou couldst
have taken a wage for that.'
Said he, 'This is the parting between
me and thee. Now I will tell thee
the interpretation of that
thou couldst not bear patiently.
As for the ship, it belonged
to certain poor men, who toiled
upon the sea; and I desired
to damage it, for behind them
there was a king who was seizing
every ship by brutal force.

As for the lad, his parents were
believers; and we were afraid
he would impose on them insolence
80   and unbelief; so we desired
that their Lord should give to them
in exchange one better than he in
purity, and nearer in tenderness.
As for the wall, it belonged
to two orphan lads in the city,
and under it was a treasure
belonging to them. Their father
was a righteous man; and thy Lord
desired that they should come of age
and then bring forth their treasure
as a mercy from thy Lord. I
did it not of my own bidding.
This is the interpretation of that
thou couldst not bear patiently.'

They will question thee concerning
Dhool Karnain. Say: 'I will
recite to you a mention of him.'
We established him in the land,
and We gave him a way to everything;
          and he followed a way
until, when he reached the setting
of the sun, he found it setting
in a muddy spring, and he found
          nearby a people.
85   We said, 'O Dhool Karnain,
either thou shalt chastise them,
or thou shalt take towards them a
          way of kindness.'
He said, 'As for the evildoer,
him we shall chastise, then he
shall be returned to his Lord
and He shall chastise him with a
          horrible chastisement.
But as for him who believes, and

does righteousness, he shall receive
as recompense the reward most fair,
and we shall speak to him, of our
    command, easiness.'
Then he followed a way
until, when he reached the rising
of the sun, he found it rising
upon a people for whom We had
not appointed any veil to shade
    them from it.

90   So; and We encompassed in knowledge what
    was with him.
Then he followed a way
until, when he reached between the
two barriers, he found this side
of them a people scarcely able to
    understand speech.
They said, 'O Dhool Karnain, behold,
Gog and Magog are doing corruption
in the earth; so shall we assign
to thee a tribute, against thy setting
up a barrier between us and
    between them?'
He said, 'That wherein my Lord has
established me is better; so aid me
forcefully, and I will set up
a rampart between you and
    between them.

95   Bring me ingots of iron!' Until,
when he had made all level between
the two cliffs, he said, 'Blow!' Until,
when he had made it a fire, he said,
'Bring me, that I may pour molten
    brass on it.'
So they were unable either to scale it
    or pierce it.
He said, 'This is a mercy
    from my Lord.
But when the promise of my Lord

comes to pass, He will make it into
powder; and my Lord's promise
is ever true.'

Upon that day We shall leave them surging on one another,
and the Trumpet shall be blown, and We shall gather them
[together,
100 and upon that day We shall present Gehenna to the unbelievers
whose eyes were covered against My remembrance, and they
were not able to hear. What, do the unbelievers reckon
that they may take My servants as friends, apart from Me?
We have prepared Gehenna for the unbelievers' hospitality.

Say: 'Shall We tell you who will be
the greatest losers in their works?
Those whose striving goes astray
in the present life, while they think
that they are working good deeds.
105 Those are they that disbelieve in the
signs of their Lord and the encounter
with Him; their works have failed,
and on the Day of Resurrection We
shall not assign to them any weight.
That is their recompense—Gehenna
for that they were unbelievers and took
My signs and My messengers in mockery.
But those who believe, and do deeds
of righteousness—the Gardens of
Paradise shall be their hospitality,
therein to dwell forever,
desiring no removal out of them.'

Say: 'If the sea were ink
for the Words of my Lord,
the sea would be spent before the Words of my Lord are spent,
though We brought replenishment the like of it.'

110 Say: 'I am only a mortal
the like of you; it is revealed to me

300

that your God
is One God.
So let him, who hopes for
the encounter with his Lord,
work righteousness, and not associate with his Lord's service
anyone.'

XIX

MARY

In the Name of God, the Merciful, the Compassionate

Kaf Ha Ya Ain Sad

The mention of thy Lord's mercy
unto His servant Zachariah;
when he called upon his Lord
    secretly
saying, 'O my Lord, behold
the bones within me are feeble
and my head is all aflame with
    hoariness.
And in calling on Thee, my Lord,
I have never been hitherto
    unprosperous.

5   And now I fear my kinsfolk
after I am gone; and my wife
is barren. So give me, from Thee,
    a kinsman
who shall be my inheritor
and the inheritor of the House
of Jacob; and make him, my Lord,
    well-pleasing.'
'O Zachariah, We give thee
good tidings of a boy, whose name
    is John.
No namesake have We given him
    aforetime.'
He said, 'O my Lord, how
shall I have a son, seeing
my wife is barren, and I
have attained to the declining
    of old age?'

10   Said He, 'So it shall be; thy

Lord says, "Easy is that for
Me, seeing that I created
thee aforetime, when thou wast
    nothing." '
He said, 'Lord, appoint to me
some sign.' Said He, 'Thy sign
is that thou shalt not speak to
men, though being without fault,
    three nights.'
So he came forth unto his
people from the Sanctuary,
then he made signal to them,
'Give you glory at dawn and
    evening.'
'O John, take the Book forcefully';
and We gave him judgment, yet a
    little child,
and a tenderness from Us,
and purity; and he was
godfearing, and cherishing
his parents, not arrogant,
    rebellious.
15   'Peace be upon him, the day
he was born, and the day he
dies, and the day he is raised
    up alive!'

And mention in the Book Mary
when she withdrew from her people
    to an eastern place,
and she took a veil apart from them;
then We sent unto her Our Spirit
that presented himself to her
    a man without fault.
She said, 'I take refuge in
the All-merciful from thee!
    If thou fearest God. . . .'
He said, 'I am but a messenger
come from thy Lord, to give thee

a boy most pure.'

20 She said, 'How shall I have a son
whom no mortal has touched, neither
have I been unchaste?'
He said, 'Even so thy Lord has said:
"Easy is that for Me; and that We
may appoint him a sign unto men
and a mercy from Us; it is
a thing decreed."'
So she conceived him, and withdrew with him
to a distant place.
And the birthpangs surprised her by
the trunk of the palm-tree. She said,
'Would I had died ere this, and become
a thing forgotten!'
But the one that was below her
called to her, 'Nay, do not sorrow;
see, thy Lord has set below thee
a rivulet.

25 Shake also to thee the palm-trunk,
and there shall come tumbling upon thee
dates fresh and ripe.
Eat therefore, and drink, and be
comforted; and if thou shouldst see
any mortal,
say, "I have vowed to the All-merciful
a fast, and today I will not speak
to any man."'
Then she brought the child to her folk
carrying him; and they said,
'Mary, thou hast surely committed
a monstrous thing!
Sister of Aaron, thy father was not
a wicked man, nor was thy mother
a woman unchaste.'

30 Mary pointed to the child then;
but they said, 'How shall we speak
to one who is still in the cradle,
a little child?'

He said, 'Lo, I am God's servant;
God has given me the Book, and
     made me a Prophet.
Blessed He has made me, wherever
I may be; and He has enjoined me
to pray, and to give the alms, so
     long as I live,
and likewise to cherish my mother;
He has not made me arrogant,
     unprosperous.
Peace be upon me, the day I was born,
and the day I die, and the day I am
     raised up alive!'

35   That is Jesus, son of Mary,
in word of truth, concerning which
     they are doubting.
It is not for God to take a son
unto Him. Glory be to Him! When He
decrees a thing, He but says to it
     'Be,' and it is.
Surely God is my Lord, and your
Lord; so serve you Him. This is
     a straight path.

But the parties have fallen into variance among themselves;
then woe to those who disbelieve for the scene of a dreadful day.
How well they will hear and see on the day they come to Us!
But the evildoers even today are in error manifest.
40   Warn thou them of the day of anguish, when the matter
shall be determined, and they yet heedless and unbelieving.
Surely We shall inherit the earth and all that are upon it,
     and unto Us they shall be returned.

And mention in the Book Abraham;
surely he was a true man, a Prophet.
When he said to his father, 'Father,
why worshippest thou that which neither
hears nor sees, nor avails thee anything?
Father, there has come to me knowledge

such as came not to thee; so follow me,
and I will guide thee on a level path.
45 Father, serve not Satan; surely Satan
is a rebel against the All-merciful.
Father, I fear that some chastisement
from the All-merciful will smite thee,
so that thou becomest a friend to Satan.'
Said he, 'What, art thou shrinking
from my gods, Abraham? Surely, if thou
givest not over, I shall stone thee;
so forsake me now for some while.'
He said, 'Peace be upon thee!
I will ask my Lord to forgive thee;
surely He is ever gracious to me.
Now I will go apart from you
and that you call upon, apart from
God; I will call upon my Lord,
and haply I shall not be, in calling
upon my Lord, unprosperous.'
50 So, when he went apart from them
and that they were serving, apart
from God, We gave him Isaac and
Jacob, and each We made a Prophet;
and We gave them of Our mercy,
and We appointed unto them
a tongue of truthfulness, sublime.

And mention in the Book Moses;
he was devoted, and he was
    a Messenger, a Prophet.
We called to him from the right side
of the Mount, and We brought him
    near in communion.
And We gave him his brother Aaron, of
    Our mercy, a Prophet.

55 And mention in the Book Ishmael;
he was true to his promise, and he was
    a Messenger, a Prophet.

He bade his people to pray
and to give the alms, and he was
 pleasing to his Lord.

And mention in the Book Idris; he was
 a true man, a Prophet.
We raised him up to a high place.

These are they whom God has blessed
 among the Prophets
of the seed of Adam, and of those
We bore with Noah, and of the seed of
 Abraham and Israel,
and of those We guided and chose.
When the signs of the All-merciful were
 recited to them,
they fell down prostrate, weeping.

60 Then there succeeded after them a succession
who wasted the prayer, and followed lusts; so
 they shall encounter error
save him who repents, and believes, and
does a righteous deed; those—they shall
enter Paradise, and they shall not
 be wronged anything;
Gardens of Eden that the All-merciful
promised His servants in the Unseen; His
 promise is ever performed.
There they shall hear no idle talk, but only
'Peace.' There they shall have their provision
 at dawn and evening.
That is Paradise which We shall give
as an inheritance to those of Our servants
 who are godfearing.

65 We come not down, save at the commandment of thy Lord.
  To Him belongs
all that is before us, and all that is behind us, and all
  between that.

And thy Lord is never forgetful,
Lord He of the heavens and earth and all that is between them.
  So serve Him,
and be thou patient in His service; knowest thou any that
  can be named with His Name?

Man says, 'What, when I am dead
shall I then be brought forth alive?'
Will not man remember that We created
him aforetime, when he was nothing?
Now, by thy Lord, We shall surely muster them, and the Satans,
then We shall parade them about Gehenna hobbling on their
            [knees.

70 Then We shall pluck forth from every party whichever of them
was the most hardened in disdain of the All-merciful;
then We shall know very well those most deserving to burn
            [there.

Not one of you there is, but he
shall go down to it; that for thy Lord
is a thing decreed, determined.
Then We shall deliver those that were
godfearing; and the evildoers We shall
leave there, hobbling on their knees
When Our signs are recited to them
as clear signs, the unbelievers say
to the believers, 'Which of the two parties
is better in station, fairer in assembly?'
75 And how many a generation We
destroyed before them, who were fairer
in furnishing and outward show!
Say: 'Whosoever is in error, let the
All-merciful prolong his term for him!
Till, when they see that they were threatened,
whether the chastisement, or the Hour,
then they shall surely know who is worse
in place, and who is weaker in hosts.'

And God shall increase those who were guided in guidance;

and the abiding things, the deeds of righteousness,
are better with thy Lord in reward, and better in return.

80   Hast thou seen him who disbelieves
in Our signs and says, 'Assuredly
I shall be given wealth and children'?
What, has he observed the Unseen, or
taken a covenant with the All-merciful?
No, indeed! We shall assuredly
write down all that he says, and We shall
prolong for him the chastisement;
and We shall inherit from him that
he says, and he shall come to Us alone.

And they have taken to them other gods
apart from God, that they might be for them
    a might.
85   No, indeed! They shall deny their
service, and they shall be against them
    pitted.
Hast thou not seen how We sent the
Satans against the unbelievers, to
    prick them?
So hasten thou not against them;
We are only numbering for them a
    number.
On the day that We shall muster
the godfearing to the All-merciful
    with pomp
and drive the evildoers into Gehenna
    herding,
90   having no power of intercession, save
those who have taken with the All-merciful
    covenant.

And they say, 'The All-merciful
has taken unto Himself a son.'
You have indeed advanced something
    hideous!

The heavens are wellnigh rent of it
and the earth split asunder, and
the mountains wellnigh fall down
      crashing
for that they have attributed
to the All-merciful a son; and it
behoves not the All-merciful to take
      a son.

None is there in the heavens and earth
but he comes to the All-merciful
as a servant; He has indeed counted
them, and He has numbered them
      exactly.   ·

95   Every one of them shall come to Him
upon the Day of Resurrection, all
      alone.
Surely those who believe and do deeds
of righteousness—unto them
the All-merciful shall assign
      love.

Now We have made it easy by thy tongue
that thou mayest bear good tidings
thereby to the godfearing, and warn a people
      stubborn.
And how many a generation We
destroyed before them! Dost thou perceive
so much as one of them, or hear of them a
      whisper?

XX

TA HA

In the Name of God, the Merciful, the Compassionate

Ta Ha

We have not sent down the Koran upon thee
for thee to be unprosperous, but only
  as a reminder to
  him who fears, a
  revelation from
Him who created the earth and the high heavens; the
  All-compassionate
    sat Himself upon the Throne;
    to Him belongs
5   all that is in the heavens and the earth
    and all that is between them, and
    all that is underneath the soil.

Be thou loud in thy speech, yet
    surely He knows the secret
    and that yet more hidden.
        God—
    there is no god but He.
To Him belong the Names Most Beautiful.

Hast thou received the story of Moses?
When he saw a fire, and said to his family,
'Tarry you here; I observe a fire.
10   Perhaps I shall bring you a brand from it,
or I shall find at the fire guidance.'
When he came to it, a voice cried, 'Moses,
I am thy Lord; put off thy shoes;
thou art in the holy valley, Towa.
I Myself have chosen thee; therefore
give thou ear to this revelation.

Verily I am God; there is
no god but I; therefore serve Me,
and perform the prayer of My remembrance.

15   The Hour is coming; I would conceal it
that every soul may be recompensed
for its labours. Let none bar thee
from it, that believes not in it
but follows after his own caprice,
or thou wilt perish. What is that,
Moses, thou hast in thy right hand?'
'Why, it is my staff,' said Moses.
'I lean upon it, and with it I
beat down leaves to feed my sheep;
other uses also I find in it.'

20   Said He, 'Cast it down, Moses!'
and he cast it down, and behold
it was a serpent sliding.
Said He, 'Take it, and fear not;
We will restore it to its first state.
Now clasp thy hand to thy arm-pit;
it shall come forth white, without evil.
That is a second sign. So We would
show thee some of Our greatest signs.

25   Go to Pharaoh; he has waxed insolent.'
'Lord, open my breast,' said Moses,
'and do Thou ease for me my task.
Unloose the knot upon my tongue,
that they may understand my words.

30   Appoint for me of my folk a familiar,
Aaron, my brother; by him confirm
my strength, and associate him with me
in my task. So shall we glorify
Thee, and remember Thee abundantly.

35   Surely Thou seest into us.'
Said He, 'Thou art granted, Moses,
thy petition. Already another time
We favoured thee, when We revealed
what was revealed unto thy mother:
"Cast him into the ark, and cast him

into the river, and let the river
throw him up on the shore. An enemy
of Mine and his shall take him."
And I loaded on thee love from Me,
40   and to be formed in My sight,
when thy sister went out, saying,
"Shall I point you to one to have charge of him?"
So We returned thee to thy mother
that she might rejoice, and not sorrow.
Then thou slewest a living soul,
and We delivered thee out of grief,
and We tried thee with many trials.
Many years among the people of Midian
thou didst sojourn, then camest hither,
Moses, according to a decree.
I have chosen thee for My service;
go therefore, thou and thy brother,
with My signs, and neglect not
45   to remember Me. Go to Pharaoh,
for he has waxed insolent; yet
speak gently to him, that haply
he may be mindful, or perchance fear.'
'O our Lord,' said Moses and Aaron,
'truly we fear he may exceed
against us, or wax insolent.'
'Fear not,' said He. 'Surely I
shall be with you, hearing and seeing.
So go you both to Pharaoh, and say,
"We are the Messengers of thy Lord, so
send forth with us the Children of Israel
and chastise them not; we have brought thee
a sign from thy Lord; and peace
be upon him who follows the guidance!
50   It has been revealed to us that
chastisement shall light upon him who
cries lies and turns his back." '

Pharaoh said, 'Who is your Lord,
Moses?' He said, 'Our Lord is He

who gave everything its creation,
then guided it.' Pharaoh said,
'And what of the former generations?'
Said Moses, 'The knowledge of them
is with my Lord, in a Book;
my Lord goes not astray, nor forgets—

55 He who appointed the earth to be
a cradle for you, and therein
threaded roads for you, and sent down
water out of heaven, and therewith
We have brought forth divers kinds
of plants. Do you eat, and pasture
your cattle! Surely in that are
signs for men possessing reason.
Out of the earth We created you,
and We shall restore you into it,
and bring you forth from it a second time.'
So We showed Pharaoh all Our signs,
but he cried lies, and refused.
'Hast thou come, Moses,' he said,
'to expel us out of our land

60 by thy sorcery? We shall assuredly
bring thee sorcery the like of it;
therefore appoint a tryst between us
and thee, a place mutually agreeable,
and we shall not fail it, neither thou.'
'Your tryst shall be upon the Feast Day.'
said Moses. 'Let the people
be mustered at the high noon.'
Pharaoh then withdrew, and gathered
his guile. Thereafter he came again,
and Moses said to them, 'O beware!
Forge not a lie against God,
lest He destroy you with a chastisement.
Whoso forges has ever failed.'

65 And they disputed upon their plan
between them, and communed secretly
saying, 'These two men are sorcerers
and their purpose is to expel you

out of your land by their sorcery,
and to extirpate your justest way.
So gather your guile; then come
in battle-line. Whoever today
gains the upper hand shall surely prosper.'

They said, 'Moses, either thou wilt cast,
or we shall be the first to cast.'
'No,' said Moses. 'Do you cast!'
And lo, it seemed to him, by their sorcery,
their ropes and their staffs were sliding;
70 and Moses conceived a fear within him.
We said unto him, 'Fear not;
surely thou art the uppermost.
Cast down what is in thy right hand,
and it shall swallow what they have fashioned;
for they have fashioned only the guile
of a sorcerer, and the sorcerer
prospers not, wherever he goes.'
And the sorcerers cast themselves down
prostrating. 'We believe,' they said,
'in the Lord of Aaron and Moses.'
Pharaoh said, 'Have you believed him
before I gave you leave? Why, he
is the chief of you, the same that taught you
sorcery; I shall assuredly cut off
alternately your hands and feet,
then I shall crucify you upon
the trunks of palm-trees; you shall know
of a certainty which of us is more terrible
in chastisement, and more abiding.'
75 They said, 'We will not prefer thee
over the clear signs that have come to us,
nor over Him who originated us.
Decide then what thou wilt decide;
thou canst only decide touching
this present life. We believe
in our Lord, that He may pardon us
our offences, and the sorcery

thou hast constrained us to practise;
God is better, and more abiding.'

Whosoever comes unto his Lord a sinner,
        for him awaits Gehenna
wherein he shall neither die nor live.
And whoso comes unto Him a believer
having done deeds of righteousness,
those—for them await the most sublime degrees;
Gardens of Eden, underneath which rivers flow,
        therein dwelling forever;
that is the recompense of the self-purified.

Also We revealed unto Moses,
'Go with My servants by night; strike
for them a dry path in the sea,
80   fearing not overtaking, neither afraid.'
Pharaoh followed them with his hosts,
but they were overwhelmed by the sea;
so Pharaoh had led his people
astray, and was no guide to them.

Children of Israel, We delivered you
from your enemy; and We made covenant
with you upon the right side of the Mount,
and sent down on you manna and quails:
'Eat of the good things wherewith
We have provided you; but exceed not
therein, or My anger shall alight on you;
and on whomsoever My anger
alights, that man is hurled to ruin.
Yet I am All-forgiving to him who
repents and believes, and does
righteousness, and at last is guided.'

85   'What has sped thee far from thy people,
Moses?' 'They are upon my tracks,'
Moses said. 'I have hastened,
Lord, only that I may please Thee.'

Said He, 'We have tempted thy people
since thou didst leave them. The Samaritan
has misled them into error.'
Then Moses returned very angry
and sorrowful to his people, saying,
'My people, did your Lord not promise
a fair promise to you? Did the time
of the covenant seem so long to you,
or did you desire that anger
should alight on you from your Lord,
so that you failed in your tryst with me?'
90   'We have not failed in our tryst
with thee,' they said, 'of our volition;
but we were loaded with fardels,
even the ornaments of the people,
and we cast them, as the Samaritan
also threw them, into the fire.'
(Then he brought out for them a Calf,
a mere body that lowed; and they said,
'This is your god, and the god
of Moses, whom he has forgotten.'
What? Did they not see that thing
returned no speech unto them, neither
had any power to hurt or profit them?
Yet Aaron had aforetime said to them,
'My people, you have been tempted
by this thing, no more; surely
your Lord is the All-merciful; therefore
follow me, and obey my commandment!'
'We will not cease,' they said, 'to cleave
to it, until Moses returns to us.')

Moses said, 'What prevented thee,
Aaron, when thou sawest them in error,
so that thou didst not follow after me?
Didst thou then disobey my commandment?'
95   'Son of my mother,' Aaron said,
'take me not by the beard, or the head!
I was fearful that thou wouldst say,

"Thou hast divided the Children of Israel,
and thou hast not observed my word." '
Moses said, 'And thou, Samaritan,
what was thy business?' 'I beheld
what they beheld not,' he said,
'and I seized a handful of dust
from the messenger's track, and cast it
into the thing. So my soul prompted me.'
'Depart!' said Moses. 'It shall be thine
all this life to cry "Untouchable!"
And thereafter a tryst awaits thee
thou canst not fail to keep. Behold
thy god, to whom all the day
thou wast cleaving! We will surely burn it
and scatter its ashes into the sea.
Your God is only the One God;
there is no god, but He alone
who in His knowledge embraces everything.'

So We relate to thee stories of what
has gone before, and We have given thee a
    remembrance from Us.
100   Whosoever turns away from it,
upon the Day of Resurrection He
    shall bear a fardel,
therein abiding forever; how evil
upon the Day of Resurrection that
    burden for them!

On the day the Trumpet is blown; and We shall muster the
                                   ⌈sinners
upon that day with eyes staring, whispering one to another,
'You have tarried only ten nights.' We know very well
what they will say, when the justest of them in the way will
    say, 'You have tarried only a day.'

105   They will question thee concerning
the mountains. Say: 'My Lord will
    scatter them as ashes;

then He will leave them a level hollow
wherein thou wilt see no crookedness
neither any curving.'

On that day they will follow the Summoner in whom is no
[crookedness;
voices will be hushed to the All-merciful, so that thou hearest
naught but a murmuring. Upon that day the intercession
will not profit, save for him to whom the All-merciful
gives leave, and whose speech He approves. He knows what is
before them and behind them, and they comprehend Him not
110 in knowledge. And faces shall be humbled unto the Living,
the Eternal. He will have failed whose burden is of evildoing;
but whosoever does deeds of righteousness, being a believer,
shall fear neither wrong nor injustice.

Even so We have sent it down
as an Arabic Koran, and We
have turned about in it something
of threats, that haply they may be
godfearing, or it may arouse in
them remembrance.
So high exalted be God, the true King!
And hasten not with the Koran ere
its revelation is accomplished unto
thee; and say, 'O my Lord, increase
me in knowledge.'

And We made covenant with Adam before,
but he forgot, and We found in
him no constancy.
115 And when We said to the angels, 'Bow
yourselves to Adam'; so they bowed
themselves, save Iblis; he refused.
Then We said, 'Adam, surely this
is an enemy to thee and thy wife.
So let him not expel you both
from the Garden, so that thou art
unprosperous.

It is assuredly given to thee
neither to hunger therein, nor
    to go naked,
neither to thirst therein, nor to
    suffer the sun.'
Then Satan whispered to him
saying, 'Adam, shall I point thee to
the Tree of Eternity, and a Kingdom
    that decays not?'
So the two of them ate of it, and
their shameful parts revealed to them,
and they took to stitching upon
themselves leaves of the Garden. And
Adam disobeyed his Lord, and
    so he erred.

120   Thereafter his Lord chose him,
and turned again unto him, and He
    guided him.
Said He, 'Get you down, both of you
together, out of it, each of you an enemy
to each; but if there comes to you from
    Me guidance,
then whosoever follows My guidance
shall not go astray, neither shall he be
    unprosperous;
but whosoever turns away from My
remembrance, his shall be a life
    of narrowness,
and on the Resurrection Day We shall
    raise him blind.'

125   He shall say, 'O my Lord, why hast
thou raised me blind, and I was
    wont to see?'
God shall say, 'Even so it is.
Our signs came unto thee, and thou
didst forget them; and so today
    thou art forgotten.'
So We recompense him who is prodigal

and believes not in the signs of his
Lord; and the chastisement of the
world to come is more terrible and
    more enduring.

Is it not a guidance to them, how many
generations We destroyed before them
in whose dwelling-places they walk?
Surely in that are signs for men
    possessing reason.
And but for a word that preceded from
thy Lord, and a stated term, it
    had been fastened.

130   So be thou patient under what they say, and
        proclaim thy Lord's praise
before the rising of the sun, and before its setting, and
        proclaim thy Lord's praise
in the watches of the night, and at the ends of the day;
    haply thou wilt be well-pleasing.
    Stretch not thine eyes to that We have given
        pairs of them to enjoy—
the flower of the present life, that We may try them therein;
and thy Lord's provision is better, and more enduring.
        And bid thy family to pray,
        and be thou patient in it;
We ask of thee no provision, but it is We who provide thee.
    And the issue ultimate is to godfearing.

They say, 'Why does he not bring us a
sign from his Lord?' Has there not come
to them the clear sign of what is in
    the former scrolls?
Had We destroyed them with a chastisement
aforetime, they would have said, 'Our Lord,
why didst Thou not send us a Messenger,
so that we might have followed Thy signs
before that we were humiliated
    and degraded?'

135   Say: 'Everyone is waiting; so wait,
and assuredly you shall know
who are the travellers on the even path,
and who is guided.'

XXI

THE PROPHETS

In the Name of God, the Merciful, the Compassionate

Nigh unto men has drawn their reckoning,
while they in heedlessness are yet turning away;
no Remembrance from their Lord comes to them
lately renewed, but they listen to it yet playing,
diverted their hearts. The evildoers whisper
one to another, 'Is this aught but a mortal
like to yourselves? What, will you take to sorcery
  with your eyes open?'
He says: 'My Lord knows what is said in the heavens
and the earth, and He is the All-hearing,
  the All-knowing.'

5 Nay, but they say: 'A hotchpotch of nightmares!
Nay, he has forged it; nay, he is a poet!
Now therefore let him bring us a sign, even
as the ancient ones were sent as Messengers.'

Not one city that We destroyed before them
believed; what then, will they not believe?
And We sent none before thee, but men to whom
We made revelation—question the People
of the Remembrance, if you do not know—
nor did We fashion them as bodies
that ate not food, neither were they immortal;
then We made true the promise We gave them
and We delivered them, and whomsoever We would;
  and We destroyed the prodigal.

10 Now We have sent down to you a Book wherein
is your Remembrance; will you not understand?
How many a city that was evildoing
We have shattered, and set up after it

another people! Then, when they perceived
Our might, behold, they ran headlong out of it.
'Run not! Return you unto the luxury
that you exulted in, and your dwelling-places;
      haply you shall be questioned.'
They said, 'Alas for us! We have been evildoers.'
15   So they ceased not to cry, until We made them
      stubble, silent and still.

We created not the heaven and the earth,
and whatsoever between them is, as playing;
had We desired to take to Us a diversion
We would have taken it to Us from Ourselves,
      had We done aught.
Nay, but We hurl the truth against falsehood
and it prevails over it, and behold,
falsehood vanishes away. Then woe to you
      for that you describe!

To Him belongs whosoever is in the heavens
and the earth; and those who are with Him
wax not too proud to do Him service.
      neither grow weary,
20   glorifying Him by night and in the daytime
      and never failing.
Or have they taken gods out of the earth
      who raise the dead?
Why, were there gods in earth and heaven
other than God, they would surely go to ruin;
so glory be to God, the Lord of the Throne,
      above that they describe!
He shall not be questioned as to what He does,
      but they shall be questioned.
Or have they taken gods apart from Him?
Say: 'Bring your proof! This is the Remembrance
of him who is with me, and the Remembrance
of those before me. Nay, but the most part
of them know not the truth, so therefore they
      are turning away.'

25 And We sent never a Messenger before thee
except that We revealed to him, saying,
'There is no god but I; so serve Me.'

They say: 'The All-merciful has taken to Him
a son.' Glory be to Him! Nay, but they
   are honoured servants
that outstrip Him not in speech, and perform
  as He commands.
He knows what is before them and behind them,
  and they intercede not
save for him with whom He is well-pleased, and they
   tremble in awe of Him.
30 If any of them says, 'I am a god
apart from Him', such a one We recompense
with Gehenna; even so We recompense
   the evildoers.

Have not the unbelievers then beheld
that the heavens and the earth were a mass
all sewn up, and then We unstitched them
and of water fashioned every living thing?
   Will they not believe?
And We set in the earth firm mountains
lest it should shake with them, and We set in it
ravines to serve as ways, that haply so
   they may be guided;
and We set up the heaven as a roof
well-protected; yet still from Our signs
   they are turning away.
It is He who created the night and the day,
  the sun and the moon,
   each swimming in a sky.

35 We have not assigned to any mortal before thee
to live forever; therefore, if thou diest,
   will they live forever?
Every soul shall taste of death; and We try you
with evil and good for a testing, then unto Us

you shall be returned.

When the unbelievers behold thee, they take thee
only for mockery: 'Ha, is this the one
who makes mention of your gods?' Yet they
in the Remembrance of the All-merciful
          are unbelievers.
Man was created of haste. Assuredly
I shall show you My signs; so demand not
          that I make haste.
They say, 'And when shall the promise come to pass,
          if you speak truly?'
40 If the unbelievers but knew when that they
shall not ward off the Fire from their faces
nor from their backs, neither shall they be helped!
Nay, but it shall come upon them suddenly,
dumbfounding them, and they shall not be able
to repel it, nor shall they be respited.

Messengers indeed were mocked at before thee,
but those that scoffed at them were encompassed
          by that they mocked at.
Say: 'Who shall guard you by night and in the daytime
from the All-merciful?' Nay, but from the Remembrance
of their Lord they are turning away.
Or have they gods that shall defend them
apart from Us? Why, they are not able
to help themselves, nor shall they be guarded
          in safety from Us.
45 Nay, but Ourselves gave these and their fathers
enjoyment of days, until their life had lasted
long while upon them. What, do they not see
how We come to the land, diminishing it
in its extremities? Or are they the victors?
Say: 'I warn you only by the Revelation';
but they that are deaf do not hear the call
          when they are warned.
If but a breath of thy Lord's chastisement
touched them, they would surely say, 'Alas for us!

We were evildoers.'
And We shall set up the just balances
for the Resurrection Day, so that not one soul
shall be wronged anything; even if it be
the weight of one grain of mustard-seed
We shall produce it, and sufficient are
    We for reckoners.

We gave Moses and Aaron the Salvation
and a Radiance, and a Remembrance
   for the godfearing
50 such as fear God in the Unseen, trembling
    because of the Hour.

  And this is a blessed Remembrance
that We have sent down; so are you
    now denying it?

  We gave Abraham aforetime
his rectitude—for We knew him—
when he said to his father and his people,
'What are these statues unto which
    you are cleaving?'
They said, 'We found our fathers
    serving them.'
55 He said, 'Then assuredly you
and your fathers have been in
    manifest error.'
They said, 'What, hast thou come to us
with the truth, or art thou one of
    those that play?'
He said, 'Nay, but your Lord
is the Lord of the heavens and the earth
who originated them, and I
am one of those that bear witness
    thereunto.
And, by God, I shall assuredly
outwit your idols, after you have gone away
    turning your backs.'

So he broke them into fragments,
all but a great one they had, for haply they
would return to it.
60 They said, 'Who has done this
with our gods? Surely he is one of
the evildoers.'
They said, 'We heard a young man
making mention of them, and he was called
Abraham.'
They said, 'Bring him before the people's eyes;
haply they shall bear witness.'
They said, 'So, art thou the man
who did this unto our gods,
Abraham?'
He said, 'No; it was this great one
of them that did it. Question them, if they
are able to speak!'
65 So they returned one to another,
and they said, 'Surely it is you who are
the evildoers.'
Then they were utterly put to confusion
saying, 'Very well indeed thou knowest
these do not speak.'
He said, 'What, and do you serve,
apart from God, that which profits you
nothing, neither hurts you? Fie upon you
and that you serve apart from God!
Do you not understand?'
They said, 'Burn him, and help your gods, if
you would do aught.'
We said, 'O fire, be coolness and safety
for Abraham!'
70 They desired to outwit him; so We made
them the worse losers,
and We delivered him, and Lot,
unto the land that We had blessed
for all beings.
And We gave him Isaac and Jacob
in superfluity, and every one

made We righteous
and appointed them to be leaders
guiding by Our command, and We revealed
to them the doing of good deeds, and
to perform the prayer, and to pay the alms,
and Us they served.

And Lot—to him We gave judgment
and knowledge; and we delivered him
from the city that had been doing
deeds of corruption; they were an evil people,
truly ungodly;
75   and We admitted him into Our mercy; he
was of the righteous.

And Noah—when he called before, and We answered
him, and delivered him and his people
from the great distress,
and We helped him against the people
who cried lies to Our signs; surely
they were an evil people, so We drowned them
all together.

And David and Solomon—when they gave
judgment concerning the tillage, when the sheep
of the people strayed there, and We bore witness
to their judgment;
and We made Solomon to understand it,
and unto each gave We judgment
and knowledge. And with David We subjected
the mountains to give glory, and the birds,
and We were doers.
80   And We taught him the fashioning of garments
for you, to fortify you against your violence;
then are you thankful?
And to Solomon the wind, strongly blowing,
that ran at his command unto the land,
that We had blessed; and We had knowledge
of everything;

and of the Satans some dived for him
and did other work besides; and We were
      watching over them.

And Job—when he called unto his Lord,
'Behold, affliction has visited me,
and Thou art the most merciful
      of the merciful.'
So We answered him, and removed
the affliction that was upon him,
and We gave his people, and the like of them
with them, mercy from Us, and a Reminder
      to those who serve.

85   And Ishmael, Idris, Dhul Kifl—each
      was of the patient,
and We admitted them into Our mercy; they
      were of the righteous.

And Dhul Nun—when he went forth enraged
and thought that We would have no power
over him; then he called out in the darkness,
'There is no god but Thou. Glory be to Thee!
      I have done evil.'
So We answered him, and delivered him
out of grief; even so do We deliver
      the believers.

And Zachariah—when he called
unto his Lord, 'O my Lord, leave me not
solitary; though Thou art the best
      of inheritors.'
So We answered him, and bestowed on him
John, and We set his wife right for him;
truly they vied with one another, hastening
to good works, and called upon Us
out of yearning and awe; and they were
      humble to Us.

And she who guarded her virginity,

so We breathed into her of Our spirit
and appointed her and her son to be a sign
    unto all beings.
'Surely this community of yours
is one community, and I am your Lord;
    so serve Me.'
But they split up their affair between them;
    all shall return to Us.
95   And whosoever does deeds of righteousness,
being a believer, no unthankfulness
shall befall his endeavour; We Ourselves
    write it down for him.

There is a ban upon any city that We have destroyed;
    they shall not return
till, when Gog and Magog are unloosed, and they slide down
    out of every slope,
and nigh has drawn the true promise, and behold, the eyes
of the unbelievers staring: 'Alas for us! We were heedless
    of this; nay, we were evildoers.'
'Surely you, and that you were serving apart from God,
    are fuel for Gehenna; you shall go down to it.'
If those had been gods, they would never have gone down
yet every one of them shall therein abide forever;   [to it;
100   there shall be sighing for them therein, and naught they
                            [shall hear.
But as for those unto whom already
the reward most fair has gone forth from Us,
    they shall be kept far from it
neither shall they hear any whisper of it,
and they shall dwell forever in that
    their souls desired;
the greatest terror shall not grieve them,
and the angels shall receive them: 'This is
    your day that you were promised.'
On the day when We shall roll up heaven as a scroll is rolled
for the writings; as We originated the first creation,
so We shall bring it back again—a promise binding on Us;
    so We shall do.

105 For We have written in the Psalms, after the
Remembrance, 'The earth shall be the inheritance
of My righteous servants.'
Surely in this is a Message delivered
unto a people who serve.

We have not sent thee, save as a mercy
unto all beings.
Say: 'It is revealed unto me only that
your God is One God; do you then surrender?'
Then, if they should turn their backs, say:
'I have proclaimed to you all equally,
even though I know not whether near or far
is that you are promised.'

110 Surely He knows what is spoken aloud
and He knows what you hide.
I know not; haply it is a trial for you
and an enjoyment for a time.

He said: 'My Lord, judge Thou with truth!
And our Lord is the All-merciful;
His succour is ever to be sought against
that you describe.'

XXII

THE PILGRIMAGE

In the Name of God, the Merciful, the Compassionate

O men, fear your Lord!
Surely the earthquake of the Hour is a mighty thing;
on the day when you behold it, every suckling woman shall
neglect the child she has suckled, and every pregnant woman
shall deposit her burden, and thou shalt see mankind drunk,
yet they are not drunk, but God's chastisement is terrible.

And among men there is such a one
that disputes concerning God without knowledge
     and follows every rebel Satan,
against whom it is written down that
whosoever takes him for a friend, him he
leads astray, and he guides him to the
     chastisement of the burning.
5   O men,
if you are in doubt as to the Uprising,
     surely We created you of dust
          then of a sperm-drop,
          then of a blood clot,
then of a lump of flesh, formed and unformed
     that We may make clear to you.
     And We establish in the wombs
     what We will, till a stated term,
     then We deliver you as infants,
     then that you may come of age;
          and some of you die,
     and some of you are kept back
unto the vilest state of life, that after
knowing somewhat, they may know nothing.
And thou beholdest the earth blackened,
then, when We send down water upon it,

it quivers, and swells, and puts forth
  herbs of every joyous kind.
That is because God—He is the Truth,
and brings the dead to life, and is powerful
   over everything,
and because the Hour is coming, no doubt of it, and
God shall raise up whosoever is within the tombs.

And among men there is such a one
that disputes concerning God without knowledge
or guidance, or an illuminating Book,
turning his side to lead astray
from God's way; for him is degradation
in this world, and on the Resurrection Day
We shall let him taste the chastisement
   of the burning:
'That is for what thy hands have forwarded
and for that God is never unjust
   unto His servants.'

And among men there is such a one
as serves God upon the very edge—
if good befalls him he is at rest in it,
but if a trial befalls him he turns
completely over; he loses this world
and the world to come; that is indeed
   the manifest loss.
He calls, apart from God, upon that
which hurts him not, and which neither
profits him anything; that is indeed
   the far error.
He calls upon him who is likelier
to hurt him, rather than to profit him—
an evil protector indeed, he,
   an evil friend!

God shall surely admit those who believe
and do righteous deeds into gardens
underneath which rivers flow; surely God does

that He desires.

15   Whosoever thinks God will not help him
in the present world and the world to come,
let him stretch up a rope to heaven,
then let him sever it, and behold
whether his guile does away with what
        enrages him.

Even so We have sent it down as signs,
clear signs, and for that God guides
        whom He desires.
Surely they that believe, and those of Jewry,
the Sabaeans, the Christians, the Magians
and the idolaters—God shall distinguish
between them on the Day of Resurrection;
assuredly God is witness
        over everything.
Hast thou not seen how to God bow all who are in the
        and all who are in the earth,   [heavens
the sun and the moon, the stars and the mountains,
        the trees and the beasts,
and many of mankind? And many merit the chastisement;
        and whom God abases,
there is none to honour him. God does whatsoever He will.

20   These are two disputants who have disputed
concerning their Lord. As for the unbelievers,
for them garments of fire shall be cut,
and there shall be poured over their heads
        boiling water
whereby whatsoever is in their bellies
and their skins shall be melted; for them await
        hooked iron rods;
as often as they desire in their anguish
to come forth from it, they shall be restored
into it, and: 'Taste the chastisement
        of the burning!'
God shall surely admit those who believe

and do righteous deeds into gardens
underneath which rivers flow; therein
they shall be adorned with bracelets of gold
and with pearls, and their apparel there
      shall be of silk;
and they shall be guided unto goodly speech,
and they shall be guided unto the path
      of the All-laudable.

25   Those who disbelieve, and bar from God's way
and the Holy Mosque that We have appointed
equal unto men, alike him who cleaves to it
      and the tent-dweller,
and whosoever purposes to violate it
wrongfully, We shall let him taste
      a painful chastisement.

And when We settled for Abraham the place
of the House: 'Thou shall not associate
with Me anything. And do thou purify
My House for those that shall go about it
and those that stand, for those that bow
      and prostrate themselves;
and proclaim among men the Pilgrimage,
and they shall come unto thee on foot
and upon every lean beast, they shall come from
      every deep ravine
that they may witness things profitable to them
and mention God's Name on days well-known
over such beasts of the flocks as He has
provided them: "So eat thereof, and feed
      the wretched poor."

30   Let them then finish with their self-neglect
and let them fulfil their vows, and go about
      the Ancient House.'
All that; and whosoever venerates
the sacred things of God, it shall be better
for him with his Lord. And permitted
to you are the flocks, except that which is
recited to you. And eschew the abomination

of idols, and eschew the speaking
    of falsehood,
being men pure of faith unto God,
not associating with Him anything;
for whosoever associates with God anything,
it is as though he has fallen from heaven
and the birds snatch him away, or the wind
sweeps him headlong into a place
    far away.
All that; and whosoever venerates
God's waymarks, that is of the godliness
    of the hearts.
There are things therein profitable
to you unto a stated term; thereafter
their lawful place of sacrifice is by
    the Ancient House.

35   We have appointed for every nation
a holy rite, that they may mention
God's Name over such beasts of the flocks
as He has provided them. Your God is One God,
so to Him surrender. And give thou good tidings
    unto the humble
who, when God is mentioned, their hearts
quake, and such as endure patiently
whatever visits them, and who perform
the prayer, and expend of what We have
    provided them.
And the beasts of sacrifice—We have appointed
them for you as among God's waymarks;
therein is good for you. So mention
God's Name over them, standing in ranks;
then, when their flanks collapse, eat of them
and feed the beggar and the suppliant.
So We have subjected them to you; haply
    you will be thankful.
The flesh of them shall not reach God,
neither their blood, but godliness from you
shall reach Him. So He has subjected them

to you, that you may magnify God for that
He has guided you. And give thou good tidings
   unto the good-doers.

Assuredly God will defend those
who believe; surely God loves not any
   ungrateful traitor.

40 Leave is given to those who fight because
they were wronged—surely God is able
   to help them—
who were expelled from their habitations
without right, except that they say
'Our Lord is God.' Had God not driven back
the people, some by the means of others,
there had been destroyed cloisters and churches,
oratories and mosques, wherein God's Name
is much mentioned. Assuredly God will
help him who helps Him—surely God is
   All-strong, All-mighty—
who, if We establish them in the land,
perform the prayer, and pay the alms,
and bid to honour, and forbid dishonour;
and unto God belongs the issue
   of all affairs.
If they cry lies to thee, so too before them
the people of Noah cried lies, and Ad
and Thamood, and the people of Abraham,
the people of Lot, and the men of Midian;
to Moses also they cried lies. And I respited
the unbelievers, then I seized them; and
   how was My horror!
How many a city We have destroyed
in its evildoing, and now it is fallen down
upon its turrets! How many a ruined well,
   a tall palace!

45 What, have they not journeyed in the land
so that they have hearts to understand with
or ears to hear with? It is not the eyes
that are blind, but blind are the hearts

within the breasts.
And they demand of thee to hasten
the chastisement! God will not fail
His promise; and surely a day
with thy Lord is as a thousand years
of your counting.
How many a city I have respited
in its evildoing; then I seized it, and to
Me was the homecoming.
Say: 'O men, I am only for you
a plain warner.'
Those who believe, and do deeds of
righteousness—theirs shall be forgiveness
and generous provision.
50   And those who strive against Our signs
to void them—they shall be the inhabitants
of Hell.

We sent not ever any Messenger
or Prophet before thee, but that Satan
cast into his fancy, when he was fancying;
but God annuls what Satan casts, then
God confirms His signs—surely God is
All-knowing, All-wise—
that He may make what Satan casts
a trial for those in whose hearts
is sickness, and those whose hearts
are hard; and surely the evildoers are
in wide schism;
and that they who have been given knowledge
may know that it is the truth from thy Lord
and believe in it, and so their hearts
be humble unto Him; and assuredly
God ever guides those who believe
to a straight path.

And the unbelievers will not cease
to be in doubt of it, until the Hour
comes on them suddenly, or there shall

come upon them the chastisement of
a barren day.

55   The Kingdom upon that day shall belong
to God, and He shall judge between them.
As for those who believe, and do deeds
of righteousness, they shall be in
Gardens of Bliss.
But as for the unbelievers, who cried
lies to Our signs, for them awaits
a humbling chastisement.
And those who emigrated in God's way
and were slain, or died, God shall provide them
with a fair provision; and surely God is the
best of providers.
He shall admit them by a gate that is
well-pleasing to them; and surely God is
All-knowing, All-clement.
All that; and whosoever chastises
after the manner that he was chastised
and then again is oppressed, assuredly
God will help him; surely God is
All-pardoning, All-forgiving.

60   That is because God makes the night to enter into the day
and makes the day to enter into the night; and that God is
All-hearing, All-seeing.
That is because God—He is the Truth, and that they call
apart from Him—that is the false; and for that God is ⌜upon
the All-high, the All-great.
Hast thou not seen how that God has sent down out of heaven
water, and in the morning the earth becomes green? God is
All-subtle, All-aware.
To Him belongs all that is in the heavens and in the earth;
surely God—He is the All-sufficient, the All-laudable.
Hast thou not seen how that God has subjected to you
all that is in the earth
and the ships to run upon the sea at His commandment,
and He holds back heaven
lest it should fall upon the earth, save by His leave?

Surely God is All-gentle to men, All-compassionate.
It is He who gave you
65   life, then He shall make you dead, then He shall give you life.
Surely man is ungrateful.

We have appointed for every nation
a holy rite that they shall perform.
Let them not therefore wrangle with thee
upon the matter, and do thou summon
unto thy Lord; surely thou art upon
a straight guidance.
And if they should dispute with thee,
do thou say, 'God knows very well
what you are doing.
God shall judge between you on the Day
of Resurrection touching that whereon
you were at variance.'
Didst thou not know that God knows all
that is in heaven and earth? Surely that
is in a Book; surely that for God is
an easy matter.
70   They serve, apart from God, that whereon
He has sent down never authority
and that whereof they have no knowledge;
and for the evildoers there shall be
no helper.
And when Our signs are recited to them,
clear signs, thou recognisest in the faces of
the unbelievers denial; wellnigh they
rush upon those who recite to them
Our signs. Say: 'Shall I tell you of
something worse than that? The Fire—God
has promised it to the unbelievers—
an evil homecoming!'

O men, a similitude is struck; so
give you ear to it. Surely those upon
whom you call, apart from God, shall never
create a fly, though they banded together

to do it; and if a fly should rob them
of aught, they would never rescue it from him.
Feeble indeed alike are the seeker
    and the sought!
They measure not God with His true measure; surely God is
    All-strong, All-mighty.

God chooses of the angels Messengers
and of mankind; surely God is
    All-hearing, All-seeing.
75 He knows whatsoever is before them
and behind them, and unto God all
    matters are returned.

O men, bow you down and prostrate yourselves,
and serve your Lord, and do good; haply so
    you shall prosper;
and struggle for God as is His due, for
He has chosen you, and has laid on you
no impediment in your religion,
being the creed of your father Abraham; He
    named you Muslims
aforetime and in this, that the Messenger
might be a witness against you, and that
you might be witnesses against mankind.
So perform the prayer, and pay the alms,
and hold you fast to God; He is your
Protector—an excellent Protector,
    an excellent Helper.

XXIII

THE BELIEVERS

In the Name of God, the Merciful, the Compassionate

Prosperous are the believers
who in their prayers are humble
and from idle talk turn away
and at almsgiving are active
5   and guard their private parts
save from their wives and what their right hands own
then being not blameworthy
(but whosoever seeks after more than that,
those are the transgressors)
and who preserve their trusts
and their covenant
and who observe their prayers.
10   Those are the inheritors
who shall inherit Paradise
therein dwelling forever.

We created man of an extraction
of clay,
then We set him, a drop, in a receptacle
secure,
then We created of the drop a clot
then We created of the clot a tissue
then We created of the tissue bones
then We garmented the bones in flesh;
thereafter We produced him as another creature.
So blessed be God, the fairest of creators!
15   Then after that you shall surely die,
then on the Day of Resurrection you
shall surely be raised up.
And We created above you seven ways,
and We were not heedless of creation.

And We sent down out of heaven water
in measure and lodged it in the earth;
and We are able to take it away.
Then We produced for you therewith
 gardens of palms and vines
 wherein are many fruits for
 you, and of them you eat,
20 and a tree issuing from the Mount of Sinai that
 bears oil and seasoning
  for all to eat.
And surely in the cattle there is a lesson for you;
 We give you to drink of
 what is in their bellies,
and many uses there are in them for you,
 and of them you eat;
and upon them, and on the ships, you are borne.

And We sent Noah to his people;
and he said, 'O my people, serve God!
You have no god other than He.
 Will you not be godfearing?''
Said the Council of the unbelievers
of his people, 'This is naught but
a mortal like yourselves, who desires
to gain superiority over you. And
if God willed, He would have sent down
angels. We never heard of this among
 our fathers, the ancients.
25 He is naught but a man bedevilled; so
 wait on him for a time.'
He said, 'O my Lord, help me,
 for that they cry me lies.'
Then We said to him, 'Make thou the Ark
under Our eyes and as We reveal,
and then, when Our command comes
 and the Oven boils,
insert in it two of every kind
and thy family—except for him
against whom the word already

has been spoken; and address Me not
concerning those who have done evil;
    they shall be drowned.
Then, when thou art seated in the Ark
and those with thee, say, "Praise belongs to
God, who has delivered us from the people
    of the evildoers."

30   And say, "O my Lord, do Thou harbour
me in a blessed harbour, for Thou art
    the best of harbourers." '
Surely in that are signs, and surely
    We put to the test.

Thereafter, after them, We produced
    another generation,
and We sent amongst them a Messenger
of themselves, saying, 'Serve God!
You have no god other than He.
    Will you not be godfearing?'
Said the Council of the unbelievers
of his people, who cried lies to the
encounter of the world to come,
and to whom We had given ease in the
present life, 'This is naught but
a mortal like yourselves, who eats
    of what you eat

35   and drinks of what you drink.
If you obey a mortal like yourselves,
    then you will be losers.
What, does he promise you that when you are
dead, and become dust and bones, you
    shall be brought·forth?
      Away, away
    with that you are promised!
There is nothing but our present life;
we die, and we live, and we shall
    not be raised up.

40   He is naught but a man who has forged
against God a lie, and we will

not believe him.'
He said, 'O my Lord, help me,
for that they cry me lies.'
He said, 'In a little they will
be remorseful.'
And the Cry seized them justly, and We
made them as scum; so away with the people
of the evildoers!

Thereafter, after them, We produced
other generations;
45 no nation outstrips its term, nor
do they put it back.
Then sent We Our Messengers successively;
whenever its Messenger came to a nation
they cried him lies, so We caused some
of them to follow others, and We made them
as but tales; so away with a people
who do not believe!

Then We sent Moses and his brother
Aaron with Our signs and a manifest
authority
unto Pharaoh and his Council;
but they waxed proud, and they were
a lofty people,
and they said, 'What, shall we believe
two mortals like ourselves, whose people
are our servants?'
50 So they cried them lies, and they were
among the destroyed.

And We gave Moses the Book, that haply
they would be guided;
and We made Mary's son, and his mother,
to be a sign, and gave them refuge
upon a height, where was a hollow
and a spring:
'O Messengers, eat of the good things

and do righteousness; surely I know
 the things you do.
Surely this community of yours
is one community, and I am your Lord;
 so fear Me.'
55 But they split in their affair between them
into sects, each party rejoicing in
 what is with them.
So leave thou them in their perplexity
 for a time.
What, do they think that We succour them with
 of wealth and children
We vie in good works for them? Nay, but
 they are not aware.

Surely those who tremble in fear of their Lord
60 and those who believe in the signs of their Lord
and those who associate naught with their Lord
and those who give what they give, their hearts
quaking that they are returning to their Lord—
those vie in good works, outracing to them.

We charge not any soul save to its capacity,
and with Us is a Book speaking truth, and
 they shall not be wronged.
65 Nay, but their hearts are in perplexity
as to this, and they have deeds besides that
 that they are doing.
Till, when We seize with the chastisement
the ones of them that live at ease,
 behold, they groan.
'Groan not today; surely you shall not be
 helped from Us.
My signs were recited to you, but upon your
 heels you withdrew,
waxing proud against it, talking foolish
 talk by night.'
70 Have they not pondered the saying, or came there
upon them that which came not upon their

347

fathers, the ancients?
Or did they not recognise their Messenger
    and so denied him?
Or do they say, 'He is bedevilled'? Nay,
he has brought them the truth, but most of them are
    averse from the truth.
Had the truth followed their caprices,
the heavens and the earth and whosoever
in them is had surely corrupted. Nay, We
brought them their Remembrance, but from their
    Remembrance they turned.
Or dost thou ask them for tribute? Yet the
tribute of thy Lord is better, and He is the
    best of providers.

75   Assuredly thou art calling them
            to a straight path;
        and surely they that believe not
        in the world to come are deviating
            from the path.
        Did We have mercy on them, and remove
        the affliction that is upon them,
        they would persist in their insolence
            wandering blindly.
        We already seized them with the chastisement,
        yet they abased not themselves to their Lord
            nor were they humble;
        until, when We open against them a door
        of terrible chastisement, lo, they are sore
            confounded at it.

80   It is He who produced for you hearing, and eyes, and
            little thanks you show.   ⌈hearts;
        It is He who scattered you in the earth, and to Him
            you shall be mustered.
        It is He who gives life, and makes to die, and to Him
        belongs the alternation of night and day; what,
            will you not understand?

        Nay, but they said the like of what

the ancients said.
They said, 'What, when we are dead
and become dust and bones, shall we be
    indeed raised up?

85   We and our fathers have been promised this
before; this is naught but the fairy-tales
    of the ancients.'
Say: 'Whose is the earth, and whoso is in it,
    if you have knowledge?'
They will say, 'God's.' Say: 'Will you not
    then remember?'
Say: 'Who is the Lord of the seven heavens
    and the Lord of the mighty Throne?'
They will say, 'God's.' Say: 'Will you not
    then be godfearing?'

90   Say: 'In whose hand is the dominion of
everything, protecting and Himself unprotected,
    if you have knowledge?'
They will say, 'God's.' Say: 'How then
    are you bewitched?'
Nay, but We brought them the truth, and they
    are truly liars.
God has not taken to Himself any son,
nor is there any god with Him; for then
each god would have taken off that he created
and some of them would have risen up
over others; glory to be God, beyond
    that they describe,
who has knowledge of the Unseen and the
Visible; high exalted be He, above
    that they associate!

95   Say: 'O my Lord, if Thou shouldst show me
    that they are promised,
O my Lord, put me not among the people
    of the evildoers.'
Assuredly, We are able to show thee
    that We promise them.
Repel thou the evil with that which is

fairer. We Ourselves know very well
    that they describe.
And say: 'O my Lord, I take refuge
in Thee from the evil suggestions
    of the Satans,
100   and I take refuge in Thee, O my Lord,
    lest they attend me.'

Till, when death comes to one of them, he says,
    'My Lord, return me;
haply I shall do righteousness in that
I forsook.' Nay, it is but a word
he speaks; and there, behind them,
is a barrier until the day that they
    shall be raised up.

For when the Trumpet is blown, that day there shall be no
    [kinship
any more between them, neither will they question one
    [another.
Then he whose scales are heavy—they are the prosperers,
105   and he whose scales are light—they have lost their souls
in Gehenna dwelling forever, the Fire smiting their faces
the while they glower there. 'What, were My signs not
    [recited
to you, and you cried them lies?' They shall say, 'Our Lord,
our adversity prevailed over us; we were an erring people.
Our Lord, bring us forth out of it! Then, if we revert,
110   we shall be evildoers indeed.' 'Slink you into it,'
He shall say, 'and do not speak to Me. There is a party
of My servants who said, "Our Lord, we believe; therefore
forgive us, and have mercy on us, for Thou art the best
of the merciful." But you took them for a laughing-stock,
till they made you forget My remembrance, mocking at them.
Now today I have recompensed them for their patient
    [endurance;
115   they are the triumphant.' He shall say, 'How long have you
tarried in the earth, by number of years?' They shall say,
'We have tarried a day, or part of a day; ask the numberers!'

He shall say, 'You have tarried but a little, did you know.
What, did you think that We created you only for sport,
    and that you would not be returned to Us?'

      Then high exalted be God,
        the King, the True!
      There is no god but He, the
      Lord of the noble Throne.

And whosoever calls upon another god
    with God, whereof he has no proof,
    his reckoning is with his Lord;
surely the unbelievers shall not prosper.

      And say: 'My Lord, forgive
and have mercy, for Thou art the best
      of the merciful.'

XXIV

LIGHT

In the Name of God, the Merciful, the Compassionate

A sura that We have sent down
and appointed; and We have sent down
in it signs, clear signs, that haply
     you will remember.

The fornicatress and the fornicator—
scourge each one of them a hundred stripes,
and in the matter of God's religion
let no tenderness for them seize you
if you believe in God and the Last Day;
and let a party of the believers
     witness their chastisement.
The fornicator shall marry none but
a fornicatress or an idolatress,
and the fornicatress—none shall marry her
but a fornicator or an idolator;
that is forbidden to the believers.

And those who cast it up on women in
wedlock, and then bring not four witnesses,
scourge them with eighty stripes, and do not
accept any testimony of theirs ever; those—
     they are the ungodly,
5   save such as repent thereafter and
make amends; surely God is All-forgiving,
     All-compassionate.
And those who cast it up on their wives
having no witnesses except themselves,
the testimony of one of them shall be
to testify by God four times that he
     is of the truthful,

and a fifth time, that the curse of
God shall be upon him, if he should
     be of the liars.
It shall avert from her the chastisement
if she testify by God four times that he
     is of the liars,
and a fifth time, that the wrath of
God shall be upon her, if he should
     be of the truthful.

10   But for God's bounty to you and His mercy
and that God turns, and is All-wise—

Those who came with the slander are a
band of you; do not reckon it evil
for you; rather it is good for you.
Every man of them shall have the sin
that he has earned charged to him; and
whosoever of them took upon himself
the greater part of it, him there awaits
     a mighty chastisement.
Why, when you heard it, did the believing
men and women not of their own account
think good thoughts, and say, 'This is
     a manifest calumny'?
Why did they not bring four witnesses
against it? But since they did not
bring the witnesses, in God's sight
     they are the liars.
But for God's bounty to you and His mercy
in the present world and the world to come
there would have visited you for your mutterings
a mighty chastisement. When you received it
on your tongues, and were speaking with your mouths
that whereof you had no knowledge, and
reckoned it a light thing, and with God it
     was a mighty thing—

15   And why, when you heard it, did you not
say, 'It is not for us to speak about

this; glory be to Thee! This is
a mighty calumny'?
God admonishes you, that you shall
never repeat the like of it again, if
you are believers.
God makes clear to you the signs; and God is
All-knowing, All-wise.
Those who love, that indecency
should be spread abroad concerning
them that believe—there awaits them
a painful chastisement
in the present world and the world to come;
and God knows, and you know not.

20   But for God's bounty to you and His mercy
and that God is All-gentle, All-compassionate—

O believers, follow not the steps of
Satan; for whosoever follows
the steps of Satan, assuredly he
bids to indecency and dishonour.
But for God's bounty to you and His mercy
not one of you would have been pure ever;
but God purifies whom He will; and God is
All-hearing, All-knowing.

Let not those of you who possess bounty
and plenty swear off giving kinsmen
and the poor and those who emigrate
in the way of God; but let them pardon
and forgive. Do you not wish that God
should forgive you? God is All-forgiving,
All-compassionate.

Surely those who cast it up on women
in wedlock that are heedless but believing
shall be accursed in the present world
and the world to come; and there awaits them
a mighty chastisement

on the day when their tongues, their hands and
their feet shall testify against them touching
       that they were doing.
25   Upon that day God will pay them in full
their just due, and they shall know that God
       is the manifest Truth.

Corrupt women for corrupt men,
and corrupt men for corrupt women;
good women for good men,
and good men for good women—
these are declared quit of what they
say; theirs shall be forgiveness
       and generous provision.

O believers, do not enter houses
other than your houses until you first
ask leave and salute the people
thereof; that is better for you; haply
       you will remember.
And if you find not anyone therein,
enter it not until leave is given
to you. And if you are told, 'Return,'
return; that is purer for you; and God knows
       the things you do.
There is no fault in you that you enter
houses uninhabited wherein enjoyment is
for you. God knows what you reveal
       and what you hide.

30   Say to the believers, that they cast down
their eyes and guard their private parts;
that is purer for them. God is aware of
       the things they work.
And say to the believing women, that they
cast down their eyes and guard their private
parts, and reveal not their adornment
save such as is outward; and let them cast
their veils over their bosoms, and not reveal

their adornment save to their husbands,
or their fathers, or their husbands' fathers,
or their sons, or their husbands' sons,
or their brothers, or their brothers' sons,
or their sisters' sons, or their women,
or what their right hands own, or such men
as attend them, not having sexual desire,
or children who have not yet attained knowledge
of women's private parts; nor let them stamp
their feet, so that their hidden ornament
may be known. And turn all together
to God, O you believers;.haply so
you will prosper.

Marry the spouseless among you, and your
slaves and handmaidens that are righteous;
if they are poor, God will enrich them
of His bounty; God is All-embracing,
All-knowing.
And let those who find not the means to
marry be abstinent till God enriches them
of His bounty. Those your right hands own
who seek emancipation, contract with
them accordingly, if you know some good
in them; and give them of the wealth of God
that He has given you. And constrain not
your slavegirls to prostitution, if they
desire to live in chastity, that you may
seek the chance goods of the present life.
Whosoever constrains them, surely God,
after their being constrained, is All-forgiving,
All-compassionate.

Now We have sent down to you signs
making all clear, and an example
of those who passed away before you,
and an admonition for the godfearing.

35   God is the Light of the heavens and the earth;

the likeness of His Light is as a niche
wherein is a lamp
(the lamp in a glass,
the glass as it were a glittering star)
kindled from a Blessed Tree,
an olive that is neither of the East nor of the West
whose oil wellnigh would shine, even if no fire touched it;
Light upon Light;
(God guides to His Light whom He will.)
(And God strikes similitudes for men,
and God has knowledge of everything.)
in temples God has allowed to be raised up,
and His Name to be commemorated therein;
therein glorifying Him, in the mornings and the evenings,
are men whom neither commerce nor trafficking
diverts from the remembrance of God
and to perform the prayer, and to pay the alms,
fearing a day when hearts and eyes shall be turned about,
that God may recompense them for their fairest works
and give them increase of His bounty;
and God provides whomsoever He will, without reckoning.

And as for the unbelievers,
their works are as a mirage in a spacious plain
which the man athirst supposes to be water,
till, when he comes to it, he finds it is nothing;
there indeed he finds God,
and He pays him his account in full; (and God is swift
at the reckoning.)
40   or they are as shadows upon a sea obscure
covered by a billow
above which is a billow
above which are clouds,
shadows piled one upon another;
when he puts forth his hand, wellnigh he cannot see it.
And to whomsoever God assigns no light,
no light has he.

Hast thou not seen how that whatsoever is in the heavens

and in the earth extols God,
and the birds spreading their wings?
Each—He knows its prayer and its extolling; and God knows
      the things they do.
To God belongs the Kingdom of the heavens and the earth,
      and to Him is the homecoming.
Hast thou not seen how God drives the clouds, then composes
      then converts them into a mass,   [them,
then thou seest the rain issuing out of the midst of them?
And He sends down out of heaven mountains, wherein is hail,
so that He smites whom He will with it, and turns it aside
      from whom He will;
wellnigh the gleam of His lightning snatches away the sight.
      God turns about the day and the night;
   surely in that is a lesson for those who have eyes.
      God has created every beast of water,
      and some of them go upon their bellies,
      and some of them go upon two feet,
      and some of them go upon four; God
      creates whatever He will; God is powerful
            over everything.

45   Now We have sent down signs making all
                  clear; God guides whomsoever He will
                        to a straight path.
                  They say, 'We believe in God and the
                  Messenger, and we obey.' Then after that
                  a party of them turn away; those—
                        they are not believers.
                  When they are called to God and His Messenger
                  that he may judge between them, lo, a party of them
                        are swerving aside;
                  but if they are in the right, they will come to
                        him submissively.
                  What, is there sickness in their hearts,
                  or are they in doubt, or do they fear
                  that God may be unjust towards them
                  and His Messenger? Nay, but those—
                        they are the evildoers.

50 　 All that the believers say, when they
are called to God and His Messenger, that he
may judge between them, is that they say,
'We hear, and we obey'; those—
　　　 they are the prosperers.
Whoso obeys God and His Messenger,
and fears God and has awe of Him, those—
　　　 they are the triumphant.
They have sworn by God the most earnest oaths,
if thou commandest them they will go forth.
Say: 'Do not swear; honourable obedience
is sufficient. Surely God is aware of
　　　 the things you do.'
Say: 'Obey God, and obey the Messenger;
then, if you turn away, only upon
him rests what is laid on him, and
upon you rests what is laid on you.
If you obey him, you will be guided.
It is only for the Messenger to deliver
　　　 the manifest Message.'

God has promised those of you who believe
and do righteous deeds that He will surely
make you successors in the land, even as He
made those who were before them successors,
and that He will surely establish their
religion for them that He has approved for them,
and will give them in exchange, after
their fear, security: 'They shall serve Me,
not associating with Me anything.'
Whoso disbelieves after that, those—
　　　 they are the ungodly.

55 　 Perform the prayer, and pay the alms,
and obey the Messenger—haply so
　　　 you will find mercy.
Think not the unbelievers able to frustrate
God in the earth; their refuge is the Fire—
　　　 an evil homecoming.

O believers, let those your right hands own
and those of you who have not reached puberty
ask leave of you three times—before
the prayer of dawn, and when you put off
your garments at the noon, and after
the evening prayer—three times of nakedness
for you. There is no fault in you or them, apart
from these, that you go about one to the other.
So God makes clear to you the signs; and God is
   All-knowing, All-wise.
When your children reach puberty, let them
ask leave, as those before them asked leave.
So God makes clear to you His signs; and God is
   All-knowing, All-wise.
Such women as are past child-bearing
and have no hope of marriage—there is no
fault in them that they put off their clothes,
so be it that they flaunt no ornament;
but to abstain is better for them; and God is
   All-hearing, All-knowing.

60   There is no fault in the blind, and there is
no fault in the lame, and there is no fault
in the sick, neither in yourselves, that you
eat of your houses, or your fathers' houses,
or your mothers' houses, or your brothers' houses,
or your sisters' houses, or the houses of
your uncles or your aunts paternal, or
the houses of your uncles or your aunts
maternal, or that whereof you own the keys,
or of your friend; there is no fault in you
that you eat all together, or in groups
   separately.
But when you enter houses, greet one another
with a greeting from God, blessed and good.
So God makes clear to you the signs; haply
   you will understand.

Those only are believers, who believe

in God and His Messenger and who, when they
are with him upon a common matter,
go not away until they ask his leave.
Surely those who ask thy leave—those are
they that believe in God and His Messenger;
so, when they ask thy leave for some affair
of their own, give leave to whom thou wilt
of them, and ask God's forgiveness
for them; surely God is All-forgiving,
      All-compassionate.
Make not the calling of the Messenger
among yourselves like your calling
one of another. God knows those of you
who slip away surreptitiously; so let those
who go against His command beware, lest
a trial befall them, or there befall them
      a painful chastisement.

Why, surely to God belongs whatsoever is in the heavens
and the earth; He ever knows what state you are upon;
and the day when they shall be returned to Him, then He
will tell them of what they did; and God knows everything.

XXV

SALVATION

In the Name of God, the Merciful, the Compassionate

Blessed be He
who has sent down the Salvation upon
His servant, that he may be a warner
to all beings;
to whom belongs the Kingdom of the heavens
and the earth; and He has not taken
to Him a son, and He has no associate
in the Kingdom; and He created
every thing, then He ordained it
very exactly.
Yet they have taken to them gods, apart
from Him, that create nothing and themselves
are created,
and have no power to hurt or profit
themselves, no power of death or life or
raising up.

5   The unbelievers say, 'This is naught but a
calumny he has forged, and other folk have
helped him to it.' So they have committed
wrong and falsehood.
They say, 'Fairy-tales of the ancients
that he has had written down, so that
they are recited to him at the dawn
and in the evening.'
Say: 'He sent it down, who knows the secret
in the heavens and earth; He is All-forgiving,
All-compassionate.'

They also say, 'What ails this Messenger
that he eats food, and goes in the markets?

Why has an angel not been sent down to him, to be
a warner with him?
Or why is not a treasure thrown to him,
or why has he not a Garden to eat of?'
The evildoers say, 'You are only following
a man bewitched!'
10   Behold, how they strike similitudes
for thee, and go astray, and are unable
to find a way!

Blessed be He
who, if He will, shall assign to thee
better than that—gardens underneath
which rivers flow, and he shall assign
to thee palaces.

Nay, but they cry lies to the Hour; and We have prepared
for him who cries lies to the Hour a Blaze. When it sees them
from a far place, they shall hear its bubbling and sighing.
And when they are cast, coupled in fetters, into a narrow place
of that Fire, they will call out there for destruction.
15   'Call not out today for one destruction, but call for many!'

Say: 'Is that better, or the Garden
of Eternity, that is promised to
the godfearing, and is their recompense
and homecoming?'
Therein they shall have what they will
dwelling forever; it is a promise
binding upon thy Lord, and of Him
to be required.

Upon the day when He shall muster them and that they
                                        [serve, apart
from God, and He shall say, 'Was it you that led these My
                                        [servants
astray, or did they themselves err from the way?' They shall
'Glory be to Thee! It did not behove us to take unto   [say,
ourselves protectors apart from Thee; but Thou gavest them

and their fathers enjoyment of days, until they forgot
20 the Remembrance, and were a people corrupt.' So they cried
lies touching the things you say, and you can neither ⌈you
turn it aside, nor find any help. Whosoever of you
does evil, We shall let him taste a great chastisement.

> And We sent not before thee any
> Envoys, but that they ate food, and went
> in the markets; and We appointed
> some of you to be a trial for others:
> 'Will you endure?' Thy Lord is ever
> All-seeing.
> Say those who look not to encounter Us,
> 'Why have the angels not been sent down
> on us, or why see we not our Lord?'
> Waxed proud they have within them, and become
> greatly disdainful.

Upon the day that they see the angels, no good tidings
that day for the sinners; they shall say, 'A ban forbidden!'
25 We shall advance upon what work they have done, and make it
a scattered dust. The inhabitants of Paradise that day,
better shall be their lodging, fairer their resting-place.
Upon the day that heaven is split asunder with the clouds
and the angels are sent down in majesty, the Kingdom
that day, the true Kingdom, shall belong to the All-merciful,
and it shall be a day harsh for the unbelievers.
Upon the day the evildoer shall bite his hands, saying,
'Would that I had taken a way along with the Messenger!
30 Alas, would that I had not taken So-and-so for a friend!
He indeed led me astray from the Remembrance, after
it had come to me; Satan is ever a forsaker of men.'

> The Messenger says, 'O my Lord, behold,
> my people have taken this Koran as a
> thing to be shunned.'
> Even so We have appointed to every
> Prophet an enemy among the sinners;
> but thy Lord suffices as a guide

and as a helper.
The unbelievers say, 'Why has the Koran
not been sent down upon him all at once?'
Even so, that We may strengthen thy
heart thereby, and We have chanted it
                    very distinctly.
35   They bring not to thee any similitude
but that We bring thee the truth, and better
            in exposition.
Those who shall be mustered to Gehenna
upon their faces—they shall be worse
in place, and gone further astray
            from the way.

We gave Moses the Book, and appointed
with him his brother Aaron as minister
and We said, 'Go to the people
who have cried lies to Our signs';
then We destroyed them utterly.
And the people of Noah, when they
cried lies to the Messengers, We
drowned them, and made them to be
a sign to mankind; and We
have prepared for the evildoers
a painful chastisement.
40   And Ad, and Thamood, and the men
of Er-Rass, and between that
generations a many—for each
We struck similitudes, and each
            We ruined utterly.
Surely they have come by the city
that was rained on by an evil rain;
what, have they not seen it? Nay,
but they look for no upraising.
And when they see thee, they take thee
in mockery only: 'What, is this he
whom God sent forth as a Messenger?
Wellnigh he had led us astray
from our gods, but that we kept

steadfast to them.' Assuredly
they shall know, when they see
the chastisement, who is further
astray from the way.

45   Hast thou seen him who has taken
his caprice to be his god?
Wilt thou be a guardian over them?
Or deemest thou that most of them
hear or understand? They are but
as the cattle; nay, they are further
astray from the way.

Hast thou not regarded thy Lord, how He has stretched out
the shadow? Had He willed,
He would have made it still.
Then We appointed the sun, to be a guide to it;
thereafter We seize it to
Ourselves, drawing it gently.
It is He who appointed the night for you to be a garment
and sleep for a rest, and day
He appointed for a rising.

50   And it is He who has loosed the winds, bearing good tidings
before His mercy; and We
sent down from heaven pure water
so that We might revive a dead land, and give to drink
of it, of that We created,
cattle and men a many.

We have indeed turned it about
amongst them, so that they may
remember; yet most men refuse all
but unbelief.

If We had willed, We would have raised up
in every city a warner.
So obey not the unbelievers, but struggle with
them thereby mightily.

55   And it is He who let forth the two seas, this one sweet,

grateful to taste, and this
salt, bitter to the tongue,
and He set between them a barrier, and a ban forbidden.
And it is He who created of
water a mortal, and made him
kindred of blood and marriage; thy Lord is All-powerful.

And they serve, apart from God, what neither
profits them nor hurts them; and the
unbeliever is ever a partisan
against his Lord.
We have sent thee not, except good tidings
to bear, and warning.
Say: 'I do not ask of you a wage for this,
except for him who wishes to take to
his Lord a way.'

60   Put thy trust in the Living God,
the Undying,
and proclaim His praise.
Sufficiently is He aware of His servants' sins
who created the heavens and the earth,
and what between them is, in six days,
then sat Himself upon the Throne,
the All-compassionate: ask any informed of Him!

But when they are told, 'Bow yourselves
to the All-merciful,' they say, 'And what
is the All-merciful? Shall we bow ourselves
to what thou biddest us?' And it increases
them in aversion.

Blessed be He
who has set in heaven constellations, and has set
among them a lamp, and
an illuminating moon.
And it is He who made the night and day a succession
for whom He desires to remember
or He desires to be thankful.

The servants of the All-merciful are
those who walk in the earth modestly
and who, when the ignorant address them,
    say, 'Peace';

65   who pass the night prostrate to their Lord
    and standing;
who say, 'Our Lord, turn Thou from us
the chastisement of Gehenna; surely
its chastisement is torment most terrible;
evil it is as a lodging-place
    and an abode';
who, when they expend, are neither prodigal
nor parsimonious, but between that is
    a just stand;
who call not upon another god with God,
nor slay the soul God has forbidden
except by right, neither fornicate,
for whosoever does that shall meet
    the price of sin—
doubled shall be the chastisement for him
on the Resurrection Day, and he shall dwell
    therein humbled,

70   save him who repents, and believes, and
does righteous work—those, God will
change their evil deeds into good deeds,
for God is ever All-forgiving,
    All-compassionate;
and whosoever repents, and does
righteousness, he truly turns to God
    in repentance.
And those who bear not false witness
and, when they pass by idle talk, pass by
    with dignity;
who, when they are reminded of the signs
of their Lord, fall not down thereat
    deaf and blind;
who say, 'Our Lord, give us refreshment of
our wives and seed, and make us a model

to the godfearing.'

75 Those shall be recompensed with the highest
heaven, for that they endured patiently,
and they shall receive therein a greeting
and—'Peace!'
Therein they shall dwell forever;
fair it is as a lodging-place
and an abode.

Say: 'My Lord esteems you not at all
were it not for your prayer, for you
have cried lies, and it shall surely be
fastened.'

XXVI

THE POETS

In the Name of God, the Merciful, the Compassionate

Ta Sin Mim

Those are the signs of the Manifest Book.

> Perchance thou consumest thyself
>   that they are not believers.
> If We will, We shall send down on them
> out of heaven a sign, so their necks
>   will stay humbled to it.
> But never fresh remembrance comes to
> them from the All-merciful, except
>   they turn away from it.

5   So they have cried lies; therefore
> assuredly tidings will come to them
>   of that they mocked at.

What, have they not regarded the earth, how many therein
  We have caused to grow of every generous kind?

>   Surely in that is a sign,
> yet most of them are not believers.
>   Surely thy Lord, He is
> the All-mighty, the All-compassionate.

And when thy Lord called to Moses,
'Go to the people of the evildoers, the

10   people of Pharaoh; will they not be godfearing?'
He said, 'My Lord, I fear they will cry me
lies, and my breast will be straitened,
and my tongue will not be loosed; so
send to Aaron. They also have a sin

against me, and I fear they will slay me.'
Said He, 'No indeed; but go, both of you,
with Our signs, and We assuredly
shall be with you, listening.

15   So go you to Pharaoh, and say,
"Verily, I am the Messenger
of the Lord of all Being; so send
forth with us the Children of Israel." '
He said, 'Did we not raise thee
amongst us as a child? Didst thou not
tarry among us years of thy life?
And thou didst the deed thou didst,
being one of the ungrateful!'
Said he, 'Indeed I did it then,
being one of those that stray;

20   so I fled from you, fearing you.
But my Lord gave me Judgment
and made me one of the Envoys.
That is a blessing thou reproachest me with,
having enslaved the Children of Israel.'
Pharaoh said, 'And what is the Lord
of all Being?' He said, 'The Lord
of the heavens and earth, and what
between them is, if you have faith.'
Said he to those about him,

25   'Do you not hear?' He said, 'Your Lord
and the Lord of your fathers, the ancients.'
Said he, 'Surely your Messenger
who was sent to you is possessed!'
He said, 'The Lord of the East and West,
and what between them is, if you
have understanding,' Said he, 'If thou
takest a god other than me,
I shall surely make thee one
of the imprisoned.' He said, 'What,
even though I brought thee something

30   manifest?' Said he, 'Bring it then,
if thou art of the truthful.' So he
cast his staff, and behold,

it was a serpent manifest.
And he drew forth his hand, and lo,
it was white to the beholders.
Said he to the Council about him,
'Surely this man is a cunning sorcerer
who desires to expel you from
your land by his sorcery; what

35 do you command?' They said, 'Put him
and his brother off a while, and
send among the cities musterers,
to bring thee every cunning sorcerer.'
So the sorcerers were assembled
for the appointed time of a fixed day.
The people were asked, 'Will you assemble?
Haply we shall follow the sorcerers
if it should be they are the victors.'

40 Then, when the sorcerers came, they said
to Pharaoh, 'Shall we indeed have a
wage, if we should be the victors?'
He said, 'Yes indeed; and you shall
then be among the near-stationed.' ⸱
Moses said to them, 'Cast you down
what you will cast.' So they cast
their ropes and their staffs, and said,
'By the might of Pharaoh we shall be
the victors.' Then Moses cast his staff
and lo, it forthwith swallowed up

45 their lying invention; so the sorcerers
were cast down, bowing themselves.
They said, 'We believe in the
Lord of all Being, the Lord of Moses
and Aaron.' Said Pharaoh, 'You have
believed him before I gave you leave.
Why, he is the chief of you, the same
that taught you sorcery; now you shall know!
I shall assuredly cut off
alternately your hands and feet,
then I shall crucify you all together.'

50 They said, 'There is no harm; surely

372

unto our Lord we are turning.
We are eager that our Lord should
forgive us our offences, for that
we are the first of the believers.'
Also We revealed unto Moses,
'Go with My servants by night; surely
you will be followed.' Then Pharaoh
sent among the cities musterers:
'Behold, these are a small troop,
55 and indeed they are enraging us;
and we are a host on our guard.'
So We expelled them from gardens
and fountains, and treasures and a
noble station; even so, and We
bequeathed them upon the Children of
60 Israel. Then they followed them
at the sunrise; and, when the two hosts
sighted each other, the companions
of Moses said, 'We are overtaken!'
Said he, 'No indeed; surely my
Lord is with me; He will guide me.'
Then We revealed to Moses,
'Strike with thy staff the sea'; and it clave,
and each part was as a mighty mount.
65 And there We brought the others on, and We
delivered Moses and those with him
all together; then We drowned the others.

  Surely in that is a sign,
yet most of them are not believers.
  Surely thy Lord, He is
the All-mighty, the All-compassionate.

And recite to them the tiding of Abraham
70 when he said to his father and his people,
  'What do you serve?'
They said, 'We serve idols, and continue
  cleaving to them.'

He said, 'Do they hear you when you call,
　　or do they profit you, or harm?'
They said, 'Nay, but we found our fathers
　　so doing.'
75　He said, 'And have you considered what
　　　　you have been serving,
you and your fathers, the elders?
They are an enemy to me, except the
　　　　Lord of all Being
who created me, and Himself guides me,
and Himself gives me to eat and drink,
80　and, whenever I am sick, heals me,
who makes me to die, then gives me life,
and who I am eager shall forgive me
my offence on the Day of Doom.
My Lord, give me Judgment, and join me
　　　　with the righteous,
and appoint me a tongue of truthfulness
　　　　among the others.
85　Make me one of the inheritors of the
　　　　Garden of Bliss.
and forgive my father, for he is one
　　　　of those astray.
Degrade me not upon the day when they
　　　　are raised up,
the day when neither wealth nor sons
　　　　shall profit
except for him who comes to God with
　　　　a pure heart.
90　And Paradise shall be brought forward
　　　　for the godfearing,
and Hell advanced for the perverse.
It shall be said to them, 'Where is that
　　　　you were serving
apart from God? Do they help you
　　　　or help themselves?'
Then they shall be pitched into it,
　　　　they and the perverse
95　and the hosts of Iblis, all together.

They shall say, as they dispute there
one with another,
'By God, we were certainly in
manifest error
when we made you equal with the
Lord of all Being.
It was naught but the sinners that
led us astray;
100   so now we have no intercessors,
no loyal friend.
O that we might return again, and be
among the believers!'

Surely in that is a sign,
yet most of them are not believers.
Surely thy Lord, He is
the All-mighty, the All-compassionate.

105   The people of Noah cried lies to the Envoys
when their brother Noah said to them,
'Will you not be godfearing?
I am for you a faithful Messenger,
so serve you God, and obey you me.
I ask of you no wage for this;
my wage falls only upon the
Lord of all Being;
110   so fear you God, and obey you me.'
They said, 'Shall we believe thee, whom
the vilest follow?'
He said, 'What knowledge have I of that
they have been doing?
Their account falls only upon my Lord,
were you but aware.
I would not drive away the believers;
115   I am naught but a plain warner.'
They said, 'If thou givest not over,
Noah, thou shalt assuredly be
one of the stoned.'
He said, 'My Lord, my people have

cried me lies,
so give true deliverance between me
and them, and deliver me and the believers
    that are with me.'
So We delivered him, and those with him,
    in the laden ship,
120   then afterwards We drowned the rest.

Surely in that is a sign,
yet most of them are not believers.
    Surely thy Lord, He is
the All-mighty, the All-compassionate.

Ad cried lies to the Envoys
when their brother Hood said to them,
    'Will you not be godfearing?
125   I am for you a faithful Messenger,
so fear you God, and obey you me.
I ask of you no wage for this;
my wage falls only upon the
    Lord of all Being.
What, do you build on every prominence
    a sign, sporting,
and do you take to you castles, haply
    to dwell forever?
130   When you assault, you assault
    like tyrants!
So fear you God, and obey you me;
and fear Him who has succoured you
    with what you know,
succoured you with flocks and sons,
    gardens and fountains.
135   Indeed, I fear for you the chastisement of
    a dreadful day.'
They said, 'Alike it is to us, whether
thou admonishest, or art not one of
    the admonishers;
this is nothing but the habit of
    the ancients,

and we shall not be chastised.'
So they cried him lies; then We destroyed them.

Surely in that is a sign,
yet most of them are not believers.
140 Surely thy Lord, He is
the All-mighty, the All-compassionate.

Thamood cried lies to the Envoys
when their brother Salih said to them,
 'Will you not be godfearing?
I am for you a faithful Messenger,
so fear you God, and obey you me.
145 I ask of you no wage for this;
my wage falls only upon the
  Lord of all Being.
Will you be left secure in this here, among
  gardens and fountains,
sown fields, and palms with slender spathes?
Will you still skilfully hew houses
  out of the mountains?
150 So fear you God, and obey you me,
and obey not the commandment
  of the prodigal
who do corruption in the earth, and set
  not things aright.'
They said, 'Thou art merely one of those
  that are bewitched;
thou art naught but a mortal, like us;
then produce a sign, if thou art
  one of the truthful.'
155 He said, 'This is a she-camel;
to her a draught and to you a draught, on
  a day appointed,
and do not touch her with malice
so that there seize you the chastisement of
  a dreadful day.'
But they hamstrung her, and in the morning
  they were remorseful,

and the chastisement seized them.

> Surely in that is a sign,
> yet most of them are not believers.
> Surely thy Lord, He is
> the All-mighty, the All-compassionate.

160 The people of Lot cried lies to the Envoys
when their brother Lot said to them,
'Will you not be godfearing?
I am for you a faithful Messenger,
so fear you God, and obey you me.
I ask of you no wage for this;
my wage falls only upon the
Lord of all Being.
165 What, do you come to male beings,
leaving your wives that your Lord created
for you? Nay, but you are a people
of transgressors.'
They said, 'If thou givest not over,
Lot, thou shalt assuredly be
one of the expelled.'
He said, 'Truly I am a detester
of what you do.
My Lord, deliver me and my people
from that they do.'
170 So We delivered him and his people
all together,
save an old woman among those that tarried;
then We destroyed the others, and We rained
on them a rain; and evil is the rain of
them that are warned.

175' Surely in that is a sign,
yet most of them are not believers.
Surely thy Lord, He is
the All-mighty, the All-compassionate.

The men of the Thicket cried lies to the Envoys

when Shuaib said to them,
'Will you not be godfearing?
I am for you a faithful Messenger,
so fear you God, and obey you me.

180   I ask of you no wage for this;
my wage falls only upon the
        Lord of all Being.
Fill up the measure, and be not cheaters,
and weigh with the straight balance,
and diminish not the goods of the people,
and do not mischief in the earth,
        working corruption.
Fear Him who created you, and the generations
        of the ancients.'

185   They said, 'Thou art merely one of those
        that are bewitched;
thou art naught but a mortal, like us;
indeed, we think that thou art
        one of the liars.
Then drop down on us lumps from heaven, if thou
        one of the truthful.'   [art
He said, 'My Lord knows very well
        what you are doing.'
But they cried him lies; then there seized them
the chastisement of the Day of Shadow;
assuredly it was the chastisement of
        a dreadful day.

190   Surely in that is a sign,
yet most of them are not believers.
        Surely thy Lord, He is
the All-mighty, the All-compassionate.

        Truly it is the revelation of
        the Lord of all Being,
brought down by the Faithful Spirit
upon thy heart, that thou mayest be
        one of the warners,
195   in a clear, Arabic tongue.

Truly it is in the Scriptures
of the ancients.

Was it not a sign for them, that it is known
to the learned of the Children of Israel?
If We had sent it down on a barbarian
and he had recited it to them, they would
not have believed in it.

200 Even so We have caused it to enter into
the hearts of the sinners,
who will not believe in it, until they
see the painful chastisement
so that it will come upon them suddenly,
while they are not aware,
and they will say, 'Shall we be respited?'
What, do they seek to hasten Our chastisement?

205 What thinkest thou? If We give them enjoyment
of days for many years,
then there comes on them that they were promised,
what will it then avail them, the enjoyment
of days they were given?

Never a city We destroyed, but it had warners
for a reminder; and never did We wrong.

210 Not by the Satans has it
been brought down;
it behoves them not, neither
are they able.
Truly, they are expelled
from hearing.

So call thou not upon another god
with God, lest thou shouldst be one of those
that are chastised.
And warn thy clan, thy nearest kin.

215 Lower thy wing to those who follow thee,
being believers;
then, if they disobey thee, say, 'I am quit

of that you do.'

Put thy trust in the All-mighty, the All-compassionate
     who sees thee when thou standest
and when thou turnest about among those who bow.
     Surely He is the All-hearing, the All-knowing.

     Shall I tell you on whom the Satans come down?
     They come down on every guilty impostor.
     They give ear, but most of them are liars.
     And the poets—the perverse follow them;
     hast thou not seen how they wander in every valley
     and how they say that which they do not?

     Save those that believe, and do righteous deeds,
          and remember God oft,
     and help themselves after being wronged; and
     those who do wrong shall surely know by what
          overturning they will be overturned.

220

225

XXVII

THE ANT

In the Name of God, the Merciful, the Compassionate

Ta Sin

Those are the signs of the Koran
and a Manifest Book,
a guidance, and good tidings
unto the believers
who perform the prayer, and pay the alms,
and have sure faith in the Hereafter.

Those who believe not in the Hereafter,
We have decked out fair for them their
    works, and they wander blindly;
5   those are they whom an evil chastisement
awaits, and they will be the greatest losers
    in the Hereafter.

Thou receivest the Koran
from One All-wise, All-knowing.

When Moses said to his people
'I observe a fire, and will bring
you news of it, or I will bring
you a flaming brand, that haply
you shall warm yourselves.'
So, when he came to it, he
was called: 'Blessed is He
who is in the fire, and he
who is about it. Glory be to
God, the Lord of all Being!
Moses, behold, it is I, God,
the All-mighty, the All-wise.

10   Cast down thy staff.' And when he
saw it quivering like a serpent
he turned about, retreating,
and turned not back. 'Moses,
fear not; surely the Envoys
do not fear in My presence,
save him who has done evil,
then, after evil, has changed
into good; All-forgiving
am I, All-compassionate.
Thrust thy hand in thy bosom
and it will come forth white
without evil—among nine
signs to Pharaoh and his people;
they are an ungodly people.'
But when Our signs came to them
visibly, they said, 'This
is a manifest sorcery';
and they denied them, though
their souls acknowledged them,
wrongfully and out of pride.
Behold, how was the end of
the workers of corruption!

15   And We gave David and Solomon knowledge
and they said, 'Praise belongs to God
who has preferred us over many of His
      believing servants.'

And Solomon was David's heir,
and he said, 'Men, we have been
taught the speech of the birds, and we
have been given of everything; surely
this is indeed the manifest bounty.'
And his hosts were mustered to Solomon,
jinn, men and birds, duly disposed;
till, when they came on the Valley of Ants,
an ant said, 'Ants, enter your
dwelling-places, lest Solomon and

his hosts crush you, being unaware!'
But he smiled, laughing at its words,
and he said, 'My Lord, dispose me
that I may be thankful for Thy blessing
wherewith Thou hast blessed me and my
father and mother, and that I may do
righteousness well-pleasing to Thee;
and do Thou admit me, by Thy mercy,
amongst Thy righteous servants.'

20   And he reviewed the birds; then he said,
'How is it with me, that I do not see
the hoopoe? Or is he among the absent?
Assuredly I will chastise him with a
terrible chastisement, or I will slaughter
him, or he bring me a clear authority.'
But he tarried not long, and said,
'I have comprehended that which thou
hast not comprehended, and I have come
from Sheba to thee with a sure tiding.
I found a woman ruling over them,
and she has been given of everything,
and she possesses a mighty throne.
I found her and her people prostrating
to the sun, apart from God; Satan
has decked out fair their deeds to them
and he has barred them from the way,
and therefore they are not guided,

25   so that they prostrate not themselves
to God, who brings forth what is hidden
in the heavens and earth; and He knows
what you conceal and what you publish.
God: there is no god but He,
the Lord of the Mighty Throne.'
Said he, 'Now we will see whether
thou hast spoken truly, or whether
thou art amongst those that lie.
Take this letter of mine, and cast it
unto them, then turn back from them
and see what they shall return.'

She said, 'O Council, see, a letter
honourable has been cast unto me.
It is from Solomon, and it is "In the Name
of God, the Merciful, the Compassionate.
Rise not up against me, but come to me
in surrender." ' She said, 'O Council,
pronounce to me concerning my affair;
I am not used to decide an affair
until you bear me witness.' They said,
'We possess force and we possess great might.
The affair rests with thee; so consider
what thou wilt command.' She said, 'Kings,
when they enter a city, disorder it
and make the mighty ones of its inhabitants
abased. Even so they too will do.
Now I will send them a present, and see
what the envoys bring back.' But when he
came to Solomon he said, 'What, would you
succour me with wealth, and what God gave me
is better than what He has given you?
Nay, but instead you rejoice in your gift!
Return thou to them; we shall assuredly
come against them with hosts they have not
power to resist, and we shall expel them
from there, abased and utterly humbled.'
He said, 'O Council, which one of you will
bring me her throne, before they come to me
in surrender?' An efreet of the jinns
said, 'I will bring it to thee, before thou
risest from thy place; I have strength for it
and I am trusty.' Said he who possessed
knowledge of the Book, 'I will bring it to
thee, before ever thy glance returns to thee.
Then, when he saw it settled before him,
he said, 'This is of my Lord's bounty
that He may try me, whether I am thankful
or ungrateful. Whosoever gives thanks
gives thanks only for his own soul's good,
and whosoever is ungrateful—my Lord

is surely All-sufficient, All-generous.'
He said, 'Disguise her throne for her,
and we shall behold whether she is guided
or if she is of those that are not guided.'
So, when she came, it was said, 'Is thy
throne like this?' She said, 'It seems
the same.' 'And we were given the knowledge
before her, and we were in surrender,
but that she served, apart from God, barred her,
for she was of a people of unbelievers.'
It was said to her, 'Enter the pavilion.'
But when she saw it, she supposed it was
a spreading water, and she bared her legs.
He said, 'It is a pavilion smoothed of
45   crystal.' She said, 'My Lord, indeed I
have wronged myself, and I surrender with
Solomon to God, the Lord of all Being.'

And We sent to Thamood their brother
Salih: 'Serve you God!' And behold,
they were two parties, that were disputing
                one with another.
He said, 'O my people, why do you seek
to hasten evil before good? Why do you
not ask forgiveness of God? Haply so
                you will find mercy.'
They said, 'We augur ill of thee and of
those that are with thee.' He said, 'Your augury
is with God; nay, but you are a people
                being proved.'
Now in the city there were nine persons
who did corruption in the land, and put
                not things right;
50   they said, 'Swear you, one to another, by
God, "We will attack him and his family
by night, then we will tell his protector,
We were not witnesses of the destruction
of his family; and assuredly we
                are truthful men."'

And they devised a device, and We
likewise devised a device, while they
    were not aware;
and behold, how was the end of their device!
For We destroyed them and their people
    all together.
Those are their houses, all fallen down
because of the evil they committed;
surely in that is a sign for a people
    who have knowledge.
And We delivered those who believed
    and were godfearing.

55   And Lot, when he said to his people,
'What, do you commit indecency
    with your eyes open?
What, do you approach men lustfully
instead of women? No, you are a people
    that are ignorant.'
And the only answer of his people
was that they said, 'Expel the folk
of Lot from your city; they are men that
    keep themselves clean!'
So We delivered him and his family,
except his wife; We decreed she should be
    of those that tarried.
And We rained on them a rain;
and evil indeed is the rain of
    them that are warned.

60   Say: 'Praise belongs to God,
and peace be on His servants
    whom He has chosen.'
What, is God better, or that
    they associate?

He who created the heavens and earth, and sent down for you
    out of heaven water;
and We caused to grow therewith gardens full of loveliness

whose trees you could never grow.
    Is there a god with God?
Nay, but they are a people who assign to Him equals!

    He who made the earth a fixed place
      and set amidst it rivers
    and appointed for it firm mountains
and placed a partition between the two seas.
    Is there a god with God?
Nay, but the most of them have no knowledge.

He who answers the constrained, when he calls unto Him,
      and removes the evil
and appoints you to be successors in the earth.
    Is there a god with God?
    Little indeed do you remember.

He who guides you in the shadows of the land and the sea
      and looses the winds,
    bearing good tidings before His mercy.
    Is there a god with God?
High exalted be God, above that which they associate!

65 Who originates creation, then brings it back again,
    and provides you out of heaven and earth.
    Is there a god with God?
Say: 'Produce your proof, if you speak truly.'
Say: 'None knows the Unseen in the heavens and earth
      except God.
      And they are not aware
      when they shall be raised;
nay, but their knowledge fails as to the Hereafter;
      nay, they are in doubt of it;
      nay, they are blind to it.

    The unbelievers say, 'What, when we are
dust, and our fathers, shall we indeed
      be brought forth?
70   We have been promised this, and our fathers

before; this is naught but the fairy-tales
of the ancients.'
Say: 'Journey in the land, then behold
how was the end of the sinners.'

Do not sorrow for them,
nor be thou straitened
for what they devise.

They say, 'When shall this promise come to
pass, if you speak the truth?'
Say: 'It may be that riding behind you
already is some part of that you seek
to hasten on.'

75   Surely thy Lord is bountiful to men; but most of them
are not thankful.
Surely thy Lord knows what their hearts conceal, and
what they publish.
And not a thing is
there hidden in heaven and earth
but it is in a Manifest Book.

Surely this Koran relates to the Children
of Israel most of that concerning which
they are at variance;
it is a guidance, and a mercy
unto the believers.
80   Surely thy Lord will decide between them
by His Judgment; He is the All-mighty,
the All-knowing.
So put thy trust in God;
thou art upon the manifest truth.

Thou shalt not make the dead to hear,
neither shalt thou make the deaf to hear the call
when they turn about, retreating.
Thou shalt not guide the blind out of their error

neither shalt thou make any to hear, save
such as believe in Our signs, and so surrender.
When the Word falls on them, We shall bring forth for them
out of the earth a beast that shall speak unto them:
'Mankind had no faith in Our signs.'

85 Upon the day when We shall muster out of every nation
a troop of those that cried lies to Our signs, duly disposed,
till, when they are come, He shall say, 'Did you cry lies to
My signs, not comprehending them in knowledge, or what
have you been doing?' And the Word shall fall upon them
because of the evil they committed, while they speak naught.

Have they not seen how We made the night
for them, to repose in it, and the day, to see?
Surely in that is a sign for a people who are believers.

On the day the Trumpet is blown, and terrified is whosoever
is in the heavens and earth, excepting whom God wills,
and every one shall come to Him, all utterly abject;
90 and thou shalt see the mountains, that thou supposest fixed,
passing by like clouds—God's handiwork, who has created
everything very well. He is aware of the things you do.
Whosoever comes with a good deed, he shall have better
than it; and they shall be secure from terror that day.
And whosoever comes with an evil deed, their faces shall be
thrust into the Fire: 'Are you recompensed but for what you
[did?'

I have only been commanded
to serve the Lord of this territory
which He has made sacred;
to Him belongs everything.
And I have been commanded
to be of those that surrender,
and to recite the Koran.
So whosoever is guided, is only guided
to his own gain; and whosoever goes
astray, say: 'I am naught but a warner.'

95 And say: 'Praise belongs to God.

He shall show you His signs
and you will recognise them.
Thy Lord is not heedless of the things you do.'

XXVIII

THE STORY

In the Name of God, the Merciful, the Compassionate

Ta Sin Mim

Those are the signs of the Manifest Book.

We will recite to thee something of the tiding
of Moses and Pharaoh truthfully, for a
    people who believe.
Now Pharaoh had exalted himself in the land
and had divided its inhabitants into sects,
abasing one party of them, slaughtering their
sons, and sparing their women; for he was of the
    workers of corruption.
Yet We desired to be gracious to those that were
abased in the land, and to make them leaders, and to
    make them the inheritors,
5   and to establish them in the land, and to show
Pharaoh and Haman, and their hosts, what they
    were dreading from them.
So We revealed to Moses' mother, 'Suckle him,
then, when thou fearest for him, cast him into
the sea, and do not fear, neither sorrow, for
We shall return him to thee, and shall appoint him
    one of the Envoys.'
So then the folk of Pharaoh picked him out
to be an enemy and a sorrow to them;
certainly Pharaoh and Haman, and their hosts,
    were of the sinners.
Said Pharaoh's wife, 'He will be a comfort
to me and thee. Slay him not; perchance he will
profit us, or we will take him for a son.' And
    they were not aware.

On the morrow the heart of Moses' mother
became empty, and she wellnigh disclosed him
had We not strengthened her heart, that she might be
    among the believers;
10   and she said to his sister, 'Follow him,'
and she perceived him from afar, even while
    they were not aware.
Now We had forbidden to him aforetime
to be suckled by any foster-mother; therefore
she said, 'Shall I direct you to the people of a
household who will take charge of him for you
    and look after him?'
So We returned him to his mother, that she might be
comforted and not sorrow, and that she might know
that the promise of God is true; but most of
    them do not know.
And when he was fully grown and in the perfection
of his strength, We gave him judgment and
knowledge; even so do We recompense
    the good-doers.
And he entered the city, at a time when its people
were unheeding, and found there two men
fighting; the one was of his own party, and
the other was of his enemies. Then the one
that was of his party cried to him to aid him
against the other that was of his enemies; so
Moses struck him, and despatched him, and said,
'This is of Satan's doing; he is surely an enemy
    misleading, manifest.'
15   He said, 'My Lord, I have wronged myself. Forgive me!'
So God forgave him, for He is the All-forgiving,
    the All-compassionate.
He said, 'My Lord, forasmuch as Thou hast
blessed me, I will never be a partisan
    of the sinners.'
Now in the morning he was in the city,
fearful and vigilant; and behold, the man
who had sought his succour on the day before
cried out to him again. Moses said to him, 'Clearly

thou art a quarreller.'

But when he would have assaulted the man who
was an enemy to them both, the man said, 'Moses,
dost thou desire to slay me, even as thou slewest
a living soul yesterday? Thou only desirest to be
a tyrant in the land; thou desirest not to be of
  them that put things right.'

Then came a man from the furthest part of the
city, running; he said, 'Moses, the Council are
conspiring to slay thee. Depart; I am one of
  thy sincere advisers.'

20 So he departed therefrom, fearful and vigilant;
he said, 'My Lord, deliver me from the people
  of the evildoers.'

And when he turned his face towards Midian
he said, 'It may be that my Lord will guide me
  on the right way.'

And when he came to the waters of Midian
he found a company of the people there
  drawing water,

and he found, apart from them, two women
holding back their flocks. He said, 'What is
your business?' They said, 'We may not draw
water until the shepherds drive off, and our father
  is passing old.'

So he drew water for them; then he turned away
to the shade, and he said, 'O my Lord, surely
I have need of whatever good Thou shalt have
  sent down upon me.'

25 Then came one of the two women to him, walking
modestly, and said, 'My father invites thee,
that he may recompense thee with the wage of thy
drawing water for us.' So when he came to him
and had related to him the story, he said,
'Be not afraid; thou hast escaped from the people
  of the evildoers.'

Said one of the two women, 'Father, hire him;
surely the best man thou canst hire is the one
  strong and trusty.'

He said, 'I desire to marry thee to one of
these my two daughters, on condition that thou
hirest thyself to me for eight years. If thou
completest ten, that shall be of thy own accord;
I do not desire to press hard upon thee.
Thou shalt assuredly find me, if God wills,
    one of the righteous.'
Said he, 'So let it be between me and thee.
Whichever of the two terms I fulfil, it shall be
no injustice to me; and God is guardian
    of what we say.'
So when Moses had accomplished the term
and departed with his household, he observed
on the side of the Mount a fire. He said to his
household, 'Tarry you here; I observe a fire.
Perhaps I shall bring you news of it,
or a faggot from the fire, that haply
    you shall warm yourselves.'
30   When he came to it, a voice cried from the right bank
of the watercourse, in the sacred hollow,
coming from the tree: 'Moses, I am God, the
    Lord of all Being.
Cast down thy staff.' And when he saw it
quivering like a serpent, he turned about
retreating, and turned not back. 'Moses,
come forward, and fear not; for surely thou
    art in security.
Insert thy hand into thy bosom, and it will
come forth white without evil; and press to thee
thy arm, that thou be not afraid. So these
shall be two proofs from thy Lord to Pharaoh
and his Council; for surely they are an
    ungodly people.'
Said he, 'My Lord, I have indeed slain
a living soul among them, and I fear that
    they will slay me.
Moreover my brother Aaron is more eloquent
than I. Send him with me as a helper
and to confirm I speak truly, for I fear they

will cry me lies.'

35 Said He, 'We will strengthen thy arm by means
of thy brother, and We shall appoint to you
an authority, so that they shall not reach you
because of Our signs; you, and whoso follows you,
shall be the victors.'

So when Moses came to them with Our signs,
clear signs, they said, 'This is nothing but a
forged sorcery. We never heard of this among
our fathers, the ancients.'

But Moses said, 'My Lord knows very well
who comes with the guidance from Him, and shall
possess the Ultimate Abode; surely the evildoers
will not prosper.'

And Pharaoh said, 'Council, I know not that you
have any god but me. Kindle me, Haman,
a fire upon the clay, and make me a tower, that I
may mount up to Moses' god; for I think that he is
one of the liars.'

And he waxed proud in the land, he and his hosts,
wrongfully; and they thought they should not be
returned to Us.

40 Therefore We seized him and his hosts, and cast them
into the sea; so behold how was the end
of the evildoers!

And We appointed them leaders, calling to the
Fire; and on the Day of Resurrection they
shall not be helped;

and We pursued them in this world with a curse,
and on the Day of Resurrection they shall be
among the spurned.

And We gave Moses the Book, after that We had
destroyed the former generations, to be examples
and a guidance and a mercy, that haply so
they might remember.

Thou wast not upon the western side
when We decreed to Moses the commandment,
nor wast thou of those witnessing;

45   but We raised up generations,
and long their lives continued.
Neither wast thou a dweller among
the Midianites, reciting to them Our
signs; but We were sending Messengers.
Thou wast not upon the side of the
Mount when We called; but for a mercy
from thy Lord, that thou mayest warn
a people to whom no warner came before
thee, and that haply they may remember.
Else, did an affliction visit them
for that their own hands have forwarded
then they might say, 'Our Lord, why
didst Thou not send a Messenger to us
that we might follow Thy signs
and so be among the believers?'
Yet when the truth came to them
from Ourselves, they said, 'Why
has he not been given the like of
that Moses was given?' But they,
did they not disbelieve also in
what Moses was given aforetime?
They said, 'A pair of sorceries
mutually supporting each other.'
They said, 'We disbelieve both.'

50   Say: 'Bring a Book from God that gives
better guidance than these, and follow it,
     if you speak truly.'
Then if they do not answer thee, know that
they are only following their caprices;
and who is further astray than he who
follows his caprice without guidance from
God? Surely God guides not the people
     of the evildoers.
Now We have brought them the Word; haply
     they may remember.
Those to whom We gave the Book before this
     believe in it

and, when it is recited to them, they say,
'We believe in it; surely it is the truth
from our Lord. Indeed, even before it
    we had surrendered.'
These shall be given their wage twice over
for that they patiently endured, and avert
evil with good, and expend of that
    We have provided them.

55   When they hear idle talk, they turn away
from it and say, 'We have our deeds, and you
your deeds. Peace be upon you! We desire
    not the ignorant.'
Thou guidest not whom thou likest, but God
guides whom He wills, and knows very well
    those that are guided.
They say, 'Should we follow the guidance
with thee, we shall be snatched from our land.'
Have We not established for them a sanctuary
secure, to which are collected the fruits of
everything, as a provision from Us? But
    most of them know not.
How many a city We have destroyed
that flourished in insolent ease! Those
are their dwelling-places, undwelt in
after them, except a little; Ourselves
    are the inheritors.
Yet thy Lord never destroyed the cities
until He sent in their mother-city
a Messenger, to recite Our signs
unto them; and We never destroyed
the cities, save that their inhabitants
    were evildoers.

60   Whatever thing you have been given
is the enjoyment of the present life
and its adornment; and what is with
God is better and more enduring.
    Will you not understand?
What, is he to whom We have promised
a fair promise, and he receives it,

like him to whom We have given the
enjoyment of the present life, then he
on the Resurrection Day shall be of those
that are arraigned?

Upon the day when He shall call to them, and He shall say,
'Where now are My associates whom you were asserting?'
Those against whom the Word is realized, they shall say,
'Our Lord, those whom we perverted, we perverted them
even as we ourselves erred. We declare our innocence
unto Thee; it was not us that they were serving.'
It shall be said, 'Call you now upon your associates!'
And they will call upon them, but they shall not answer them,
and they shall see the chastisement—ah, if they had been
[guided!
65 Upon the day when He shall call to them, and He shall say,
'What answer gave you to the Envoys?' Upon that day
the tidings will be darkened for them, nor will they ask
[each other.

But as for him who repents, and believes,
and works righteousness, haply he shall be
among the prosperers.
Thy Lord creates whatsoever He will
and He chooses; they have not the choice.
Glory be to God! High be He exalted above
that they associate!
And thy Lord knows what their breasts conceal
and what they publish.

70   And He is God;
there is no god but He.
His is the praise
in the former as in the latter;
His too is the Judgment,
and unto Him you shall be returned.

Say: 'What think you? If God should make
the night unceasing over you, until

the Day of Resurrection, what god other
than God shall bring you illumination?
Will you not hear?'
Say: 'What think you? If God should make
the day unceasing over you, until
the Day of Resurrection, what god other
than God shall bring you night to repose in?
Will you not see?
Of His mercy He has appointed for you
night and day, for you to repose in
and seek after His bounty, that haply
you will be thankful.'

Upon the day when He shall call to them, and He shall say,
'Where now are My associates whom you were asserting?'
And We shall draw out from every nation a witness, and say,
75 'Produce your proof!' Then will they know that Truth is
[God's,
and there shall go astray from them that they were forging.

Now Korah was of the people of Moses; he
became insolent to them, for We had given him
treasures such that the very keys of them
were too heavy a burden for a company of
men endowed with strength. When his people
said to him, 'Do not exult; God loves not
those that exult;
but seek, amidst that which God has given thee,
the Last Abode, and forget not thy portion
of the present world; and do good, as God has
been good to thee. And seek not to work
corruption in the earth; surely God loves not the
workers of corruption.'
He said, 'What I have been given is only
because of a knowledge that is in me.' What,
did he not know that God had destroyed before
him generations of men stronger than he
in might, and more numerous in multitude?
And yet the sinners shall not be questioned

concerning their sins.
So he went forth unto his people in his
adornment. Those who desired the present life
said, 'Would that we possessed the like of that
Korah has been given! Surely he is a man
of mighty fortune.'
80 But those to whom knowledge had been given
said, 'Woe upon you! The reward of God
is better for him who believes, and works
righteousness; and none shall receive it
except the steadfast.'
So We made the earth to swallow him and his dwelling
and there was no host to help him, apart from God,
and he was helpless;
and in the morning those who had longed to be
in his place the day before were saying,
'Ah, God outspreads and straitens His provision
to whomsoever He will of His servants. Had
God not been gracious to us, He would have made
us to be swallowed too. Ah, the unbelievers
do not prosper.'

That is the Last Abode;
We appoint it for those who desire not
exorbitance in the earth, nor corruption.
The issue ultimate is to the godfearing.
Whoso brings a good deed shall have better
than it; and whoso brings an evil deed—
those who have done evil deeds shall only
be recompensed for that they were doing.

85 He who imposed the Recitation upon thee
shall surely restore thee to a place of homing.
Say: 'My Lord knows very well who comes
with guidance, and who is in manifest error.'
Thou didst not hope that the Book should be
cast unto thee, except it be as a mercy
from thy Lord; so be thou not a partisan
of the unbelievers. Let them not bar thee

from the signs of God, after that they have been
sent down to thee. And call upon thy Lord,
and be thou not of the idolaters.

And call not upon another god with God;
    there is no god but He.
  All things perish, except His Face.
   His is the Judgment,
and unto Him you shall be returned.

XXIX

THE SPIDER

In the Name of God, the Merciful, the Compassionate

Alif Lam Mim

Do the people reckon that they will be left to say
    'We believe,' and will not be tried?
We certainly tried those that were before them,
and assuredly God knows those who speak truly,
    and assuredly He knows the liars.
Or do they reckon, those who do evil deeds, that
    they will outstrip Us? Ill they judge!
Whoso looks to encounter God, God's term is coming;
    He is the All-hearing, the All-knowing.

5   Whosoever struggles, struggles only to his
    own gain; surely God is All-sufficient
        nor needs any being.
And those who believe, and do righteous deeds,
We shall surely acquit them of their evil
deeds, and shall recompense them the best of
        what they were doing.
We have charged man, that he be kind to his
parents; but if they strive with thee to make thee
associate with Me that whereof thou hast no
knowledge, then do not obey them; unto Me
you shall return, and I shall tell you
        what you were doing.
And those who believe, and do righteous deeds
assuredly We shall admit them
        among the righteous.

Some men there are who say, 'We believe
in God,' but when such a man is hurt

in God's cause, he makes the persecution
of men as it were God's chastisement;
then if help comes from thy Lord, he will say
'We were with you.' What, does not God
know very well what is in the breasts
  of all beings?
10 God surely knows the believers, and He knows
  the hypocrites.

The unbelievers say to the believers,
'Follow our path, and let us carry
your offences'; yet they cannot carry
anything, even of their own offences;
  they are truly liars.
They shall certainly carry their loads,
and other loads along with their loads,
and upon the Day of Resurrection they
shall surely be questioned concerning
  that they were forging.

Indeed, We sent Noah to his people,
and he tarried among them a thousand years,
all but fifty; so the Flood seized them, while
  they were evildoers.
Yet We delivered him, and those who were
in the ship, and appointed it for a sign
  unto all beings.

15 And Abraham, when he said to his people,
'Serve God, and fear Him; that is better for
  you, did you know.
You only serve, apart from God, idols
and you create a calumny; those you serve,
apart from God, have no power to
provide for you. So seek after your
provision with God, and serve Him,
and be thankful to Him; unto Him
  you shall be returned.
But if you cry me lies, nations cried lies before

you; and it is only for the Messenger to deliver
    the Manifest Message.'
(Have they not seen how God originates
creation, then brings it back again? Surely
    that is an easy matter for God.
Say: 'Journey in the land, then behold how
He originated creation; then God causes
the second growth to grow; God is powerful
    over everything,

20   chastising whom He will, and having mercy
on whomsoever He will, and unto Him
    you shall be turned.
You are not able to frustrate Him
either in the earth or in heaven;
and you have not, apart from God, either
    protector or helper.
And those who disbelieve in God's signs
and the encounter with Him—they despair
of My mercy, and there awaits them
    a painful chastisement.)
But the only answer of his people was
that they said, 'Slay him, or burn him!'
Then God delivered him from the fire;
surely in that are signs for a people
    who believe.
And he said, 'You have only taken to
yourselves idols, apart from God, as
a mark of mutual love between you in
the present life; then upon the Day of
Resurrection you will deny one another,
and you will curse one another,
and your refuge will be the Fire, and you
    will have no helpers.'

25   But Lot believed him; and he said, 'I will
flee to my Lord; He is the All-mighty,
    the All-wise.'
And We gave him Isaac and Jacob, and We
appointed the Prophecy and the Book to be
among his seed; We gave him his wage in

this world, and in the world to come he shall be
    among the righteous.

And Lot, when he said to his people
'Surely you commit such indecency
as never any being in all the world
    committed before you.
What, do you approach men, and cut
the way, and commit in your assembly
dishonour?' But the only answer
of his people was that they said,
'Then bring us the chastisement of God, if
    thou speakest truly.'
He said, 'My Lord, help me against the people
    that work corruption.'

30   And when Our messengers came to Abraham
with the good tidings, they said, 'We shall
destroy the people of this city, for its people
    are evildoers.'
He said, 'Lot is in it.' They said, 'We
know very well who is in it; assuredly
We shall deliver him and his family,
except his wife; she has become
    of those that tarry.'
When that Our messengers came to Lot
he was troubled on their account
and distressed for them; but they said,
'Fear not, neither sorrow, for surely we
shall deliver thee and thy family,
except thy wife; she has become
    of those that tarry.
We shall send down upon the people
of this city wrath out of heaven
    for their ungodliness.'
And indeed, We have left thereof a
sign, a clear sign, unto a people
    who understand.

35   And to Midian their brother Shuaib;

he said, 'O my people, serve God,
and look you for the Last Day;
and do not mischief in the land,
    working corruption.'
But they cried lies to him; so
the earthquake seized them, and
morning found them in their habitation
    fallen prostrate.

And Ad, and Thamood—it has become
clear to you from their dwelling-places;
and Satan decked out fair to them
their works, and barred them from the way,
    though they saw clearly.

And Korah, and Pharaoh, and Haman;
Moses came to them with the clear signs, but
they waxed proud in the earth, yet they
    outstripped Us not.
Each We seized for his sin; and of them
against some We loosed a squall of pebbles
and some were seized by the Cry, and some
We made the earth to swallow, and some We
drowned; God would never wrong them, but
    they wronged themselves.

40   The likeness of those who have taken
to them protectors, apart from God,
is as the likeness of the spider that takes
to itself a house; and surely the frailest
of houses is the house of the spider,
    did they but know.
God knows whatever thing they call upon
apart from Him; He is the All-mighty,
    the All-wise.
And those similitudes—We strike them
for the people, but none understands them
    save those who know.
God created the heavens and the earth

with the truth; surely in that is a sign
    to the believers.

Recite what has been revealed to thee
of the Book, and perform the prayer;
prayer forbids indecency and dishonour.
God's remembrance is greater; and God knows
    the things you work.

45   Dispute not with the People of the Book
save in the fairer manner, except for
those of them that do wrong; and say,
'We believe in what has been sent down
to us, and what has been sent down to you;
our God and your God is One, and to Him
    we have surrendered.'

Even so We have sent down to thee
the Book. Those to whom We have given
the Book believe in it; and some of these
believe in it; and none denies Our signs but
    the unbelievers.
Not before this didst thou recite any
Book, or inscribe it with thy right hand,
for then those who follow falsehood
    would have doubted.
Nay; rather it is signs, clear signs
in the breasts of those who have been given
knowledge; and none denies Our signs but
    the evildoers.
They say, 'Why have signs not been sent
down upon him from his Lord?' Say:
'The signs are only with God, and I am only
    a plain warner.'
50   What, is it not sufficient for them that
We have sent down upon thee the Book
that is recited to them? Surely in that is
a mercy, and a reminder to a people
    who believe.

Say: 'God suffices as a witness between
    me and you.'
He knows whatsoever is in the heavens
and earth. Those who believe in vanity
and disbelieve in God—those,
    they are the losers.
And they demand of thee to hasten
the chastisement! But for a stated term
the chastisement would have come upon them;
but it shall come upon them suddenly, when
    they are not aware.
They demand of thee to hasten the
chastisement! Lo, Gehenna encompasses
    the unbelievers.

55   Upon the day the chastisement shall overwhelm them
    from above them and from under their feet, and He shall say,
        'Taste now what you were doing!'

O My servants who believe, surely
My earth is wide; therefore Me
    do you serve!
Every soul shall taste of death; then unto Us
    you shall be returned.
And those who believe, and do righteous deeds,
We shall surely lodge them in lofty
chambers of Paradise, underneath which
rivers flow, therein dwelling forever;
and excellent is the wage of
    those who labour,
such men as are patient, and put their
    trust in their Lord.

60   How many a beast that bears not its own
provision, but God provides for it and you!
    He is the All-hearer, the All-knower.

If thou askest them,
'Who created the heavens and the earth

and subjected the sun and the moon?'
　　　they will say, 'God.'
　How then are they perverted?
God outspreads and straitens His provision
to whomsoever He will of His servants;
　　　God has knowledge of everything.

　　　If thou askest them,
'Who sends down out of heaven water, and
therewith revives the earth after it is dead?'
　　　they will say, 'God.'
　　　Say: 'Praise belongs to God.'
Nay, but most of them have no understanding.

This present life is naught but a diversion
and a sport; surely the Last Abode is Life,
　　　did they but know.

65　　　When they embark in the ships, they call on
God; making their religion sincerely His;
but when He has delivered them to the land,
　　　they associate others
with Him, that they may be ungrateful for what
We have given them, and take their enjoyment;
　　　they will soon know!
Have they not seen that We have appointed
a sanctuary secure, while all about them
the people are snatched away? What, do they
believe in vanity, and do they disbelieve
　　　in God's blessing?
And who does greater evil than he who
forges against God a lie, or cries lies
to the truth when it comes to him? What,
is there not in Gehenna a lodging
　　　for the unbelievers?

But those who struggle in Our cause, surely
We shall guide them in Our ways; and God is
　　　with the good-doers.

XXX

THE GREEKS

In the Name of God, the Merciful, the Compassionate

Alif Lam Mim

    The Greeks have been vanquished
    in the nearer part of the land;
    and, after their vanquishing,
      they shall be the victors
      in a few years.
    To God belongs the Command
      before and after,
      and on that day
    the believers shall rejoice in
      God's help; God
    helps whomsoever He will; and
      He is the All-mighty, the
      All-compassionate.

5   The promise of God! God fails not His promise,
      but most men do not know it.
    They know an outward part of the present life,
      but of the Hereafter they are heedless.
    What, have they not considered within themselves?
    God created not the heavens and the earth,
    and what between them is, save with the truth
    and a stated term; yet most men disbelieve
      in the encounter with their Lord.
    What, have they not journeyed in the land and
    beheld how was the end of those before them?
    They were stronger than themselves in might,
    and they ploughed up the earth and cultivated it
    more than they themselves have cultivated it;
    and their Messengers came to them with the clear

signs; and God would never wrong them, but
themselves they wronged.
Then the end of those that did evil was evil,
for that they cried lies to the signs of God
and mocked at them.

10   God originates creation, then
brings it back again,
then unto Him you shall be returned.

Upon the day when the Hour is come, the sinners shall be
[confounded;
no intercessors shall they have amongst their associates, and
shall disbelieve in their associates.   [they
Upon the day when the Hour is come, that day they shall be
[divided;
as for those who believed, and did deeds of righteousness,
walk with joy in a green meadow,   [they shall
15 but as for those who disbelieved, and cried lies to Our signs
and the encounter of the Hereafter, they shall be arraigned
into the chastisement.

So glory be to God
both in your evening hour
and in your morning hour.
His is the praise
in the heavens and earth,
alike at the setting sun
and in your noontide hour.
He brings forth the living from the dead,
and brings forth the dead from the living,
and He revives the earth after it is dead;
even so you shall be brought forth.

And of His signs
is that He created you of dust; then lo,
you are mortals, all scattered abroad.
20   And of His signs
is that He created for you, of yourselves,

spouses, that you might repose in them,
and He has set between you love and mercy.
Surely in that are signs for a people who consider.
And of His signs
is the creation of the heavens and earth
and the variety of your tongues and hues.
Surely in that are signs for all living beings.
And of His signs
is your slumbering by night and day,
and your seeking after His bounty.
Surely in that are signs for a people who hear.
And of His signs
He shows you lightning, for fear and hope,
and that He sends down out of heaven water
and He revives the earth after it is dead.
Surely in that are signs for a people who understand.
And of His signs
is that the heaven and earth stand firm
by His command; then, when He calls you
once and suddenly, out of the earth, lo
you shall come forth.

25   To Him belongs whosoever is in the heavens and the earth;
all obey His will.
And it is He who originates creation,
then brings it back again,
and it is very easy for Him.
His is the loftiest likeness in the heavens and the earth;
He is the All-mighty, the All-wise.

He has struck for you a similitude
from yourselves; do you have, among
that your right hands own, associates
in what We have provided for you
so that you are equal in regard to it,
you fearing them as you fear each other?
So We distinguish the signs for a people
who understand.
Nay, but the evildoers follow their own

caprices, without knowledge; so who shall
guide those whom God has led astray?
    They have no helpers.

So set thy face to the religion,
a man of pure faith—God's original
upon which He originated mankind.
There is no changing God's creation.
That is the right religion; but
    most men know it not—

30   turning to Him. And fear you Him,
and perform the prayer, and be not
    of the idolaters,
even of those who have divided up
their religion, and become sects,
each several party rejoicing in
    what is theirs.

When some affliction visits mankind, they
call unto their Lord, turning to Him; then,
when He lets them taste mercy from Him,
lo, a party of them assign associates
    to their Lord,
that they may be ungrateful for what We have
given them. 'Take your enjoyment; certainly
    you will soon know.'
Or have We sent down any authority
upon them, such as speaks of that they
    associate with Him?

35   And when We let men taste mercy, they
rejoice in it; but if some evil befalls them
for that their own hands have forwarded,
    behold, they despair.
Have they not seen that God outspreads and
straitens His provision to whom He will?
Surely in that are signs for a people
    who believe.

And give the kinsman his right,

and the needy, and the traveller;
that is better for those who desire
God's Face; those—they are
   the prosperers.
And what you give in usury,
that it may increase upon the
people's wealth, increases not
with God; but what you give in
alms, desiring God's Face,
those—they receive recompense
   manifold.

God is He that created you, then He provided for you,
then He shall make you dead, then He shall give you life;
is there any of your associates does aught of that?
Glory be to Him! High be He exalted above that
   they associate!

40   Corruption has appeared in the land and sea, for that
men's own hands have earned, that He may let them taste
some part of that which they have done, that haply so
   they may return.

Say: 'Journey in the land, then behold
how was the end of those that were before;
   most of them were idolaters.'

So set thy face to the true religion
before there comes a day from God that
cannot be turned back; on that day
   they shall be sundered apart.
Whoso disbelieves, his unbelief shall be
charged against him; and whosoever
does righteousness—for themselves
   they are making provision,
that He may recompense those who believe
and do righteous deeds of His bounty;
   He loves not the unbelievers.

45   And of His signs

is that He looses the winds, bearing good tidings
and that He may let you taste of His mercy,
and that the ships may run at His commandment,
and that you may seek His bounty; haply so
     you will be thankful.

Indeed, We sent before thee Messengers
unto their people, and they brought them
the clear signs; then We took vengeance
upon those who sinned; and it was
ever a duty incumbent upon Us, to
     help the believers.

God is He that looses the winds, that stir up clouds,
and He spreads them in heaven how He will, and shatters
                       [them;
then thou seest the rain issuing out of the midst of them,
and when He smites with it whomsoever of His servants
     He will, lo, they rejoice,
although before it was sent down on them before that
     they had been in despair.

So behold the marks of God's mercy,
how He quickens the earth after it
was dead; surely He is the quickener
of the dead, and He is powerful
     over everything.

50   But if We loose a wind, and they see it growing yellow,
     they remain after that unbelievers.

Thou shalt not make the dead to hear,
neither shalt thou make the deaf to hear the call
     when they turn about, retreating.
Thou shalt not guide the blind out of their error
     neither shalt thou make any to hear
except for such as believe in Our signs, and so surrender.

God is He that created you of weakness, then He appointed
after weakness strength, then after strength He appointed

weakness and grey hairs; He creates what He will, and
He is the All-knowing, the All-powerful.

Upon the day when the Hour is come, the sinners shall swear
55 they have not tarried above an hour; so they were perverted.
But those who have been given knowledge and faith shall say,
'You have tarried in God's Book till the Day of the Uprising,
This is the Day of the Uprising, but you did not know.'
So that day their excuses will not profit the evildoers,
  nor will they be suffered to make amends.

  Indeed, We have struck for the people
  in this Koran every manner of
  similitude; and if thou bringest them
  a sign, those who are unbelievers
  will certainly say, 'You do nothing
   but follow falsehood.'
  Even so God seals the hearts of
   those that know not.

60   So be thou patient;
  surely God's promise is true;
  and let not those who have not sure faith
   make thee unsteady.

XXXI

LOKMAN

In the Name of God, the Merciful, the Compassionate

Alif Lam Mim

Those are the signs of the Wise Book
for a guidance and a mercy to the good-doers
who perform the prayer, and pay the alms,
and have sure faith in the Hereafter.
Those are upon guidance from their Lord;
    those are the prosperers.

5   Some men there are who buy diverting talk
to lead astray from the way of God
without knowledge, and to take it in
mockery; those—there awaits them
    a humbling chastisement.
And when Our signs are recited to such
a man he turns away, waxing proud, as
though he heard them not, and in his ears
were heaviness; so give him good tidings of
    a painful chastisement.
Surely those who believe, and do deeds
of righteousness, there awaits them
    Gardens of Bliss
therein to dwell forever—God's promise
in truth; and He is the All-mighty,
    the All-wise.
He created the heavens without pillars
you can see, and He cast on the earth
firm mountains, lest it shake with you,
and He scattered abroad in it all manner of
crawling thing. And We sent down out of
heaven water, and caused to grow in it of

every generous kind.

10   This is God's creation; now show me
what those have created that are apart
from Him! Nay, but the evildoers are in
     manifest error.

Indeed, We gave Lokman wisdom:
'Give thanks to God. Whosoever gives thanks
gives thanks only for his own soul's good,
and whosoever is ungrateful—surely God
is All-sufficient, All-laudable.'
And when Lokman said to his son,
admonishing him, 'O my son, do not
associate others with God; to associate
others with God is a mighty wrong.'
(And We have charged man concerning his
parents—his mother bore him in weakness
upon weakness, and his weaning was in
two years—'Be thankful to Me, and to
thy parents; to Me is the homecoming.
But if they strive with thee to make thee
associate with Me that whereof thou hast no
knowledge, then do not obey them. Keep them
company honourable in this world; but
follow the way of him who turns to Me.
Then unto Me you shall return, and
I shall tell you what you were doing.')

15   'O my son, if it should be but the
weight of one grain of mustard-seed, and
though it be in a rock, or in the heavens,
or in the earth, God shall bring it forth;
surely God is All-subtle, All-aware.
O my son, perform the prayer, and
bid unto honour, and forbid dishonour.
And bear patiently whatever may befall
thee; surely that is true constancy.
Turn not thy cheek away from men in
scorn, and walk not in the earth exultantly;
God loves not any man proud and boastful.

Be modest in thy walk, and lower thy voice;
the most hideous of voices is the ass's.'

Have you not seen how that God has subjected to you what-
   is in the heavens and earth,   ⌜soever
and He has lavished on you His blessings, outward and
                ⌜inward?

    And among men there is such a one
    that disputes concerning God without knowledge
    or guidance, or an illuminating Book;
20   and when it is said to them, 'Follow
    what God has sent down,' they say,
    'No; but we will follow such things
    as we found our fathers doing.'
    What? Even though Satan were calling them
    to the chastisement of the burning?

    And whosoever submits his will to God,
    being a good-doer, has laid hold
    of the most firm handle; and unto God is
      the issue of all affairs.
    And whoso disbelieves, let not his disbelief
    grieve thee; unto Us they shall return,
    and We shall tell them what they did.
    Surely God knows all the thoughts
      within the breasts.
    To them We give enjoyment a little, then
    We compel them to a harsh chastisement.

      If thou askest them,
     'Who created the heavens and the earth?'
      they will say, 'God.'
      Say: 'Praise belongs to God.'
    Nay, but most of them have no knowledge.

25   To God belongs all that is in the heavens and the earth;
   surely God—He is the All-sufficient, the All-laudable.

Though all the trees in the earth were
pens, and the sea—seven seas after it
    to replenish it,
yet would the Words of God not be spent.
   God is All-mighty, All-wise.

Your creation and your upraising are as
    but as a single soul.
God is All-hearing, All-seeing.

Hast thou not seen how that God makes the night to enter
          [into the day
and makes the day to enter into the night.
and He has subjected the sun and the moon, each of them
     to a stated term,   [running
and that God is aware of what you do?
That is because God—He is the Truth, and that they call
apart from Him—that is the false; and for that God is [upon
   the All-high, the All-great.
30 Hast thou not seen how that the ships run upon the sea by the
blessing of God, that He may show you some of His signs?
     Surely in that are signs for every man
       enduring, thankful.
   And when the waves cover them like shadows
   they call upon God, making their religion
   sincerely His; but when He has delivered them
   to the land, some of them are lukewarm.
   And none denies Our signs, except every
     ungrateful traitor.

   O men, fear your Lord, and dread a day
   when no father shall give satisfaction
   for his child, and no child shall give
   satisfaction for his father whatever.
   Surely God's promise is true; so let not
   the present life delude you, and let not
   the Deluder delude you concerning God.

   Surely God—He has knowledge of the Hour;

He sends down the rain; He knows what is in the wombs.
No soul knows what it shall earn tomorrow, and
no soul knows in what land it shall die.
Surely God is All-knowing, All-aware.

XXXII

PROSTRATION

In the Name of God, the Merciful, the Compassionate

Alif Lam Mim

The sending down of the Book, wherein no doubt is,
    from the Lord of all Being.

Or do they say, 'He has forged it'? Say:
'Not so; it is the truth from thy Lord
that thou mayest warn a people to whom no
warner came before thee, that haply so
    they may be guided.

God is He that created the heavens and the earth,
and what between them is, in six days,
then seated Himself upon the Throne.
Apart from Him, you have no protector
neither mediator; will you not remember?
He directs the affair from heaven to earth,
then it goes up to Him in one day, whose measure is
    a thousand years of your counting.

5   He is the knower of the Unseen and the Visible,
the All-mighty, the All-compassionate,
    who has created all things well.
And He originated the creation of man
    out of clay,
then He fashioned his progeny of an extraction of
    mean water,
then He shaped him, and breathed His spirit in him.
And He appointed for you hearing, and sight, and hearts;
    little thanks you show.

They say, 'What, when we have gone astray

in the earth, shall we indeed be in a
new creation?'
10   Nay, but they disbelieve in the encounter
with their Lord.
Say: 'Death's angel, who has been charged
with you, shall gather you, then to your Lord
you shall be returned.'

Ah, if thou couldst see the guilty hanging their heads before
           [their Lord!
'Our Lord, we have seen and heard; now return us, that we
    righteousness, for we have sure faith.'   [may do
'If We had so willed, We could have given every soul its
         [guidance;
but now My Word is realized—"Assuredly I shall fill
    with jinn and men all together."   [Gehenna
So now taste, for that you forgot the encounter of this your
         [day!
We indeed have forgotten you. Taste the chastisement of
    for that you were doing!'   [eternity

15   Only those believe in Our signs who, when
they are reminded of them, fall down prostrate
and proclaim the praise of their Lord,
    not waxing proud.
Their sides shun their couches as they call on their
Lord in fear and hope; and they expend of that
    We have provided them.
No soul knows what comfort is laid up
for them secretly, as a recompense for that
    they were doing.
What? Is he who has been a believer
like unto him who has been ungodly?
    They are not equal.
As for those who believe, and do deeds of
righteousness, there await them the Gardens
of the Refuge, in hospitality for that
    they were doing.
20   But as for the ungodly, their refuge

shall be the Fire; as often as they desire
to come forth from it, they shall be restored
into it, and it shall be said to them,
'Taste the chastisement of the Fire, which
      you cried lies to.'
And We shall surely let them taste the nearer
chastisement, before the greater; haply so
      they will return.
And who does greater evil than he who
is reminded of the signs of his Lord, then
turns away from them? We shall take vengeance
      upon the sinners.

Indeed, We gave Moses the Book; so be not
in doubt concerning the encounter with him;
and We appointed it for a guidance to the
      Children of Israel.
And We appointed from among them leaders
guiding by Our command, when they
endured patiently, and had sure faith
      in Our signs.

25   Surely thy Lord will distinguish between them
on the Resurrection Day, touching that whereon
      they were at variance.

Is it not a guidance to them, how many
generations We destroyed before them
in whose dwelling-places they walk?
Surely in that are signs; what,
      will they not hear?
Have they not seen how We drive the water
to the dry land and bring forth crops therewith
whereof their cattle and themselves eat? What,
      will they not see?

They also say, 'When shall be this Victory,
      if you speak truly?'
Say: 'On the Day of Victory their faith
shall not profit the unbelievers, nor shall

they be respited.'
So turn thou away from them, and wait;
        they too are waiting.

XXXIII

THE CONFEDERATES

In the Name of God, the Merciful, the Compassionate

O Prophet, fear God,
and obey not the unbelievers
and the hypocrites. God is All-knowing,
All-wise.
And follow what is revealed to thee
from thy Lord; surely God is aware of
the things you do.
And put thy trust in God; God suffices
as a guardian.

God has not assigned to any man two hearts within
his breast; nor has He made your wives, when you
divorce, saying, 'Be as my mother's back,' truly
your mothers, neither has He made your adopted sons
your sons in fact. That is your own saying, the
words of your mouths; but God speaks the truth, and
guides on the way.

5 Call them after their true fathers; that is more
equitable in the sight of God. If you know not
who their fathers were, then they are your brothers
in religion, and your clients. There is no fault
in you if you make mistakes, but only in what
your hearts premeditate. God is All-forgiving,
All-compassionate.
The Prophet is nearer to the believers than their
selves; his wives are their mothers. Those who are
bound by blood are nearer to one another
in the Book of God than the believers and the
emigrants; nevertheless you should act towards
your friends honourably; that stands inscribed
in the Book.

And when We took compact from the Prophets,
and from thee, and from Noah, and Abraham,
Moses, and Jesus, Mary's son; We took from them
    a solemn compact,
that He might question the truthful concerning their
truthfulness; and He has prepared for the unbelievers
    a painful chastisement.

O believers, remember God's blessing upon you
when hosts came against you, and We loosed
against them a wind, and hosts you saw not; and God sees
    the things you do.

10   When they came against you from above you
and from below you, and when your eyes swerved
and your hearts reached your throats, while you thought
    thoughts about God;
there it was that the believers were tried, and
    shaken most mightily.
And when the hypocrites, and those in whose hearts is
sickness, said, 'God and His Messenger promised us
    only delusion.'
And when a party of them said, 'O people of
Yathrib, there is no abiding here for you,
therefore return!' And a part of them were asking
leave of the Prophet, saying, 'Our houses are
exposed'; yet they were not exposed; they desired
    only to flee.
And if entrance had been forced against them
from those quarters, and then they had been asked to
apostatise, they would have done so, and but tarried
    about it briefly.

15   Yet they had made covenant with God before that, that
they would not turn their backs; and covenants with God
    shall be questioned of.
Say: 'Flight will not profit you, if you flee from
death or slaying; you will be given enjoyment of days
    then but little.'
Say: 'Who is he that shall defend you from God, if
He desires evil for you, or desires mercy for you?'

They shall find for themselves, apart from God,
   neither protector nor helper.
God would surely know those of you who hinder, and
those who say to their brothers, 'Come to us,' and come
   to battle but little,
being niggardly towards you. When fear comes
upon them, thou seest them looking at thee, their eyes
rolling like one who swoons of death; but when the
fear departs, they flay you with sharp tongues, being
niggardly to possess the good things. Those have never
believed; God has made their works to fail; and
   that is easy for God.

20 They think the Confederates have not departed;
and if the Confederates come, they will wish that
they were desert-dwellers among the Bedouins
asking for news of you. If they were among you, they
   would fight but little.
You have had a good example in God's Messenger
for whosoever hopes for God and the Last Day, and
   remembers God oft.
When the believers saw the Confederates
they said, 'This is what God and His Messenger
promised us, and God and His Messenger have
spoken truly.' And it only increased them in
   faith and surrender.
Among the believers are men who were true
to their covenant with God; some of them
have fulfilled their vow by death, and some
are still awaiting, and they have not
   changed in the least;
that God may recompense the truthful ones
for their truthfulness, and chastise the
hypocrites, if He will, or turn again
unto them. Surely God is All-forgiving,
   All-compassionate.
25 And God sent back those that were unbelievers
in their rage, and they attained no good; God
spared the believers of fighting. Surely God is

All-strong, All-mighty.
And He brought down those of the People of the
Book who supported them from their fortresses
and cast terror in their hearts; some you slew,
   some you made captive.
And He bequeathed upon you their lands,
their habitations, and their possessions,
and a land you never trod. God is powerful
   over everything.

O Prophet, say to thy wives: 'If you desire
the present life and its adornment, come now,
I will make you provision, and set you free
   with kindliness.
But if you desire God and His Messenger
and the Last Abode, surely God has prepared
for those amongst you such as do good
   a mighty wage.'
30 Wives of the Prophet, whosoever among you
commits a flagrant indecency, for her
the chastisement shall be doubled; that is
   easy for God.
But whosoever of you is obedient to God and His
Messenger, and does righteousness, We shall pay her
her wage twice over; We have prepared for her
   a generous provision.
Wives of the Prophet, you are not as other
women. If you are godfearing, be not
abject in your speech, so that he in whose
heart is sickness may be lustful; but speak
   honourable words.
Remain in your houses; and display not
your finery, as did the pagans of old.
And perform the prayer, and pay the alms,
and obey God and His Messenger.
People of the House, God only desires
to put away from you abomination
   and to cleanse you.
And remember that which is recited in your

houses of the signs of God and the Wisdom;
  God is All-subtle, All-aware.

35   Men and women who have surrendered,
   believing men and believing women,
   obedient men and obedient women,
   truthful men and truthful women,
   enduring men and enduring women,
   humble men and humble women,
   men and women who give in charity,
   men who fast and women who fast,
   men and women who guard their private parts,
   men and women who remember God oft—
   for them God has prepared forgiveness
     and a mighty wage.

  It is not for any believer, man or
  woman, when God and His Messenger
  have decreed a matter, to have the choice
  in the affair. Whosoever disobeys
  God and His Messenger has gone astray
   into manifest error.

When thou saidst to him whom God had blessed
and thou hadst favoured, 'Keep thy wife to thyself,
and fear God,' and thou wast concealing
within thyself what God should reveal,
fearing other men; and God has better right
for thee to fear Him. So when Zaid had accomplished
what he would of her, then We gave her in marriage
to thee, so that there should not be any fault
in the believers, touching the wives of their
adopted sons, when they have accomplished
what they would of them; and God's commandment
   must be performed.
There is no fault in the Prophet, touching what
God has ordained for him—God's wont with those
who passed away before; and God's commandment
  is doom decreed;

who were delivering the Messages of God,
and were fearing Him, and fearing not any one
except Him; and God suffices
  as a reckoner.
40 Muhammad is not the father of any one
of your men, but the Messenger of God,
and the Seal of the Prophets; God has knowledge
  of everything.

 O believers, remember God oft,
and give Him glory at the dawn and in the evening.
It is He who blesses you, and His angels,
to bring you forth from the shadows into the light.
He is All-compassionate to the believers.
Their greeting, on the day when they shall meet Him,
will be 'Peace!' And He has prepared for them
  a generous wage.

 O Prophet, We have sent thee as a
witness, and good tidings to bear
and warning, calling unto God by His
leave, and as a light-giving lamp.
45 Give good tidings to the believers that
there awaits them with God great bounty.
 And obey not the unbelievers
and the hypocrites; heed not their hurt,
but put thy trust in God; God suffices
  as a guardian.

 O believers, when you marry believing women
and then divorce them before you touch them,
you have no period to reckon against them;
so make provision for them, and set them free
  with kindliness.

 O Prophet, We have made lawful for thee
thy wives whom thou hast given their wages
and what thy right hand owns, spoils of war
that God has given thee, and the daughters of thy

uncles paternal and aunts paternal, thy
uncles maternal and aunts maternal, who
have emigrated with thee, and any woman
believer, if she give herself to the Prophet
and if the Prophet desire to take her in
marriage, for thee exclusively, apart
   from the believers—
50 We know what We have imposed upon them
touching their wives and what their right hands own—
that there may be no fault in thee; God is
   All-forgiving, All-compassionate.
Thou mayest put off whom thou wilt of them,
and whom thou wilt thou mayest take to thee;
and if thou seekest any thou hast set aside
there is no fault in thee. So it is likelier
they will be comforted, and not sorrow,
and every one of them will be well-pleased.
with what thou givest her. God knows what
is in your hearts; God is All-knowing,
   All-clement.
Thereafter women are not lawful to thee,
neither for thee to take other wives in exchange
for them, though their beauty please thee, except
what thy right hand owns; God is watchful
   over everything.

O believers, enter not the houses of
the Prophet, except leave is given you
for a meal, without watching for its hour.
But when you are invited, then enter; and
when you have had the meal, disperse,
neither lingering for idle talk;
that is hurtful to the Prophet, and he
is ashamed before you; but God is not
ashamed before the truth. And when you
ask his wives for any object, ask them
from behind a curtain; that is cleaner
for your hearts and theirs. It is not
for you to hurt God's Messenger, neither

to marry his wives after him, ever;
surely that would be, in God's sight,
a monstrous thing.
Whether you reveal anything, or whether
you conceal it, surely God has knowledge
of everything.

55 There is no fault in the Prophet's wives
touching their fathers, their sons, their brothers,
their brothers' sons, their sisters' sons,
their women, and what their right hands own.
And fear you God; surely God is witness
of everything.

God and His angels bless the Prophet.
O believers, do you also bless him, and
pray him peace.
Those who hurt God and His Messenger—
them God has cursed in the present world and
the world to come, and has prepared for them
a humbling chastisement.
And those who hurt believing men and
believing women, without that they have
earned it, have laid upon themselves calumny
and manifest sin.

O Prophet, say to thy wives and daughters
and the believing women, that they draw
their veils close to them; so it is likelier·
they will be known, and not hurt. God is
All-forgiving, All-compassionate.

60 Now, if the hypocrites do not give over,
and those in whose hearts there is sickness
and they that make commotion in the city,
We shall assuredly urge thee against them
and then they will be thy neighbours there
only a little;
cursed they shall be, and wheresoever

they are come upon they shall be seized
    and slaughtered all—
God's wont with those who passed away
before; and thou shalt find no changing
    the wont of God.

The people will question thee concerning
the Hour. Say: 'The knowledge of it is only
with God; what shall make thee know? Haply
    the Hour is nigh.'
God has cursed the unbelievers, and prepared
    for them a Blaze,
65   therein to dwell for ever; they shall find
    neither protector nor helper.

Upon the day when their faces are turned about in the Fire
they shall say, 'Ah, would we had obeyed God and the
    [Messenger!'
They shall say, 'Our Lord, we obeyed our chiefs and great
    [ones,
and they led us astray from the way. Our Lord, give them
chastisement twofold, and curse them with a mighty curse!'

O believers, be not as those who hurt
Moses, but God declared him quit of
what they said, and he was high honoured
    with God.
70   O believers, fear God, and speak words hitting
    the mark,
and He will set right your deeds for you
and will forgive you your sins. Whosoever
obeys God and His Messenger has won a mighty
    triumph.

We offered the trust to the heavens and the earth
and the mountains, but they refused to carry it
and were afraid of it; and man carried it. Surely
    he is sinful, very foolish.

That God may chastise the hypocrites,
men and women alike, and the idolaters,
men and women alike; and that God may
turn again unto the believers, men and
women alike. God is All-forgiving,
    All-compassionate.

XXXIV

SHEBA

In the Name of God, the Merciful, the Compassionate

Praise belongs to God
to whom belongs whatsoever is in the heavens
and whatsoever is in the earth.
To Him belongs praise also in the Hereafter;
He is the All-wise, the All-aware.
He knows what penetrates into the earth, and
what comes forth from it,
what comes down from heaven, and what goes up to it;
He is the All-compassionate, the All-forgiving.

The unbelievers say, 'The Hour will never
come to us.' Say: 'Yes indeed, by my Lord,
it shall come to you, by Him who knows
the Unseen; not so much as the weight of
an ant in heaven and earth escapes from Him,
neither is aught smaller than that, or greater,
but it is in a Manifest Book;
that He may recompense those who believe, and do
righteous deeds; theirs shall be forgiveness
and generous provision.
5   And those who strive against Our signs
to void them—theirs shall be a chastisement
of painful wrath.'
Those who have been given the knowledge see
that what has been sent down to thee from thy
Lord is the truth, and guides to the path of
the All-mighty, the All-laudable.

The unbelievers say, 'Shall we point you to a
man who will tell you, when you have been
utterly torn to pieces, then you shall be in

a new creation?'
What, has he forged against God a lie, or
is he possessed? Not so; but those who
believe not in the Hereafter are in chastisement
      and far error.
Have they not regarded what lies before them
and what lies behind them of heaven and earth?
Did We will, We would make the earth to
swallow them, or We would drop down on them
lumps from heaven. Surely in that is a sign to
      every penitent servant.

10   And We gave David bounty from Us:
'O you mountains, echo God's praises
with him, and you birds!' And We softened
for him iron: 'Fashion wide coats of mail,
and measure well the links.'—And do ye
righteousness, for surely I see
      the things you do.
And to Solomon the wind; its morning course
was a month's journey, and its evening course
was a month's journey. And We·made
the Fount of Molten Brass to flow for him.
And of the jinn, some worked before him
by the leave of his Lord; and such of them
as swerved away from Our commandment,
We would let them taste the chastisement
      of the Blaze;
fashioning for him whatsoever he would—
places of worship, statues, porringers
like water-troughs, and anchored cooking-pots.
'Labour, O House of David, in thankfulness;
for few indeed are those that are thankful
      among My servants.'
And when We decreed that he should die,
naught indicated to them that he was dead
but the Beast of the Earth devouring his staff;
and when he fell down, the jinn saw clearly
that, had they only known the Unseen,

they would not have continued in the
      humbling chastisement.

For Sheba also there was a sign in
their dwelling-place—two gardens,
one on the right and one on the left:
'Eat of your Lord's provision, and give thanks
to Him; a good land, and a Lord
      All-forgiving.'

15   But they turned away; so We loosed on
them the Flood of Arim, and We gave them,
in exchange for their two gardens,
two gardens bearing bitter produce
and tamarisk-bushes, and here and there
      a few lote-trees.
Thus We recompensed them for their unbelief;
and do We ever recompense any but
      the unbeliever?
And We set, between them and the cities
that We have blessed, cities apparent
and well We measured the journey between them:
'Journey among them by night and day
      in security!'
But they said, 'Our Lord, prolong the
stages of our travel'; and they wronged
themselves, so We made them as but tales,
and We tore them utterly to pieces.
Surely in that are signs for every man
      enduring, thankful.
Iblis proved true his opinion of them,
and they followed him, except a party
      of the believers.

20   Yet he had no authority over them,
but that We might know him who believed
in the Hereafter from him who was in
doubt thereof. Thy Lord is Guardian
      over everything.

Say: 'Call on those you have asserted

apart from God; they possess not so much
as the weight of an ant in the heavens
nor in the earth; they have no partnership
in either of them, nor has He in them
   any supporter.'
Intercession will not avail with Him
save for him to whom He gives leave;
till, when terror is lifted from their hearts,
they will say, 'What said your Lord?'
They will say, 'The truth; and He is
   the All-high, the All-great.'

Say: 'Who provides for you out of the heavens and the
    Say: 'God.'   [earth?'
Surely, either we or you are upon right guidance, or in
   manifest error.

Say: 'You will not be questioned concerning our sins, neither
   shall we be questioned as to what you do.'
25 Say: 'Our Lord will bring us together, then make deliverance
    between us by the truth.
   He is the Deliverer, the All-knowing.'

Say: 'Show me those you have joined to Him as associates!
   No indeed; rather He is God,
   the All-mighty, the All-wise.'

We have sent thee not, except to mankind
entire, good tidings to bear, and warning;
   but most men do not know it.
They say, 'When shall this promise come to
   pass, if you speak the truth?'
Say: 'You have the tryst of a day that you
shall not put back by a single hour
   nor put it forward.'

30   The unbelievers say, 'We will not believe
   in this Koran, nor in that before it.'

Ah, if thou couldst see when the evildoers are stationed
[before
their Lord, bandying argument the one against the other!
Those that were abased will say to those that waxed proud,
'Had it not been for you, we would have been believers.'
Those that waxed proud will say to those that were abased,
'What, did we bar you from the guidance after it came to
Nay, rather you were sinners.' [you?
And those that were abased will say to those that waxed
[proud,
'Nay, but devising night and day, when you were ordering us
to disbelieve in God, and to set up compeers to Him.'
They will be secretly remorseful when they see the chastise-
and We put fetters on the necks of the unbelievers; [ment
shall they be recompensed except for what they were doing?

We sent no warner into any city
except its men who lived at ease said,
'We disbelieve in the Message you
have been sent with.'
They also said, 'We are more abundant
in wealth and children, and we shall not
be chastised.'
35   Say: 'My Lord outspreads and straitens
His provision to whomsoever He will,
but most men do not know it.'
It is not your wealth nor your children
that shall bring you nigh in nearness to Us,
except for him who believes, and does
righteousness; those—there awaits them
the double recompense for that they did,
and they shall be in the lofty chambers
in security.
And those who strive against Our signs
to void them—those shall be arraigned
into the chastisement.
Say: 'My Lord outspreads and straitens
His provision to whomsoever He will
of His servants; and whatever thing

you shall expend, He will replace it.
He is the best of providers.'

Upon the day when He shall muster them all together,
then He shall say to the angels, 'Was it you these were
[serving?'

40   They shall say, 'Glory be to Thee! Thou art our Protector,
apart from them; nay rather, they were serving the jinn;
most of them believed in them.'
'Therefore today none of you shall have power to profit
or hurt another.' And We shall say to the evildoers,
'Taste the chastisement of the Fire, which you cried lies to!'

And when Our signs are recited to them,
clear signs, they say, 'This is naught but
a man who desires to bar you from that
your fathers served'; and they say,
'This is nothing but a forged calumny.'
And the unbelievers say to the truth, when
it has come to them, 'This is nothing but
manifest sorcery.'
We have not given them any Books to
study, nor have We sent them before thee
any warner.
Those that were before them also cried lies,
yet they reached not a tenth of what We gave
them; they cried lies to My Messengers, and
how was My horror!

45   Say: 'I give you but one admonition,
that you stand unto God, two by two
and one by one, and then reflect: no
madness is in your comrade. He is
naught but a warner unto you, before a
terrible chastisement.'
Say: 'I have asked no wage of you;
that shall be yours. My wage falls
only upon God; and He is witness
over everything.'
Say: 'My Lord hurls the truth—the Knower

of the Unseen.'
Say: 'Truth has come; falsehood originates not,
          nor brings again.'
Say: 'If I go astray, I go astray
only to my own loss; if I am guided,
it is by what my Lord reveals to me.
          He is All-hearing, Ever-nigh.'

50   Ah, if thou couldst see when they are terrified, and there is no
escape, and they are seized from a place near at hand,
and they say, 'We believe in it'; but how can they reach
          from a place far away,
seeing they disbelieved in it before, guessing at the Unseen
          from a place far away?
And a barrier is set between them and that they desire,
as was done with the likes of them aforetime; they were in
          doubt disquieting.

XXXV

THE ANGELS

In the Name of God, the Merciful, the Compassionate

Praise belongs to God, Originator of the heavens and earth,
  who appointed the angels to be messengers
    having wings two, three and four,
    increasing creation as He wills.
  Surely God is powerful over everything.
Whatsoever mercy God opens to men, none can withhold and
  whatsoever He withholds, none can loose after Him.
    He is the All-mighty, the All-wise.

  O men, remember God's blessing upon you;
  is there any creator, apart from God, who
  provides for you out of heaven and earth?
      There is no god but He:
      how then are you perverted?

  If they cry lies to thee, Messengers before thee
  were cried lies to; and unto God all
      matters are returned.

5   O men, God's promise is true; so let not
    the present life delude you, and let not
    the Deluder delude you concerning God.
    Surely Satan is an enemy to you; so
    take him for an enemy. He calls his party
    only that they may be among the inhabitants
        of the Blaze.
    Those who disbelieve—there awaits them
        a terrible chastisement;
    but those who believe, and do deeds of
    righteousness—theirs shall be forgiveness
        and a great wage.

And what of him, the evil of whose deeds
has been decked out fair to him, so that he
thinks it is good? God leads astray
whomsoever He will, and whomsoever He will
He guides; so let not thy soul be wasted
in regrets for them; God has knowledge of
    the things they work.

10   God is He that looses the winds, that stir up cloud,
    then We drive it to a dead land
and therewith revive the earth, after it is dead.
    Even so is the Uprising.

    Whosoever desires glory,
the glory altogether belongs to God.
    To Him good words go up,
and the righteous deed—He uplifts it;
but those who devise evil deeds—theirs shall be
    a terrible chastisement,
and their devising shall come to naught.

    God created you of dust
    then of a sperm-drop,
    then He made you pairs.
No female bears or brings forth, save with His knowledge;
    and none is given long life who is given long life
neither is any diminished in his life, but it is in a Book.
    Surely that is easy for God.

Not equal are the two seas; this is sweet, grateful to taste,
    delicious to drink,
    and that is salt, bitter to the tongue.
    Yet of both you eat
fresh flesh, and bring forth out of it ornaments
    for you to wear;
and thou mayest see the ships cleaving through it,
    that you may seek
of His bounty, and so haply you will be thankful.
He makes the night to enter into the day

and makes the day to enter into the night,
and He has subjected the sun and the moon, each of them
       to a stated term.   [running
    That is God, your Lord; to Him belongs the Kingdom;
    and those you call upon, apart from Him, possess
        not so much as the skin of a date-stone.

15   If you call upon them, they will not hear your prayer,
    and if they heard, they would not answer you; and
      on the Day of Resurrection they will disown
          your partnership.
    None can tell thee like One who is aware.

O men, you are the ones that have need of God;
He is the All-sufficient, the All-laudable.
    If He will, He can put you away
    and bring a new creation; that
    is surely no great matter for God.

No soul laden bears the load of another;
and if one heavy-burdened calls for its
load to be carried, not a thing of it
will be carried, though he be a near
kinsman. Thou warnest only those
who fear their Lord in the Unseen
and perform the prayer; and whosoever
purifies himself, purifies himself
only for his own soul's good. To God
    is the homecoming.

20   Not equal are the blind and the seeing man,
      the shadows and the light,
      the shade and the torrid heat;
    not equal are the living and the dead.
    God makes to hear whomsoever He will;
thou canst not make those in their tombs to hear—
      thou art naught but a warner.
    Surely We have sent thee with the truth
    good tidings to bear, and warning;
    not a nation there is, but there has

passed away in it a warner.
If they cry thee lies, those before them
also cried lies; their Messengers
came to them with the clear signs,
the Psalms, the Illuminating Book;
then I seized the unbelievers, and
how was My horror!

25   Hast thou not seen how that God sends down out of heaven
                              [water,
and therewith We bring forth fruits of diverse hues?
And in the mountains are streaks white and red, of diverse
         and pitchy black;   [hues,
men too, and beasts and cattle—diverse are their hues.
Even so only those of His servants
fear God who have knowledge; surely God is
    All-mighty, All-forgiving.

Surely those who recite the Book of God
and perform the prayer, and expend of that
We have provided them, secretly and in public,
look for a commerce that comes not to naught,
that He may pay them in full their wages
and enrich them of His bounty; surely He is
    All-forgiving, All-thankful.
And that We have revealed to thee of the
Book is the truth, confirming what is before it;
God is aware of and sees His servants.
Then We bequeathed the Book on those of Our
servants We chose; but of them some
wrong themselves, some of them are lukewarm,
and some are outstrippers in good works
by the leave of God; that is the great bounty.

30   Gardens of Eden they shall enter; therein
they shall be adorned with bracelets of gold
and with pearls, and their apparel there
    shall be of silk.
And they shall say, 'Praise belongs to God
who has put away all sorrow from us. Surely

our Lord is All-forgiving, All-thankful,
who of His bounty has made us to dwell
in the abode of everlasting life
wherein no weariness assails us
        neither fatigue.'

As for the unbelievers, theirs shall be the fire of Gehenna;
they shall neither be done with and die, nor shall its chastise-
                                                [ment
be lightened for them. Even so We recompense every.
                                        [ungrateful one.
Therein they shall shout, 'Our Lord, bring us forth, and
we will do righteousness, other than what we have done.'
'What, did We not give you long life, enough to remember in
for him who would remember? To you the warner came;
35   so taste you now! The evildoers shall have no helper.'

God knows the Unseen in the heavens and the earth;
        He knows the thoughts within the breasts.
It is He who appointed you viceroys in the earth.
So whosoever disbelieves, his unbelief shall be
charged against him; their unbelief increases
the disbelievers only in hate in God's sight;
their unbelief increases the disbelievers only
                in loss.
Say: 'Have you considered your associates on whom
you call, apart from God? Show me what they have
created in the earth; or have they a partnership
in the heavens?' Or have We given them a Book,
so that they are upon a clear sign from it?
Nay, but the evildoers promise one another
                naught but delusion.

God holds the heavens and the earth, lest they remove;
did they remove, none would hold them after Him.
        Surely He is All-clement, All-forgiving.

40   They have sworn by God the most earnest oaths
that if a warner came to them, they would be

more rightly guided than any one of the nations;
but when a warner came to them, it increased them
        only in aversion,
   waxing proud in the land, and devising
   evil; but evil devising encompasses
   only those who do it. So do they expect
   anything but the wont of the ancients?
   And thou shalt never find any changing
        the wont of God,
   and thou shalt never find any altering
        the wont of God.
   What, have they not journeyed in the land and
   beheld how was the end of those before them?
   They were stronger than themselves in might;
but God—there is naught in the heavens or the earth
   that can frustrate Him. Surely He is
        All-knowing, All-powerful.

If God should take men to task for what they have earned
He would not leave upon the face of the earth
one creature that crawls; but He is deferring them
        to a stated term.
   But when their term is come—surely God
        sees His servants.

XXXVI

YA SIN

In the Name of God, the Merciful, the Compassionate

Ya Sin

By the Wise Koran,
thou art truly among the Envoys
on a straight path;
the sending down of the All-mighty, the All-wise,
5   that thou mayest warn a people whose fathers were
never warned, so they are heedless.
The Word has been realised against most of them,
yet they do not believe.
Surely We have put on their necks fetters
up to the chin, so their heads are raised;
and We have put before them a barrier and
behind them a barrier; and We have covered
them, so they do not see.
Alike it is to them whether thou hast warned them
or thou hast not warned them, they do not believe.
10   Thou only warnest him who follows the Remembrance
and who fears the All-merciful in the Unseen; so
give him the good tidings of forgiveness
and a generous wage.
Surely it is We who bring the dead to life
and write down what they have forwarded
and what they have left behind; everything
We have numbered in a clear register.

Strike for them a similitude—
the inhabitants of the city, when
the Envoys came to it;
when We sent unto them two men,
but they cried them lies, so We

450

sent a third as reinforcement.
They said, 'We are assuredly
   Envoys unto you.'
They said, 'You are naught but
mortals like us; the All-merciful
has not sent down anything. You
   are speaking only lies.'

15   They said, 'Our Lord knows we are
   Envoys unto you;
and it is only for us to deliver
   the Manifest Message.'
They said, 'We augur ill of you. If
you give not over, we will stone you
and there shall visit you from us
   a painful chastisement.'
They said, 'Your augury is with you;
if you are reminded? But you are a
   prodigal people.'
Then came a man from the furthest part of
the city, running; he said, 'My people,
   follow the Envoys!

20   Follow such as ask no wage of you,
   that are right-guided.
And why should I not serve Him who
originated me, and unto whom
   you shall be returned?
What, shall I take, apart from Him, gods
whose intercession, if the All-merciful
desires affliction for me, shall not
avail me anything, and who will
   never deliver me?
Surely in that case I should be in
   manifest error.
Behold, I believe in your Lord;
   therefore hear me!'

25   It was said, 'Enter Paradise!'
He said, 'Ah, would that my people
   had knowledge
that my Lord has forgiven me

and that He has placed me
among the honoured.'
And We sent not down upon his
people, after him, any host
out of heaven; neither would We
send any down.
It was only one Cry and lo, they were
silent and still.
Ah, woe for those servants! Never
comes unto them a Messenger, but
they mock at him.
30   What, have they not seen how many
generations We have destroyed
before them,
and that it is not unto them
that they return?
They shall every one of them be arraigned
before Us.

And a sign for them is the dead land, that We quickened
and brought forth from it grain, whereof they eat;
and We made therein gardens of palms and vines,
and therein We caused fountains to gush forth,
35   that they might eat of its fruits and their hands' labour.
What, will they not be thankful?
Glory be to Him, who created all the pairs
of what the earth produces, and of themselves,
and of what they know not.
And a sign for them is the night; We strip it of the
day and lo, they are in darkness.
And the sun—it runs to a fixed resting-place;
that is the ordaining of the All-mighty, the All-knowing.
And the moon—We have determined it by stations,
till it returns like an aged palm-bough.
40   It behoves not the sun to overtake the moon, neither
does the night outstrip the day,
each swimming in a sky.
And a sign for them is that We carried their seed
in the laden ship,

and We have created for them the like of it
    whereon they ride;
    and if We will, We drown them,
    then none have they to cry to,
    neither are they delivered,
    save as a mercy from Us, and enjoyment
        for a while.

45   And when it is said to them, 'Fear what is before you
    and what is behind you; haply you will find mercy'—
    yet never any sign of the signs of their Lord
    comes to them, but they are turning away from it.
    And when it is said to them, 'Expend of that God has
    provided you,' the unbelievers say to the believers,
    'What, shall we feed such a one whom, if God willed,
    He would feed? You are only in manifest error!'

    They also say, 'When shall this promise come to
        pass, if you speak truly?'
    They are awaiting only for one Cry to seize them
        while they are yet disputing,
50   then they will not be able to make any testament,
        nor will they return to their people.
    And the Trumpet shall be blown; then behold, they are
        from their tombs unto their Lord. [sliding down
    They say, 'Alas for us! Who roused us out of our sleeping-
                                                    [place?
    This is what the All-merciful promised, and the Envoys
                                                    [spoke truly.'
    'It was only one Cry; then behold, they are all arraigned
                                                    [before Us.
    So today no soul shall be wronged anything, and you shall
                                                    [not be
    recompensed, except according to what you have been
                                                    [doing.
55   See, the inhabitants of Paradise today are busy in their
                                                    [rejoicing,
    they and their spouses, reclining upon couches in the shade;
    therein they have fruits, and they have all that they call for.

'Peace!'—such is the greeting, from a Lord All-
[compassionate.
'Now keep yourselves apart, you sinners, upon this day!
60 Made I not covenant with you, Children of Adam, that you
should not serve Satan—surely he is a manifest foe to you—
and that you should serve Me? This is a straight path.
He led astray many a throng of you; did you not understand?
This is Gehenna, then, the same that you were promised;
roast well in it today, for that you were unbelievers!'
65 Today We set a seal on their mouths, and their hands speak
[to Us,
and their feet bear witness as to what they have been earning.

Did We will, We would have obliterated
their eyes, then they would race to the path,
but how would they see?
Did We will, We would have changed them
where they were, then they could not go on,
nor could they return.
And to whomsoever We give long life,
We bend him over in His constitution; what,
do they not understand?

We have not taught him poetry; it is not
seemly for him. It is only a Remembrance
and a Clear Koran,
70 that he may warn whosoever is living,
and that the Word may be realized against
the unbelievers.

Have they not seen how that We have created for them
of that Our hands wrought cattle that they own?
We have subdued them to them, and some of them they
and some they eat; [ride,
other uses also they have in them, and beverages.
What, will they not be thankful?
Yet they have taken, apart from God, gods;
haply they might be helped.
75 They cannot help them, though they be hosts

made ready for them.
So do not let their saying grieve thee;
assuredly We know what they keep secret
and what they publish.

Has not man regarded how that We created him
of a sperm-drop?
Then lo, he is a manifest adversary.
And he has struck for Us a similitude
and forgotten his creation;
he says, 'Who shall quicken the bones
when they are decayed?'
Say: 'He shall quicken them, who originated them
the first time; He knows all creation,
80   who has made for you out of the green tree
fire and lo, from it you kindle.'
Is not He, who created the heavens and earth,
able to create the like of them? Yes indeed;
He is the All-creator, the All-knowing.
His command, when He desires a thing, is to say to it
'Be,' and it is.
So glory be to Him, in whose hand is the dominion
of everything,
and unto whom you shall be returned.

XXXVII

THE RANGERS

In the Name of God, the Merciful, the Compassionate

By the rangers ranging
and the scarers scaring
and the reciters of a Remembrance,
surely your God is One,
5   Lord of the heavens and the earth, and of what between them
Lord of the Easts.   [is,
We have adorned the lower heaven with the adornment of
[the stars
and to preserve against every rebel Satan;
they listen not to the High Council.
for they are pelted from every side,
rejected, and theirs is an everlasting chastisement,
10   except such as snatches a fragment,
and he is pursued by a piercing flame.

So ask them for a pronouncement—
Are they stronger in constitution, or
those We created? We created them
of clinging clay.
Nay, thou marvellest; and they scoff
and, when reminded, do nôt remember
and, when they see a sign, would scoff;
15   and they say, 'This is nothing but
manifest sorcery.
What, when we are dead and become
dust and bones, shall we indeed
be raised up?
What, and our fathers, the ancients?'
Say: 'Yes, and in all lowliness.'

For it is only a single scaring, then behold, they are watching

20 and they say, 'Woe, alas for us! This is the Day of Doom.'
'This is the Day of Decision, even that you cried lies to.
Muster those who did evil, their wives, and that they were
[serving,
apart from God, and guide them unto the path of Hell!
25 And halt them, to be questioned: "Why help you not one
[another?" '
No indeed; but today they resign themselves in submission
and advance one upon another, asking each other questions.
These say, 'Why, you of old would come to us from the
[right hand.'
Those say, 'No; on the contrary, you were not believers;
we had no authority over you; no, you were an insolent
[people.
30 So our Lord's Word is realised against us; we are tasting it.
Therefore we perverted you, and we ourselves were
[perverts.'
So all of them on that day are sharers in the chastisement.
Even so We do with the sinners; for when it was said to
[them,
'There is no god but God,' they were ever waxing proud,
35 saying, 'What, shall we forsake our gods for a poet
[possessed?'
'No indeed; but he brought the truth, and confirmed the
[Envoys.
Now certainly you shall be tasting the painful chastisement,
and not be recompensed, except according to what you were
[doing.'

         Except for God's sincere servants;
40   for them awaits a known provision,
           fruits—and they high-honoured
             in the Gardens of Bliss
   .   upon couches, set face to face,
       a cup from a spring being passed round to them,
45   white, a delight to the drinkers,
       wherein no sickness is, neither intoxication;
           and with them wide-eyed maidens
             restraining their glances

as if they were hidden pearls.
They advance one upon another, asking each other questions.
One of them says, 'I had a comrade
50 who would say, "Are you a confirmer?
What, when we are dead and become
dust and bones, shall we indeed
 be requited?" '
He says, 'Are you looking down?'
Then he looks, and sees him in the midst of Hell.
He says, 'By God, wellnigh thou didst destroy me;
55 But for my Lord's blessing, I were one of the arraigned.
What, do we then not die
except for our first death, and are we not chastised?
This is indeed the mighty triumph,
and for the like of this let the workers work.'

60 Is that better as a hospitality,
 or the Tree of Ez-Zakkoum?
We have appointed it as a trial
 for the evildoers.
It is a tree that comes forth in
 the root of Hell;
its spathes are as the heads of Satans,
and they eat of it, and of it fill
 their bellies,
65 then on top of it they have a brew
 of boiling water,
then their return is unto Hell.
They found their fathers erring,
and they run in their footsteps.
Before them erred most of the ancients,
70 and We sent among them warners;
and behold, how was the end of
 them that were warned,
except for God's sincere servants.

Noah called to Us; and how excellent
 were the Answerers!
And We delivered him and his people

from the great distress,
75   and We made his seed the survivors,
and left for him among the later folk
'Peace be upon Noah among all beings!'
Even so We recompense the good-doers;
he was among Our believing servants.
80   Then afterwards We drowned the rest.

Of his party was also Abraham;
when he came unto his Lord with
    a pure heart,
when he said to his father and his folk,
    'What do you serve?
Is it a calumny, gods apart from God,
    that you desire?
85   What think you then of the Lord
    of all Being?'
And he cast a glance at the stars,
and he said, 'Surely I am sick.'
But they went away from him,
    turning their backs.
Then he turned to their gods, and said,
    'What do you eat?
90   What ails you, that you speak not?'
And he turned upon them smiting them
    with his right hand.
Then came the others to him hastening.
He said, 'Do you serve what you hew,
and God created you and what you make?'
95   They said, 'Build him a building, and cast him
    into the furnace!'
They desired to outwit him; so We made
    them the lower ones.
He said, 'I am going to my Lord;
    He will guide me.
My Lord, give me one of the righteous.'
Then We gave him the good tidings of
    a prudent boy;
100   and when he had reached the age of

running with him,
he said, 'My son, I see in a dream
that I shall sacrifice thee; consider,
        what thinkest thou?'
He said, 'My father, do as thou art
bidden; thou shalt find me, God willing,
        one of the steadfast.'
When they had surrendered, and he flung him
        upon his brow,
We called unto him, 'Abraham,

105   thou hast confirmed the vision;
even so We recompense the good-doers.
This is indeed the manifest trial.'
And We ransomed him with a mighty sacrifice,
and left for him among the later folk
        'Peace be upon Abraham!'

110   Even so We recompense the good-doers;
he was among Our believing servants.
Then We gave him the good tidings of
Isaac, a Prophet, one of the righteous.
And We blessed him, and Isaac;
and of their seed some are good-doers,
and some manifest self-wrongers.

We also favoured Moses and Aaron,
115   and We delivered them and their people
        from the great distress.
And We helped them, so that they
        were the victors;
and We gave them the Manifesting Book,
and guided them in the straight path,
and left for them among the later folk
120   'Peace be upon Moses and Aaron!'
Even so We recompense the good-doers;
they were among Our believing servants.

Elias too was one of the Envoys;
when he said to his people, 'Will you
        not be godfearing?

125 Do you call on Baal, and abandon the
  Best of creators?
God, your Lord, and the Lord of your
  fathers, the ancients?'
But they cried him lies; so they will be
  among the arraigned,
except for God's sincere servants;
and We left for him among the later folk
130 'Peace be upon Elias!'
Even so We recompense the good-doers;
he was among Our believing servants.

Lot too was one of the Envoys;
when We delivered him and his people
  all together,
135 save an old woman among those that tarried;
  then We destroyed the others,
and you pass by them in the morning and
in the night; will you not understand?

Jonah too was one of the Envoys;
140 when he ran away to the laden ship
and cast lots, and was of the rebutted,
then the whale swallowed him down,
  and he blameworthy.
Now had he not been of those that
  glorify God,
he would have tarried in its belly
until the day they shall be raised;
145 but We cast him upon the wilderness,
  and he was sick,
and We caused to grow over him
  a tree of gourds.
Then We sent him unto a hundred
  thousand, or more,
and they believed; so We gave them enjoyment
  for a while.

So ask them for a pronouncement—

Has thy Lord daughters, and they sons?

150 Or did We create the angels
females, while they were witnesses?
Is it not of their own calumny
that they say,
'God has begotten?' They are truly liars.
Has He chosen daughters above sons?
What ails you then, how you judge?

155 What, and will you not remember?
Or have you a clear authority?
Bring your Book, if you speak truly!

They have set up a kinship between Him and the jinn;
and the jinn know that they shall be arraigned.
Glory be to God
above that they describe,

160 except for God's sincere servants.
But as for you, and that you serve,
you shall not tempt any against Him
except him who shall roast in Hell.
None of us is there, but has a known station;

165 we are the rangers,
we are they that give glory.

What though they would say,
'If only we had had a Reminder from the ancients,
then were we God's sincere servants.'

170 But they disbelieved in it; soon they shall know!
Already Our Word has preceded to Our servants, the Envoys;
assuredly they shall be helped,
and Our host—they are the victors.
So turn thou from them for a while,

175 and see them; soon they shall see!
What, do they seek to hasten Our chastisement?
When it lights in their courtyard, how evil will be the
of them that are warned!   [morning
So turn thou from them for a while,
and see; soon they shall see!

180 Glory be to thy Lord. the Lord of Glory,

above that they describe!
And peace be upon the Envoys;
and praise belongs to God, the Lord of all Being.

XXXVIII

SAD

In the Name of God, the Merciful, the Compassionate

Sad

By the Koran, containing the Remembrance—
nay, but the unbelievers glory in their schism.
How many a generation We destroyed before them,
and they called, but time was none to escape.

Now they marvel that a warner has come to them
from among them; and the unbelievers say,
    'This is a lying sorcerer.
What, has he made the gods One God? This is
    indeed a marvellous thing.'
5 And the Council of them depart, saying
'Go! Be steadfast to your gods; this is
    a thing to be desired.
We have not heard of this in the last religion;
    this is surely an invention.
What, has the Remembrance been sent down on him
out of us all?' Nay, but they are in doubt
of My Remembrance; nay, they have not yet
    tasted My chastisement.
Or have they the treasuries of thy Lord's mercy,
    the All-mighty, the All-giving?
Or is theirs the kingdom of the heavens and earth
and of what between them is? Why, then let them
    ascend the cords!
10 A very host of parties is routed there!

Cried lies before them the people of Noah,
and Ad, and Pharaoh, he of the tent-pegs,
and Thamood, and the people of Lot, and
the men of the Thicket—those were the parties;

not one, that cried not lies to the Messengers,
    so My retribution was just.
These are only awaiting for a single Cry,
    to which there is no delay.

15   They say, 'Our Lord, hasten to us our share
    before the Day of Reckoning.'
Bear patiently what they say, and remember
Our servant David, the man of might;
    he was a penitent.
With him We subjected the mountains to give glory
    at evening and sunrise,
and the birds, duly mustered, every one
    to him reverting;
We strengthened his kingdom, and gave him wisdom
    and speech decisive.
20   Has the tiding of the dispute come to thee?
    When they scaled the Sanctuary,
when they entered upon David, and he took
fright at them; and they said, 'Fear not;
two disputants we are—one of us has
injured the other; so judge between us
justly, and transgress not, and guide us
    to the right path.'
'Behold, this my brother has ninety-nine
ewes, and I have one ewe. So he said,
"Give her into my charge"; and he overcame
    me in the argument.'
Said he, 'Assuredly he has wronged thee
in asking for thy ewe in addition to
his sheep; and indeed many intermixers
do injury one against the other,
save those who believe, and do deeds of
righteousness—and how few they are!'
And David thought that We had only
tried him; therefore he sought forgiveness
of his Lord, and he fell down, bowing,
    and he repented.
Accordingly We forgave him that,

and he has a near place in Our presence
and a fair resort.

25   'David, behold, We have appointed thee
a viceroy in the earth; therefore judge
between men justly, and follow not caprice,
lest it lead thee astray from the way of God.
Surely those who go astray from the way
of God—there awaits them a terrible
chastisement, for that they have forgotten
    the Day of Reckoning.'

We have not created the heavens and earth,
and what between them is, for vanity;
such is the thought of the unbelievers,
wherefore woe unto the unbelievers
    because of the Fire!
Or shall We make those who believe and do
righteous deeds as the workers of corruption
in the earth, or shall We make the godfearing
    as the transgressors?
A Book We have sent down to thee, Blessed,
that men possessed of minds may ponder its signs
    and so remember.

And We gave unto David Solomon;
how excellent a servant he was!
    He was a penitent.
30   When in the evening were presented to him
    the standing steeds,
he said, 'Lo, I have loved the love of
good things better than the remembrance
of my Lord, until the sun was hidden
    behind the veil.
Return them to me!' And he began to stroke
    their shanks and necks.
Certainly We tried Solomon, and We
cast upon his throne a mere body;
    then he repented.
He said, 'My Lord, forgive me, and

give me a kingdom such as may not
befall anyone after me; surely Thou
    art the All-giver.'

35 So We subjected to him the wind, that ran
at his commandment, softly, wherever
    he might light on,
and the Satans, every builder and diver
and others also, coupled in fetters:
'This is Our gift; bestow or withhold
    without reckoning.'
And he had a near place in Our presence
    and a fair resort.

40 Remember also Our servant Job;
when he called to his Lord, 'Behold,
Satan has visited me with weariness
    and chastisement.'
'Stamp thy foot! This is a laving-place
    cool, and a drink.'
And We gave to him his family, and
the like of them with them, as a mercy
from us, and a reminder unto men
    possessed of minds;
and, 'Take in thy hand a bundle of
rushes, and strike therewith, and do not
fail in thy oath.' Surely We found him
    a steadfast man.
How excellent a servant he was!
    He was a penitent.

45 Remember also Our servants Abraham,
Isaac and Jacob—men of might they
    and of vision.
Assuredly We purified them with a
quality most pure, the remembrance
    of the Abode,
and in Our sight they are of the chosen,
    the excellent.
Remember also Our servants Ishmael,

Elisha, and Dhul Kifl; each is among
the excellent.

This is a Remembrance; and for the godfearing
is a fair resort,
50   Gardens of Edén, whereof the gates
are open to them,
wherein they recline, and wherein
they call for fruits abundant, and
sweet potions,
and with them maidens restraining their glances
of equal age.
'This is what you were promised for the
Day of Reckoning;
this is Our provision, unto which
there is no end.'
55   All this; but for the insolent awaits
an ill resort,
Gehenna, wherein they are roasted—
an evil cradling!
All this; so let them taste it—boiling
water and pus,
and other torments of the like kind
coupled together.

'This is a troop rushing in with you; there is no Welcome
they shall roast in the Fire.'   [for them;
60 They say, 'No, it is you have no Welcome; you forwarded it
how evil a stablishment!'   [for us;
They say, 'Our Lord, whoso forwarded this for us, give him
chastisement in the Fire!'   [a double
They say, 'How is it with us, that we do not see men here
counted among the wicked?   [that we
What, did we take them for a laughing-stock? Or have our
swerved away from them?'   [eyes

Surely that is true—the disputing of
the inhabitants of the Fire.

65   Say: 'I am only a warner.
        There is not any god but God,
        the One, the Omnipotent,
    Lord of the heavens and earth, and of what between them is,
        the All-mighty, the All-forgiving.'
        Say: 'It is a mighty tiding
        from which you are turning away.
        I had no knowledge of the High Council
            when they disputed.

70 This alone is revealed to me, that I am only a clear warner.'

        When thy Lord said to the angels,
        'See, I am creating a mortal
            of a clay.
        When I have shaped him, and breathed
        My spirit in him, fall you down,
            bowing before him!'
        Then the angels bowed themselves
            all together,
        save Iblis; he waxed proud, and was
        one of the unbelievers.

75   Said He, 'Iblis, what prevented thee
        to bow thyself before that I created
            with My own hands?
        Hast thou waxed proud, or art thou
            of the lofty ones?'
        Said he, 'I am better than he;
        Thou createdst me of fire, and him Thou
            createdst of clay.'
        Said He, 'Then go thou forth hence;
            thou art accursed.
        Upon thee shall rest My curse, till
            the Day of Doom.'

80   Said he, 'My Lord, respite me till
            the day they shall be raised.'
        Said He, 'Thou art among the ones
            that are respited
        until the day of the known time.'
        Said he, 'Now, by Thy glory,

I shall pervert them all together,
excepting those Thy servants among them
    that are sincere.'

85   Said He, 'This is the truth, and the
truth I say; I shall assuredly
fill Gehenna with thee, and with
whosoever of them follows thee,
    all together.'

Say: 'I ask of you no wage for it,
neither am I of those who take things
    upon themselves.
It is nothing but a reminder
    unto all beings,
and you shall surely know its tiding
    after a while.'

XXXIX

THE COMPANIES

In the Name of God, the Merciful, the Compassionate

The sending down of the Book is from God
　　the All-mighty, the All-wise.
We have sent down to thee the Book with the truth;
　　so worship God, making thy religion
　　　　His sincerely.
Belongs not sincere religion to God?
And those who take protectors, apart from Him—
　　'We only serve them that they may bring
　　us nigh in nearness to God'—surely God
shall judge between them touching that whereon
　　　　they are at variance.
5 　　 Surely God guides not him who is a liar,
　　　　unthankful.
Had God desired to take to Him a son,
He would have chosen whatever He willed of that
He has created. Glory be to Him! He is God,
　　　　the One, the Omnipotent.

He created the heavens and the earth in truth,
　　wrapping night about the day, and
　　wrapping the day about the night;
and He has subjected the sun and the moon, each of them
　　to a stated term.　　　　　　　　　[running
Is not He the All-mighty, the All-forgiving?
　　He created you of a single soul, then
　　from it He appointed its mate;
and He sent down to you of the cattle eight couples.
　　He creates you in your mothers' wombs
　　　　creation after creation
　　　　in threefold shadows.
　　That then is God, your Lord;

to Him belongs the Kingdom;
there is no god but He;
so how are you turned about?
If you are unthankful, God is independent of you,
yet He approves not unthankfulness in His servants;
but if you are thankful, He will approve it in you.
And no soul laden bears the load of another. Then
to your Lord shall you return, and He will tell you
what you have been doing.

10   He knows the thoughts within the breasts.

When some affliction visits a man, he
calls upon his Lord, turning to him; then
when He confers on him a blessing from Him
he forgets that he was calling to before
and sets up compeers to God, to lead
astray from His way. Say: 'Enjoy thy
unbelief a little; thou shalt be among
the inhabitants of the Fire.'
Or is he who is obedient in the watches
of the night, bowing himself and standing,
he being afraid of the world to come
and hoping for the mercy of his Lord . . .?
Say: 'Are they equal—those who know and
those who know not?' Only men possessed
of minds remember.
Say: 'My servants who believe, fear your
Lord. For those who do good in this world
good, and God's earth is wide. Surely the
patient will be paid their wages in full
without reckoning.'
Say: 'I have been commanded to serve God
making my religion His sincerely; and
I have been commanded to be the first of
those that surrender.'

15   Say: 'Truly I fear, if I should rebel
against my Lord, the chastisement
of a dreadful day.'
Say: 'God I serve, making my religion

His sincerely;
so serve what you will apart from Him.'
Say: 'Surely the losers are they who
lose themselves and their families
on the Day of Resurrection; is not that
  the manifest loss?
Above them they shall have overshadowings
of the Fire, and underneath them
overshadowings; that it is wherewith God
frightens His servants: "O My servants,
  so fear you Me!" '
Those who eschew the serving of idols
and turn penitent to God, for them is
good tidings! So give thou good tidings
to My servants who give ear to the Word
and follow the fairest of it. Those are they
whom God has guided; those—they are men
  possessed of minds.

20 He against whom the word of chastisement
is realized—shalt thou deliver him
  out of the Fire?
But those who fear their Lord—for them
await lofty chambers, above which are
built lofty chambers, underneath which
rivers flow—God's promise; God fails
  not the tryst.

Hast thou not seen how that God has sent down out of heaven
  and threaded it as springs in the earth,   [water
then He brings forth therewith crops of diverse hues,
then they wither, and thou seest them turning yellow,
  then He makes them broken orts?
Surely in that is a reminder for men
  possessed of minds.

Is he whose breast God has expanded
unto Islam, so he walks in a light
from his Lord . . .? But woe to those
whose hearts are hardened against

the remembrance of God! Those are
in manifest error.
God has sent down the fairest discourse as
a Book, consimilar in its oft-repeated,
whereat shiver the skins of those who fear
their Lord; then their skins and their hearts
soften to the remembrance of God.
That is God's guidance, whereby
He guides whomsoever He will;
and whomsoever God leads astray,
no guide has he.

25   Is he who guards himself with his face
against the evil of the chastisement
on the Day of Resurrection . . .? And it
is said to the evildoers, 'Taste now
that you were earning!'
Those that were before them cried lies, then
the chastisement came upon them from whence
they were not aware;
so God let them taste degradation
in this present life; and the chastisement
of the world to come is assuredly greater,
did they but know.

Indeed We have struck for the people
in this Koran every manner of similitude;
haply they will remember;
an Arabic Koran, wherein there is no crookedness;
haply they will be godfearing.

30   God has struck a similitude—a man
in whom partners disagreeing share,
and a man the property of one man.
Are the two equal in likeness? Praise
belongs to God! Nay, but most of them
do not know.

Thou art mortal, and they are mortal;
then on the Day of Resurrection before your Lord

you shall dispute.

But who does greater evil than he who
lies against God and cries lies to the
very truth, when it comes to him?
Is there not in Gehenna a lodging
      for the unbelievers?
And he who has come with the very
truth and confirms it, those—they
      are the godfearing.

35   They shall have whatsoever they will
with their Lord; that is the recompense
      of the good-doers,
that God may acquit them of the worst
of what they did, and recompense them
with the wages of the fairest of
      what they were doing.
Shall not God suffice His servant, though
they frighten thee with those apart from
Him? And whomsoever God leads astray,
      no guide has he.
But whomso God guides, none shall lead
him astray; is not God All-mighty,
      All-vengeful?

If thou askest them,
'Who created the heavens and the earth?'
      they will say, 'God.'
Say: 'What think you? That you call upon
apart from God—if God desires
affliction for me, shall they remove
His affliction? Or if He desires
mercy for me, shall they withhold His
mercy?' Say: 'God is enough for me;
in Him all those put their trust
      who put their trust.'

40   Say: 'My people, act according to
your station; I am acting; and
      soon you will know

to whom will come a chastisement
degrading him, and upon whom lights
a lasting chastisement.'

Surely We have sent down upon thee
the Book for mankind with the truth.
Whosoever is guided, is only guided
to his own gain, and whosoever goes
astray, it is only to his own loss;
thou art not a guardian over them.

God takes the souls at the time of their death,
and that which has not died, in its sleep;
He withholds that against which He has decreed death,
but looses the other till a stated term.
Surely in that are signs for a people who reflect.
Or have they taken intercessors apart from God?
Say: 'What, even though they have no power whatever
and no understanding?'
45   Say: 'To God belongs intercession altogether.
His is the kingdom of the heavens and the earth;
then unto Him you will be returned.'

When God is mentioned alone, then shudder
the hearts of those who believe not in the Hereafter,
but when those apart from Him are mentioned
behold, they rejoice.
Say: 'O God, Thou originator of the heavens and the earth
who knowest the Unseen and the Visible,
Thou shalt judge between Thy servants touching that
they are at variance.'   [whereon

If the evildoers possessed all that is in the earth,
and the like of it with it, they would offer it to
ransom themselves from the evil of the chastisement
on the Day of Resurrection; yet there would appear
to them from God that they never reckoned with, and
there would appear to them the evils of that they
have earned, and they would be encompassed by

that they mocked at.

50   When some affliction visits a man, he
calls unto Us; then, when We confer on
him a blessing from Us, he says, 'I was
given it only because of a knowledge.'
Nay, it is a trial, but most of them
         do not know it.
So said those that were before them; but
that they earned did not avail them,
in that the evils of that they earned
smote them. The evildoers of these men,
they too shall be smitten by the evils
of that they earned; they will not be able
         to frustrate it.

Do they know that God outspreads and straitens
   His provision to whomsoever He will?
Surely in that are signs for a people who believe.

Say: 'O my people who have been prodigal
against yourselves, do not despair of
God's mercy; surely God forgives sins
altogether; surely He is the All-forgiving,
         the All-compassionate.
55   Turn unto your Lord and surrender to Him,
ere the chastisement comes upon you, then
         you will not be helped.
And follow the fairest of what has been
sent down to you from your Lord, ere the
chastisement comes upon you suddenly
         while you are unaware.'
Lest any soul should say, 'Alas for me,
in that I neglected my duty to God,
         and was a scoffer,'
or lest it should say, 'If only God
had guided me, I should have been
         among the godfearing,'
or lest it should say, when it sees

the chastisement, 'O that I might
return again, and be among
 the good-doers.'
60   'Yes indeed! My signs did come to thee,
but thou hast cried them lies, and thou
hast waxed proud, and become one of
 the unbelievers.'

And upon the Day of Resurrection thou shalt see those who
                ⌈lied
against God, their faces blackened; is there not in Gehenna
 a lodging for those that are proud?

But God shall deliver those that were godfearing
in their security; evil shall not visit them,
 neither shall they sorrow.

God is the Creator of every thing;
He is Guardian over every thing;
unto Him belong the keys of the heavens and the earth.
And those who disbelieve in the signs of God,
 those—they are the losers.

65   Say: 'Is it other than God you bid me serve,
 you ignorant ones?'
It has been revealed to thee, and to those before thee,
'If thou associatest other gods with God,
thy work shall surely fail and thou wilt be
 among the losers.'
Nay, but God do thou serve; and be thou
 among the thankful.

They measure not God with His true measure.
The earth altogether shall be His handful
on the Day of Resurrection, and the heavens
 shall be rolled up in His right hand.
Glory be to Him! High be He exalted above
 that they associate!

For the Trumpet shall be blown, and whosoever is in the
[heavens
and whosoever is in the earth shall swoon, save whom God
[wills.
Then it shall be blown again, and lo, they shall stand,
[beholding.
And the earth shall shine with the light of its Lord, and the
[Book
shall be set in place, and the Prophets and witnesses shall be
[brought,
and justly the issue be decided between them, and they not
[wronged.
70   Every soul shall be paid in full for what it has wrought; and
knows very well what they do.   [He
Then the unbelievers shall be driven in companies into
[Gehenna
till, when they have come thither, then its gates will be
[opened
and its keepers will say to them, 'Did not Messengers come
[to you
from among yourselves, reciting to you the signs of your
[Lord
and warning you against the encounter of this your day?'
They shall say, 'Yes indeed; but the word of the chastisement
has been realized against the unbelievers.'
It shall be said, 'Enter the gates of Gehenna, to dwell therein
forever.' How evil is the lodging of those that are proud!
Then those that feared their Lord shall be driven in com-
[panies
into Paradise, till, when they have come thither, and its gates
are opened, and its keepers will say to them, 'Peace be upon
Well you have fared; enter in, to dwell forever.' [you!
And they shall say, 'Praise belongs to God, who has been
[true
in His promise to us, and has bequeathed upon us the earth,
for us to make our dwelling wheresoever we will in Para-
How excellent is the wage of those that labour! [dise.'
75   And thou shalt see the angels encircling about the Throne
proclaiming the praise of their Lord; and justly the issue

shall be decided between them; and it shall be said,
'Praise belongs to God, the Lord of all Being.'

XL

THE BELIEVERS

In the Name of God, the Merciful, the Compassionate

Ha Mim

The sending down of the Book is from God
  the All-mighty, the All-knowing,
Forgiver of sins, Accepter of penitence,
    Terrible in retribution,
      the Bountiful;
      there is no god but He,
and unto Him is the homecoming.

None but the unbelievers dispute concerning
the signs of God; so 'let not their going
  to and fro in the land delude thee.
The people of Noah before them also cried
lies, and the parties after them; every
nation purposed against their Messenger
to seize him, and disputed with falsehood
that they might rebut thereby the truth.
Then I seized them; and how was My retribution!
Even so the Word of thy Lord was realised
against the unbelievers, that they are the inhabitants of
      the Fire.

Those who bear the Throne, and those round about it
proclaim the praise of their Lord, and believe in Him,
  and they ask forgiveness for those who believe:
  'Our Lord, Thou embracest every thing in mercy
  and knowledge; therefore forgive those who have
repented, and follow Thy way, and guard them against
      the chastisement of Hell.
Our Lord, and admit them to the Gardens of Eden

that Thou hast promised them and those who were
                                        [righteous
of their fathers, and their wives, and their seed; surely
      Thou art the All-mighty, the All-wise.
And guard them against evil deeds; whomsoever
Thou guardest against evil deeds on that day,
on him Thou hast had mercy; and that is indeed
      the mighty triumph.

10 It shall be proclaimed to the unbelievers, 'Surely God's
                                        [hatred
is greater than your hatred one of another, when you were
            unto belief, and disbelieved.'   [called
They shall say, 'Our Lord, Thou hast caused us to die two
                                        [deaths
and Thou hast given us twice to live; now we confess our
            Is there any way to go forth?'   [sins.

      That is because, when God was called to alone,
      you disbelieved; but if others are associated
      with Him, then you believe. Judgment belongs to
      God, the All-high, the All-great.

      It is He who shows you His signs
      and sends down to you out of heaven provision;
      yet none remembers but he who repents.
      So call unto God, making your religion
      His sincerely, though the unbelievers be averse.

15   Exalter of ranks is He, Possessor of the Throne,
            casting the Spirit of His bidding upon
                  whomever He will of His servants,
            that he may warn them of the Day of Encounter,
      the day they sally forth, and naught of theirs is hidden from
                                        [God.
      'Whose is the Kingdom today?' 'God's, the One, the Omni-
                                        [potent.
      Today each soul shall be recompensed for that it has earned;
            no wrong today.

Surely God is swift at the reckoning.'

And warn them against the Day of the Imminent
when, choking with anguish, the hearts are in the throats
and the evildoers have not one loyal friend,
no intercessor to be heeded.

20   He knows the treachery of the eyes
and what the breasts conceal.

God shall decide justly, and those they call on,
apart from Him, shall not decide by any means.
surely God is the All-hearing, the All-seeing.

What, have they not journeyed in the land and
beheld how was the end of those before them?
They were stronger than themselves in might
and left firmer traces in the earth; yet God
seized them in their sins, and they had none
to defend them from God.
That was because their Messengers came to them
with the clear signs; but they disbelieved,
so God seized them. Surely He is All-strong,
terrible in retribution.

We also sent Moses with Our signs and
a clear authority,
25   to Pharaoh, Haman and Korah; they said,
'A lying sorcerer!'
And when he brought them the truth from
Us, they said, 'Slay the sons of those
who believe with him, and spare their
women.' But the guile of the unbelievers
is ever in error.
And Pharaoh said, 'Let me slay Moses,
and let him call to his Lord. I fear
that he may change your religion, or
that he may cause corruption to appear
in the land.'

And Moses said, 'I take refuge in
my Lord and your Lord from every man
who is proud, and believes not in the
      Day of Reckoning.'
Then said a certain man, a believer
of Pharaoh's folk that kept hidden
his belief, 'What, will you slay a man
because he says, "My Lord is God,"
yet he has brought you the clear signs
from your Lord? If he is a liar,
his lying is upon his own head; but
if he is truthful, somewhat of that he
promises you will smite you. Surely
God guides not him who is prodigal
      and a liar.

30   O my people, today the kingdom is
yours, who are masters in the land.
But who will help us against the might
of God, if it comes upon us?' Said
Pharaoh, 'I only let you see what
I see; I only guide you in the way
      of rectitude.'
Then said he who believed, 'My people,
truly I fear for you the like of the
      day of the parties,
the like of the case of Noah's people,
      Ad, Thamood,
and those after them; and God desires not
      wrong for His servants.

35   O my people, I fear for you the Day
      of Invocation,
the day you turn about, retreating,
having none to defend you from God;
and whomsoever God leads astray,
      no guide has he.
Joseph brought you the clear signs before,
yet you continued in doubt concerning
that he brought you until, when he
perished, you said, "God will never

send forth a Messenger after him."
Even so God leads astray the prodigal
   and the doubter.'
(Those who dispute concerning the signs
of God, without any authority
come to them, very hateful is that
in the sight of God and the believers;
so God sets a seal on every heart
   proud, arrogant.)
Pharaoh said, 'Haman, build for me
a tower, that haply so I may reach
   the cords,
the cords of the heavens, and look upon
Moses' God; for I think that he is
   a liar.'

40 So the evil of his deeds was decked out
fair to Pharaoh, and he was barred from
the way, and Pharaoh's guile came only
   to ruin.
Then said he who believed, 'My people,
follow me, and I will guide you in the way
   of rectitude.
O my people, surely this present life
is but a passing enjoyment; surely
the world to come is the abode of
   stability.
Whosoever does an evil deed shall be
recompensed only with the like of it,
but whosoever does a righteous deed,
be it male or female, believing—those shall
enter Paradise, therein provided
   without reckoning.
O my people, how is it with me, that
I call you to salvation, and you call
   me to the Fire?

45 You call me to disbelieve in God, and
to associate with Him that whereof I
have no knowledge, while I call you to
  the All-mighty, the All-forgiving.

No doubt that what you call me to has
no call heard, in this world or in the
world to come, that to God we return,
and that the prodigal are the inhabitants
        of the Fire.
You will remember what I say to you.
I commit my affair to God; surely God
        sees His servants.'
So God guarded him against the evil
things of their devising, and there
encompassed the folk of Pharaoh the evil
        chastisement,
the Fire, to which they shall be exposed
morning and evening; and on the day
when the Hour is come: 'Admit the folk
of Pharaoh into the most terrible
        chastisement!'

50   And when they argue one with the other in the Fire, and the
                                                        [weak
        say unto those who waxed proud, 'Why, we were your
                                                        [followers;
        will you avail us now against any part of the Fire?' Then
        those who waxed proud shall say, 'Every one of us is in it;
        indeed, God already has passed judgment between His ser-
                                                        [vants.'
        And those who are in the Fire will say to the keepers of
                                                        [Gehenna,
        'Call on your Lord, to lighten for us one day of the chastise-
                                                        [ment!'
        They shall say, 'Did not your Messengers bring you the
                                                        [clear signs?'
        They shall say, 'Yes indeed.' They shall say, 'Then do you
                                                        [call!'
        But the calling of the unbelievers is only in error.

            Surely We shall help Our Messengers
            and those who have believed, in the
            present life, and upon the day when

the witnesses arise,
55   upon the day when their excuses
shall not profit the evildoers,
and theirs shall be the curse, and
theirs the evil abode.

We also gave Moses the guidance,
and We bequeathed upon the Children
of Israel the Book for a guidance
and for a reminder to men possessed
of minds.
So be thou patient;
surely God's promise is true.
And ask forgiveness for thy sin, and
proclaim the praise of thy Lord at evening and dawn.

Those who dispute concerning the signs
of God, without any authority
come to them, in their breasts is only
pride, that they shall never attain.
So seek thou refuge in God;
surely He is the All-hearing, the All-seeing.

Certainly the creation of the heavens and earth is greater
than the creation of men;
but most men know it not.

60   Not equal are the blind and the seeing man,
those who believe and do deeds of righteousness,
and the wrongdoer.
Little do you reflect.
The Hour is coming, no doubt of it, but most men
do not believe.

Your Lord has said, 'Call upon Me
and I will answer you. Surely those
who wax too proud to do Me service
shall enter Gehenna utterly abject.'

It is God who made for you the night, to repose in it,
        and the day, to see.
Surely God is bountiful to men, but most men
        are not thankful.
That then is God, your Lord, the Creator of everything;
        there is no god but He.
        How then are you perverted?
65   Even so perverted are they who deny
        the signs of God.

It is God who made for you the earth a fixed place
        and heaven for an edifice;
And He shaped you, and shaped you well,
        and provided you with the good things.
That then is God, your Lord, so blessed be God,
        the Lord of all Being.

        He is the Living One;
        there is no god but He.
So call upon Him, making your religion
His sincerely. Praise belongs to God,
        the Lord of all Being.

Say: 'I am forbidden to serve those you call on
        apart from God
since the clear signs came to me from my Lord;
        and I am commanded to surrender to
        the Lord of all Being.'

It is He who created you of dust
        then of a sperm-drop,
        then of a blood-clot,
    then He delivers you as infants,
    then that you may come of age,
    then that you may be old men—
though some of you there are who die before it—
    and that you may reach a stated term;
        haply you will understand.
70   It is He who gives life, and makes to die;

and when He decrees a thing, He but says to it
'Be,' and it is.

Hast thou not regarded those who dispute
concerning the signs of God, how they
are turned about?
Those who cry lies to the Book and that
wherewith We sent Our Messengers—
soon they will know!

When the fetters and chains are on their necks, and they
[dragged
into the boiling water, then into the Fire they are poured;
then it is said to them, 'Where are those you associated,
apart from God?' They shall say, 'They have gone astray
[from us;
nay, but it was nothing at all that we called upon aforetime.'
Even so God leads astray the unbelievers.
75 'That is because you rejoiced in the earth without right, and
were exultant. Enter the gates of Gehenna, to dwell therein
forever.' How evil is the lodging of those that are proud!

So be thou patient;
surely God's promise is true.
Whether We show thee a part of that We
promise them, or We call thee unto Us,
to Us they shall be returned.

We sent Messengers before thee; of some
We have related to thee, and some We
have not related to thee. It was not for
any Messenger to bring a sign, save by
God's leave. When God's command comes,
justly the issue shall be decided; then
the vain-doers shall be lost.

It is God who appointed for you the cattle,
some of them to ride
and of some you eat;

80   other uses also you have in them;
     and that on them you may attain a need in your breasts,
        and upon them and on the ships you are carried.
     And He shows you His signs; then which of God's signs
                do you reject?

        What, have they not journeyed in the land and
        beheld how was the end of those before them?
        They were stronger than themselves in might
        and left firmer traces in the earth; yet
        that they earned did not avail them.
        So, when their Messengers brought them
        the clear signs, they rejoiced in what
        knowledge they had, and were encompassed by
                that they mocked at.
        Then, when they saw Our might, they said,
        'We believe in God alone, and we disbelieve
        in that we were associating with Him.'
85   But their belief when they saw Our might
        did not profit them—the wont of God, as
        in the past, touching His servants; then
                the unbelievers shall be lost.

XLI

DISTINGUISHED

In the Name of God, the Merciful, the Compassionate

Ha Mim

A sending down from the Merciful, the Compassionate.
A Book whose signs have been distinguished as
an Arabic Koran for a people having knowledge,
    good tidings to bear, and warning, but
most of them have turned away, and do not give ear.
They say, 'Our hearts are veiled from what thou callest us to,
    and in our ears is a heaviness,
    and between us and thee there is a veil;
        so act; we are acting!'
5   Say: 'I am only a mortal, like you are.
To me it has been revealed that your God is One God; so go
    straight with Him, and ask for His forgiveness;
            and woe to the idolaters
who pay not the alms, and disbelieve in the world to come.
Surely those who believe, and do righteous deeds
        shall have a wage unfailing.'

    Say: 'What, do you disbelieve in Him who
    created the earth in two days, and do you
    set up compeers to Him? That is the
            Lord of all Being.
    And He set therein firm mountains over it,
    and He blessed it, and He ordained therein
    its diverse sustenance in four days, equal
            to those who ask.
10   Then He lifted Himself to heaven when it was
    smoke, and said to it and to the earth, "Come
    willingly, or unwillingly!" They said,
            "We come willingly."
So He determined them as seven heavens

491

in two days, and revealed its commandment
in every heaven.'
And We adorned the lower heaven with lamps, and to
[preserve;
that is the ordaining of the All-mighty, the All-knowing.
But if they turn away, then say, 'I warn you
of a thunderbolt like to the thunderbolt of
Ad and Thamood.'
When the Messengers came unto them from
before them and from behind them, saying,
'Serve none but God,' they said, 'Had our
Lord willed, surely He would have sent down
angels; so we disbelieve in the Message
you were sent with.'
As for Ad, they waxed proud in the earth
without right, and they said, 'Who is
stronger than we in might?' What, did they
not see that God, who created them, was
stronger than they in might? And they
denied Our signs.
15   Then We loosed against them a wind
clamorous in days of ill fortune, that
We might let them taste the chastisement
of degradation in the present life;
and the chastisement of the world to
come is even more degrading, and they
shall not be helped.
As for Thamood, We guided them, but
they preferred blindness above guidance,
so the thunderbolt of the chastisement
of humiliation seized them for that
they were earning.
And We delivered those who believed and
were godfearing.

Upon the day when God's enemies are mustered to the Fire,
[duly disposed,
till when they are come to it, their hearing, their eyes and
[their skins

bear witness against them concerning what they have been
[doing,
20 and they will say to their skins, 'Why bore you witness
[against us?'
They shall say, 'God gave us speech, as He gave everything
[speech.
He created you the first time, and unto Him you shall be
[returned.
Not so did you cover yourselves, that your hearing, your
[eyes
and your skins should not bear witness against you; but you
[thought
that God would never know much of the things that you were
[working.
That then, the thought you thought about your Lord, has
[destroyed you,
and therefore you find yourselves this morning among the
[losers.'

Then if they persist, the Fire shall be a
lodging for them; and if they ask amends
yet no amends shall be made to them.
We have allotted them comrades, and
they have decked out fair to them that
which is before them and behind them.
So against them has been realized the
Word concerning nations that passed away
before them, men and jinn alike; surely
they were losers.

25   The unbelievers say, 'Do not give ear
to this Koran, and talk idly about it;
haply you will overcome.'
So We shall let the unbelievers taste
a terrible chastisement,
and shall recompense them with the worst
of what they were working.
That is the recompense of God's enemies—
the Fire, wherein they shall have the Abode

of Eternity as a recompense, for that
they denied Our signs.
And the unbelievers shall say, 'Our Lord,
show us those that led us astray, both
jinn and men, and we shall set them
underneath our feet, that they may be
among the lower ones.'
30   Those who have said, 'Our Lord is God.'
then have gone straight, upon them the
angels descend, saying, 'Fear not,
neither sorrow; rejoice in Paradise
that you were promised.
We are your friends in the present life
and in the world to come; therein you
shall have all that your souls desire,
all that you call for,
as hospitality from One All-forgiving,
One All-compassionate.'
And who speaks fairer than he who
calls unto God and does righteousness
and says, 'Surely I am of them
that surrender'?

Not equal are the good deed and the evil deed.
Repel with that which is fairer
and behold, he between whom and thee
there is enmity shall be as if he were
a loyal friend.
35   Yet none shall receive it, except the
steadfast; none shall receive it, except a man
of mighty fortune.

If a provocation
from Satan should provoke thee,
seek refuge in God;
He is the All-hearing, the All-knowing.

And of His signs
are the night and the day, the sun and the moon.

Bow not yourselves to the sun and moon,
but bow yourselves to God who created them,
if Him you serve.

And if they wax proud,
yet those who are with thy Lord do glorify Him
by night and day, and grow not weary.

And of His signs
is that thou seest the earth humble;
then, when We send down water upon it,
it quivers, and swells.
Surely He who quickens it is He who
quickens the dead; surely He is powerful
over everything.

40   Those who blaspheme Our signs are not hidden from Us.
What, is he who shall be cast into the Fire better, or
he who comes on the Day of Resurrection in security?
Do what you will; surely He sees
the things you do.

Those who disbelieve in the Remembrance
when it comes to them—and surely it is
a Book Sublime;
falsehood comes not to it from before it
nor from behind it; a sending down from
One All-wise, All-laudable.
Naught is said to thee but what already
was said to the Messengers before thee.
Surely thy Lord is a Lord of forgiveness
and of painful retribution.
If We had made it a barbarous Koran,
they would have said, 'Why are its signs
not distinguished? What, barbarous
and Arabic?' Say: 'To the believers
it is a guidance, and a healing;
but those who believe not, in their ears
is a heaviness, and to them it is a

blindness; those—they are called
from a far place.'

45 And We gave Moses the Book; and there was
difference concerning it, and but for a Word
that preceded from thy Lord, it had been
decided between them; and they are in doubt
of it disquieting.

Whoso does righteousness, it is to his own gain,
and whoso does evil, it is to his own loss.
Thy Lord wrongs not His servants.
To Him is referred the knowledge of the Hour.
Not a fruit comes forth from its sheath,
no female bears or brings forth, save with His knowledge.

Upon the day when He shall call to them, 'Where now are
[My associates?'
they shall say, 'We proclaim to Thee, there is not a witness
[among us.'
Then that they called upon before will go astray from
and they will think that they have no asylum.   [them,

Man wearies not of praying for good; but
when evil visits him, then he is cast down
and desperate.
50 And if We let him taste mercy from Us
after hardship that has visited him, he
surely says, 'This is mine; I think not
the Hour is coming. If I am returned
to my Lord, surely the reward most fair
with Him will be mine.' Then We shall tell
the unbelievers the things they have done,
and assuredly We shall let them taste
a harsh chastisement.
And when We bless man, he turns away
and withdraws aside; but when evil
visits him, he is full of endless prayers.

Say: 'What think you? If it is from God,
then you disbelieve in it, who is further
astray than he who is in wide schism?'

We shall show them Our signs in the horizons and
in themselves, till it is clear to them
that it is the truth. Suffices it not
as to thy Lord, that He is witness over
everything?
Are they not in doubt touching the encounter
with their Lord? Does He not encompass
everything?

XLII

COUNSEL

In the Name of God, the Merciful, the Compassionate

Ha Mim
Ain Sin Qaf

So reveals to thee, and to those before thee,
　　God, the All-mighty, the All-wise.
To Him belongs whatsoever is in the heavens
and whatsoever is in the earth; and He is
　　the All-high, the All-glorious.
The heavens wellnigh are rent above them,
when the angels proclaim the praise of their
Lord, and ask forgiveness for those on earth.
Surely God—He is the All-forgiving, the All-compassionate.
And those who have taken to them protectors
apart from Him—God is Warden over them;
　　thou art not a guardian over them.

5　　　And so We have revealed to thee an
Arabic Koran, that thou mayest warn
the Mother of Cities and those who
dwell about it, and that thou mayest
warn of the Day of Gathering, wherein
is no doubt—a party in Paradise,
　　and a party in the Blaze.

If God had willed, He would have made them
one nation; but He admits whomsoever He will
into His mercy, and the evildoers shall have
　　neither protector nor helper.
Or have they taken to them protectors apart
from Him? But God—He is the Protector;
He quickens the dead, and He is powerful
　　over everything.

498

And whatever you are at variance on,
the judgment thereof belongs to God.
   That then is God, my Lord;
in Him I have put my trust, and to Him
     I turn, penitent.
The Originator of the heavens and the earth;
He has appointed for you, of yourselves, pairs,
    and pairs also of the cattle,
therein multiplying you. Like Him there is naught;
   He is the All-hearing, the All-seeing.

10   To Him belong the keys of the heavens and the earth.
He outspreads and straitens His provision to whom He will;
   surely He has knowledge of everything.

He has laid down for you as religion
that He charged Noah with, and that
We have revealed to thee, and that We
charged Abraham with, Moses and Jesus:
'Perform the religion, and scatter not
regarding it.' Very hateful is that
    for the idolaters,
that thou callest them to. God chooses
unto Himself whomsoever He will,
and He guides to Himself whosoever
    turns, penitent.
They scattered not, save after knowledge
had come to them, being insolent
one to another; and but for a Word
that preceded from thy Lord until a
stated term, it had been decided
between them. But those to whom the Book
has been given as an inheritance
after them, behold, they are in doubt
    of it disquieting.
Therefore call thou, and go straight as
thou hast been commanded; do not follow
their caprices. And say: 'I believe
in whatever Book God has sent down; I
have been commanded to be just between

you. God is our Lord and your Lord.
We have our deeds, and you have your deeds;
there is no argument between us and you;
God shall bring us together, and unto Him
    is the homecoming.'

15   And those who argue concerning God
after that answer has been made to Him,
their argument is null and void in the
sight of their Lord; anger shall rest
upon them, and there awaits them a
    terrible chastisement.
God it is who has sent down the Book
with the truth, and also the Balance.
And what shall make thee know? Haply
    the Hour is nigh.
Those that believe not therein seek to
hasten it; but those who believe in it
go in fear of it, knowing that it is
the truth. Why, surely those who are
in doubt concerning the Hour are indeed
    in far error.

God is All-gentle to His servants,
providing for whomsoever He will.
He is the All-strong, the All-mighty.

Whoso desires the tillage of the world
to come, We shall give him increase
in his tillage; and whoso desires the
tillage of this world, We shall give him
of it, but in the world to come he
    will have no share.

20   Or have they associates who have laid
down for them as religion that for which
God gave not leave? But for the Word of
Decision, it had been decided between
them. For the evildoers there awaits a
    painful chastisement.

Thou seest the evildoers going in fear
of that they have earned, that is about
to fall on them; but those who believe
and do righteous deeds are in Meadows
of the Gardens; whatsoever they will
they shall have with their Lord; that is
    the great bounty.
That is the good tidings God gives to His
servants who believe and do righteous
deeds. Say: 'I do not ask of you
a wage for this, except love for the
kinsfolk; and whosoever gains a good
deed, We shall give him increase of good
in respect of it. Surely God is
    All-forgiving, All-thankful.'
Or do they say, 'He has forged against
God a lie?' But if God wills, He
will set a seal on thy heart; and God
blots out falsehood and verifies the
truth by His words; He knows the thoughts
    within the breasts.
It is He who accepts repentance from His
servants, and pardons evil deeds; He knows
    the things you do.
And He answers those who believe
and do righteous deeds, and He
gives them increase of His bounty.
And the unbelievers—for them awaits a
    terrible chastisement.
Had God expanded His provision to His
servants, they would have been insolent
in the earth; but He sends down
in measure whatsoever He will;
surely He is aware of and sees
    His servants.

And it is He who sends down the rain
    after they have despaired,
    and He unfolds His mercy;

25

He is the Protector, the All-laudable.
And of His signs
is the creation of the heavens and earth
and the crawling things He has scattered abroad in them;
and He is able to gather them whenever He will.

Whatever affliction may visit you is for
what you own hands have earned; and He
pardons much.
30 You are not able to frustrate Him in the
earth; and, apart from God, you have
neither protector nor helper.

And of His signs
are the ships that run on the sea like landmarks;
and if He wills, He stills the wind, and
they remain motionless on its back.
Surely in that are signs for every man
enduring, thankful.
Or He wrecks them for what they have earned; and He
pardons much;
and that those who dispute concerning Our signs may know
they have no asylum.

Whatever thing you have been given is
the enjoyment of the present life; but
what is with God is better and more
enduring for those who believe and put
their trust in their Lord.
35 And those who avoid the heinous sins
and indecencies and when they are angry
forgive,
and those who answer their Lord, and
perform the prayer, their affair being
counsel between them, and they expend of
that We have provided them,
and who, when insolence visits them,
do help themselves—
and the recompense of evil is evil

the like of it; but whoso pardons
and puts things right, his wage falls
upon God; surely He loves not
    the evildoers.
And whosoever helps himself after he
has been wronged—against them
    there is no way.

40   The way is only open against those who do
wrong to the people, and are insolent in
the earth wrongfully; there awaits them a
    painful chastisement.
But surely he who bears patiently
and is forgiving—surely that is
    true constancy.

Whomsoever God leads astray, he has no protector
after him; and thou shalt see the evildoers,
when they see the chastisement, saying, 'Is there
    any way to be sent back?'
And thou shalt see them, as they are exposed to it,
abject in humbleness, looking with furtive glance;
and the believers shall say, 'Surely the losers
are they who lose themselves and their families
on the Day of Resurrection; surely the evildoers
    are in lasting chastisement.

45   They have no protectors to help them, apart from God,
and whomsoever God leads astray, no way has he.'

Answer your Lord, before there comes a
day from God that cannot be turned
back; upon that day you shall have
    no shelter, no denial.

But if they turn away, We sent thee
not to be a guardian over them. It is
for thee only to deliver the Message.

And when We let man taste mercy from
Us, he rejoices in it; but if some

evil befalls him for that his own hands
have forwarded, then surely man is
  unthankful.

To God belongs the Kingdom of the heavens and the earth;
  He creates what He will;
  He gives to whom He will females,
  and He gives to whom He will males
or He couples them, both males and females;
  and He makes whom He will barren.
Surely He is All-knowing, All-powerful.

50   It belongs not to any mortal that
        God should speak to him, except
        by revelation, or from behind
          a veil,
        or that He should send a messenger
        and he reveal whatsoever He will,
        by His leave; surely He is
          All-high, All-wise.
        Even so We have revealed to thee a
        Spirit of Our bidding. Thou knewest
        not what the Book was, nor belief;
        but We made it a light, whereby We
        guide whom We will of Our servants. And thou,
        surely thou shalt guide unto a
          straight path—
the path of God, to whom belongs whatsoever is in
the heavens, and whatsoever is in the earth. Surely
        unto God all things come home.

XLIII

ORNAMENTS

In the Name of God, the Merciful, the Compassionate

Ha Mim

By the Clear Book,
behold, We have made it an Arabic Koran;
haply you will understand;
and behold, it is in the Essence of the Book, with Us;
sublime indeed, wise.
Shall We turn away the Remembrance from you, for
that you are a prodigal people?

5   How many a Prophet We sent among
the ancients,
but not a Prophet came to them,
without they mocked at him;
so We destroyed men stronger in
valour than they, and the example
of the ancients passed away.

If thou askest them, 'Who created
the heavens and earth?' they will say,
'The All-mighty, the All-knowing
created them.'
He who appointed the earth to be
a cradle for you, and appointed
ways for you therein, that haply
you may be guided;

10   and who sent down out of heaven water
in measure; and We revived thereby
a land that was dead; even so you
shall be brought forth;
and who created the pairs, all of them,

and appointed for you ships and cattle
    such as you ride,
that you may be seated on their backs
and then remember your Lord's blessing
when you are seated on them, and say,
'Glory be to Him, who has subjected
this to us, and we ourselves were not
    equal to it;
surely unto our Lord we are turning.'

Yet they have assigned to Him a part
of His own servants! Man is clearly
    unthankful.
Or has He taken to Himself, from that
He creates, daughters, and favoured you
    with sons?
And when any of them is given the good
tidings of that he has likened to the
All-merciful, his face is darkened, and
    he chokes inwardly.
What, one who is reared amid ornaments
and, when the time of altercation comes,
    is not to be seen?
And they have made the angels, who are
themselves servants of the All-merciful,
females. What, did they witness their
creation? Their witness shall be written
    down, and they shall be questioned.
They say, 'Had the All-merciful so
willed, we would not have served them.'
They have no knowledge of that; they are
    only conjecturing.
Or did We bring them a Book aforetime
    to which they hold?
Nay, but they say, 'We found our fathers
upon a community, and we are guided
    upon their traces.'
Even so We sent never before thee
any warner into any city, except that

its men who lived at ease said, 'We
indeed found our fathers upon a
community, and we are following
      upon their traces.'
Say: 'What, though I should bring you a
better guidance than you found your
fathers upon?' They say, 'We disbelieve
      in that you were sent with.'
So We took vengeance upon them;
and behold how was the end of them
      that cried lies.

25 And when Abraham said to his father
and his people, 'Surely I am quit of
      that you serve,
except Him who originated me;
      and He will guide me.'
And he made it a word enduring
among his posterity; haply so
      they would return.
Nay, but I gave these and their fathers
enjoyment of days, until the truth
came unto them, and a manifest
      Messenger.
And when the truth came to them, they
said, 'This is a sorcery, and in it
      we are unbelievers.'

30 They say, 'Why was this Koran not sent
down upon some man of moment in the
      two cities?'
What, is it they who divide the mercy
of thy Lord? We have divided between
them their livelihood in the present
life, and raised some of them above
others in rank, that some of them may
take others in servitude; and the
mercy of thy Lord is better than that
      they amass.
And were it not that mankind would be

one nation, We would have appointed for
those who disbelieve in the All-merciful
roofs of silver to their houses, and stairs
       whereon to mount,
and doors to their houses, and couches
       whereon to recline,
and ornaments; surely all this is but
the enjoyment of the present life,
and the world to come with thy Lord is
       for the godfearing.

35   Whoso blinds himself to the Remembrance
of the All-merciful, to him We assign a
       Satan for comrade;
and they bar them from the way, and they
       think they are guided,
till, when he comes to Us, he says,
'Would there had been between me and
thee the distance of the two Easts!'
       An evil comrade!
It shall not profit you today, since
you did evil, that you are partners in
       the chastisement.

What, shalt thou make the deaf to hear,
       or shalt thou guide the blind
and him who is in manifest error?
40   Whether We take thee away,
We shall take vengeance upon them,
       or We show thee a part
of that We promised them, surely
       We have power over them.
So hold thou fast unto that which has
       been revealed unto thee;
surely thou art upon a straight path.
       Surely it is a Reminder
to thee and to thy people; and assuredly
       you will be questioned.
Ask those of Our Messengers We sent
       before thee: Have We

appointed, apart from the All-merciful,
   gods to be served?

45   We also sent Moses with Our signs to
Pharaoh and his Council, and he said,
'Surely I am the Messenger of the
      Lord of all Being.'
But when he brought them Our signs, lo,
      they laughed at them.
And not a sign We showed them, but
it was greater than its sister sign;
and We seized them with chastisement,
      that haply they should return.
And they said, 'Sorcerer, pray to thy
Lord for us by the covenant He has
made with thee, and surely we shall
      be right-guided.'
But when We removed from them the
chastisement, behold, they broke
      their troth.

50   And Pharaoh proclaimed among his
people: 'O my people, do I not
possess the kingdom of Egypt, and
these rivers flowing beneath me? What,
      do you not see?
Or am I better than this man, who is
      contemptible
and scarcely makes things clear?
Why then have bracelets of gold not
been cast on him, or angels not come
      with him conjoined?'
So he made his people unsteady, and
they obeyed him; surely they were an
      ungodly people.

55   So, when they had angered Us, We took
vengeance on them, and We drowned them
      all together;
and We made them a thing past, and
We appointed them for an example

509

to later folk.

And when the son of Mary is
cited as an example, behold,
thy people turn away from it
and say, 'What, are our gods
better, or he?' They cite not
him to thee, save to dispute;
nay, but they are a people
contentious. He is only a
servant We blessed, and We
made him to be an example
to the Children of Israel.

60   Had We willed, We would have appointed
angels among you to be successors in
      the earth.
It is knowledge of the Hour; doubt not
concerning it, and follow me. This is
      a straight path.
Let not Satan bar you; he is for you
      a manifest foe.

And when Jesus came with the
clear signs he said, 'I have
come to you with wisdom, and
that I may make clear to you
some of that whereon you are
at variance; so fear you God
and obey you me. Assuredly
God is my Lord and your Lord;
therefore serve Him; this is
      a straight path.'

65   But the parties among them fell into
variance; so woe unto those who did
evil, because of the chastisement of
      a painful day.
Are they looking for aught but the Hour,

that it shall come upon them suddenly,
    when they are not aware?

Friends on that day shall be foes to one another, but the god-
                               [fearing—
'O My servants, today no fear is on you, neither do you
                               [sorrow'—
even those who believed in Our signs, and had surrendered
                               [themselves:
70 'Enter Paradise, you and your wives, walking with joy!'
There shall be passed around them platters of gold, and cups,
therein being whatever the souls desire, and the eyes delight
      'And therein you shall dwell forever.   [in.
This is the Paradise that you have been given for an in-
        for the things that you were doing.   [heritance
Therein you have abundant fruits, whereof you may eat.'
But the evildoers dwell forever in the chastisement of
                               [Gehenna
75 that is not abated for them and therein they are sore con-
                               [founded.
We never wronged them, but they themselves did the wrong.
And they shall call, 'O Malik, let thy Lord have done with
      He will say, 'You will surely tarry.'   [us!'
'We brought you the truth, but most of you were averse to
                               [the truth.'

      Or have they contrived some matter? We
         too are contriving.
80   Or do they think We hear not their secret
      and what they conspire together? Yes indeed,
      and Our messengers are present with them
         writing it down.

     . Say: 'If the All-merciful has a son,
      then I am the first to serve him.
      Glory be to the Lord of the heavens
      and the earth, the Lord of the Throne,
         above that they describe.'
      Then leave them alone to plunge and play,

until they encounter that day of theirs
    which they are promised.
And it is He who in heaven is God
and in earth is God; He is the All-wise,
    the All-knowing.

85   Glory be to Him, to whom belongs the
Kingdom of the heavens and the earth
and all that between them is; with Him
is the knowledge of the Hour, and to Him
    you shall be returned.
Those they call upon, apart from Him,
have no power of intercession, save
such as have testified to the truth,
    and that knowingly.
If thou askest them, 'Who created you?'
    they will say, 'God.'
    How then are they perverted?

And for his saying, 'My Lord, surely
these are a people who believe not'—
yet pardon them, and say, 'Peace!'
    Soon they will know.

XLIV

SMOKE

In the Name of God, the Merciful, the Compassionate

Ha Mim

By the Clear Book.
We have sent it down in a blessed night
(We are ever warning)
therein every wise bidding determined
as a bidding from Us,
(We are ever sending)
5   as a mercy from thy Lord
(surely He is the All-hearing, the All-knowing)
Lord of the heavens and earth, and all that between them is,
if you have faith.
There is no god but He;
He gives life and makes to die;
your Lord and the Lord of your fathers, the ancients.

Nay, but they are in doubt, playing.
So be on the watch for a day when heaven shall bring
a manifest smoke
10   covering the people; this is a painful chastisement.
'O our Lord, remove Thou from us the chastisement;
we are believers.'
How should they have the Reminder,
seeing a clear Messenger already came to them, then
they turned away from him
and said, 'A man tutored, possessed!'
'Behold, We are removing the chastisement a little;
behold, you revert!'
15   Upon the day when We shall assault most mightily,
then We shall take Our vengeance.

Already before them We tried the people

of Pharaoh, and a noble Messenger
    came unto them,
saying, 'Deliver to me God's servants;
I am for you a faithful Messenger,'
and, 'Rise not up against God; behold,
I come to you with a clear authority,
and I take refuge in my Lord and
your Lord, lest you should stone me.

20   But if so be that you believe me not,
    go you apart from me!'
And he called to his Lord, saying,
  'These are a sinful people.'
'Then set thou forth with My servants
in a watch of the night; surely you
    will be followed.
And leave the sea becalmed; they are
    a drowned host.'
They left how many gardens and fountains,

25   sown fields, and how noble a station,
and what prosperity they had rejoiced in!
Even so; and We bequeathed them upon
    another people.
Neither heaven nor earth wept for them,
    nor were they respited;
and We delivered the Children of Israel
    from the humbling chastisement,

30   from Pharaoh; surely he was a high one,
    of the prodigals;
and We chose them, out of a knowledge,
    above all beings.
and gave them signs wherein there was a
    manifest trial.

    These men do say,
'There is nothing but our first death;
    we shall not be revived.

35   Bring us our fathers, if you speak truly!'
Are they better, or the people of Tubba'
and those before them whom We destroyed?

They were surely sinners.

We created not the heavens and earth,
and all that between them is, in play;
We created them not save in truth; but
    most of them know it not.

40 Surely the Day of Decision shall be
    their appointed time, all together,
    the day a master shall avail nothing
    a client, and they shall not be helped,
    save him upon whom God has mercy; He is
    the All-mighty, the All-compassionate.

    Lo, the Tree of Ez-Zakkoum
    is the food of the guilty,
45 like molten copper, bubbling in the belly
    as boiling water bubbles.
'Take him, and thrust him into the midst of Hell,
then pour over his head the chastisement of
        boiling water!'
'Taste! Surely thou art the mighty, the noble.
50 This is that concerning which you were doubting.'

Surely the godfearing shall be in a station secure
        among gardens and fountains,
robed in silk and brocade, set face to face.
    Even so; and We shall espouse them
        to wide-eyed houris,
55 therein calling for every fruit, secure.
    They shall not taste therein of death,
        save the first death,
And He shall guard them against the chastisement of Hell—
    a bounty from thy Lord; that is the mighty triumph.

Now We have made it easy by thy tongue,
    that haply they may remember.
So be on the watch; they too are on the watch.

XLV

HOBBLING

In the Name of God, the Merciful, the Compassionate

Ha Mim

> The sending down of the Book is from God,
> the All-mighty, the All-wise.

> Surely in the heavens and earth there are signs
> for the believers;
> and in your creation,
> and the crawling things He scatters abroad, there are signs
> for a people having sure faith,
> and in the alternation of night and day,
> and the provision God sends down from heaven,
> and therewith revives the earth after it is dead,
> and the turning about of the winds, there are signs
> for a people who understand.

5 Those are the signs of God that We recite to thee in truth;
in what manner of discourse then, after God and His signs,
will they believe?

> Woe to every guilty impostor
> who hears the signs of God being recited to him,
> then perseveres in waxing proud, as if he has
> not heard them; so give him the good tidings of
> a painful chastisement.
> And when he knows anything of Our signs, he
> takes them in mockery; those—for them awaits
> a humbling chastisement.
> Behind them Gehenna; and that they have earned
> shall not avail them aught, nor those they took
> as protectors, apart from God; for them awaits

516

a mighty chastisement.

10   This is guidance;
and those who disbelieve in the signs of their
Lord, there awaits them a painful chastisement
    of wrath.

God is He who has subjected to you the sea, that
the ships may run on it at His commandment, and
  that you may seek His bounty; haply so
    you will be thankful.
And He has subjected to you what is in the heavens
and what is in the earth, all together, from Him.
  Surely in that are signs for a people
    who reflect.

Say unto those who believe, that they forgive
those who do not look for the days of God,
  that He may recompense a people for that
    they have been earning.

Whoso does righteousness, it is to his own gain,
and whoso does evil, it is to his own loss; then
  to your Lord you shall be returned.

15   Indeed, We gave the Children of Israel
the Book, the Judgment, and the Prophethood,
and We provided them with good things,
and We preferred them above all beings.
We gave them clear signs of the Command;
so they differed not, except after the
knowledge had come to them, being
insolent one to another. Surely
thy Lord will decide between them
on the Day of Resurrection touching
   their differences.
Then We set thee upon an open way
of the Command; therefore follow it,
and follow not the caprices of those

who do not know.
Surely they will not avail thee aught
against God. Surely the evildoers are
friends one of the other; God is the friend
    of the godfearing.

This is clear proofs for men,
and a guidance, and a mercy
to a people having sure faith.

20   Or do those who commit evil deeds
think that We shall make them as those
who believe and do righteous deeds,
equal their living and their dying?
        How ill they judge!
God created the heavens and the earth
in truth, and that every soul may be
recompensed for what it has earned;
    they shall not be wronged.

Hast thou seen him who has taken
his caprice to be his god, and God
has led him astray out of a knowledge,
and set a seal upon his hearing
and his heart, and laid a covering
on his eyes? Who shall guide him
after God? What, will you not remember?

        They say,
'There is nothing but our present life;
we die, and we live, and nothing but
Time destroys us.' Of that they have
no knowledge; they merely conjecture.
And when Our signs are recited to them,
clear signs, their only argument is
that they say, 'Bring us our fathers,
        if you speak truly.'
25   Say:
'God gives you life, then makes you die,

then He shall gather you to the Day
of Resurrection, wherein is no doubt,
but most men do not know.'

To God belongs the Kingdom of the heavens and the earth.

And on the day when the Hour is come,
upon that day the vain-doers shall lose.
And thou shalt see every nation hobbling on their knees,
every nation being summoned unto its Book: 'Today
you shall be recompensed for that you were doing.
This is Our Book, that speaks against you the truth;
We have been registering all that you were doing.'

And as for those who have believed
and done deeds of righteousness,
their Lord shall admit them into
His mercy; that is the manifest
             triumph.
But as for those who have disbelieved:
'Were not My signs recited to you, and
you waxed proud, and were a sinful
             people?
And when it was said, "God's promise
is true, and the Hour, there is no
doubt of it," you said, "We know not
what the Hour may be; we have only
a surmise, and are by no means
             certain." '
And the evil deeds that they have done shall appear to
                                          [them,
and they shall be encompassed by that they mocked at.
And it shall be said, 'Today We do forget you, even
as you forgot the encounter of this your day; and your
refuge is the Fire, and you shall have no helpers.
That is for that you took God's signs in mockery,
             and the present life deluded you.'
So today they shall not be brought forth from it,
             nor will they be suffered to make amends.

35   So to God belongs praise,
the Lord of the heavens and the Lord of the earth,
       Lord of all Being.
His is the Domination in the heavens and the earth;
He is the All-mighty, the All-wise.

XLVI

THE SAND-DUNES

In the Name of God, the Merciful, the Compassionate

Ha Mim

> The sending down of the Book is from God,
> the All-mighty, the All-wise.

We have not created the heavens and the earth,
and what between them is, save with the truth
and a stated term; but the unbelievers are
turning away from that they were warned of.
Say: 'Have you considered that you call upon
apart from God? Show me what they have
created of the earth; or have they a partnership
in the heavens? Bring me a Book before
this, or some remnant of a knowledge,
> if you speak truly.'
And who is further astray than he who calls,
apart from God, upon such a one as shall not
answer him till the Day of Resurrection?
5 Such as are heedless of their calling, and when
mankind are mustered, shall be enemies to them,
> and shall deny their service.

And when Our signs are recited to them,
clear signs, the unbelievers say to the
truth when it has come to them, 'This is
> manifest sorcery.'
Or do they say, 'He has forged it'?
Say: 'If I have forged it, you have no
power to help me against God. He knows
very well what you are pressing upon;
He suffices as a witness between me
and you; He is the All-forgiving,

521

the All-compassionate.'
Say: 'I am not an innovation among
the Messengers, and I know not what
shall be done with me or with you.
I only follow what is revealed to me;
    I am only a clear warner.'
Say: 'Have you considered? If it be from
God, and you disbelieve in it, and a
witness from among the Children of Israel
bears witness to its like, and believes,
and you wax proud, God guides not the people
        of the evildoers.'

10   The unbelievers say, as regards the
        believers, 'If it had been aught good,
        they had not outstripped us to it.'
        And since they are not guided by it,
        certainly they will say, 'This is an
                old calumny!'
        Yet before it was the Book of Moses
        for a model and a mercy; and this is
        a Book confirming, in Arabic tongue,
        to warn the evildoers, and good tidings
                to the good-doers.

        Surely those who say, 'Our Lord is God'
                and then go straight,
        no fear shall be on them, neither shall they sorrow.
        Those are the inhabitants of Paradise,
        therein dwelling forever, as a recompense for that
                they have been doing.

        We have charged man, that he be kind to his
        parents; his mother bore him painfully, and
        painfully she gave birth to him; his bearing
        and his weaning are thirty months. Until,
        when he is fully grown, and reaches forty
        years, he says, 'O my Lord, dispose me
        that I may be thankful for Thy blessing

wherewith Thou hast blessed me and my
father and mother, and that I may do
righteousness well-pleasing to Thee;
and make me righteous also in my seed.
Behold, I repent to Thee, and am among
  those that surrender.'

15 Those are they from whom We shall accept
the best of what they have done, and We
shall pass over their evil deeds. They are
among the inhabitants of Paradise—
the promise of the very truth, which
  they were promised.
But he who says to his father and his
mother, 'Fie upon you! Do you promise me
that I shall be brought forth, when already
generations have passed away before me?'
while they call upon God for succour—
'Woe upon thee! Believe; surely God's
promise is true'; then he says, 'This is
naught but the fairy-tales of the ancients'—
such men are they against whom has been
realized the Word concerning nations that
passed away before them, men and jinn alike;
  they were losers.
All shall have their degrees, according to
what they have wrought, and that He may
pay them in full for their works, and they
  not being wronged.

Upon the day when the unbelievers are exposed to the Fire:
'You dissipated your good things in your present life,
and you took your enjoyment in them; therefore today you
shall be recompensed with the chastisement of humiliation
for that you waxed proud in the earth without right, and
  for your ungodliness.'

20 And remember the brother of Ad, when he
warned his people beside the sand-dunes—
and already warners had passed away

alike before him and behind him—
saying, 'Serve none but God! Truly
I fear for you the chastisement of
       a dreadful day.'
They said, 'What, hast thou come to
pervert us from our gods? Then bring us
that thou promisest us, if indeed
       thou speakest truly.'
He said, 'Knowledge is only with God,
and I deliver to you the Message with
which I was sent; but I see you are
       an ignorant people.'
Then, when they saw it as a sudden cloud
coming towards their valleys, they said,
'This is a cloud, that shall give us
rain!' 'Not so; rather it is that you
sought to hasten—a wind, wherein is a
       painful chastisement,
destroying everything by the commandment
of its Lord.' So in the morning there was
naught to be seen but their dwelling-places.
Even so do We recompense the people
       of the sinners.

25   And We had established them in that
wherein We have not established you,
and We appointed for them hearing, and
sight, and hearts; and yet their hearing,
their sight and their hearts availed them
nothing, since they denied the signs
of God, and they were encompassed by
       that they mocked at.
And We destroyed the cities about you,
and We turned about the signs, that haply
       they would return.
Then why did those not help them
that they had taken to themselves
as mediators, gods apart from God?
Not so; but they went astray from them,
and that was their calumny, and what

they had been forging.

And when We turned to thee a company of jinn
giving ear to the Koran; and when they were
in its presence they said, 'Be silent!'
Then, when it was finished, they turned back
    to their people, warning.
They said, 'Our people, we have heard a Book
that was sent down after Moses, confirming
what was before it, guiding to the truth and
    to a straight path.

30   O our people, answer God's summoner, and
believe in Him, and He will forgive you
some of your sins, and protect you from a
    painful chastisement.
Whosoever answers not God's summoner
cannot frustrate God in the earth, and he
has no protectors apart from Him; those are
    in manifest error.'

What, have they not seen that God
who created the heavens and earth,
not being wearied by creating them,
is able to give life to the dead?
Yes indeed; He is powerful over
    everything.

Upon the day when the unbelievers are exposed to the Fire:
'Is not this the truth?' They shall say, 'Yes, by our Lord!'
He shall say, 'Then taste the chastisement of your unbelief!'

So be thou patient,
as the Messengers possessed of constancy were also patient.
    Seek not to hasten it for them—
it shall be as if, on the day they see that they are promised,
35 they had not tarried but for an hour of a single day.
    A Message to be delivered !
And shall any be destroyed but the people of the ungodly?

XLVII

MUHAMMAD

In the Name of God, the Merciful, the Compassionate

Those who disbelieve and bar from God's way,
God will send their works astray.
But those who believe and do righteous deeds
and believe in what is sent down to Muhammad —
and it is the truth from their Lord—
He will acquit them of their evil deeds,
and dispose their minds aright.
That is because those who disbelieve follow falsehood,
and those who believe follow the truth from their Lord.
Even so God strikes their similitudes for men.

When you meet the unbelievers, smite their necks,
then, when you have made wide slaughter among them,
tie fast the bonds;
5   then set them free, either by grace or ransom,
till the war lays down its loads.
So it shall be; and if God had willed,
He would have avenged Himself upon them;
but that He may try some of you by means of others.
And those who are slain in the way of God, He
will not send their works astray.
He will guide them, and dispose their minds aright,
and He will admit them to Paradise,
that He has made known to them.

O believers, if you help God, He will help
you, and confirm your feet. But as for the
unbelievers, ill chance shall befall them!
He will send their works astray.
10   That is because they have been averse to
what God has sent down, so He has made

their works to fail.
What, have they not journeyed in the land and
beheld how was the end of those before them?
God destroyed them; the unbelievers shall have
       the likes thereof.
That is because God is the Protector
of the believers, and that the unbelievers
       have no protector.
God shall surely admit those who believe
and do righteous deeds into gardens
underneath which rivers flow. As for the
unbelievers, they take their enjoyment
and eat as cattle eat; and the Fire shall
       be their lodging.
How many a city that was stronger in might
than thy city which has expelled thee
have We destroyed! And there was no
       helper for them.

15   What, is he who is upon a clear sign
from his Lord like unto such a one
unto whom his evil deeds have been
decked out fair, and they have followed
       their caprices?
This is the similitude of Paradise
which the godfearing have been promised:
therein are rivers of water unstaling,
rivers of milk unchanging in flavour,
and rivers of wine—a delight
       to the drinkers,
rivers, too, of honey purified;
and therein for them is every fruit,
and forgiveness from their Lord—
Are they as he who dwells forever
in the Fire, such as are given to
drink boiling water, that tears their
       bowels asunder?

And some of them there are give ear to

thee, till, when they go forth from thee,
they say to those who have been given
knowledge, 'What said he just now?'
Those are they upon whose hearts God
has set a seal, and they have followed
      their caprices.
But those who are guided aright, them
He increases in guidance, and gives them
      their godfearing.

20   Are they looking for aught but the Hour,
that it shall come upon them suddenly?
Already its tokens have come; so, when
it has come to them, how shall they have
      their Reminder?

      Know thou therefore that
      there is no god but God,
and ask forgiveness for thy sin, and
for the believers, men and women. God
knows your going to and fro, and
      your lodging.

Those who believe say, 'Why has a sura
not been sent down?' Then, when a clear
sura is sent down, and therein fighting
is mentioned, thou seest those in whose
hearts is sickness looking at thee as
one who swoons of death; but better
for them would be obedience, and words
      honourable.
Then, when the matter is resolved, if
they were true to God, it would be
      better for them.
If you turned away, would you then haply
work corruption in the land, and break your
      bonds of kin?

25   Those are they whom God has cursed,
and so made them deaf, and blinded
      their eyes.

What, do they not ponder the Koran?
Or is it that there are locks upon
      their hearts?

Those who have turned back in their traces
after the guidance has become clear to them,
Satan it was that tempted them, and God
      respited them.
That is because they said to those who were
averse to what God sent down, 'We will
obey you in some of the affair'; and God
      knows their secrets.
How shall it be, when the angels
take them, beating their faces and
      their backs?
30   That is because they have followed what
angers God, and have been averse to
His good pleasure, so He has made
      their works to fail.
Or did those in whose hearts is sickness
think that God would not bring to light
      their rancour?
Did We will, We would show them to thee,
then thou wouldst know them by their mark;
and thou shalt certainly know them in
the twisting of their speech; and God
      knows your deeds.
And We shall assuredly try you
until We know those of you who
struggle and are steadfast, and try
      your tidings.

Those who disbelieve and bar from God's way
and make a breach with the Messenger
after the guidance has become clear to them,
they will nothing hurt God, and He will make
      their works to fail.

35   O believers, obey God, and obey

the Messenger, and do not make your
  own works vain.
Those who disbelieve and bar from God's way
and then die disbelieving, them God
    will not forgive.
So do not faint and call for peace;
you shall be the upper ones, and God
is with you, and will not deprive you
        of your works.
The present life is naught but a sport
and a diversion; and if you believe
and are godfearing, He will give you
your wages, and will not ask of you
        your goods.
If He asks you for them, and presses you,
you are niggardly, and He brings to light
        your rancour.

40   Ha, there you are; you are called upon
to expend in God's way, and some of
you are niggardly. Whoso is niggardly
is niggardly only to his own soul. God is
the All-sufficient; you are the needy ones.
If you turn away, He will substitute
another people instead of you, then they will
        not be your likes.

XLVIII

VICTORY

In the Name of God, the Merciful, the Compassionate

Surely We have given thee
a manifest victory,
that God may forgive thee thy former and thy latter sins,
and complete His blessing upon thee, and guide thee
on a straight path,
and that God may help thee
with mighty help.

It is He who sent down the Shechina
into the hearts of the believers, that
they might add faith to their faith—
to God belong the hosts of the heavens and the earth;
God is All-knowing, All-wise—
5 and that He may admit the believers,
men and women alike, into gardens
underneath which rivers flow, therein
to dwell forever, and acquit them of
their evil deeds; that is in God's sight
a mighty triumph;
and that He may chastise the hypocrites,
men and women alike, and the idolaters,
men and women alike, and those who think
evil thoughts of God; against them
shall be the evil turn of fortune. God
is wroth with them, and has cursed them,
and has prepared for them Gehenna—
an evil homecoming!
To God belong the hosts of the heavens and the earth;
God is All-mighty, All-wise.

Surely We have sent thee

as a witness,
good tidings to bear, and warning, that
you may believe in God and His Messenger
and succour Him, and reverence Him, and
that you may give Him glory at the dawn
and in the evening.

10   Those who swear fealty to thee
swear fealty in truth to God;
God's hand is over their hands.
Then whosoever breaks his oath
breaks it but to his own hurt;
and whoso fulfils his covenant
made with God, God will give him
a mighty wage.

The Bedouins who were left behind
will say to thee, 'We were occupied
by our possessions and our families;
so ask forgiveness for us!' They say
with their tongues what is not in their
hearts. Say: 'Who can avail you
aught against God, if He desires
hurt for you, or desires profit for
you? Nay, but God is ever aware of
the things you do.
Nay, but you thought that the Messenger
and the believers would never return to
their families, and that was decked out
fair in your hearts, and you thought
evil thoughts, and you were a
people corrupt.'

Whoso believes not in God and His Messenger,
We have prepared for the unbelievers
a Blaze.
To God belongs the kingdom of the heavens
and of the earth; whomsoever He will

He forgives, and whomsoever He will
He chastises; God is All-forgiving,
 All-compassionate.

15 The Bedouins who were left behind
will say, when you set forth after
spoils, to take them, 'Let us follow
you,' desiring to change God's words.
Say: 'You shall not follow us; so
God said before.' Then they will say,
'Nay, but you are jealous of us.'
Nay, but they have not understood
 except a little.
Say to the Bedouins who were left
behind: 'You shall be called against
a people possessed of great might
to fight them, or they surrender.
If you obey, God will give you a
goodly wage; but if you turn your
backs, as you turned your backs
before, He will chastise you with a
 painful chastisement.'

There is no fault in the blind, and there is
no fault in the lame, and there is no fault
in the sick. And whosoever obeys
God and His Messenger, He will admit
him into gardens underneath which
rivers flow; but whosoever turns his
back, him He will chastise with a
 painful chastisement.
God was well pleased with the believers
when they were swearing fealty to thee
under the tree, and He knew what was
in their hearts, so He sent down the
Shechina upon them, and rewarded them with
 a nigh victory
and many spoils to take; and God is ever
 All-mighty, All-wise.

20   God has promised you many spoils
to take; these He has hastened to
you, and has restrained the hands of
men from you, and that it may be a
sign to the believers, and to guide you
      on a straight path,
and other spoils you were not able
to take; God had encompassed
them already. God is powerful
      over everything.
If the unbelievers had fought you, they
would have turned their backs, and then found
      neither protector nor helper;
the wont of God, as in the past before,
and thou shalt never find any changing
      the wont of God.
It is He who restrained their hands
from you, and your hands from them, in
the hollow of Mecca, after that He
made you victors over them. God sees
      the things you do.

25   They are the ones who disbelieved,
and barred you from the Holy Mosque
and the offering, detained so as
not to reach its place of sacrifice.
If it had not been for certain men
believers and certain women believers
whom you knew not, lest you should
trample them, and there befall you
guilt unwittingly on their account
(that God may admit into His mercy
whom He will), had they been separated
clearly, then We would have chastised
the unbelievers among them with a
      painful chastisement.
When the unbelievers set in their hearts
fierceness, the fierceness of pagandom,
then God sent down His Shechina upon
His Messenger and the believers, and

fastened to them the word of godfearing
to which they have better right and are
worthy of; and God has knowledge
      of everything.
God has indeed fulfilled the vision He
vouchsafed to His Messenger truly:
'You shall enter the Holy Mosque,
if God wills, in security, your
heads shaved, your hair cut short,
not fearing.' He knew what you
knew not, and appointed ere that a
      nigh victory.

It is He who has sent His Messenger with
the guidance and the religion of truth, that
He may uplift it above every religion.
      God suffices as a witness.

Muhammad is the Messenger of God,
and those who are with him are hard
against the unbelievers, merciful
one to another. Thou seest them
bowing, prostrating, seeking bounty
from God and good pleasure. Their
mark is on their faces, the trace of
prostration. That is their likeness
in the Torah, and their likeness
in the Gospel: as a seed that puts
forth its shoot, and strengthens it,
and it grows stout and rises straight
upon its stalk, pleasing the sowers,
that through them He may enrage
the unbelievers. God has promised
those of them who believe and do deeds
of righteousness forgiveness and
      a mighty wage.

XLIX

APARTMENTS

In the Name of God, the Merciful, the Compassionate

O believers, advance not before God
and His Messenger; and fear God. God is
All-hearing, All-knowing.

O believers, raise not your voices above
the Prophet's voice, and be not loud
in your speech to him, as you are loud
one to another, lest your works fail
while you are not aware.
Surely those who lower their voices in
the presence of God's Messenger, those
are they whose hearts God has tested for
godfearing; they shall have forgiveness
and a mighty wage.
Surely those who call unto thee from
behind the apartments, the most of them
do not understand.
5 And if they had patience, until thou
comest out to them, that would be better
for them; and God is All-forgiving,
All-compassionate.

O believers, if an ungodly man
comes to you with a tiding, make
clear, lest you afflict a people
unwittingly, and then repent of
what you have done.
And know that the Messenger of God
is among you. If he obeyed you
in much of the affair, you would
suffer; but God has endeared to you
belief, decking it fair in your hearts,

and He has made detestable to you
unbelief and ungodliness and
disobedience. Those—they are
    the right-minded,
by God's favour and blessing; God is
    All-knowing, All-wise.

If two parties of the believers fight,
put things right between them; then,
if one of them is insolent against
the other, fight the insolent one
till it reverts to God's commandment.
If it reverts, set things right between
them equitably, and be just. Surely
    God loves the just.

10   The believers indeed are brothers;
so set things right between your
two brothers, and fear God; haply so
    you will find mercy.

O believers, let not any people
scoff at another people who may be
better than they; neither let women
scoff at women who may be better
than themselves. And find not fault
with one another, neither revile one
another by nicknames. An evil name
is ungodliness after belief. And
whoso repents not, those—they are
    the evildoers.

O believers, eschew much suspicion;
some suspicion is a sin. And do not
spy, neither backbite one another;
would any of you like to eat the
flesh of his brother dead? You would
abominate it. And fear you God;
assuredly God turns, and He is
    All-compassionate.

O mankind, We have created you
male and female, and appointed you
races and tribes, that you may know
one another. Surely the noblest
among you in the sight of God is
the most godfearing of you. God is
          All-knowing, All-aware.

The Bedouins say, 'We believe.'
Say: 'You do not believe; rather
say, "We surrender"; for belief
has not yet entered your hearts.
If you obey God and His Messenger,
He will not diminish you anything
of your works. God is All-forgiving,
          All-compassionate.'
The believers are those who believe
in God and His Messenger, then have
not doubted, and have struggled
with their possessions and their selves
in the way of God; those—they are
          the truthful ones.
Say: 'What, would you teach God
what your religion is, and God knows
what is in the heavens and what is
in the earth? And God has knowledge
          of everything.'
They count it as a favour to thee
that they have surrendered! Say:
'Do not count your surrendering
as a favour to me; nay, but
rather God confers a favour
upon you, in that He has guided
you to belief, if it be that
          you are truthful.
God knows the Unseen of the heavens
and of the earth; and God sees
          the things you do.'

L

QAF

In the Name of God, the Merciful, the Compassionate

Qaf

By the glorious Koran!

Nay, but they marvel that a warner has come to
them from among them; and the unbelievers say,
'This is a marvellous thing!
What, when we are dead and become dust? That
is a far returning!'
We know what the earth diminishes of them;
with Us is a book recording.
Nay, but they cried lies to the truth
when it came to them, and so they are
in a case confused.
What, have they not beheld heaven above them,
how We have built it, and decked it out fair,
and it has no cracks?
And the earth—We stretched it forth, and cast on it
firm mountains,
and We caused to grow therein of every joyous kind
for an insight
and a reminder to every penitent servant.
And We sent down out of heaven
water blessed,
and caused to grow thereby gardens
and grain of harvest
and tall palm-trees with spathes compact,
a provision for the servants,
and thereby We revived a land that was dead.
Even so is the coming forth.

Cried lies before them the people of Noah

and the men of Er-Rass, and Thamood, and
Ad and Pharaoh, the brothers of Lot, the
men of the Thicket, the people of Tubba'.
Every one cried lies to the Messengers,
    and My threat came true.

What, were We wearied by the first creation?
No indeed; but they áre in uncertainty
    as to the new creation.

15   We indeed created man; and We know
    what his soul whispers within him,
    and We are nearer to him than the
        jugular vein.

    When the two angels meet together,
    sitting one on the right, and one
        on the left,
    not a word he utters, but by him
    is an observer ready.
And death's agony comes in truth; that is what thou wast
                [shunning!
And the Trumpet shall be blown; that is the Day of the
                [Threat.
20 And every soul shall come, and with it a driver and a witness.
'Thou wast heedless of this; therefore We have now removed
from thee thy covering, and so thy sight today is piercing.'
And his comrade shall say, 'This is what I have, made ready.'
'Cast, you twain, into Gehenna every froward unbeliever,
every hinderer of the good, transgressor, disquieter,
25 who set up with God another god; therefore, you twain, cast
                [him
into the terrible chastisement.' And his comrade shall say,
'Our Lord, I made him not insolent, but he was in far error.'
He shall say, 'Dispute not before Me! For I sent you before-
                [hand
the threat. The Word is not changed with Me; I wrong not
                [My servants.'

Upon the day We shall say unto Gehenna, 'Art thou filled?'
30   And it shall say, 'Are there any more to come?' And Paradise
shall be brought forward to the godfearing, not afar: 'This is
that you were promised; it is for every mindful penitent.'

> Whosoever fears the All-merciful
> in the Unseen, and comes with a
>   penitent heart:
> 'Enter it in peace! This is the
>   Day of Eternity.'
> Therein they shall have whatever
> they will; and with Us there is
>   yet more.

35
> How many a generation We destroyed before them
> that was stronger in valour than they, then
> they searched about in the land; was there
>   any asylum?
> Surely in that there is a reminder to him
> who has a heart, or will give ear with a
>   present mind.

> We created the heavens and the earth, and
> what between them is, in six days, and no
>   weariness touched Us.

> So be thou patient under what they say, and
>   proclaim thy Lord's praise
> before the rising of the sun, and before its setting, and
>   proclaim thy Lord's praise
> in the night, and at the ends of the prostrations.

40
> And listen thou for the day
> when the caller shall call from a near place.
>   On the day they hear
> the Cry in truth, that is the day of coming forth.
> It is We who give life, and make to die,
>   and to Us is the homecoming.

Upon the day when the earth is split asunder from about them
as they hasten forth; that is a mustering easy for Us.

We know very well what they say;
thou art not a tyrant over them.
45   Therefore remind by the Koran him
who fears My threat.

LI

THE SCATTERERS

In the Name of God, the Merciful, the Compassionate

By the swift scatterers
and the burden-bearers
and the smooth runners
and the partitioners,
5   surely that you are promised is true, and
surely the Doom is about to fall!

By heaven with all its tracks
surely you speak at variance, and
perverted therefrom are some.

10   Perish the conjecturers
who are dazed in perplexity
asking, 'When shall be the Day of Doom?'
Upon the day when they shall be tried at the Fire:
'Taste your trial! This is that you were seeking to hasten.'

15 Surely the godfearing shall be among gardens and fountains
taking whatsoever their Lord has given them;
they were good-doers before that.
Little of the night would they slumber,
and in the mornings they would ask for forgiveness;
and the beggar and the outcast had a share in their wealth.

20   In the earth are signs for those having sure faith;
and in your selves; what, do you not see?
And in heaven is your provision, and that you are promised.
So by the Lord of heaven and earth, it is as surely true
as that you have speech.

Hast thou received the story of

the honoured guests of Abraham?
25   When they entered unto him, saying
'Peace!' he said 'Peace! You
are a people unknown to me.'
Then he turned to his household
and brought a fattened calf,
and he laid it before them
saying, 'Will you not eat?'
Then he conceived a fear of them.
They said, 'Be not afraid!'
And they gave him good tidings
of a cunning boy. Then came
forward his wife, clamouring,
and she smote her face, and
said, 'An old woman, barren!'
30   They said, 'So says thy Lord; He
is the All-wise, the All-knowing.'
Said he, 'And what is your business,
envoys?' They said, 'We have been
sent to a people of sinners, to
loose upon them stones of clay
marked with thy Lord for the prodigal.'
So We brought forth such believers
35   as were in it, but We found not
therein except one house of those
that have surrendered themselves.
And therein We left a sign to those
who fear the painful chastisement.

And also in Moses, when We sent him
unto Pharaoh, with a clear authority,
but he turned his back, with his court,
saying, 'A sorcerer, or a man possessed!'
40   So We seized him and his hosts, and We
cast them into the sea, and he blameworthy.

And also in Ad, when We loosed against them
        the withering wind
that left nothing it came upon, but made it

as stuff decayed.

And also in Thamood, when it was said to them,
    'Take your enjoyment for a while!'
Then they turned in disdain from the commandment
of their Lord, and the thunderbolt took them
    and they themselves beholding
45   and they were not able to stand upright, and
        were not helped.

And the people of Noah before; surely
    they were an ungodly people.

And heaven—We built it with might,
    and We extend it wide.
And the earth—We spread it forth;
    O excellent Smoothers!
And of everything created We two kinds;
    haply you will remember.

50   Therefore flee unto God!
I am a clear warner from Him to you.
And set not up with God another god;
I am a clear warner from Him to you.

Even so not a Messenger came to those before them
but they said, 'A sorcerer, or a man possessed!'
What, have they bequeathed it one to another?
    Nay, but they are an insolent people.

So turn thou from them;
    thou wilt not be reproached.
55   And remind;
    the Reminder profits the believers.

I have not created jinn and mankind
    except to serve Me.
I desire of them no provision,
neither do I desire that they should feed Me.

Surely God is the All-provider,
the Possessor of Strength, the Ever-Sure

The evildoers shall have their portion,
like the portion of their fellows; so
let them not hasten Me!
60   So woe to the unbelievers, for that day of theirs
that they are promised.

LII

THE MOUNT

In the Name of God, the Merciful, the Compassionate

By the Mount
and a Book inscribed
in a parchment unrolled,
by the House inhabited
5   and the roof uplifted
and the sea swarming,
surely thy Lord's chastisement is about to fall;
there is none to avert it.

Upon the day when heaven spins dizzily
10   and the mountains are in motion,
woe that day unto those that cry lies,
such as play at plunging,
the day when they shall be pitched into the fire of Gehenna:
'This is the fire that you cried lies to!
15   What, is this magic, or is it you that do not see?
Roast in it! And bear you patiently, or bear not patiently,
equal it is to you; you are only being recompensed for
that you were working.'

Surely the godfearing shall be in gardens and bliss,
rejoicing in that their Lord has given them;
and their Lord shall guard them against the chastisement of
'Eat and drink, with wholesome appetite, for [Hell.
that you were working.'
·20   .   Reclining upon couches ranged in rows;
and We shall espouse them to wide-eyed houris.
And those who believed, and their seed followed them
in belief, We shall join their seed with them, and We
shall not defraud them of aught of their work;
every man shall be pledged for what he earned.

And We shall succour them with fruits and flesh
    such as they desire
while they pass therein a cup one to another
wherein is no idle talk, no cause of sin,
and there go round them youths, their own,
    as if they were hidden pearls.

25   They advance one upon another, asking each other questions.
    They say, 'We were before among our people, ever
        going in fear,
and God was gracious to us, and guarded us
against the chastisement of the burning wind;
we were before ever calling upon Him; surely
He is the All-benign, the All-compassionate.'

Therefore remind!
by thy Lord's blessing thou art not a soothsayer
    neither possessed.

30   Or do they say, 'He is a poet for whom
we await Fate's uncertainty'? Say:
'Await! I shall be awaiting with you.'

Or do their intellects bid them do this?
    Or are they an insolent people?
Or do they say, 'He has invented it?'
    Nay, but they do not believe.
Then let them bring a discourse like it,
    if they speak truly.

35   Or were they created out of nothing?
    Or are they the creators?
Or did they create the heavens and earth?
    Nay, but they have not sure faith.
Or are thy Lord's treasuries in their keeping?
    Or are they the registrars?
Or have they a ladder whereon they listen?
Then let any of them that has listened bring
    a clear authority.

Or has He daughters, and they sons?

40   Or askest thou them for a wage, and so they
               are weighed down with debt?
Or is the Unseen in their keeping, and so
        they are writing it down?
Or desire they to outwit? The unbelievers,
        they are the outwitted.
Or have they a god, other than God?
Glory be to God, above that which
        they associate!

Even if they saw lumps falling from heaven,
        they would say, 'A massed cloud!'
45   Then leave them, till they encounter their day
        wherein they shall be thunderstruck,
the day when their guile shall avail them naught,
        and they shall not be helped.
And there surely awaits the evildoers a
chastisement beyond even that, but
        most of them know it not.

And be thou patient under the judgment of thy Lord;
        surely thou art before Our eyes.
And proclaim the praise of thy Lord
        when thou arisest,
and proclaim the praise of thy Lord
in the night, and at the declining of the stars.

LIII

THE STAR

In the Name of God, the Merciful, the Compassionate

By the Star when it plunges,
your comrade is not astray, neither errs,
nor speaks he out of caprice.
This is naught but a revelation revealed,
5   taught him by one terrible in power,
very strong; he stood poised,
being on the higher horizon,
then drew near and suspended hung,
two bows'-length away, or nearer,
10   then revealed to his servant that he revealed.
His heart lies not of what he saw;
what, will you dispute with him what he sees?

Indeed, he saw him another time
by the Lote-Tree of the Boundary
15   nigh which is the Garden of the Refuge,
when there covered the Lote-Tree that which covered;
his eye swerved not, nor swept astray.
Indeed, he saw one of the greatest signs of his Lord.

Have you considered El-Lat and El-'Uzza
20   and Manat the third, the other?
What, have you males, and He females?
That were indeed an unjust division.
They are naught but names yourselves
have named, and your fathers; God has
sent down no authority touching them.
They follow only surmise, and what the
souls desire; and yet guidance has
come to them from their Lord.
Or shall man have whatever he fancies?

25   And to God belongs the First and the Last.

How many an angel there is in the heavens whose
intercession avails not anything, save after
that God gives leave to whomsoever He wills
    and is well-pleased.
Those who do not believe in the world to come
name the angels with the names of females.
They have not any knowledge thereof; they follow
only surmise, and surmise avails naught against truth.
30   So turn thou from him who turns away
    from Our Remembrance, and desires only
        the present life.
That is their attainment of knowledge.
    Surely thy Lord knows very well
    those who have gone astray from
    His way, and He knows very well
        those who are guided.

To God belongs whatsoever is in the heavens
and whatsoever is in the earth, that He may
recompense those who do evil for what they
have done, and recompense those who have done
    good with the reward most fair.

    Those who avoid the heinous sins and
    indecencies, save lesser offences—
surely thy Lord is wide in His forgiveness.

Very well He knows you, when He produced you
from the earth, and when you were yet unborn
in your mothers' wombs; therefore hold not
yourselves purified; God knows very well
      him who is godfearing.

Hast thou considered him who turns his back
35   and gives a little, and then grudgingly?
Does he possess the knowledge of the Unseen,
    and therefore he sees?

Or has he not been told of what is in the
     scrolls of Moses,
and Abraham, he who paid his debt in full?
That no soul laden bears the load of another,
40   and that a man shall have to his account only
     as he has laboured,
and that his labouring shall surely be seen,
then he shall be recompensed for it with the
     fullest recompense,
and that the final end is unto thy Lord,
and that it is He who makes to laugh, and
     that makes to weep,
45   and that it is He who makes to die, and
     that makes to live,
and that He Himself created the two kinds,
     male and female,
of a sperm-drop, when it was cast forth,
and that upon Him rests the second growth,
and that it is He who gives wealth and riches,
50   and that it is He who is the Lord of Sirius,
and that He destroyed Ad, the ancient,
and Thamood, and He did not spare them,
and the people of Noah before—certainly
they did exceeding evil, and were insolent—
55   and the Subverted City He also overthrew,
so that there covered it that which covered.
Then which of thy Lord's bounties disputest thou?

This is a warner, of the warners of old.
The Imminent is imminent; apart from God
     none can disclose it.
Do you then marvel at this discourse,
60   and do you laugh, and do you not weep,
     while you make merry?

So bow yourselves before God, and serve Him!

LIV

THE MOON

In the Name of God, the Merciful, the Compassionate

The Hour has drawn nigh: the moon is split.

Yet if they see a sign they turn away, and they say
    'A continuous sorcery!'
They have cried lies, and followed their caprices;
    but every matter is settled.
And there have come to them such tidings as contain
    a deterrent—
a Wisdom far-reaching; yet warnings do not avail.
5   So turn thou away from them.

Upon the day when the Caller shall call unto a horrible thing,
abasing their eyes, they shall come forth from the tombs as if
    they were scattered grasshoppers,
running with outstretched necks to the Caller. The unbelievers
    shall say, 'This is a hard day!'

The people of Noah cried lies before them;
they cried lies to Our servant, and said,
'A man possessed!' And he was rejected.
10   And so he called unto his Lord, saying,
'I am vanquished; do Thou succour me!'
Then We opened the gates of heaven unto
    water torrential,
and made the earth to gush with fountains,
and the waters met for a matter decreed.
And We bore him upon a well-planked vessel
    well-caulked
running before Our eyes—a recompense for
    him denied.
15   And We left it for a sign.

Is there any that will remember?
How then were My chastisement and My warnings?
Now We have made the Koran easy for Remembrance.
Is there any that will remember?

Ad cried lies.
How then were My chastisement and My warnings?
We loosed against them a wind
clamorous in a day of ill fortune continuous,
20   plucking up men as if they were stumps of
uprooted palm-trees.
How then were My chastisement and My warnings?
Now We have made the Koran easy for Remembrance.
Is there any that will remember?

Thamood cried lies to the warnings
and said, 'What, shall we follow
a mortal, one out of ourselves?
Then indeed we should be in error
and insanity!
25   Has the Reminder been cast upon him
alone among us? Nay, rather he is
an impudent liar.'
'They shall surely know tomorrow
who is the impudent liar.
We shall send the She-camel as a
trial for them; so watch thou them
and keep patience.
And tell them that the water is to
be divided between them, each drink
for each in turn.'
Then they called their comrade, and
he took in hand, and hamstrung her.
30 How then were My chastisement and My warnings?
We loosed against them one Cry,
and they were as the wattles of a
pen-builder.
Now We have made the Koran easy for Remembrance.
Is there any that will remember?

The people of Lot cried lies to the warnings.
We loosed against them a squall of pebbles
except the folk of Lot; We delivered them
    at the dawn—

35   a blessing from Us; even so We recompense
        him who is thankful.
He had warned them of Our assault, but
    they disputed the warnings.
Even his guests they had solicited of him;
so We obliterated their eyes, saying,
'Taste now My chastisement and My warnings!'
In the morning early there came upon them
    a settled chastisement:
'Taste now My chastisement and My warnings!'
40 Now We have made the Koran easy for Remembrance.
    Is there any that will remember?

The warnings came also to Pharaoh's folk.
They cried lies to Our signs, all of them,
so We seized them with the seizing of One
    mighty, omnipotent.

What, are your unbelievers better than those?
Or have you an immunity in the Scrolls? Or
do they say, 'We are a congregation that
    shall be succoured?'
45 Certainly the host shall be routed, and
    turn their backs.

Nay, but the Hour is their tryst,
and the Hour is very calamitous
    and bitter.
Surely the sinners are in error
    and insanity!

The day when they are dragged on their faces into the Fire:
'Taste now the touch of Sakar!'

Surely We have created everything

in measure.

50   Our commandment is but one word,
       as the twinkling of an eye.

We have destroyed the likes of you;
is there any that will remember?

Every thing that they have done
     is in the Scrolls,
and everything, great and small,
     is inscribed.

Surely the godfearing shall dwell amid gardens
     and a river
55   in a sure abode, in the presence of
     a King Omnipotent.

LV

THE ALL-MERCIFUL

In the Name of God, the Merciful, the Compassionate

The All-merciful has taught the Koran.
He created man
and He has taught him the Explanation.

The sun and the moon to a reckoning,
and the stars and the trees bow themselves;
and heaven—He raised it up, and set
.the Balance.
(Transgress not in the Balance,
and weigh with justice, and skimp not in the Balance.)
And earth—He set it down for all beings,
therein fruits, and palm-trees with sheaths,
and grain in the blade, and fragrant herbs.
O which of your Lord's bounties will you and you deny?

He created man of a clay
like the potter's,
and He created the jinn
of a smokeless fire.
O which of your Lord's bounties will you and you deny?

Lord of the Two Easts,
Lord of the Two Wests,
O which of your Lord's bounties will you and you deny?

He let forth the two seas that meet together,
between them a barrier they do not overpass.
O which of your Lord's bounties will you and you deny?
From them come forth the pearl and the coral.
O which of your Lord's bounties will you and you deny?
His too are the ships that run, raised up in the sea like land-
[marks.

25   O which of your Lord's bounties will you and you deny?

    All that dwells upon the earth is perishing, yet still
      abides the Face of thy Lord, majestic, splendid.
    O which of your Lord's bounties will you and you deny?
Whatsoever is in the heavens and the earth implore Him;
      every day He is upon some labour.
30   O which of your Lord's bounties will you and you deny?

     We shall surely attend to you at leisure,
      you weight and you weight!
    O which of your Lord's bounties will you and you deny?
    O tribe of jinn and of men, if you are able to
    pass through the confines of heaven and earth,
    pass through them! You shall not pass through
      except with an authority.
    O which of your Lord's bounties will you and you deny?
35   Against you shall be loosed
      a flame of fire, and molten
    brass; and you shall not be helped.
    O which of your Lord's bounties will you and you deny?
    And when heaven is split asunder,
    and turns crimson like red leather—
    O which of your Lord's bounties will you and you deny?
    on that day none shall be questioned
    about his sin, neither man nor jinn.
40   O which of your Lord's bounties will you and you deny?
    The sinners shall be known by their mark,
and they shall be seized by their forelocks and their feet.
    O which of your Lord's bounties will you and you deny?
    This is Gehenna, that sinners cried lies to;
    they shall go round between it and between
      hot, boiling water.
45   O which of your Lord's bounties will you and you deny?

    But such as fears the Station of his Lord,
    for them shall be two gardens—
    O which of your Lord's bounties will you and you deny?
    abounding in branches—

O which of your Lord's bounties will you and you deny?
50   therein two fountains of running water—
O which of your Lord's bounties will you and you deny?
        therein of every fruit two kinds—
O which of your Lord's bounties will you and you deny?
    reclining upon couches lined with brocade,
    the fruits of the gardens nigh to gather—
55   O which of your Lord's bounties will you and you deny?
    therein maidens restraining their glances,
    untouched before them by any man or jinn—
O which of your Lord's bounties will you and you deny?
    lovely as rubies, beautiful as coral—
O which of your Lord's bounties will you and you deny?
60 Shall the recompense of goodness be other than goodness?
O which of your Lord's bounties will you and you deny?

    And besides these shall be two gardens—
O which of your Lord's bounties will you and you deny?
    green, green pastures—
65   O which of your Lord's bounties will you and you deny?
    therein two fountains of gushing water—
O which of your Lord's bounties will you and you deny?
      therein fruits,
      and palm-trees, and pomegranates—
O which of your Lord's bounties will you and you deny?
70   therein maidens good and comely—
O which of your Lord's bounties will you and you deny?
    houris, cloistered in cool pavilions—
O which of your Lord's bounties will you and you deny?
    untouched before them by any man or jinn—
75   O which of your Lord's bounties will you and you deny?
reclining upon green cushions and lovely druggets—
O which of your Lord's bounties will you and you deny?

Blessed be the Name of thy Lord, majestic, splendid.

LVI

THE TERROR

In the Name of God, the Merciful, the Compassionate

When the Terror descends
(and none denies its descending)
abasing, exalting,
when the earth shall be rocked
5 and the mountains crumbled
and become a dust scattered,
and you shall be three bands—

Companions of the Right (O Companions of the Right!)
Companions of the Left (O Companions of the Left!)
10 and the Outstrippers: the Outstrippers
those are they brought nigh the Throne,
in the Gardens of Delight
(a throng of the ancients
and how few of the later folk)
15 upon close-wrought couches
reclining upon them, set face to face,
immortal youths going round about them
with goblets, and ewers, and a cup from a spring
(no brows throbbing, no intoxication)
20 and such fruits as they shall choose,
and such flesh of fowl as they desire,
and wide-eyed houris
as the likeness of hidden pearls,
a recompense for that they laboured.
Therein they shall hear no idle talk, no cause of sin,
25 only the saying 'Peace, Peace!'

The Companions of the Right (O Companions of the Right!)
mid thornless lote-trees and serried acacias,
30 and spreading shade and outpoured waters,

and fruits abounding
unfailing, unforbidden,
and upraised couches.
Perfectly We formed them, perfect,
35   and We made them spotless virgins,
chastely amorous, like of age
for the Companions of the Right.
A throng of the ancients
and a throng of the later folk.

40   The Companions of the Left (O Companions of the Left!)
mid burning winds and boiling waters
and the shadow of a smoking blaze
neither cool, neither goodly;
and before that they lived at ease,
45   and persisted in the Great Sin,
ever saying,
'What, when we are dead and become
dust and bones, shall we indeed
be raised up?
What, and our fathers, the ancients?'

Say: 'The ancients, and the later folk
shall be gathered to the appointed time
of a known day.
50   Then you erring ones, you that cried lies,
you shall eat of a tree called Zakkoum,
and you shall fill therewith your bellies
and drink on top of that boiling water
55   lapping it down like thirsty camels.'
This shall be their hospitality on the
Day of Doom.

We created you; therefore why will you
not believe?

Have you considered the seed you spill?
Do you yourselves create it, or are We
the Creators?

561

60 We have decreed among you Death; We shall
  not be outstripped;
that We may exchange the likes of you,
and make you to grow again in a fashion
  you know not.
You have known the first growth; so why
  will you not remember?

Have you considered the soil you till?
Do you yourselves sow it, or are We
  the Sowers?
65 Did We will, We would make it broken
orts, and you would remain bitterly
   jesting—
'We are debt-loaded; nay, we have been
   robbed!'

Have you considered the water you drink?
Did you send it down from the clouds, or
  did We send it?
Did We will, We would make it bitter; so
  why are you not thankful?

70 Have you considered the fire you kindle?
Did you make its timber to grow, or
  did We make it?
We Ourselves made it for a reminder, and
  a boon to the desert-dwellers.

Then magnify the Name of thy Lord, the All-mighty.

No! I swear by the fallings of the stars
75 (and that is indeed a mighty oath, did
   you but know it)
it is surely a noble Koran
in a hidden Book
none but the purified shall touch,
a sending down from the Lord of all Being.
80 What, do you hold this discourse in disdain, and

do you make it your living to cry lies?

Why, but when the soul leaps to the throat of the dying
and that hour you are watching
(And We are nigher him than you, but you do not see Us)
85   why, if you are not at Our disposa ,
do you not bring back his soul, if you speak truly?

Then, if he be of those brought nigh the Throne,
there shall be repose and ease, and a Garden of Delight;
90   and if he be a Companion of the Right:
'Peace be upon thee, Companion of the Right!'
But if he be of them that cried lies, and went astray,
there shall be a hospitality of boiling water
and the roasting in Hell.

95   Surely this is the truth of certainty.
Then magnify the Name of thy Lord, the All-mighty.

LVII

IRON

In the Name of God, the Merciful, the Compassionate

All that is in the heavens and the earth magnifies God;
    He is the All-mighty, the All-wise.
To Him belongs the Kingdom of the heavens and the earth;
He gives life, and He makes to die, and He is powerful
          over everything.
He is the First and the Last, the Outward and the Inward;
    He has knowledge of everything.
It is He that created the heavens and the earth
      in six days
    then seated Himself upon the Throne.
He knows what penetrates into the earth,
    and what comes forth from it,
what comes down from heaven, and what goes up unto it.
He is with you wherever you are; and God sees
      the things you do.
5   To Him belongs the Kingdom of the heavens and the earth;
    and unto Him all matters are returned.
He makes the night to enter into the day
    and makes the day to enter into the night.
He knows the thoughts within the breasts.

Believe in God and His Messenger, and expend of
that unto which He has made you successors. And
those of you who believe and expend shall have
      a mighty wage.
How is it with you, that you believe not in God
seeing that the Messenger is calling you to
believe in your Lord, and He has taken compact
    with you, if you are believers?
It is He who sends down upon His servant signs,
clear signs, that He may bring you forth from

the shadows into the light. Surely God is to you
     All-gentle, All-compassionate.
10   How is it with you, that you expend not in the
way of God, and to God belongs the inheritance
of the heavens and the earth? Not equal is he
among you who spent, and who fought before the
victory; those are mightier in rank than they
who spent and fought afterwards; and unto each
God has promised the reward most fair; and God
     is aware of the things you do.
Who is he that will lend to God a good loan,
and He will multiply it for him, and his shall be
     a generous wage?

Upon the day when thou seest the believers, men and women,
their light running before them, and on their right hands.
'Good tidings for you today! Gardens underneath which
rivers flow, therein to dwell for ever; that is indeed
     the mighty triumph.'
Upon the day when the hypocrites, men and women, shall say
to those who have believed, 'Wait for us, so that we may
borrow your light!' It shall be said, 'Return you back
behind, and seek for a light!' And a wall shall be set up
between them, having a door in the inward whereof is
mercy, and against the outward thereof is chastisement.
They shall be calling unto them, 'Were we not with you?'
They shall say, 'Yes indeed; but you tempted yourselves,
and you awaited, and you were in doubt, and fancies
deluded you, until God's commandment came, and the
Deluder deluded you concerning God. Therefore today
no ransom shall be taken from you, neither from those who
disbelieved. Your refuge is the Fire, that is your master—
     an evil homecoming!'

15   Is it not time that the hearts of those
who believe should be humbled to the
Remembrance of God and the Truth which
He has sent down, and that they should
not be as those to whom the Book was

given aforetime, and the term seemed
over long to them, so that their hearts
have become hard, and many of them
      are ungodly?
Know that God revives the earth after
it was dead. We have indeed made clear
for you the signs, that haply you will
      understand.
Surely those, the men and the women,
who make freewill offerings and have
lent to God a good loan, it shall be
multiplied for them, and theirs shall be
      a generous wage.
And those who believe in God and His
Messengers—they are the just men
and the martyrs in their Lord's sight;
they have their wage, and their light.
But the unbelievers, who have cried lies
to Our signs, they are the inhabitants
      of Hell.
Know that the present life is but a
sport and a diversion, an adornment
and a cause for boasting among you,
and a rivalry in wealth and children.
It is as a rain whose vegetation
pleases the unbelievers; then it
withers, and thou seest it turning
yellow, then it becomes broken orts.
And in the world to come there is a
      terrible chastisement,
20   and forgiveness from God and good pleasure;
and the present life is but the joy
      of delusion.
Race to forgiveness from your Lord,
and a Garden the breadth whereof is
as the breadth of heaven and earth,
made ready for those who believe in
God and His Messengers. That is the
bounty of God; He gives it unto

whomsoever He will; and God is of
    bounty abounding.
No affliction befalls in the earth
or in yourselves, but it is in a
Book, before We create it; that is
    easy for God;
that you may not grieve for what
escapes you, nor rejoice in what has
come to you; God loves not any man
    proud and boastful,
such as are niggardly, and bid men
to be niggardly. And whosoever
turns away, God is the All-sufficient,
    the All-laudable.

25 Indeed, We sent Our Messengers with
the clear signs, and We sent down
with them the Book and the Balance
so that men might uphold justice.
And We sent down iron, wherein is
great might, and many uses for men,
and so that God might know who
helps Him, and His Messengers,
in the Unseen. Surely God is
    All-strong, All-mighty.
And We sent Noah, and Abraham,
and We appointed the Prophecy and
the Book to be among their seed; and
some of them are guided, and many of
    them are ungodly.

Then We sent, following
in their footsteps, Our
Messengers; and We sent,
following, Jesus son of
Mary, and gave unto him
    the Gospel.
And We set in the hearts of those who
followed him tenderness and mercy.

And monasticism they invented—We
did not prescribe it for them—only
seeking the good pleasure of God; but
they observed it not as it should be
observed. So We gave those of them
who believed their wage; and many of
           them are ungodly.

O believers, fear God, and believe
in His Messenger, and He will give you
a twofold portion of His mercy, and
He will appoint for you a light whereby
you shall walk, and forgive you; God is
      All-forgiving, All-compassionate;
that the People of the Book may know
that they have no power over anything
of God's bounty, and that bounty is in
the hand of God; He gives it unto
whomsoever He will; and God is of
          bounty abounding.

LVIII

THE DISPUTER

In the Name of God, the Merciful, the Compassionate

God has heard the words of her that disputes with thee
concerning her husband, and makes complaint unto God.
God hears the two of you conversing together; surely
God is All-hearing, All-seeing.

Those of you who say, regarding their wives, 'Be as
my mother's back,' they are not truly their mothers;
their mothers are only those who gave them birth, and
they are surely saying a dishonourable saying, and a
falsehood.
Yet surely God is All-pardoning, All-forgiving.
And those who say, regarding their wives, 'Be as my
mother's back,' and then retract what they have said,
they shall set free a slave, before the two of them
touch one another. By that you are admonished; and
God is aware of the things you do.

5 But whosoever finds not the means, then let him fast
two successive months, before the two of them touch
one another. And if any man is not able to, then
let him feed sixty poor persons—that, that you may
believe in God and His Messenger. Those are God's
bounds; and for the unbelievers there awaits yet
a painful chastisement.

Surely those who oppose God and His Messenger
shall be frustrated as those before them were
frustrated. Now We have sent down signs,
clear signs; and for the unbelievers awaits
a humbling chastisement,
upon the day when God shall raise them up all
together, then He shall tell them what they did.

God has numbered it, and they have forgotten it.
God is witness over everything.

Hast thou not seen that God knows whatsoever is in
the heavens, and whatsoever is in the earth? Three
men conspire not secretly together, but He is the
fourth of them, neither five men, but He is the
sixth of them, neither fewer than that, neither
more, but He is with them, wherever they may be;
then He shall tell them what they have done, on the ·
Day of Resurrection. Surely God has knowledge
of everything.

Hast thou not regarded those who were forbidden
to converse secretly together, then they return
to that they were forbidden, and they converse
secretly together in sin and enmity, and in
disobedience to the Messenger? Then, when they
come to thee, they greet thee with a greeting
God never greeted thee withal; and they say
within themselves, 'Why does God not chastise
us for what we say?' Sufficient for them shall
be Gehenna, at which they shall be roasted—
an evil homecoming!

10 O believers, when you conspire secretly, then
conspire not together in sin and enmity and
disobedience to the Messenger, but conspire
in piety and godfearing. Fear God, unto whom
you shall be mustered.
Conspiring secretly together is of Satan,
that the believers may sorrow; but he will
not hurt them anything, except by the leave
of God. And in God let the believers
put all their trust.

O believers, when it is said to you
'Make room in the assemblies', then
make room, and God will make room for
you; and when it is said, 'Move up',

move up, and God will raise up in rank
those of you who believe and have been
given knowledge. And God is aware of
    the things you do.
O believers, when you conspire with
the Messenger, before your conspiring
advance a freewill offering; that is
better for you and purer. Yet if you
find not means, God is All-forgiving,
    All-compassionate.
Are you afraid, before your conspiring,
to advance freewill offerings? If you
do not so, and God turns again unto
you, then perform the prayer, and
pay the alms, and obey God and
His Messenger. God is aware of
    the things you do.

15   Hast thou not regarded those who have taken
for friends a people against whom God is
wrathful? They belong neither to you nor
to them; and they swear upon falsehood,
    and that wittingly.
God has made ready for them a chastisement
terrible; surely they—evil are the things
    they have been doing.
They have taken their oaths as a covering,
and barred from God's way; so there awaits them
    a humbling chastisement.
Neither their riches nor their children
shall avail them anything against God;
those—they are the inhabitants of the Fire,
    therein dwelling forever.
Upon the day when God shall raise them up all
together, and they will swear to Him, as they
swear to you, and think they are on something.
    Surely, they are the liars!
20   Satan has gained the mastery over them, and
caused them to forget God's Remembrance.

Those are Satan's party; why, Satan's party,
    surely, they are the losers!

Surely those who oppose God and His Messenger,
those are among the most abject. God has
written, 'I shall assuredly be the victor,
I and My Messengers.' Surely God is
    All-strong, All-mighty.

Thou shalt not find any people who believe
in God and the Last Day who are loving to
anyone who opposes God and His Messenger, not
though they were their fathers, or their sons,
or their brothers, or their clan. Those—
He has written faith upon their hearts, and
He has confirmed them with a Spirit from
Himself; and He shall admit them into
gardens underneath which rivers flow, therein
to dwell forever, God being well-pleased with
them, and they well-pleased with Him. Those are
God's party; why, surely God's party—they are
    the prosperers.

LIX

THE MUSTERING

In the Name of God, the Merciful, the Compassionate

All that is in the heavens and the earth magnifies God;
    He is the All-mighty, the All-wise.

It is He who expelled from their habitations
the unbelievers among the People of the Book
at the first mustering. You did not think
that they would go forth, and they thought
that their fortresses would defend them
against God; then God came upon them from
whence they had not reckoned, and He cast
terror into their hearts as they destroyed
their houses with their own hands, and the
hands of the believers; therefore take heed,
        you who have eyes!
Had God not prescribed dispersal for them,
He would have chastised them in this world;
and there awaits them in the world to come
        the chastisement of the Fire.
That is because they made a breach with
God and His Messenger; and whosoever
makes a breach with God, God is terrible
        in retribution.

5   Whatever palm-trees you cut down, or
left standing upon their roots, that was
by God's leave, and that He might degrade
        the ungodly.
And whatever spoils of war God has given
unto His Messenger from them, against
that you pricked neither horse nor camel;
but God gives authority to His Messengers

over whomsoever He will. God is powerful
over everything.
Whatsoever spoils of war God has given to
His Messenger from the people of the cities
belongs to God, and His Messenger, and
the near kinsman, orphans, the needy
and the traveller, so that it be not a
thing taken in turns among the rich of you.
Whatever the Messenger gives you, take;
whatever he forbids you, give over.
And fear God; surely God is terrible
in retribution.
It is for the poor emigrants, who were
expelled from their habitations and their
possessions, seeking bounty from God
and good pleasure, and helping God
and His Messenger; those—they are
the truthful ones.
And those who made their dwelling in
the abode, and in belief, before them,
love whosoever has emigrated to them,
not finding in their breasts any need
for what they have been given, and
preferring others above themselves, even
though poverty be their portion. And
whoso is guarded against the avarice
of his own soul, those—they are
the prosperers.

10   And as for those who came after them,
they say, 'Our Lord, forgive us and our
brothers, who preceded us in belief,
and put Thou not into our hearts any
rancour towards those who believe. Our
Lord, surely Thou art the All-gentle,
the All-compassionate.'

Hast thou not regarded the hypocrites, saying
to their brothers of the People of the Book who
disbelieve, 'If you are expelled, we will go

forth with you, and we will never obey anyone
in regard to you. If you are fought against,
we will help you.' And God bears witness that
　　　they are truly liars.
If those are expelled, they will not go forth
with them, and if they are fought against, they
will not help them. Even if they helped them,
they would surely turn their backs, then they
　　　would not be helped.
Why, you arouse greater fear in their hearts
than God; that is because they are a people
　　　who understand not.
They will not fight against you all together
except in fortified cities, or from behind walls.
Their valour is great, among themselves; you
think of them as a host; but their hearts are
scattered; that is because they are a people
　　　who have no sense.
15　Like those who a short time before them tasted
the mischief of their action; there awaits them
　　　a painful chastisement.
Like Satan, when he said to man, 'Disbelieve';
then, when he disbelieved, he said, 'Surely
I am quit of you. Surely I fear God, the
　　　Lord of all Being.'
Their end is, both are in the Fire, there
dwelling forever; that is the recompense
　　　of the evildoers.

O believers, fear God. Let every soul
consider what it has forwarded for the
morrow. And fear God; God is aware of
　　　the things you do.
Be not as those who forgot God, and so He
caused them to forget their souls; those—
　　　they are the ungodly.
20　Not equal are the inhabitants of the
Fire and the inhabitants of Paradise.
The inhabitants of Paradise—they

are the triumphant.

If We had sent down this Koran upon a mountain,
thou wouldst have seen it humbled, split asunder
out of the fear of God.
And those similitudes—We strike them for men;
haply they will reflect.

He is God;
there is no god but He.
He is the knower of the Unseen and the Visible;
He is the All-merciful, the All-compassionate.

He is God;
there is no god but He.
He is the King, the All-holy, the All-peaceable,
the All-faithful, the All-preserver,
the All-mighty, the All-compeller,
the All-sublime.
Glory be to God, above that they associate!

He is God,
the Creator, the Maker, the Shaper.
To Him belong the Names Most Beautiful.
All that is in the heavens and the earth magnifies Him;
He is the All-mighty, the All-wise.

LX

THE WOMAN TESTED

In the Name of God, the Merciful, the Compassionate

O believers, take not My enemy and your enemy
for friends, offering them love, though they
have disbelieved in the truth that has come to
you, expelling the Messenger and you because
you believe in God your Lord. If you go forth to
struggle in My way and seek My good pleasure,
secretly loving them, yet I know very well
what you conceal and what you publish; and
whosoever of you does that, has gone astray
  from the right way.
If they come on you, they will be enemies to
you, and stretch against you their hands and
their tongues, to do you evil, and they wish that
  you may disbelieve.
Neither your blood-kindred nor your children
shall profit you upon the Day of Resurrection;
He shall distinguish between you. And God sees
  the things you do.

You have had a good example in Abraham, and
those with him, when they said to their people,
'We are quit of you and that you serve, apart
from God. We disbelieve in you, and between
us and you enmity has shown itself, and
hatred for ever, until you believe in God alone.'
(Except that Abraham said unto his father,
'Certainly I shall ask pardon for thee; but I
have no power to do aught for thee against God.')
'Our Lord, in Thee we trust; to Thee we turn; to
  Thee is the homecoming.
5 Our Lord, make us not a temptation to those who

disbelieve; and forgive us. Our Lord, Thou art
    the All-mighty, the All-wise.'
You have had a good example in them for whoever
hopes for God and the Last Day. And whosoever
turns away, surely God is the All-sufficient,
    the All-laudable.
It may be God will yet establish between you
and those of them with whom you are at enmity
love. God is All-powerful; God is All-forgiving,
    All-compassionate.

God forbids you not, as regards those who have not
fought you in religion's cause, nor expelled you
from your habitations, that you should be kindly
to them, and act justly towards them; surely
    God loves the just.
God only forbids you as to those who have fought
you in religion's cause, and expelled you from
your habitations, and have supported in your
expulsion, that you should take them for friends.
And whosoever takes them for friends, those—
    they are the evildoers.

10   O believers, when believing women come to you
as emigrants, test them. God knows very well
their belief. Then, if you know them to be
believers, return them not to the unbelievers.
They are not permitted to the unbelievers,
nor are the unbelievers permitted to them.
Give the unbelievers what they have expended;
and there is no fault in you to marry them
when you have given them their wages. Do not
hold fast to the ties of unbelieving women,
and ask what you have expended, and let them
ask what they have expended. That is God's
judgment; He judges between you; and God is
    All-knowing, All-wise.
And if any of your wives slips away from you
to the unbelievers, and then you retaliate, ·

give those whose wives have gone away the like
of what they have expended. And fear God, in
      whom you believe.

O Prophet, when believing women come to thee,
swearing fealty to thee upon the terms that
they will not associate with God anything,
and will not steal, neither commit adultery,
nor slay their children, nor bring a calumny
they forge between their hands and their feet,
nor disobey thee in aught honourable, ask God's
forgiveness for them; God is All-forgiving,
      All-compassionate.

O believers, take not for friends a people
against whom God is wrathful, and who have
despaired of the world to come, even as the
unbelievers have despaired of the inhabitants
      of the tombs.

LXI

THE RANKS

In the Name of God, the Merciful, the Compassionate

All that is in the heavens and the earth magnifies God;
.He is the All-mighty, the All-wise.

O you who believe, wherefore do you say
what you do not?
Very hateful is it to God, that you say
what you do not.
God loves those who fight in His way in
ranks, as though they were a building
well-compacted.

5
And when Moses said to his people,
'O my people, why do you hurt me,
though you know I am the Messenger
of God to you?' When they swerved,
God caused their hearts to swerve;
and God guides never the people
of the ungodly.

And when Jesus son of
Mary said, 'Children of
Israel, I am indeed the
Messenger of God to you,
confirming the Torah
that is before me, and
giving good tidings of
a Messenger who shall
come after me, whose
name shall be Ahmad.'
Then, when he brought them the clear signs,
they said, 'This is a manifest sorcery.'

And who does greater evil than he who
forges against God falsehood, when he
is being called unto surrender?
And God guides never the people
    of the evildoers.

They desire to extinguish with their mouths the light
of God; but God will perfect His light, though
    the unbelievers be averse.
It is He who has sent His Messenger with
the guidance and the religion of truth, that
he may uplift it above every religion, though
    the unbelievers be averse.

10   O believers, shall I direct you to a
commerce that shall deliver you from
    a painful chastisement?
You shall believe in God and His
Messenger, and struggle in the way of
God with your possessions and your
selves. That is better for you,
    did you but know.
He will forgive you your sins and admit
you into gardens underneath which
rivers flow, and to dwelling-places
goodly in Gardens of Eden; that is
    the mighty triumph;
and other things you love, help from God
and a nigh victory. Give thou good tidings
    to the believers!

O believers, be you God's helpers, as
Jesus, Mary's son, said to the Apostles.
    'Who will be my helpers
    unto God?' The Apostles
    said, 'We will be helpers
      of God.'
And a party of the Children of Israel
believed, and a party disbelieved.

So We confirmed those who believed
against their enemy, and they became
masters.

LXII

CONGREGATION

In the Name of God, the Merciful, the Compassionate

All that is in the heavens and the earth magnifies God,
the King, the All-holy,
the All-mighty, the All-wise.
It is He who has raised up from among the common people
a Messenger from among them, to recite His signs to them
⌈and
to purify them, and to teach them the Book and the Wisdom,
though before that they were in manifest error,
and others of them who have not yet joined them. And He is
the All-mighty, the All-wise.

That is the bounty of God;
He gives it to whom He will,
and God is of bounty
abounding.

5   The likeness of those who have been loaded with the Torah,
then they have not carried it, is as the likeness of an ass
carrying books. Evil is the likeness of the people
who have cried lies to God's signs. God guides never
the people of the evildoers.

Say: 'You of Jewry, if you assert that
you are the friends of God, apart from
other men, then do you long for death,
if you speak truly.'
But they will never long for it, because of
that their hands have forwarded; God knows
the evildoers.
Say: 'Surely death, from which you flee,
shall encounter you; then you shall be

583

returned to the Knower of the Unseen and
the Visible, and He will tell you that
you have been doing.'

O believers, when proclamation is made for prayer on
the Day of Congregation, hasten to God's remembrance
and leave trafficking aside; that is better for you,
did you but know.

10   Then, when the prayer is finished, scatter in the land
and seek God's bounty, and remember God frequently;
haply you will prosper.

But when they see merchandise or diversion
they scatter off to it, and they leave thee
standing.
Say: 'What is with God is better
than diversion and merchandise.
God is the best of providers.'

LXIII

THE HYPOCRITES

In the Name of God, the Merciful, the Compassionate

When the hypocrites come to thee they say,
'We bear witness that thou art indeed
the Messenger of God.' And God knows
that thou art indeed His Messenger, and
God bears witness that the hypocrites
                are truly liars.
They have taken their oaths as a covering,
then they have barred from the way of God.
Surely they—evil are the things they
                have been doing.
That is because they have believed, then
they have disbelieved; therefore a seal
has been set on their hearts, and they
                do not understand.
When thou seest them, their bodies please
thee; but when they speak, thou listenest
to their speech, and it is as they were
propped-up timbers. They think every cry
is against them. They are the enemy;
so beware of them. God assail them! How
                they are perverted!
5   And when it is said to them, 'Come now,
and God's Messenger will ask forgiveness
for you,' they twist their heads, and thou
seest them turning their faces away,
                waxing proud.
Equal it is for them, whether thou askest
forgiveness for them or thou askest not
forgiveness for them; God will never
forgive them. God guides not the people
                of the ungodly.

Those are they that say, 'Do not expend
on them that are with God's Messenger
until they scatter off'; yet unto God
belong the treasuries of the heavens
and of the earth, but the hypocrites
   do not understand.
They say, 'If we return to the City,
the mightier ones of it will expel
the more abased'; yet glory belongs
unto God, and unto His Messenger
and the believers, but the hypocrites
   do not know it.

O believers, let not your possessions
neither your children divert you from
God's remembrance; whoso does that,
   they are the losers.

10 Expend of what We have provided you
before that death comes upon one of you
and he says, 'O my Lord, if only
Thou wouldst defer me unto a near
term, so that I may make freewill
offering, and so I may become
   one of the righteous.'
But God will never defer any soul when
its term comes. And God is aware of
   the things you do.

LXIV

MUTUAL FRAUD

In the Name of God, the Merciful, the Compassionate

All that is in the heavens and the earth magnifies God.
His is the Kingdom, and His is the praise,
and He is powerful over everything.

It is He who created you. One of you is an unbeliever,
and one of you a believer; and God sees
the things you do.
He created the heavens and the earth with the truth,
and He shaped you, and shaped you well; and unto Him
is the homecoming.
He knows whatever is in the heavens and the earth, and
He knows what you conceal and what you publish.
God knows the thoughts within the breasts.

5   Has there not come to you the tidings of those
that disbelieved before, then tasted the mischief
of their action, and there yet awaits them a
painful chastisement?
That is because their Messengers came to them
with the clear signs, and then they said, 'What,
shall mortals be our guides?' Therefore they
disbelieved, and turned away; and God was in
no need of them. And God is All-sufficient,
All-laudable.

The unbelievers assert that they will
never be raised up. Say: 'Yes indeed,
by my Lord! You shall be raised up,
then you shall be told the things you did.
That is easy for God.'

587

Therefore believe in God and
His Messenger, and in the
Light which We have sent down.
And God is aware of the things you do.

Upon the day when He shall gather you
for the Day of Gathering; that shall
be the Day of Mutual Fraud. And
whosoever believes in God, and does
righteousness, God will acquit him
of his evil deeds, and admit him
into gardens underneath which
rivers flow, therein to dwell for
ever and ever; that is the mighty
   triumph.

10 And those who disbelieved and cried
lies to Our signs, those shall be
the inhabitants of the Fire.
therein to dwell forever—an evil
   homecoming!

No affliction befalls, except it be
by the leave of God. Whosoever
believes in God, He will guide his
heart. And God has knowledge of
   everything.

And obey God, and obey the Messenger;
but if you turn your backs, it is
only for the Messenger to deliver
  the Manifest Message.

   God—
  there is no god but He.
 And in God let the believers
  put their trust.

O believers, among your wives and children

there is an enemy to you; so beware of them.
But if you pardon, and overlook, and if you
forgive, surely God is All-forgiving,
      All-compassionate.
15   Your wealth and your children are
only a trial; and with God is
      a mighty wage.
So fear God as far as you are able,
and give ear, and obey, and expend
well for yourselves. And whosoever
is guarded against the avarice
of his own soul, those—they are
      the prosperers.
If you lend to God a good loan, He
will multiply it for you, and will
forgive you. God is All-thankful,
      All-clement,
Knower He of the Unseen and the Visible,
      the All-mighty, the All-wise.

LXV

DIVORCE

In the Name of God, the Merciful, the Compassionate

O Prophet, when you divorce women, divorce them
when they have reached their period. Count the
period, and fear God your Lord. Do not expel
them from their houses, nor let them go forth,
except when they commit a flagrant indecency.
Those are God's bounds; whosoever trespasses
the bounds of God has done wrong to himself.
Thou knowest not, perchance after that God will
   bring something new to pass.
Then, when they have reached their term, retain
them honourably, or part from them honourably.
And call in to witness two men of equity from
among yourselves; and perform the witnessing
to God Himself. By this then is admónished
whosoever believes in God and the Last Day.
And whosoever fears God, He will appoint for him
a way out, and He will provide for him from
   whence he never reckoned.

And whosoever puts his trust in God,
He shall suffice him. God attains his
purpose. God has appointed a measure
  for everything.

As for your women who have despaired of further
menstruating, if you are in doubt, their period
shall be three months, and those who have not
menstruated as yet. And those who are with child,
their term is when they bring forth their burden.
Whoso fears God, God will appoint for him, of His
   command, easiness.

5   That is God's command, that He has sent down
unto you. And whosoever fears God, He will
acquit him of his evil deeds, and He will give him
         a mighty wage.
Lodge them where you are lodging, according to
your means, and do not press them, so as to
straiten their circumstances. If they are with
child, expend upon them until they bring forth
their burden. If they suckle for you, give them
their wages, and consult together honourably.
If you both make difficulties, another woman shall
         suckle for him.
Let the man of plenty expend out of his plenty.
As for him whose provision is stinted to him,
let him expend of what God has given him. God
charges no soul save with what He has given him.
God will assuredly appoint, after difficulty,
         easiness.

         How many a city turned in disdain
         from the commandment of its Lord
         and His Messengers; and then We
         made with it a terrible reckoning
         and chastised it with a horrible
            chastisement.
         So it tasted the mischief of its
         action, and the end of its affair
            was loss.
10   God prepared for them a terrible
         chastisement. So fear God, O men
            possessed of minds!

         Believers, God has sent down to you, for a
         remembrance, a Messenger reciting to
         you the signs of God, clear signs, that
         He may bring forth those who believe
         and do righteous deeds from the shadows
         into the light. Whosoever believes in
         God, and does righteousness, He will

admit him to gardens underneath which
rivers flow; therein they shall dwell
for ever and ever. God has made for him
a goodly provision.

It is God who created seven heavens, and of earth their like,
between them the Command descending,
that you may know that God is powerful over everything
and that God encompasses everything in knowledge.

LXVI

THE FORBIDDING

In the Name of God, the Merciful, the Compassionate

O Prophet, why forbiddest thou what God has
made lawful to thee, seeking the good pleasure
of thy wives? And God is All-forgiving,
   All-compassionate.

God has ordained for you the absolution of
your oaths. God is your Protector, and He is
  the All-knowing, the All-wise.

And when the Prophet confided to one of his
wives a certain matter; and then, when she
told of it, and God disclosed that to him,
he made known part of it, and turned aside
from part; then, when he told her of it,
she said, 'Who told thee this?' He said,
'I was told of it by the All-knowing,
   the All-aware.'
If you two repent to God, yet your hearts
certainly inclined; but if you support one
another against him, God is his Protector,
and Gabriel, and the righteous among the
believers; and, after that, the angels are
   his supporters.

5 It is possible that, if he divorces you,
his Lord will give him in exchange wives
better than you, women who have surrendered,
believing, obedient, penitent, devout,
given to fasting, who have been married
   and virgins too.

Believers, guard yourselves and your families
against a Fire whose fuel is men and stones,
and over which are harsh, terrible angels who
disobey not God in what He commands them and
  do what they are commanded.
'O you unbelievers, do not excuse yourselves
today; you are only being recompensed for
  what you were doing.'
Believers, turn to God in sincere repentance;
it may be that your Lord will acquit you
of your evil deeds, and will admit you
into gardens underneath which rivers flow.

Upon the day when God will not degrade the Prophet
and those who believe with him, their light running
before them, and on their right hands; and they say,
'Our Lord, perfect for us our light, and forgive us;
  surely Thou art powerful over everything.'

O Prophet, struggle with the unbelievers and the hypocrites,
and be thou harsh with them; their refuge shall be Gehenna—
  an evil homecoming!

10   God has struck a similitude
for the unbelievers—the wife of
Noah, and the wife of Lot; for
they were under two of Our
righteous servants, but they
betrayed them, so they availed
them nothing whatsoever
against God; so it was said,
'Enter, you two, the Fire with
  those who enter.'
God has struck a similitude
for the believers—the wife of
Pharaoh, when she said, 'My
Lord, build for me a house in
Paradise, in Thy presence, and
deliver me from Pharaoh

and his work, and do Thou
deliver me from the people
    of the evildoers.'
And Mary, Imran's daughter,
who guarded her virginity,
so We breathed into her of
Our Spirit, and she confirmed
the Words of her Lord and His
Books, and became one of
    the obedient.

LXVII

THE KINGDOM

In the Name of God, the Merciful, the Compassionate

Blessed be He in whose hand is the Kingdom—
He is powerful over everything—
who created death and life, that He might try·you
which of you is fairest in works; and He is
the All-mighty, the All-forgiving—
who created seven heavens one upon another.
Thou seest not in the creation
of the All-merciful any imperfection.
Return thy gaze; seest thou any fissure?
Then return thy gaze again, and again, and thy gaze comes
back to thee dazzled, aweary.
5 And We adorned the lower heaven with lamps, and made
[them
things to stone Satans; and We have prepared for them
the chastisement of the Blaze.

And for those who disbelieve in their Lord
there awaits the chastisement of Gehenna—
an evil homecoming!
When they are cast into it they will hear it sighing, the
while it boils and wellnigh bursts asunder with rage. As
often as a troop is cast into it, its keepers ask them,
'Came there no warner to you?' They say, 'Yes indeed, a
warner came to us; but we cried lies, saying, "God has
not sent down anything; you are only in great error."'
10 They also say, 'If we had only heard, or had understood,
we would not have been of the inhabitants of the Blaze.'
So they confess their sins. Curse the inhabitants of the Blaze!

Surely those who fear their Lord
in the Unseen—

there awaits them forgiveness
and a great wage.

Be secret in your speech, or proclaim it,
He knows the thoughts within the breasts.
Shall He not know, who created? And
He is the All-subtle, the All-aware.

15　It is He who made the earth submissive to you; therefore
walk in its tracts, and eat of His provision; to
Him is the Uprising.

Do you feel secure that He who is in heaven
will not cause the earth to swallow you,
the while it rocks?
Do you feel secure that He who is in heaven
will not loose against you a squall of pebbles,
then you shall know how My warning is?

Those that were before them also cried lies;
then how was My horror!

Have they not regarded the birds above them
spreading their wings, and closing them?
Naught holds them but the All-merciful. Surely
He sees everything.

20　Or who is this that shall be a host for you
to help you, apart from the All-merciful?
The unbelievers are only in delusion.
Or who is this that shall provide for you
if He withholds His provision? No, but
they persist in disdain and aversion.

What, is he who walks prone upon his face
better guided than he who walks upright
on a straight path?

Say: 'It is He who produced you, and

appointed for you hearing and sight and hearts;
     little thanks you show!'
Say: 'It is He who scattered you in the earth,
    and unto Him you shall be mustered.'

25   They say, 'When shall this promise come to pass,
     if you speak truly?'
Say: 'The knowledge is with God; I am
    only a clear warner.'
Then, when they see it nigh at hand, the faces of
the unbelievers will be vexed, and it will be said,
    'This is what you were promised.'

Say: 'What think you? If God destroys me
and those with me, or has mercy on us,
then who will protect the unbelievers from
    a painful chastisement?'
Say: 'He is the All-merciful. We believe
in Him, and in Him we put all our trust.
Assuredly, you will soon know who is
    in manifest error.'
30   Say: 'What think you? If in the morning
your water should have vanished into
the earth, then who would bring you
     running water?'

LXVIII

THE PEN

In the Name of God, the Merciful, the Compassionate

Nun

By the Pen, and what they inscribe,
thou art not, by the blessing of thy Lord,
    a man possessed.
Surely thou shalt have a wage unfailing;
surely thou art upon a mighty morality.
So thou shalt see, and they will see,
    which of you is the demented.

Surely thy Lord knows very well
those who have gone astray from
    His way, and He knows very well
    those who are guided.

So obey thou not those who cry lies. They
wish that thou shouldst compromise, then
    they would compromise.
And obey thou not every mean swearer,
backbiter, going about with slander,
hinderer of good, guilty aggressor,
coarse-grained, moreover ignoble,
    because he has wealth and sons.
When Our signs are recited to him, he
says, 'Fairy-tales of the ancients!'
We shall brand him upon the muzzle!

Now We have tried them, even as We tried
the owners of the garden when they swore
    they would pluck in the morning
and they added not the saving words.

599

Then a visitation from thy Lord visited
   it, while they were sleeping,
20   and in the morning it was as if it were
     a garden plucked.
In the morning they called to one another,
'Come forth betimes upon your tillage,
   if you would pluck!'
So they departed, whispering together,
'No needy man shall enter it today
   against your will.'
25   And they went forth early, determined
    upon their purpose.
But when they saw it, they said, 'Surely
    we are gone astray;
nay, rather we have been robbed!'
Said the most moderate of them,
'Did I not say to you, "Why do you
   not give glory?" '
They said, 'Glory be to God, our Lord;
   truly, we were evildoers.'
30   And they advanced one upon another,
    blaming each other.
They said, 'Woe, alas for us! Truly,
    we were insolent.
It may be that our Lord will give us
in exchange a better than it; to our
   Lord we humbly turn.'

Such is the chastisement; and the chastisement
of the world to come is assuredly greater,
   did they but know.
Surely for the godfearing shall be Gardens of
   Bliss with their Lord.
35   What, shall we make those who have surrendered
    like to the sinners?

What ails you then, how you judge?
Or have you a Book wherein you study? Surely
therein you shall have whatever you choose!

Or have you oaths from Us, reaching to the
Day of Resurrection? Surely you shall have
  whatever you judge!
40 Ask them, which of them will guarantee that!
  Or do they have associates? Then
  let them bring their associates,
    if they speak truly.

Upon the day when the leg shall be bared, and they shall be
    to bow themselves, but they cannot;   [summoned
humbled shall be their eyes, and abasement shall overspread
                [them,
for they had been summoned to bow themselves while they
              [were whole.

  So leave Me with him who
  cries lies to this discourse!
  We will draw them on little by little
    whence they know not;
45 and I shall respite them—assuredly
    My guile is sure.

  Or askest thou them for a wage, and so they
    are weighed down with debt?
  Or is the Unseen in their keeping, and so
    they are writing it down?

So be thou patient under the judgment of thy Lord,
and be not as the Man of the Fish, when he called,
    choking inwardly.
Had there not overtaken him a blessing from his Lord
he would have been cast upon the wilderness,
    being condemned.
50 But his Lord had chosen him, and He placed him
    among the righteous.

  The unbelievers wellnigh strike thee down
  with their glances, when they hear the
  Reminder, and they say, 'Surely he is

a man possessed!'
And it is nothing but a Reminder
unto all beings.

LXIX

THE INDUBITABLE

In the Name of God, the Merciful, the Compassionate

The Indubitable!
What is the Indubitable?
And what will teach thee what is the Indubitable?

Thamood and Ad cried lies to the Clatterer.
As for Thamood, they were destroyed by the
Screamer;
and as for Ad, they were destroyed by a
wind clamorous, violent
that He compelled against them seven nights
and eight days, uninterruptedly, and thou
mightest see the people laid prostrate in it
as if they were the stumps of fallen down
palm-trees.
Now dost thou see any remnant of them?

Pharaoh likewise, and those before him,
and the Subverted Cities—they committed
error,
and they rebelled against the Messenger
of their Lord, and He seized them with a
surpassing grip.

Lo, when the waters rose, We bore you in
the running ship
that We might make it a reminder for you
and for heeding ears to hold.

So, when the Trumpet is blown with a single blast
and the earth and the mountains are lifted up and
crushed with a single blow,

15   then, on that day, the Terror shall come to pass,
      and heaven shall be split, for upon that day it
            shall be very frail,
      and the angels shall stand upon its borders, and
      upon that day eight shall carry above them the
            Throne of thy Lord.
      On that day you shall be exposed, not one secret
            of yours concealed.
    Then as for him who is given his book in his right hand,
20   he shall say, 'Here, take and read my book! Certainly
      I thought that I should encounter my reckoning.' So he
            shall be in a pleasing life
            in a lofty Garden,
            its clusters nigh to gather.
    'Eat and drink with wholesome appetite for that you did
            long ago, in the days gone by.'
25   But as for him who is given his book in his left hand,
      he shall say, 'Would that I had not been given my book
      and not known my reckoning! Would it had been the end!
            My wealth has not availed me,
            my authority is gone from me.'
30   'Take him, and fetter him, and then roast him in Hell,
      then in a chain of seventy cubits' length insert him!
      Behold, he never believed in God the All-mighty, and
35   he never urged the feeding of the needy; therefore he
      today has not here one loyal friend, neither any food
      saving foul pus, that none excepting the sinners eat.'

            No! I swear by that you see
            and by that you do not see,
40   it is the speech of a noble Messenger.
       It is not the speech of a poet
            (little do you believe)
       nor the speech of a soothsayer
            (little do you remember).
       A sending down from the Lord of all Being.

       Had he invented against Us any sayings,
45   We would have seized him by the right hand,

then We would surely have cut his life-vein
and not one of you could have defended him.

Surely it is a Reminder to the godfearing;
but We know that some of you will cry lies.
50   Surely it is a sorrow to the unbelievers;
yet indeed it is the truth of certainty.

Then magnify the Name of thy Lord, the All-mighty.

LXX

THE STAIRWAYS

In the Name of God, the Merciful, the Compassionate

A questioner asked of a chastisement about to fall
    for the unbelievers, which none may avert,
      from God, the Lord of the Stairways.
To Him the angels and the Spirit mount up in a day
    whereof the measure is fifty thousand years.

5   So be thou patient with a sweet patience;
        behold, they see it as if far off, but We
            see it is nigh.

Upon the day when heaven shall be as molten copper
    and the mountains shall be as plucked wool-tufts,
10   no loyal friend shall question loyal friend, as
they are given sight of them. The sinner will wish that he
might ransom himself from the chastisement of that day even
by his sons, his companion wife, his brother, his kin who
sheltered him, and whosoever is in the earth, all together,
    so that then it might deliver him.

15   Nay, verily it is a furnace
        snatching away the scalp,
        calling him who drew back
          and turned away,
        who amassed and hoarded.

Surely man was created fretful,
20   when evil visits him, impatient,
        when good visits him, grudging,
          save those that pray
        and continue at their prayers,
those in whose wealth is a right known

25   for the beggar and the outcast,
        who confirm the Day of Doom
    and go in fear of the chastisement of their Lord
    (from their Lord's chastisement none feels secure)
        and guard their private parts
30 save from their wives and what their right hands own,
            then not being blameworthy
        (but whoso seeks after more than that,
            they are the transgressors),
            and who preserve their trusts
                and their covenant,
            and perform their witnessings,
            and who observe their prayers.
35   Those shall be in Gardens, high-honoured.

What ails the unbelievers, running with outstretched necks
                                    ⌜towards thee
        on the right hand and on the left hand in knots?
What, is every man of them eager to be admitted to a Garden
                                    ⌜of Bliss?
        Not so; for We have created them
            of what they know.

40   No! I swear by the Lord of the Easts and Wests,
                surely We are able
            to substitute a better than they; We shall
                not be outstripped.

        Then leave them alone to plunge and play
        until they encounter that day of theirs
            which they are promised,
        the day they shall come forth from the
        tombs hastily, as if they were hurrying
            unto a waymark,
        humbled their eyes, overspreading
        them abasement. That is the day
            which they were promised.

607

LXXI

NOAH

In the Name of God, the Merciful, the Compassionate

We sent Noah to his people, saying,
'Warn thy people, ere there come on them
 a painful chastisement.'
He said, 'O my people, I am unto you
 a clear warner,
saying, "Serve God, and fear Him, and
 obey you me,
and He will forgive you your sins, and
defer you to a stated term; God's term,
when it comes, cannot be deferred,
 did you but know." '

5 He said, 'My Lord, I have called my
people by night and by day, but my
calling has only increased them
 in flight.
And whenever I called them, that Thou
mightest forgive them, they put their
fingers in their ears, and wrapped them
in their garments, and persisted, and
 waxed very proud.
Then indeed I called them openly;
then indeed I spoke publicly
unto them, and I spoke unto them
 secretly,
and I said, "Ask you forgiveness
of your Lord; surely He is ever
 All-forgiving,

10 and He will loose heaven upon you
 in torrents
and will succour you with wealth
and sons, and will appoint for you

gardens, and will appoint for you
rivers.
What ails you, that you look not for
majesty in God,
seeing He created you by stages?
Have you not regarded how God
created seven heavens one upon
another,
15 and set the moon therein for a light
and the sun for a lamp?
And God caused you to grow out of
the earth,
then He shall return you into it,
and bring you forth.
And God has laid the earth for you
as a carpet,
that thereof you may thread ways,
ravines." '
20 Noah said, 'My Lord, they have
rebelled against me, and followed him
whose wealth and children increase him
only in loss,
and have devised a mighty device
and have said, "Do not leave your
gods, and do not leave Wadd,
nor Suwa',
Yaghuth, Ya'uq, neither Nasr."
And they have led many astray.
Increase Thou not the evildoers
save in error!'
25 And because of their transgressions
they were drowned, and admitted
into a Fire,
for they found not, apart from God,
any to help them.
And Noah said, 'My Lord, leave not
upon the earth of the unbelievers
even one.
Surely, if Thou leavest them, they

will lead Thy servants astray, and
will beget none but unbelieving
      libertines.
My Lord, forgive me and my parents
and whosoever enters my house
as a believer, and the believers,
men and women alike; and do
Thou not increase the evildoers
      save in ruin!'

LXXII

THE JINN

In the Name of God, the Merciful, the Compassionate

Say: 'It has been revealed to me that a
company of the jinn gave ear, then they
said, "We have indeed heard a Koran
wonderful,
guiding to rectitude. We believe in it,
and we will not associate with our Lord
anyone.
He—exalted be our Lord's majesty!—
has not taken to Himself either consort
or a son.
The fool among us spoke against God
outrage,
5   and we had thought that men and jinn
would never speak against God
a lie.
But there were certain men of mankind
who would take refuge with certain men
of the jinn, and they increased them in
vileness,
and they thought, even as you also
thought, that God would never raise up
anyone.
And we stretched towards heaven, but we
found it filled with terrible guards and
meteors.
We would sit there on seats to hear; but
any listening now finds a meteor in wait
for him.
10   And so we know not whether evil is
intended for those in the earth, or
whether their Lord intends for them

611

rectitude.
And some of us are the righteous, and
some of us are otherwise; we are sects
        differing.
Indeed, we thought that we should never
be able to frustrate God in the earth,
neither be able to frustrate Him
        by flight.
When we heard the guidance, we believed
in it; and whosoever believes in his
Lord, he shall fear neither paltriness nor
        vileness.
And some of us have surrendered,
and some of us have deviated.
Those who have surrendered sought
        rectitude;
15   but as for those who have deviated,
they have become firewood for
        Gehenna!" '

Would they but go straight on the way,
We would give them to drink of water
        copious,
that We might try them therein.
And whosoever turns away from the
Remembrance of his Lord, He will
thrust him into chastisement
        rigorous.
The places of worship belong to God;
so call not, along with God, upon
        anyone.
When the servant of God stood calling
on Him, they were wellnigh upon him
        in swarms.

20   Say: 'I call only upon my Lord,
and I do not associate with Him
        anyone.'
Say: 'Surely I possess no power

over you, either for hurt or for
    rectitude.'
Say: 'From God shall protect me not
    anyone,
and I shall find, apart from Him, no
    refuge,
excepting a Deliverance from God
and His Messages. And whoso rebels
against God and His Messenger,
for him there awaits the Fire of
Gehenna; therein they shall dwell
    forever.'

25   Until, when they see that which
they are promised, then they will know
who is weaker in helpers and fewer in
    numbers.
Say: 'I do not know whether that
which you are promised is nigh, or
whether my Lord will appoint for it
    a space;
Knower He of the Unseen, and
He discloses not His Unseen to
    anyone,
save only to such a Messenger as
He is well-pleased with; then He
despatches before him and behind him
    watchers,
that He may know they have delivered
the Messages of their Lord; and He
encompasses all that is with them,
and He has numbered everything in
    numbers.'

LXXIII

ENWRAPPED

In the Name of God, the Merciful, the Compassionate

O thou enwrapped in thy robes,
keep vigil the night, except a little
(a half of it, or diminish a little,
or add a little), and chant the Koran
very distinctly.
5 Behold, We shall cast upon thee a weighty word;
surely the first part of the night is heavier in
tread, more upright in speech,
surely in the day thou hast long business.
And remember the Name of thy Lord, and devote thyself
very devoutly.   ⌜unto Him
Lord of the East and the West;
there is no god but He;
so take Him for a Guardian.
10 And bear thou patiently what they say,
and forsake them graciously.
Leave Me to those who cry lies,
those prosperous ones, and respite them a little,
for with Us there are fetters, and a furnace, and
food that chokes, and a painful chastisement,
upon the day when the earth and the mountains shall quake
and the mountains become a slipping heap of sand.

15 Surely We have sent unto you a Messenger
as a witness over you, even as We sent to
Pharaoh a Messenger,
but Pharaoh rebelled against the Messenger,
so We seized him remorselessly.
If therefore you disbelieve, how will you
guard yourselves against a day that shall make
the children grey-headed?

Whereby heaven shall be split, and its promise
    shall be performed.

Surely this is a Reminder; so let
him who will take unto his Lord
    a way.

Thy Lord knows that thou keepest vigil
nearly two-thirds of the night, or a half
of it, or a third of it, and a party of
those with thee; and God determines
the night and the day. He knows that you
will not number it, and He has turned
towards you. Therefore recite of the Koran
so much as is feasible. He knows that some
of you are sick, and others journeying
in the land, seeking the bounty of God,
and others fighting in the way of God. So
recite of it so much as is feasible.
And perform the prayer, and pay the alms,
and lend to God a good loan. Whatever
good you shall forward to your souls'
account, you shall find it with God as
better, and mightier a wage. And ask
God's forgiveness; God is All-forgiving,
    All-compassionate.

LXXIV

SHROUDED

In the Name of God, the Merciful, the Compassionate

O thou shrouded in thy mantle,
          arise, and warn!
     Thy Lord magnify
     thy robes purify
5   and defilement flee!
Give not, thinking to gain greater
and be patient unto thy Lord.

For when the Trump is sounded
     that day will be a harsh day,
10   for the unbelievers not easy.
Leave Me with him whom I created alone,
     and appointed for him ample wealth
     and sons standing before him,
     and made all things smooth for him;
15   then he is eager that I should do more.
Nay! He is forward unto Our signs;
and I shall constrain him to a hard ascent.
Lo! He reflected, and determined—
     death seize him, how he determined!
20 Again, death seize him, how he determined!
          Then he beheld,
     then he frowned, and scowled,
     then he retreated, and waxed proud.
He said, 'This is naught but a trumped-up sorcery;
25   this is nothing but mortal speech.'
     I shall surely roast him in Sakar;
     and what will teach thee what is Sakar?
     It spares not, neither leaves alone
          scorching the flesh;
30   over it are nineteen.

616

We have appointed only angels to be
masters of the Fire, and their number
We have appointed only as a trial for
the unbelievers, that those who were
given the Book may have certainty,
and that those who believe may increase
            in belief,
and that those who were given the Book
and those who believe may not be
            in doubt,
and that those in whose hearts there is
sickness, and the unbelievers, may say,
'What did God intend by this as a
            similitude?'
So God leads astray whomsoever He will,
and He guides whomsoever He will; and
none knows the hosts of thy Lord but He.
And it is naught but a Reminder to
            mortals.

35   Nay! By the moon
    and the night when it retreats
    and the dawn when it is white,
surely it is one of the greatest things
      as a warner to mortals,
40   to whoever of you desires to go forward or lag behind.
Every soul shall be pledged for what it has earned,
      save the Companions of the Right;
in Gardens they will question concerning the sinners,
      'What thrusted you into Sakar?'
They shall say, 'We were not of those who prayed, and
45   we fed not the needy,
      and we plunged along with the plungers,
      and we cried lies to the Day of Doom,
        till the Certain came to us.'
Then the intercession of the intercessors shall not profit them.

50   What ails them, that they turn away
      from the Reminder,

as if they were startled asses fleeing
  before a lion?
Nay, every man of them desires to be
  given scrolls unrolled.
No indeed; but they do not fear the
  Hereafter.
No indeed; surely it is a Reminder; so
  whoever wills shall remember it.
55   And they will not remember, except that
God wills; He is worthy to be feared,
  worthy to forgive.

LXXV

THE RESURRECTION

In the Name of God, the Merciful, the Compassionate

No! I swear by the Day of Resurrection.
No! I swear by the reproachful soul.
What, does man reckon We shall not gather his bones?
Yes indeed; We are able to shape again his fingers.
5   Nay, but man desires to continue on as a libertine,
asking, 'When shall be the Day of Resurrection?'

But when the sight is dazed
and the moon is eclipsed,
and the sun and moon are brought together,
10   upon that day man shall say, 'Whither to flee?'
No indeed; not a refuge!
Upon that day the recourse shall be to thy Lord.
Upon that day man shall be told his former deeds and his
nay, man shall be a clear proof against himself,   [latter;
15   even though he offer his excuses.

Move not thy tongue with it
to hasten it;
Ours it is to gather it, and to recite it.
So, when We recite it, follow thou its recitation.
Then Ours it is to explain it.

20   No indeed; but you love the hasty world,
and leave be the Hereafter.
Upon that day faces shall be radiant,
gazing upon their Lord;
and upon that day faces shall be scowling,
25   thou mightest think the Calamity has been wreaked on them.

No indeed; when it reaches the clavicles

and it it said, 'Who is an enchanter?'
and he thinks that it is the parting
and leg is intertwined with leg,
upon that day unto thy Lord shall be the driving.

30 For he confirmed it not, and did not pray,
but he cried it lies, and he turned away,
then he went to his household arrogantly.

Nearer to thee and nearer
35 then nearer to thee and nearer!
What, does man reckon he shall be left to
roam at will?
Was he not a sperm-drop spilled?
Then he was a blood-clot, and He created and formed,
and He made of him two kinds, male and female.
40 What, is He not able to quicken the dead?

LXXVI

MAN

In the Name of God, the Merciful, the Compassionate

Has there come on man a while of time
when he was a thing unremembered?

We created man of a sperm-drop, a mingling, trying him;
and We made him hearing, seeing.
Surely We guided him upon the way
whether he be thankful or unthankful.
Surely We have prepared for the unbelievers
chains, fetters, and a Blaze.
5   Surely the pious shall drink of a cup
whose mixture is camphor,
a fountain whereat drink the servants of God,
making it to gush forth plenteously.
They fulfil their vows, and fear a day whose evil is
upon the wing;
they give food, for the love of Him, to the needy,
the orphan, the captive:
'We feed you only for the Face of God;
we desire no recompense from you, no
thankfulness;
10   for we fear from our Lord a frowning day,
inauspicious.'
So God has guarded them from the evil of
that day, and has procured them radiancy
and gladness,
and recompensed them for their patience
with a Garden, and silk;
therein they shall recline upon couches,
therein they shall see neither sun nor
bitter cold;
near them shall be its shades, and its clusters hung

meekly down,
15 and there shall be passed around them vessels of
          silver, and goblets of crystal,
        crystal of silver that they have measured
              very exactly.
And therein they shall be given to drink a cup whose
          mixture is ginger,
      therein a fountain whose name is called Salsabil.
        Immortal youths shall go about them;
      when thou seest them, thou supposest them
              scattered pearls,
20   when thou seest them then thou seest bliss
              and a great kingdom.
      Upon them shall be green garments of silk
          and brocade; they are adorned with
      bracelets of silver, and their Lord shall
          give them to drink a pure draught.
    'Behold, this is a recompense for you, and
          your striving is thanked.'

      Surely We have sent down the Koran on thee,
              a sending down;
      so be thou patient under the judgment of thy Lord,
      and obey not one of them, sinner or unbeliever.
25   And remember the Name of thy Lord
              at dawn and in the evening
      and part of the night; bow down before Him
      and magnify Him through the long night.

      Surely these men love the hasty world, and
          leave be behind them a heavy day.
      We created them, and We strengthened their
      joints; and, when We will, We shall exchange
              their likes.

          Surely this is a Reminder; so he
          who will, takes unto his Lord
                  a way.
30   But you will not unless God wills;

surely God is ever All-knowing,
    All-wise.
For He admits into His mercy
whomsoever He will; as for the
evildoers, He has prepared for them
    a painful chastisement.

LXXVII

THE LOOSED ONES

In the Name of God, the Merciful, the Compassionate

By the loosed ones successively
storming tempestuously
by the scatterers scattering
and the severally severing
and those hurling a reminder
5   excusing or warning,
surely that which you are promised is about to fall!

When the stars shall be extinguished,
when heaven shall be split
10   when the mountains shall be scattered
and when the Messengers' time is set
to what day shall they be delayed?
To the Day of Decision.
And what shall teach thee what is the Day of Decision?
15   Woe that day unto those who cry it lies!

Did We not destroy the ancients,
and then follow them with the later folk?
So We serve the sinners.
Woe that day unto those who cry it lies!

20   Did We not create you of a mean water,
that We laid within a sure lodging
till a known term decreed?
We determined; excellent determiners are We.
Woe that day unto those who cry it lies!

25   Made We not the earth to be a housing
for the living and for the dead?
Set We not therein soaring mountains?

Sated you with sweetest water?
Woe that day unto those who cry it lies!

Depart to that you cried was lies!
30   Depart to a triple-massing shadow
unshading against the blazing flame
that shoots sparks like dry faggots,
sparks like to golden herds.
Woe that day unto those who cry it lies!

35   This is the day they shall not speak
neither be given leave, and excuse themselves.
Woe that day unto those who cry it lies!

'This is the Day of Decision; We have joined you with the
[ancients;
if you have a trick, try you now to trick Me!'
40   Woe that day unto those who cry it lies!

Truly the godfearing shall dwell amid shades and fountains,
and such fruits as their hearts desire:
'Eat and drink, with wholesome appetite, for
that you were working.'
Even so do We recompense the good-doers.
45   Woe that day unto those who cry it lies!

'Eat and take your joy a little; you are sinners!'
Woe that day unto those who cry it lies!

When it is said to them, 'Prostrate yourselves!' they pros-
[trate not.
Woe that day unto those who cry it lies!

50   In what discourse after this will they believe?

LXXVIII

THE TIDING

In the Name of God, the Merciful, the Compassionate

Of what do they question one another?
Of the mighty tiding
whereon they are at variance.
No indeed; they shall soon know!
5   Again, no indeed; they shall soon know!

Have We not made the earth as a cradle
and the mountains as pegs?
And We created you in pairs,
and We appointed your sleep for a rest;
10   and We appointed night for a garment,
and We appointed day for a livelihood.
And We have built above you seven strong ones,
and We appointed a blazing lamp
and have sent down out of the rain-clouds water cascading
15   that We may bring forth thereby grain and plants,
and gardens luxuriant.

Surely the Day of Decision is an appointed time,
the day the Trumpet is blown, and you shall come in troops,
and heaven is opened, and become gates,
20   and the mountains are set in motion, and become a vapour.
Behold, Gehenna has become an ambush,
for the insolent a resort,
therein to tarry for ages,
tasting therein neither coolness nor any drink
25   save boiling water and pus
for a suitable recompense.
They indeed hoped not for a reckoning,
and they cried loud lies to Our signs;
and everything We have numbered in a Book.

30   'Taste! We shall increase you not save in chastisement.'

       Surely for the godfearing awaits a place of security,
               gardens and vineyards
      and maidens with swelling breasts, like of age,
               and a cup overflowing.
35   Therein they shall hear no idle talk, no cry of lies,
    for a recompense from thy Lord, a gift, a reckoning,
Lord of the heavens and earth, and all that between them is,
              the All-merciful
      of whom they have no power to speak.
Upon the day when the Spirit and the angels stand in ranks
they shall speak not, save him to whom the All-merciful has
        given leave, and who speaks aright.

       That is the true day; so whosoever wills
         takes unto his Lord a resort.
40   Lo, We have warned you of a nigh chastisement,
upon the day when a man shall behold what his hands have
                        [forwarded,
  and the unbeliever shall say, 'O would that I were dust!'

LXXIX

THE PLUCKERS

In the Name of God, the Merciful, the Compassionate

By those that pluck out vehemently
and those that draw out violently,
by those that swim serenely
and those that outstrip suddenly
5   by those that direct an affair!

Upon the day when the first blast shivers
and the second blast follows it,
hearts upon that day shall be athrob
and their eyes shall be humbled.
10   They shall say, 'What, are we being restored
as we were before?
What, when we are bones old and wasted?'
They shall say, 'That then were a losing return!'
But it shall be only a single scare,
and behold, they are awakened.

15   Hast thou received the story of Moses?
When his Lord called to him in the holy
valley, Towa: 'Go to Pharaoh; he has
waxed insolent. And say, "Hast thou the
will to purify thyself, and that I
should guide thee to thy Lord, then thou
20   shalt fear?" ' So he showed him the great
sign, but he cried lies, and rebelled,
then he turned away hastily, then he
mustered and proclaimed, and he said,
'I am your Lord, the Most High!' So
25   God seized him with the chastisement
of the Last World and the First.
Surely in that is a lesson for him who fears!

What, are you stronger in constitution
or the heaven He built?
He lifted up its vault, and levelled it,
and darkened its night, and brought forth its forenoon;
30   and the earth—after that He spread it out,
therefrom brought forth its waters and its pastures,
and the mountains He set firm,
an enjoyment for you and your flocks.

Then, when the Great Catastrophe comes
35   upon the day when man shall remember what he has striven,
and Hell is advanced for whoever sees,
then as for him who was insolent
and preferred the present life,
surely Hell shall be the refuge.
40   But as for him who feared the Station of his Lord
and forbade the soul its caprice,
surely Paradise shall be the refuge.

They will question thee concerning
the Hour, when it shall berth.
What art thou about, to mention it?
Unto thy Lord is the final end of it.
45   Thou art only the warner of him who fears it.
It shall be as if, on the day they see it,
they have but tarried for an evening, or its forenoon.

LXXX

HE FROWNED

In the Name of God, the Merciful, the Compassionate

He frowned and turned away
that the blind man came to him.
And what should teach thee? Perchance he would cleanse him,
or yet remember, and the Reminder profit him.
5   But the self-sufficient,
to him thou attendest
though it is not thy concern, if he does not cleanse himself.
And he who comes to thee eagerly
and fearfully,
10   to him thou payest no heed.

No indeed; it is a Reminder
(and whoso wills, shall remember it)
upon pages high-honoured,
uplifted, purified,
15   by the hands of scribes noble, pious.

Perish Man! How unthankful he is!
Of what did He create him?
Of a sperm-drop
He created him, and determined him,
20   then the way eased for him,
then makes him to die, and buries him,
then, when He wills, He raises him.
No indeed! Man has not accomplished His bidding.

Let Man consider his nourishment.
25   We poured out the rains abundantly,
then We split the earth in fissures
and therein made the grains to grow
and vines, and reeds,

and olives, and palms,
30   and dense-tree'd gardens,
and fruits, and pastures,
an enjoyment for you and your flocks.

And when the Blast shall sound,
upon the day when a man shall flee from his brother,
35   his mother, his father,
his consort, his sons,
every man that day shall have business to suffice him.
Some faces on that day shall shine
laughing, joyous;
40   some faces on that day shall be dusty
o'erspread with darkness—
those—they are the unbelievers, the libertines.

LXXXI

THE DARKENING

In the Name of God, the Merciful, the Compassionate

When the sun shall be darkened,
when the stars shall be thrown down,
when the mountains shall be set moving,
when the pregnant camels shall be neglected,
5   when the savage beasts shall be mustered,
when the seas shall be set boiling,
when the souls shall be coupled,
when the buried infant shall be asked for what sin she was
10   when the scrolls shall be unrolled,   [slain,
when heaven shall be stripped off,
when Hell shall be set blazing,
when Paradise shall be brought nigh,
then shall a soul know what it has produced.

15   No! I swear by the slinkers,
the runners, the sinkers,
by the night swarming,
by the dawn sighing,
truly this is the word of a noble Messenger
20   having power, with the Lord of the Throne secure,
obeyed, moreover trusty.

Your companion is not possessed;
he truly saw him on the clear horizon;
he is not niggardly of the Unseen.

25   And it is not the word of an accursed Satan;
where then are you going?

It is naught but a Reminder

unto all beings,
for whosoever of you who would go straight;
but will you shall not, unless God wills,
the Lord of all Being.

LXXXII

THE SPLITTING

In the Name of God, the Merciful, the Compassionate

When heaven is split open,
when the stars are scattered,
when the seas swarm over,
when the tombs are overthrown,
5   then a soul shall know its works, the former and the latter.

O Man! What deceived thee as to thy generous Lord
who created thee and shaped thee and wrought thee in
[symmetry
and composed thee after what form He would?

No indeed; but you cry lies to the Doom;
10   yet there are over you watchers
noble, writers
who know whatever you do.

Surely the pious shall be in bliss,
and the libertines shall be in a fiery furnace
15   roasting therein on the Day of Doom,
nor shall they ever be absent from it.

And what shall teach thee what is the Day of Doom?
Again, what shall teach thee what is the Day of Doom?
A day when no soul shall possess aught to succour another
[soul;
that day the Command shall belong unto God.

LXXXIII

THE STINTERS

In the Name of God, the Merciful, the Compassionate

Woe to the stinters
who, when they measure against the people, take full measure
but, when they measure for them or weigh for them, do skimp.
Do those not think that they shall be raised up
5   unto a mighty day
a day when mankind shall stand before the Lord of all Being?

No indeed; the Book of the libertines is in Sijjin;
and what shall teach thee what is Sijjin?
A book inscribed.
Woe that day unto those who cry it lies,
10   who cry lies to the Day of Doom;
and none cries lies to it but every guilty aggressor.
When our signs are recited to him, he says,
'Fairy-tales of the ancients!'
No indeed; but that they were earning has rusted
upon their hearts.
15   No indeed; but upon that day they shall be veiled
from their Lord,
then they shall roast in Hell.
Then it shall be said to them, 'This is that you cried lies to.'

No indeed; the book of the pious is in Illiyun;
and what shall teach thee what is Illiyun?
20   A book inscribed,
witnessed by those brought nigh.
Surely the pious shall be in bliss,
upon couches gazing;
thou knowest in their faces the radiancy of bliss
25   as they are given to drink of a wine sealed
whose seal is musk—so after that let the strivers strive—

635

and whose mixture is Tasnim,
a fountain at which do drink those brought nigh.

Behold, the sinners were laughing at the believers,
30   when they passed them by winking at one another,
and when they returned to their people they returned blithely,
and when they saw them they said, 'Lo, these men are astray!'
          Yet they were not sent as watchers over them.
So today the believers are laughing at the unbelievers,
35   upon couches gazing.
Have the unbelievers been rewarded what they were doing?

LXXXIV

THE RENDING

In the Name of God, the Merciful, the Compassionate

When heaven is rent asunder
and gives ear to its Lord, and is fitly disposed;
when earth is stretched out
and casts forth what is in it, and voids itself,
5   and gives ear to its Lord, and is fitly disposed!

O Man! Thou art labouring unto thy Lord laboriously,
and thou shalt encounter Him.
Then as for him who is given his book in his right hand,
he shall surely receive an easy reckoning
and he will return to his family joyfully.
10   But as for him who is given his book behind his back,
he shall call for destruction
and he shall roast at a Blaze.
He once lived among his family joyfully;
he surely thought he would never revert.
15   Yes indeed; his Lord had sight of him.

No! I swear by the twilight
and the night and what it envelops
and the moon when it is at the full,
you shall surely ride stage after stage.

20   Then what ails them, that they believe not,
and when the Koran is recited to them they do not bow?
Nay, but the unbelievers are crying lies,
and God knows very well what they are secreting.

So give them good tidings of a painful chastisement,
25   except those that believe, and do righteous deeds—
theirs shall be a wage unfailing.

LXXXV

THE CONSTELLATIONS

In the Name of God, the Merciful, the Compassionate

By heaven of the constellations,
by the promised day,
by the witness and the witnessed,
slain were the Men of the Pit,
5   the fire abounding in fuel,
when they were seated over it
and were themselves witnesses of what they did with the
[believers.
They took revenge on them only because they believed in
the All-mighty, the All-laudable,   [God
to whom belongs the Kingdom of the heavens and the earth,
and God is Witness over everything.

10   Those who persecute the believers, men and women,
and then have not repented, there awaits' them the
chastisement of Gehenna, and there awaits them
the chastisement of the burning.
Those who believe, and do righteous deeds, for them
await gardens underneath which rivers flow; that is
the great triumph.

Surely thy Lord's assault is terrible.
Surely it is He who originates, and brings again,
and He is the All-forgiving, the All-loving,
15   Lord of the Throne, the All-glorious,
Performer of what He desires.

Hast thou received the story of the hosts,
Pharaoh and Thamood?
Nay, but the unbelievers still cry lies,
20   and God is behind them, encompassing.

Nay, but it is a glorious Koran,
in a guarded tablet.

LXXXVI

THE NIGHT-STAR

In the Name of God, the Merciful, the Compassionate

By heaven and the night-star!
And what shall teach thee what is the night-star?
The piercing star!
Over every soul there is a watcher.

5 So let man consider of what he was created;
he was created of gushing water
issuing between the loins and the breast-bones.
Surely He is able to bring him back
upon the day when the secrets are tried,
10 and he shall have no strength, no helper.

By heaven of the returning rain,
by earth splitting with verdure,
surely it is a decisive word;
it is no merriment.

15 They are devising guile,
and I am devising guile.
So respite the unbelievers; delay with them awhile.

LXXXVII

THE MOST HIGH

In the Name of God, the Merciful, the Compassionate

Magnify the Name of thy Lord the Most High
    who created and shaped,
    who determined and guided,
    who brought forth the pasturage
5   then made it a blackening wrack.

We shall make thee recite, to forget not
    save what God wills;
    surely He knows what is spoken aloud
    and what is hidden.
We shall ease thee unto the Easing.

Therefore remind, if the Reminder profits,
10   and he who fears shall remember,
    but the most wretched shall flout it,
even he who shall roast in the Great Fire,
then he shall neither die therein, nor live.

Prosperous is he who has cleansed himself,
15 and mentions the Name of his Lord, and prays.

Nay, but you prefer the present life;
and the world to come is better, and more enduring.

Surely this is in the ancient scrolls,
    the scrolls of Abraham and Moses.

LXXXVIII

THE ENVELOPER

In the Name of God, the Merciful, the Compassionate

Hast thou received the story of the Enveloper?

Faces on that day humbled,
labouring, toilworn,
roasting at a scorching fire,
5   watered at a boiling fountain,
no food for them but cactus thorn
unfattening, unappeasing hunger.

Faces on that day jocund,
with their striving well-pleased,
10   in a sublime Garden,
hearing there no babble;
therein a running fountain,
therein uplifted couches
and goblets set forth
15   and cushions arrayed
and carpets outspread.

What, do they not consider how the camel was created,
how heaven was lifted up,
how the mountains were hoisted,
20   how the earth was outstretched?
Then remind them! Thou art only a reminder;
thou art not charged to oversee them.

But he who turns his back, and disbelieves,
God shall chastise him with the greatest chastisement.
25   Truly, to Us is their return;
then upon Us shall rest their reckoning.

LXXXIX

THE DAWN

In the Name of God, the Merciful, the Compassionate

By the dawn and ten nights,
by the even and the odd,
by the night when it journeys on!
Is there in that an oath for a mindful man?

5   Hast thou not seen how thy Lord did with Ad,
Iram of the pillars,
the like of which was never created in the land,
and Thamood, who hollowed the rocks in the valley,
and Pharaoh, he of the tent-pegs,
10   who all were insolent in the land
and worked much corruption therein?
Thy Lord unloosed on them a scourge of chastisement;
surely thy Lord is ever on the watch.

As for man, whenever his Lord tries him,
and honours him, and blesses him,
15   then he says, 'My Lord has honoured me.'
But when he tries him and stints for him
his provision,
then he says, 'My Lord has despised me.'

No indeed; but you honour not the orphan,
and you urge not the feeding of the needy,
20   and you devour the inheritance greedily,
and you love wealth with an ardent love.

No indeed! When the earth is ground to powder,
and thy Lord comes, and the angels rank on rank,
and Gehenna is brought out, upon that day
man will remember; and how shall the Reminder be for him?

25   He shall say, 'O would that I had forwarded for
        my life!' Upon that day none shall chastise as
                        He chastises,
                none shall bind as He binds.

                'O soul at peace, return unto thy Lord,
                    well-pleased, well-pleasing!
                Enter thou among My servants!
30   Enter thou My Paradise!'

XC

THE LAND

In the Name of God, the Merciful, the Compassionate

No! I swear by this land,
and thou art a lodger in this land;
by the begetter, and that he begot,
indeed, We created man in trouble.
5   What does he think none has power over him,
saying, 'I have consumed wealth abundant'?
What, does he think none has seen him?

Have We not appointed to him two eyes,
and a tongue, and two lips,
10   and guided him on the two highways?
Yet he has not assaulted the steep;
and what shall teach thee what is the steep?
The freeing of a slave,
or giving food upon a day of hunger
15   to an orphan near of kin
or a needy man in misery;
then that he become of those who believe
and counsel each other to be steadfast,
and counsel each other to be merciful.

Those are the Companions of the Right Hand.
And those who disbelieve in Our signs,
they are the Companions of the Left Hand;
20   over them is a Fire covered down.

XCI

THE SUN

In the Name of God, the Merciful, the Compassionate

By the sun and his morning brightness
and by the moon when she follows him,
and by the day when it displays him
and by the night when it enshrouds him!
5   By the heaven and That which built it
and by the earth and That which extended it!
By the soul, and That which shaped it
and inspired it to lewdness and godfearing!
Prosperous is he who purifies it,
10   and failed has he who seduces it.

Thamood cried lies in their insolence
when the most wretched of them uprose,
then the Messenger of God said to them,
'The She-camel of God; let her drink!'
But they cried him lies, and hamstrung her,
15   so their Lord crushed them for their sin, and levelled them:
and He fears not the issue thereof.

XCII

THE NIGHT

In the Name of God, the Merciful, the Compassionate

By the night enshrouding
and the day in splendour
and That which created the male and the female,
surely your striving is to diverse ends.

5   As for him who gives and is godfearing
and confirms the reward most fair,
We shall surely ease him to the Easing.
But as for him who is a miser, and self-sufficient,
and cries lies to the reward most fair,
10   We shall surely ease him to the Hardship;
his wealth shall not avail him when he perishes.

Surely upon Us rests the guidance,
and to Us belong the Last and the First.

Now I have warned you of a Fire that flames,
15   whereat none but the most wretched shall be roasted,
even he who cried lies, and turned away;
and from which the most godfearing shall be removed,
even he who gives his wealth to purify himself
and confers no favour on any man for recompense,
20   only seeking the Face of his Lord the Most High;
and he shall surely be satisfied.

XCIII

THE FORENOON

In the Name of God, the Merciful, the Compassionate

By the white forenoon
and the brooding night!
Thy Lord has neither forsaken thee nor hates thee
and the Last shall be better for thee than the First.
5   Thy Lord shall give thee, and thou shalt be satisfied.

Did He not find thee an orphan, and shelter thee?
Did He not find thee erring, and guide thee?
Did He not find thee needy, and suffice thee?

10   As for the orphan, do not oppress him,
and as for the beggar, scold him not;
and as for thy Lord's blessing, declare it.

XCIV

THE EXPANDING

In the Name of God, the Merciful, the Compassionate

Did We not expand thy breast for thee
and lift from thee thy burden,
the burden that weighed down thy back?
Did We not exalt thy fame?

So truly with hardship comes ease,
truly with hardship comes ease.
So when thou art empty, labour,
and let thy Lord be thy Quest.

XCV

THE FIG

In the Name of God, the Merciful, the Compassionate

By the fig and the olive
and the Mount Sinai
and this land secure!
We indeed created Man in the fairest stature
5   then We restored him the lowest of the low—
save those who believe, and do righteous deeds;
they shall have a wage unfailing.

What then shall cry thee lies as to the Doom?
Is not God the justest of judges?

XCVI

THE BLOOD-CLOT

In the Name of God, the Merciful, the Compassionate

Recite: In the Name of thy Lord who created,
created Man of a blood-clot.
Recite: And thy Lord is the Most Generous,
who taught by the Pen,
5   taught Man.that he knew not.

No indeed; surely Man waxes insolent,
for he thinks himself self-sufficient.
Surely unto thy Lord is the Returning.

What thinkest thou? He who forbids
10   a servant when he prays—
What thinkest thou? If he were upon guidance
or bade to godfearing—
What thinkest thou? If he cries lies, and turns away—
Did he not know that God sees?

15   No indeed; surely, if he gives not over,
We shall seize him by the forelock,
a lying, sinful forelock.
So let him call on his concourse!
We shall call on the guards of Hell.

No indeed; do thou not obey him,
and bow thyself, and draw nigh.

XCVII

POWER

In the Name of God, the Merciful, the Compassionate

Behold, We sent it down on the Night of Power;
And what shall teach thee what is the Night of Power?
The Night of Power is better than a thousand months;
 in it the angels and the Spirit descend,
 by the leave of their Lord, upon every command.
5   Peace it is, till the rising of dawn.

XCVIII

THE CLEAR SIGN

In the Name of God, the Merciful, the Compassionate

The unbelievers of the People of the Book
and the idolaters would never leave off,
till the Clear Sign came to them,
a Messenger from God, reciting pages purified,
therein true Books.
And they scattered not, those that were given the Book,
excepting after the Clear Sign came to them.
They were commanded only to serve God,
making the religion His sincerely,
men of pure faith, and to perform
the prayer, and pay the alms—that is
the religion of the True.

5   The unbelievers of the People of the Book
and the idolaters shall be in the Fire of Gehenna,
therein dwelling forever;
those are the worst of creatures.
But those who believe, and do righteous deeds,
those are the best of creatures;
their recompense is with their Lord—
Gardens of Eden, underneath which rivers flow,
therein dwelling for ever and ever.
God is well-pleased with them, and they are well-pleased
[with Him;
that is for him who fears his Lord.

XCIX

THE EARTHQUAKE

In the Name of God, the Merciful, the Compassionate

When earth is shaken with a mighty shaking
and earth brings forth her burdens,
and Man says, 'What ails her?'
upon that day she shall tell her tidings
for that her Lord has inspired her.

Upon that day men shall issue in scatterings to see their
[works,
and whoso has done an atom's weight of good shall see it,
and whoso has done an atom's weight of evil shall see it.

C

THE CHARGERS

In the Name of God, the Merciful, the Compassionate

By the snorting chargers,
by the strikers of fire,
by the dawn-raiders
blazing a trail of dust,
5   cleaving there with a host!
Surely Man is ungrateful to his Lord,
and surely he is a witness against that!
Surely he is passionate in his love for good things.
Knows he not that when that which is in the tombs is over-
[thrown,
10   and that which is in the breasts is brought out—
surely on that day their Lord shall be aware of them!

CI

THE CLATTERER

In the Name of God, the Merciful, the Compassionate

The Clatterer! What is the Clatterer?
And what shall teach thee what is the Clatterer?
The day that men shall be like scattered moths,
and the mountains shall be like plucked wool-tufts.

5 Then he whose deeds weigh heavy in the Balance
    shall inherit a pleasing life,
  but he whose deeds weigh light in the Balance
    shall plunge in the womb of the Pit.
    And what shall teach thee what is the Pit?
      A blazing Fire!

CII

RIVALRY

In the Name of God, the Merciful, the Compassionate

Gross rivalry diverts you,
even till you visit the tombs.
No indeed; but soon you shall know.
Again, no indeed; but soon you shall know.
5 No indeed; did you know with the knowledge of certainty,
you shall surely see Hell.
Again, you shall surely see it with the eye of certainty
then you shall be questioned that day concerning true bliss.

CIII

AFTERNOON

In the Name of God, the Merciful, the Compassionate

By the afternoon!
Surely Man is in the way of loss,
save those who believe, and do righteous deeds,
and counsel each other unto the truth,
and counsel each other to be steadfast.

CIV

THE BACKBITER

In the Name of God, the Merciful, the Compassionate

Woe unto every backbiter, slanderer,
who has gathered riches and counted them over
thinking his riches have made him immortal!

No indeed; he shall be thrust into the Crusher;
and what shall teach thee what is the Crusher?
The Fire of God kindled
roaring over the hearts
covered down upon them,
in columns outstretched.

CV

THE ELEPHANT

In the Name of God, the Merciful, the Compassionate

Hast thou not seen how thy Lord did with the Men of the
[Elephant?
Did He not make their guile to go astray?
And He loosed upon them birds in flights,
hurling against them stones of baked clay
5   and He made them like green blades devoured.

CVI

KORAISH

In the Name of God, the Merciful, the Compassionate

For the composing of Koraish,
their composing for the winter and summer caravan!

So let them serve the Lord of this House
who has fed them against hunger.
and secured them from fear.

CVII

CHARITY

In the Name of God, the Merciful, the Compassionate

Hast thou seen him who cries lies to the Doom?
That is he who repulses the orphan
and urges not the feeding of the needy.

So woe to those that pray
5   and are heedless of their prayers,
to those who make display
and refuse charity.

CVIII

ABUNDANCE

In the Name of God, the Merciful, the Compassionate

Surely We have given thee abundance;
so pray unto thy Lord and sacrifice.
Surely he that hates thee, he is the one cut off.

CIX

THE UNBELIEVERS

In the Name of God, the Merciful, the Compassionate

Say: 'O unbelievers,
I serve not what you serve
and you are not serving what I serve,
nor am I serving what you have served,
neither are you serving what I serve.

5   To you your religion, and to me my religion!'

CX

HELP

In the Name of God, the Merciful, the Compassionate

When comes the help of God, and victory,
and thou seest men entering God's religion in throngs,
then proclaim the praise of thy Lord, and seek His forgive-
for He turns again unto men.　　　[ness;

CXI

PERISH

In the Name of God, the Merciful, the Compassionate

Perish the hands of Abu Lahab, and perish he!
His wealth avails him not, neither what he has earned;
he shall roast at a flaming fire
and his wife, the carrier of the firewood,
5   upon her neck a rope of palm-fibre.

CXII

SINCERE RELIGION

In the Name of God, the Merciful, the Compassionate

Say: 'He is God, One,
God, the Everlasting Refuge,
who has not begotten, and has not been begotten,
and equal to Him is not any one.'

CXIII

DAYBREAK

In the Name of God, the Merciful, the Compassionate

Say: 'I take refuge with the Lord of the Daybreak
    from the evil of what He has created,
    from the evil of darkness when it gathers,
    from the evil of the women who blow on knots,
5   from the evil of an envier when he envies.'

CXIV

MEN

In the Name of God, the Merciful, the Compassionate

Say: 'I take refuge with the Lord of men.
    the King of men,
    the God of men,
from the evil of the slinking whisperer
5   who whispers in the breasts of men
    of jinn and men.'

INDEX

makes coats of mail, 329,
438.
and Solomon, 329, 383.
Death, angel of, 424.
Debts, 42.
Dhool Karnain (Alexander the
Great), 298–300.
Dhul Kifl, prophet, 330, 468.
Dhul Nun (Jonah), 96, 131,
208, 330, 461, 601.
Divorce, 31–34, 432, 590–1.

Eden, Gardens of, 187, 242,
292, 307, 316, 447, 468,
481, 653.
El-Hijr, 257.
Elias (Elijah), 131, 460–1.
Elisha, 131, 468.
El-Judi (Ararat), 216.
El-Lat, pagan idol, 550.
El-'Uzza, pagan idol, 550.
Emigration, 70, 85, 87, 177–8,
262, 271, 340, 574.
Er-Rakeem, 288.
Er-Rass, 365, 540.
Ezra, 182.
Ez-Zakkoum, 458, 515, 561.

Fasting, 24–25.
Flood, the, 404.
Food, laws concerning, 22,
99–100, 115, 135, 138–9,
271, 272.
of the Jews, 58, 139, 272.
Freewill offerings, 39–41, 89,
186, 188, 191, 566, 571.

Gabriel, 12, 593.
Gambling, prohibition of, 30,
99, 114.
Gehenna, 28, 46, 65, 70, 80,
86–87, 90, 93, 96, 144,
165, 173, 183, 185, 188–
9, 192, 225, 242, 248, 250,
255, 261, 275–6, 278, 281,
285, 300, 308–9, 316, 325,
331, 365, 368, 409–10,
448, 454, 468, 470, 475,
478, 487, 516, 531, 541,
547, 558, 594, 596, 612–
13, 626, 638, 643, 653.
Gog and Magog, 299, 331.
Goliath, 36.
Gospel, the, 45, 54, 107, 111,
117, 161, 192, 535, 567.
Greeks, the, 411.

Haman, minister of Pharaoh,
392, 396, 407, 483, 485.
Hami, cattle, 116.
Harut and Marut, 12.
Hell, 113, 224, 292, 374, 435,
458, 468, 486, 515, 523,
547, 555, 561, 596, 603,
606, 626.
Hood, prophet, 151, 217–18,
376.
Hour, the, 166, 267, 279, 290,
312, 333–4, 339, 363, 412,
417, 421, 435, 437, 487,
500, 510, 528, 553, 555,
629.
Hunain, battle of, 181.
Hypocrites, 85, 93, 175, 187–8,
191, 434, 436, 574, 585–6.

Iblis, 5, 143, 255, 281, 294,
319, 374, 469.
Idolaters, 30, 110, 137, 139,
181, 262, 268, 436, 531,
653.
Idris, 307, 330.
Illiyun, 635.
Imran, 49.
Inheritance, laws of, 73–74, 77,
97.
Iram, 643.
Isaac, 17, 57, 96, 131, 226,
230, 306, 405, 460, 467.
Ishmael, 16–17, 57, 96, 131,
306, 330, 467.
Islam, 47, 100, 136, 473.
Israel, 58, 307.
children of, 6, 15, 28, 58,
101, 105, 111, 118, 158,
207, 274, 286, 313, 316,
318, 373, 380, 389, 425,
487, 510, 514, 517, 522,
580–1.

Jacob, 16–17, 57, 96, 131, 226,
230, 235–7, 306, 405, 467.
Jesus, 11, 36, 51–54, 57, 95–97,
107, 112, 117–19, 131,
182, 305, 346, 428, 499,
510, 567, 580–1.
his birth, 304.
his miracles, 52, 117.
not crucified, 95.
not divine, 14, 102, 111, 119,
182, 205, 305, 309, 325.
Jews, 8, 14–15, 17–18, 55, 79,
95, 103, 106–8, 110–11,